WITHDRAWN

SHAKESPEARE'S MARLOWE

Dedicated to
John J. Wright

Shakespeare's Marlowe
The Influence of Christopher Marlowe on Shakespeare's Artistry

ROBERT A. LOGAN
University of Hartford, USA

ASHGATE

Published by
Ashgate Publishing Limited
Gower House
Croft Road
Aldershot
Hampshire GU11 3HR
England

Ashgate Publishing Company
Suite 420
101 Cherry Street
Burlington, VT 05401-4405
USA

Reprinted 2007

Ashgate website: http://www.ashgate.com

British Library Cataloguing in Publication Data
Logan, Robert A., 1935-
Shakespeare's Marlowe
    1.Shakespeare, William, 1564-1616 – Criticism and interpretation 2.Shakespeare, William, 1564-1616 – Sources 3.Marlowe, Christopher, 1564-1593 – Influence
    I.Title
    822.3'3

Library of Congress Cataloging-in-Publication Data
Logan, Robert A., 1935-
    Shakespeare's Marlowe / by Robert Logan.
      p. cm.
    Includes bibliographical references and index.
    ISBN-13: 978-0-7546-5763-7 (alk. paper)
    ISBN-10: 0-7546-5763-9 (alk. paper)
    1. Shakespeare, William, 1564-1616—Literary style. 2. Shakespeare, William, 1564-1616—Technique. 3. Marlowe, Christopher, 1564-1593—Influence. 4. Marlowe, Christopher, 1564-1593—Literary style. 5. Marlowe, Christopher, 1564-1593—Technique. 6. Shakespeare, William, 1564-1616—Criticism, Textual. 7. Marlowe, Christopher, 1564-1593—Criticism, Textual. 8. English drama—Early modern and Elizabethan, 1500-1600--History and criticism. I. Title.

PR2958.M3L64 2006
822.3'3—dc22

    ISBN-13: 978-0-7546-5763-7

2006018482

Printed and bound in Great Britain by TJ International Ltd, Padstow, Cornwall.

Contents

Acknowledgments

In a study of influence, the danger and the advantage are often one and the same: tunnel vision. Because I have restricted myself primarily to Marlowe's influence on Shakespeare, I have spoken only infrequently of the multiplicity of other cultural and literary influences on Shakespeare. To be sure, I have been limited by considerations of space. But the chief reason is that Shakespeare himself had a kind of tunnel vision when he saw or read Marlowe's works. He evidently experienced an intense degree of engagement, an infatuation of sorts, which accounts ultimately for the power, complexity, and duration of Marlowe's influence on his artistry.

Those most responsible for alerting me to the perils of tunnel vision, as well as to several other pitfalls, are Matthew Proser, who generously posed questions and made helpful comments about the manuscript in its earliest form; Sara Deats, whose superior editorial skills, abundant suggestions, and constant encouragement proved, truly, a bounty overplus; and Roslyn Knutson, who read the first and fifth chapters and, with breathtaking candor, offered invaluable commentary, especially on matters pertaining to the separation of fact and speculation. I am also most grateful to Charles Ross, a friend and former department chair, who kindly urged me forward at every turn. I wish to thank as well Erika Gaffney, senior editor at Ashgate, whose intelligence, clarity, and graciousness guided me serenely through the final stages of publication, and Dean Joseph Voelker of the University of Hartford who magnanimously put funds at my disposal when I needed them most. My strongest personal debt is to John Wright who, throughout, manifested extraordinary depth and intensity in unstinting acts of loving support.

> *perspectives, which rightly gazed upon*
> *Show nothing but confusion—eyed awry,*
> *Distinguish form.*
>
> (*Richard II*, II, ii, 18–20)

Chapter 1

Marlowe and Shakespeare: Repositioning the Question of Sources and Influence

I

Among the many forces attributed to the fashioning of Shakespeare's professional life, the influence of Christopher Marlowe has long been considered indisputable. However, although not readily acknowledged, attempts to pin down and define this influence have frequently resulted in inconclusiveness. To be sure, the scholarship resulting from the tracking processes has often proved illuminating, especially when it causes us to reflect on the methodology used in detecting influence or encourages us to scrutinize the aesthetic aims and historical contexts of each writer's works. But endeavors to make definite the lines of influence have been seriously hampered by problems encountered in trying to fathom what is historically unknowable. As a result, discussions of Marlowe's effect on Shakespeare, as well as Shakespeare's on Marlowe, have all too often blurred the line that separates fact from speculation.

For those scholars who concentrate exclusively on making definite the links between the two writers' works, delineating influence is almost guaranteed to breed frustration and, in consequence, to intensify their eagerness to describe bonds that are explicit. Apart from the difficulties emerging from the narrowness of the pursuit, such efforts have resulted in the development of two overlapping propensities: forcing conclusions and allowing speculation to harden into fact. Examples of fabricated links that have been used to connect Marlowe with Shakespeare abound. In *Two Gentlemen of Verona*, for instance, the story of *Hero and Leander* is mentioned twice (I, i, 21–26 and III, i, 117–20).[1] But, in spite of the number of times Marlowe has been suggested as a source, in neither allusion is there anything specific enough to connect the references to his *Hero and Leander*; moreover, no evidence exists to ascertain that the play was written after the poem. A second example of this same supposed source appears in *As You Like It*. Attempting to ground Orlando's love in commonsense realism, Rosalind pooh-poohs the romantic notion of dying for love (IV, i, 87–100). One of her examples is Leander who, she claims, drowned because of a cramp. But neither this detail nor the dire fate of the young lover appears in Marlowe's rendering of the tale. Evidently, the myth of Hero and Leander enjoyed a general currency such that every reference to it (especially after the writer's death) need not be attributed to Marlowe. *As You Like It* also presents other opportunities for forced links when Touchstone says, "... it strikes a man more dead than a great reckoning in a little room" (III, iii, 12–13). Some scholars find in this an echo of the line from *The Jew of Malta,* "Infinite riches in a little room" (I, i, 37);[2] others, more biographically inclined, see in it a reference to Ingram Frizer's striking Marlowe dead in a room in Eleanor Bull's house during a quarrel over "le recknynge." In neither case is the "source" more than zealous speculation.

Those scholars who move beyond source hunting in tracing the influence of Marlowe and Shakespeare also encounter impediments. This is particularly true when the explanations of influence within a single Shakespearean play become entangled in complexity or lead to irresolvable difficulties. *The Merchant of Venice* is a case in point. As I will later demonstrate, not only does the play contain influence from diverse Marlovian sources, some clearer than others, but also different degrees and kinds of Marlovian influence—the degrees ranging from specific to general to uncertain.

Anyone who examines Shakespeare's works seeking to explain Marlowe's influence is certain to meet up with these and other impediments, beginning with whether the influence is from Marlowe or from someone else. Probably the greatest single obstacle is a question that finally resists a definite or conclusive answer—as, say, the influence of magic in *Doctor Faustus* on magic in *The Tempest.* But even this hindrance can be offset if, by shifting our perspective, we understand and accept three principles: (1) Marlowe's influence cannot usually be reduced to uncomplicated explanations; (2) much of it relies on deduction and conjecture rather than hard evidence; and, most important, (3) the study of influence should never be considered an end in itself but primarily a *process,* one that expands critical inquiry through fresh perspectives and raises new issues about the theatrical and literary resourcefulness of each writer. The following chapters regard both influence and the study of influence as such. Consequently, they are dedicated to the larger purpose of arriving at a clearer and richer understanding of the creative distinctiveness of both Marlowe and Shakespeare.

Given this objective, the present study proposes to build upon what we can determine of the nature and the extent of Marlowe's influence on Shakespeare's theatrical and literary practices. By "theatrical practices," I mean those strategies that Shakespeare devised to give the production of his plays maximum effectiveness, whether measured *pragmatically,* by the plays' degree of commercial success, or *aesthetically,* by such ingredients as conflict and tension, spectacles (visual and verbal), and climactic moments. "Literary practices" include the shaping of a specific intellectual and emotional content in conjunction with the manipulation of the play's style, structure, and characterizations.

I intend to follow the progression of Shakespeare toward an unabashed acceptance of Marlowe's influence, taking into account how, over time, he shifted from moments of a commonly supposed defensive belittlement—most often in the form of parody—to an enthusiastic adaptation of his fellow playwright's dramaturgical techniques and stylistic tendencies in language and syntax. Along the way, I will consider not only what Shakespeare appropriated and, through refinements, made his own, but also what he rejected, especially in the realm of Marlovian values.

I begin the following discussion by exemplifying the need to separate evidence from presupposition, questioning in particular the validity of the long-posited critical tradition of a hostile "rivalry" between the two dramatists and its bearing on influence—a speculation that, unfortunately, has hardened into a fact. I then outline the possible reach of Marlowe's influence, clarifying what in the past we have meant by "sources" and "influence" and what, because of advances in contextualizing dramatic works, we can mean now. This section leads to an analysis of the significance of a study of Marlowe's influence (primarily) and the various forms of influence, from the most to the least definite, that the ensuing chapters encompass. I conclude the discussion with a brief examination of the preconceptions and expectations of a study of Marlowe's influence on Shakespeare.

II

By the early 1590s, Marlowe and Shakespeare were living in London and actively writing for the city's commercial theater. Born in 1564, a little over two months apart, each had established himself as a playwright by his mid-20s. But, as is well known, Marlowe began composing plays before Shakespeare and rapidly gained recognition and prominence. No evidence has been found to tell us whether Marlowe and Shakespeare ever actually met or whether Shakespeare acted in one of Marlowe's plays, but both are quite likely.[3] As every student of sixteenth-century drama knows, in 1592 Robert Greene[4] in *A Groatsworth of Wit*, writing to "those gentlemen his quondam acquaintance, that spend their wits in making plays" [usually identified with Marlowe, Nashe, and Lodge], ridiculed the multitalented Shakespeare, saying, "an upstart crow, beautified with our feathers, that with his *Tiger's heart wrapt in a player's hide*, supposes he is as well able to bombast out a blank verse as the best of you: and being an absolute *Iohannes fac totum*, is in his own conceit the only Shake-scene in a country."[5] The first italicized phrase parodies a line from Part 3 of *Henry VI*,[6] and Greene gives the playwright one final thrust with the unsubtle pun "Shake-scene." James Shapiro repeats a point of general scholarly agreement in saying that Greene appears to be addressing Marlowe when, earlier in *A Groatsworth*, he speaks of the "famous gracer of tragedians."[7] Because Greene is able to make fun of Shakespeare and to refer to Marlowe as "famous" [even though he also attacks him],[8] we understand that the two dramatists were well-known, successful figures on the London theater scene. The specific meanings of Greene's vitriolic remarks in *A Groatsworth* and Henry Chettle's protest against them in his Epistle to *Kind-Harts Dreame*, written two and one-half months after the satiric pamphlet, remain unclear.[9] But, for my purposes here, the importance of the two documents lies less in their content than in their demonstration of the visible professional status and notable reputations of Marlowe and Shakespeare. Given their standing as it is characterized in these documents, it would be less conceivable that they did not meet than that they did.

But there is even more conclusive evidence to consider. Philip Henslowe's entries in his *Diary* for the ten performances of *The Jew of Malta* and fifteen of *Henry VI* in 1592 indicate in the entries for March 10 and 11, April 4 and 5, May 4 and 5, and May 19 and 20 that *The Jew of Malta* and *Henry VI* were played in succession.[10]

Henslowe's information helps us to envision the working milieu within which Marlowe and Shakespeare were writing and producing their plays; seeing each other on something like a daily basis at the theater promotes the likelihood that the two playwrights, even if not close friends, knew one another and that they almost certainly knew each other's works as staged plays. Moreover, although no evidence exists to establish the fact, it is conceivable that Shakespeare acted in *The Jew of Malta* at the Rose in 1592–93 or at the theater in Newington Butts in 1594.

During Marlowe's lifetime, the popularity of his plays, Robert Greene's unintentionally elevating remarks about him as a dramatist in *A Groatsworth of Wit*, including the designation "famous," and the many imitations of *Tamburlaine* suggest that he was for a brief time considered England's foremost dramatist.[11] That he had a firm sense of his success cannot be doubted; in the Prologue to the second part of *Tamburlaine*, he exclaims:

> The general welcomes Tamburlaine received
> When he arrivèd last upon our stage
> Hath made our poet pen his second part … (2 Prologue, 1–3)

Marlowe's sense of his professional status is not surprising: he vigorously expresses his self-awareness as an innovator in the Prologue to the first part of *Tamburlaine*; in the same play, he declares his fervor toward the powers of the poet through the warrior leader's well-known speech on beauty and poetry (1 V, i, 135–90); and in *Hero and Leander*, he reveals a self-referential literary consciousness.[12] But, by 1592, well before Marlowe's untimely death in 1593, Shakespeare was also making his mark on the London theatrical world and receiving major critical attention—largely because of his *Henry VI* plays.[13] Henslowe's *Diary* shows that, in March of 1592, *The Jew of Malta* and Part 1 of *Henry VI*—that is, the plays of both writers—were being presented in repertory at the Rose Theater,[14] and that, within the two years following, as the title pages of *Edward II* and the 1595 quarto of Part 3 of *Henry VI* indicate, the Earl of Pembroke's Men were performing the two writers' plays.[15] These documents clearly establish both the co-presence of the two dramatists and their attempt to attract the same sources of production for the staging of their plays, thereby increasing the opportunities for influence and creating what several critics have seen as a plausible context for an unfriendly rivalry.

For us now, the term "rivalry" can be employed to mean competition that is friendly, unfriendly, or vigorously antagonistic, and the context can be either personal or professional. But Shakespeare uses the word "rival" throughout his works without a connotation of hostility to mean exclusively either a competitor or an associate, a companion. In *A Midsummer Night's Dream*, he plays upon both meanings of the word when Helena says to Demetrius and Lysander: "You both are rivals, and love Hermia, / And now both rivals to mock Helena" (III, ii, 155–56). Almost always, Shakespeare creates situations of rivalry that characterize suitors, not professional rivals. Roslyn Knutson points out that in Q2/F of *Hamlet*, the phrase "rivals of my watch" is in Q1 "partners of my watch," suggesting the likelihood that this is the accepted contemporary meaning given to the word and that this is "a sense in which 'rival' might apply to sixteenth-century businesses."[16]

Since the *Henry VI* plays were actually beginning to be performed by 1592 and since the possibility exists that *The Comedy of Errors* and *The Taming of the Shrew* may have been written and even staged before that time, then for roughly two or three years, 1590–93, both Marlowe and Shakespeare were endeavoring to capture the attention of the same public theater audiences. Their simultaneous, similar professional activities could lead one to conclude logically but only speculatively that there was an unfriendly rivalry between the two men. More fancifully, one might even imagine that the two playwrights were vigorously antagonistic as each attempted to dominate the London stage. Considering the competition implicit in the commercial aspect of their working conditions, apart from any personal elements that may have appertained, it might seem reasonable to assume that a professional rivalry of considerable enmity developed between them.

But there is no solid evidence for such a rivalry. In fact, as we know from Marlowe's seeming inattention to Shakespeare in most of his works and Shakespeare's relatively gentle parodying and implicit admiration of Marlowe in his works, there is undeniable evidence to the contrary.[17] Even so, critical tradition has long assumed that Marlowe was Shakespeare's chief early professional rival and that their rivalry was contentious. The emphasis on Shakespeare's hostility is put strongly in Jonathan Bate's metaphorical assertion that "Shakespeare was the rival who killed Marlowe."[18] The up-and-coming playwright is here cast as a ruthless Tamburlaine figure out to trample Marlowe's professional reputation. But the claim derives from fiction, not fact, for there is no evidence to support it. The fullest treatment of the supposed contestation between the two dramatists is James Shapiro's *Rival Playwrights: Marlowe, Jonson, Shakespeare*, published in 1991.[19] In characterizing Shakespeare's sense of emulation with Marlowe, Shapiro invokes the first six lines of Sonnet 86 to support, through the image of the merchant ship, his major argument: that Shakespeare well understood how theatrical commercialism encourages competition.[20] But, as we have just seen, in the sixteenth century healthy competition and emulation do not automatically carry with them the implication of hostility that our contemporary use of the term "rivalry" frequently connotes.

Shapiro does not comment on the standard critical tenet that, when Shakespeare discusses another poet (Sonnets 78–86), he might well be alluding to the object of a specific poetic rivalry—even though many scholars and critics are convinced that the figure portrayed is Marlowe. One of the latest advocates of this view is Jonathan Bate.[21] But, as with other proponents of this stance, Bate lacks concrete evidence and, thus, the correspondence between Marlowe and the Rival Poet seems forced. I would offer instead that Shakespeare composes Sonnets 78–86 with less parochialism and more artistry than Bate suggests. That is, Shakespeare writes with a calculated evasiveness that encourages his readers to focus on the consequences of a rivalry rather than on a particularized, topical rivalry, much less one whose participants can be identified. Chiefly, of course, he uses the situation of rivalry as an artistic strategy for idealizing and celebrating the Young Man. Wooing the Young Man with "the proud full sail of his great verse" (Sonnet 86, line 1), the Poet becomes the speaker's rival for the attention and affection of the Young Man. Thus, the rivalry never becomes a matter of professional enmity. During the course of the sonnet cycle, Shakespeare depicts another situation of personal rivalry: the Young Man forms a liaison with the Dark Lady and the speaker again becomes a rival, this time for the affections of both the Young Man and the Dark Lady. Here, the focus is consistently on the psychology of rivalry. Consequently, it is no surprise that Shakespeare finds in the conflict and tension inherent in a personal rivalry a handy device for his poetry and dramas and that he frequently exploits it. What is surprising, however, is that Sonnets 78–86 are used by critics as the grounds for establishing a professional rivalry between Marlowe and Shakespeare.

In making the assertion that "Shakespeare was the rival who killed Marlowe," Bate specifically invokes Harold Bloom's generalized view[22] that literary recreation originates in a writer's anxiety about what Bate declares is "the burden of tradition"[23] and the need to turn it into "the shock of the new."[24] Bate contends that "For Bloom, writers are the most powerful readers of previous writers; their creativity functions by means of what he calls 'strong misreading.' All poems are thus 'antithetical' to their precursor poems. Indeed, 'A poem is not an overcoming of anxiety but is that anxiety.'"[25] From these ideas, Bate concludes (as Bloom does not) "that some of Shakespeare's works are antithetical readings of Marlovian precursors; that they *are* his anxiety about Marlowe."[26] Although Bate's endorsement of Bloom's principle when it is applied to a few of Shakespeare's early reactions to Marlowe sometimes appears to have merit,[27] I find overall that Bloom's formula does not fit Shakespeare's absorption of Marlovian influence, which seems to me less anxious and more complicated. Moreover, the conclusion drawn by Bate suffers from overstatement, just as all too often the evidence he adduces and interprets fails to persuade because, in his exuberance, he presses too hard. The arguments of Bate and Bloom lead to unwarranted inferences about the psychology of composition in Shakespeare. Bate would seem to endorse, as Shapiro actually does, Marjorie Garber's reading of Hal's victory over Hotspur as a metaphor for Shakespeare's vanquishing of his rival Marlowe.[28] But, in Shakespeare's efforts to establish his creative individuality, there is no documentary proof to support so bellicose an attitude. Nor is there evidence to support Bloom's transhistorical assertion of strife and anxiety through influence as requisite ingredients in the psychology of composition.

Scott McMillin and Sally-Beth MacLean offer the more probable context of playing companies and the theater, if, nevertheless, another speculative source for Marlowe's influence on Shakespeare and for the latter's learning process in emulating Marlowe.[29] Their chief concern is with the Queen's Men and hence with Marlowe as their chief competitor because he is "at the centre of the commercial drama in the late 1580s and early 1590s."[30] They posit that, if Shakespeare was hired by the Queen's Men early in his career—and they conjecture that he was—then he was "participating in plays which called Marlowe the enemy and knowing in his own talent that he must write in the enemy's way."[31] Consequently, Shakespeare "learned his method for rewriting the plays of the Queen's Men from no one more obviously than the Marlowe whom the Queen's Men were trying to reject."[32] Without becoming specific, McMillin and MacLean suggest that Shakespeare changed to a more individual style of writing as soon as he left the company but kept some of the plots of the Queen's Men's history plays when he went on to write his own.[33] Moreover, they suggest that, through his practice of imitating and adapting Marlowe's plays, Shakespeare acquired a knowledge of Marlowe's artistry that became ingrained. Although McMillin and MacLean speak speculatively about what Shakespeare might have learned early on and how he emulated Marlowe, they do so without assuming that he became a serious, hostile rival. Marlowe's ability to command the attention of an audience must have intrigued Shakespeare from the moment he first set foot in London, whether or not the learning process occurred as McMillin and MacLean characterize it. Moreover, he must have found great satisfaction and excitement in working at the Rose with someone of Marlowe's expertise. Marlowe's innovative employment of language and syntax, in addition to fashioning a nontraditional dramaturgy, could not have helped but influence Shakespeare, subliminally as well as consciously, especially after he saw that Marlowe's introduction of new theatrical and literary techniques were bringing him acclaim and a steadfast commercial success. As I shall contend, overt signs of influence began to emerge as Shakespeare gained in self-confidence, coincidentally only after Marlowe's death and at about the time he became associated with the Chamberlain's Men—in 1594.

While Marlowe was alive, the awareness the two dramatists had of each other's work probably had the beneficial effect of heightening the desire of each to promote his creative individuality. At the same time, their mutual interest in playwriting and production undoubtedly included an increased consciousness of ways of meeting the practical challenges of becoming a commercial success. Shakespeare's engagement with Marlowe's plays after he died only expanded the opportunities for influence. Roslyn Knutson offers the possibility that, after Marlowe's death, Shakespeare may have been asked by the Chamberlain's Men to write a play in response to the continuing popularity of *The Jew of Malta*, indicated by its revival in 1594, and that he therefore wrote *The Merchant of Venice*;[34] if so, we can assume that Shakespeare was aware of what he would need to do to replicate Marlowe's commercial success and, yet, at the same time provide a play with attractive, fresh material. Furthermore, taken as a whole, their texts make abundantly clear that each playwright displayed an eagerness to contribute some novel manifestation of his artistic talent to the rapid development of England's burgeoning theatrical tradition—largely through innovations in genre, language, and stage spectacle. While Marlowe lived, their co-presence in this endeavor must have augmented their knowledge of each other's purely creative efforts, as well as intensifying their self-motivation. It undoubtedly also increased the possibilities of accepting and rejecting each other's influence.

Marlowe's premature death in 1593 occurred without any feelings of rivalry having surfaced in his writings. The absence of any evidence of rivalry on Marlowe's part means that Shakespeare did not have to regard his fellow playwright as a contentious professional rival. As a result, Marlowe's influence on Shakespeare very likely gained in strength, enabling the latter to see Marlowe as something of an exemplar.

As Chapters 2 and 4 below detail, Shakespeare's keen sense of emulation and Marlowe's unmistakable influence on him became visible, if largely in general ways, in *Titus Andronicus* and *Richard III* (e.g., the dominating villain-hero, the exuberant overreaching of Titus, Aaron, and Richard, and the explosive Machiavellian intrigues), and overtly in *Richard II*. There, the playwright makes pointed use of Doctor Faustus's expression of wonderment at the second appearance of Helen of Troy, "Was this the face that launched a thousand ships,"[35] as he sets before us a tale from English history that in situation and characterization noticeably resembles *Edward II*.[36]

If in fact there was dual authorship[37] in the writing of *Titus Andronicus*, then it would suggest that, during the period that Marlowe and Shakespeare were in London together working side by side (1590–93), Shakespeare was receptive to collaboration and was therefore less concerned with professional rivalry than is usually thought. The collaboration would also indicate that he left himself open to a close association with fellow playwrights and that this, in turn, increased the opportunities for an exchange of ideas and influence.

III

Of greater significance than the point at which the sense of emulation emerges as documentable evidence is the firmness with which Marlowe's influence rooted itself in Shakespeare and developed, for it continued to thrive for 18 years after Marlowe's death, roughly from 1593–1611,[38] the remainder of Shakespeare's career. The catalogue of works that may be considered as possibly bearing the marks of Marlowe's influence numbers a remarkable 20. Eight Shakespearean texts—including *Julius Caesar*, if we assume as most do that its date of composition was later than that of *The Massacre At Paris*[39]—actually quote lines from Marlowe's works; these plays are indicated by the asterisks in the following list: *Venus and Adonis, Richard III, The Taming of the Shrew, Titus Andronicus, King John, Richard II,* Romeo and Juliet, The Merchant of Venice,* Henry IV*, Part 2,* *As You Like It,* Henry V, Julius Caesar,* The Merry Wives of Windsor,* Hamlet, Troilus and Cressida,* King Lear,* Macbeth, Antony and Cleopatra, The Tempest*, plus the Sonnets. Under scrutiny, these many possibilities of influence reveal that, among those contemporaries of Shakespeare that we know about, Marlowe had the strongest continuing impact on Shakespeare's psychology as he composed his works. Such an influence, amazing in its own right, is too forceful and persistent to be neglected or taken lightly.

For Marlowe, the direct influence of Shakespeare seems to have been limited to the composition of *Edward II*. But, as Shapiro characterizes it,[40] the influence on that play is important. Marlowe's knowledge of the *Henry VI* plays appears to have set him on a new course in his writing of a play with an historical subject, a course vastly different in substance and technique from that of the *Tamburlaine* plays. Shapiro, who orders the composition of Shakespeare's plays as 2 *Henry VI*, 3 *Henry VI*, then 1 *Henry VI*, lists the verbal echoes in *Edward II* from Parts 2 and 3 of the *Henry VI* plays, discusses the similarities in the situation of a weak English king embroiled in court politics, and points to a style that has less declamation, fewer set speeches, less adorned verse, and greater dramatic interaction between characters.[41] He also notices that the end of the play contains more standard Marlovian fare than the beginning.[42] Predictably, for Shakespeare, the influence of Marlowe differed considerably. A longer life, in combination with an extraordinary multiconsciousness and a strong critical faculty in his response to Marlowe's works, naturally made the possibilities for accepting and rejecting his contemporary's influence greater and more complex.

By "influence," I mean not simply the conscious or subconscious selection of elements in another writer's work but, more significantly, the use(s) to which they are put. That is, only when we go beyond a simple identification and examine, for instance, the uses in *Antony and Cleopatra* to which Shakespeare put Marlowe's portrayal of heroic figures acting out uncharacteristic gender roles in *Dido, Queen of Carthage*, do the characteristics of creative individuality in Marlowe and Shakespeare emerge. In his 1997 edition of *The Anxiety of Influence*, Harold Bloom says, "'Influence' is a metaphor, one that implicates a matrix of relationships—imagistic, temporal, spiritual, psychological—all of them ultimately defensive in their nature."[43] I am not convinced as Bloom is that the "relationships," especially after 1600, are "ultimately defensive," but he is assuredly correct in seeing a "matrix of relationships." As Bloom and others have indicated, now that the traditional pursuit of source studies to establish a definite link between two works seems nearly exhausted, the critical interest in influence assumes an increased importance. Stephen Greenblatt asserted several years ago that "[s]ource study is, as we all know, the elephants' graveyard of literary history."[44] But, as Richard Levin has stated more recently, "… a source is not a text or event; it is always a *relationship* between that text or event and the play, and there are many possible kinds of relationships that are homogenized under the single word 'source.'"[45] Also unlike Greenblatt, Stephen J. Lynch sees that "the old notion of particular and distinct sources has given way to new notions of boundless and heterogeneous intertextuality."[46] He parallels Levin when he criticizes traditional Shakespearean scholarship for viewing sources "as static building blocks that Shakespeare picked over, rearranged, and artfully improved."[47] Moreover, he understands that "the sources themselves can be reexamined as products of intertextuality," that they are "dynamic and often inconsistent texts involving layers of implicit and subtextual suggestions."[48] Lynch is trying, as he says, "to bridge the gap between traditional assumptions about authorial power and control and poststructuralist claims that authors neither create nor control texts but are themselves products of preexistent cultural discourses."[49] He realizes that Shakespeare "made deliberate and intentional choices"[50] but that all of his

> revisionary strategies were shaped and influenced by multiple forces beyond authorial control—not only the historical, political, and religious contexts of early modern England, but also the more particular forces that would bear upon a professional playwright, such as contemporary stage practices, generic decorum, audience expectations, the number and quality of available actors, state censorship, and even the geographical locus and marginal cultural status of the theater itself.[51]

Lynch does not mention Marlowe among "the more particular forces," but certainly he needs to be included, not only because of his influence as Shakespeare's chief professional emulator but also because he must have sharpened Shakespeare's awareness of the multitude and complexity of the other "particular forces."

Still another recent critic, M.L. Stapleton, expresses a similar liberating attitude toward sources, an attitude enlightening in its scope and complexity: "Even a perfunctory analysis of Shakespeare's use of his predecessors underscores the inadequacy of a word such as 'source,' which implies a fixed locus of emanation, and hence is not descriptive of his practice (always polyglot, multiplex)."[52] As Levin, Lynch, and Stapleton are implying, the next logical step for those interested in examining sources is to use as starting points what has been harvested through existing source studies in order to proceed to a more, free-ranging intertextual study of influences with an expanded consciousness of the delimiting forces at work on authors as they are in the act of composing.[53] In taking on such a project, I recognize that, at times, the influence of Marlowe on Shakespeare and Shakespeare on Marlowe will remain lost, deep in the shadows of the two writers' psyches. But, as I have indicated, the study of influences is not simply a matter of examining similar content but a process that leads to new questions and more encompassing issues. Lynch looks at it this way when he says that source texts create "hypertexts" of "alternative textual possibilities."[54] So, yes, significant influences may be invisible and, consequently, extensive definite influence may forever be impossible to pin down. Yet, the act of trying to establish influence through such means as educated guesses and speculation can often result in a clearer sense of the psychology of influence and composition, chiefly in Shakespeare. It can also raise new questions about the formation of works, including the need to appeal to audiences for both aesthetic and commercial reasons, and it can lead to new ways of answering these questions (e.g., through the findings of theater history in combination with textual studies). More specifically, it can result in an enhanced understanding of the dramaturgical strategies of each writer and, subsequently, assess the importance of such strategies as a force exerting pressure during the act of composing. In not being limited to the significance of connections and differences between the two writers, the chapters that follow demonstrate the kinds of critical inquiry that a refashioned study of influence can generate—as, for example, the role Marlowe played in encouraging Shakespeare's break with conventions and in developing ambivalence and ambiguity as a major artistic strategy.

These new possibilities make it necessary to reassess the merits of pursuing Marlowe's influence—in conjunction, of course, with the discoveries of traditional source studies. I begin with a look at variations in methodology and some basic definitions. Charney and Shapiro are the most thorough and recent of the commentators who express an interest in the links between Marlowe and Shakespeare. An examination of their methodology affirms a crucial but often overlooked, self-evident truth: that any understanding of influence, in this case, Marlowe's on Shakespeare, is tied closely to the criteria being used to measure the influence. I agree with Charney when he says, "In making the comparison between Marlowe and Shakespeare, it all depends on what criteria are invoked."[55] Acknowledging that the criteria may not be the same for all critics, I also agree with Charney when he adds with greater specificity that "Dramaturgic criteria are likely to yield more positive results than those drawn from an ideational, thematic or strictly verbal approach."[56] In the chapters that follow, I make explicit the similarities and differences in methodology between me and my predecessors.

Scholarly consensus holds that, with the possible exception of the influence of the *Henry VI* trilogy on *Edward II*, the flow of influence has gone in one direction, from Marlowe to Shakespeare. The evidence adduced lies in verbal echoes and in several, less definite likenesses found in Shakespeare's plays, *Venus and Adonis*, and the Sonnets. In order to invest the evidence with significance, I need to address two vital, related questions: By what criteria is the range of influence established? How does the nature of this influence make the relationship between the two writers significant? These questions lead to other, related questions. The specifics of identifiable sources apart, how do Marlowe's works act as a force in Shakespeare's writings? Largely unacknowledged, the difficulty has been to delineate the force, to move beyond simply proving there is one, in order to understand how the texts of Marlowe function as examples or prototypes for Shakespeare. Part of what produces this difficulty is still another, fundamental question of definition: What is the difference between a source and an influence? It is all well and good to notice the reworking of Tamburlaine's "Holla, ye pampered jades of Asia! / What, can ye draw but twenty miles a day" (2 *Tamburlaine*, IV, iii, 1–2) in Pistol's humorously garbled question:

> Shall pack-horses
> And hollow pampered jades of Asia,
> Which cannot go but thirty mile a day,
> Compare with Caesars, and with Cannibals,
> And Trojan Greeks? (2 *Henry IV*, II, iv, 157–61)

But what does our identification of a specific source tell us about the nature of the influence—that is, the choice and use that Shakespeare made of it? It tells us that Shakespeare chose to allude to a theatrical coup in Marlowe's play that he knew had seized the imagination of Marlowe's audiences, himself included. The allusion also suggests Shakespeare's fascination with Marlowe's "high astounding terms" (1 *Tamburlaine*, Prologue 5) and, more generally, his fascination with the powers of theatrical language; moreover, the action alluded to may well have broadened his understanding of the opportunities for visual innovation through unexpected spectacle. To be sure, the comic reworking of Tamburlaine's words is an in-joke for those seasoned playgoers who would recognize the specific phrase, the inflated Marlovian style, and the accompanying stage business that are being ridiculed. With a self-indulgent boldness, Shakespeare reaches beyond the theatrical illusion to invoke a frame of reference more real to him than to his audience but with enough confidence in himself and in his relationship with his audience to produce a mutual sense of jocularity. Moreover, although the passage overtly belittles Marlowe's propensity for dramatic excess, it also pays tribute to his success. Is it of personal and also of cultural significance that the passage directs us to the figure of Tamburlaine and that it parodies the conquering hero's words? It suggests that both the artistic and the commercial sides of Shakespeare were attentive to Marlowe's early success. Moreover, it intimates that the patriarchal notion of a manly hero, unconventional though Tamburlaine is in some respects, held full sway and was widely compelling. Does it suggest further that by parodying such a figure Shakespeare is refusing to align himself with the cultural forces of conventionality? Probably not. Shakespeare's perspective is more purely aesthetic and pragmatic—a playwright and businessman attuned to what makes a fellow playwright successful. Finally, how does this bit of evidence fit into a more complete characterization of Marlowe's influence on Shakespeare?[57] The answer to this is the subject of this book and will become clear only after I have demonstrated how the manifold elements of Marlowe's influence affected the career path that Shakespeare took.

At this point, I want to resolve the question of definition as quickly and as neatly as possible. In so doing, I will also be clarifying the criteria needed to measure influence. If scholars and critics did not use the terms "sources" and "influences" interchangeably, then we might conclude that a source study identifies with as much concreteness as possible the verbal, characterological, and situational likenesses between two works, whereas a study of influences draws conclusions and inferences about the psychology of composition from such likenesses. A source usually signifies a factual, tangible, definable origin of words, characters, or actions in a text. Sources receive their name because they are clear and direct, and, more often than not, writers use them consciously, as Shakespeare appears to do when, in *The Merry Wives of Windsor* (III, i, 16–28), Evans sings lines from Marlowe's poem "The Passionate Shepherd to His Love."[58] An influence, on the other hand, although it must have had a concrete source, may or may not be able to be identified as a source, as something factual, tangible, or definable; the effects of the source may be all that we have left to study for our suppositional conclusions. For example, however likely, I can affirm only speculatively that Shakespeare's use of the damned villain-hero of *Macbeth* owes something of its origin to Marlowe's damned villain-hero in *Doctor Faustus*. Only under the best of conditions can an originating text be identified as the cause and an influence as the effect. The originating text passes through the transforming chambers of the writer's psyche to emerge as a force whose inception can be difficult to recognize; in such a case, one can only guess at the origins of the influence. But complications can also arise even before the journey begins. What if the impression of the originating text is general, not specific—for example, in understanding *The Jew of Malta* as an influence on *The Merchant of Venice*? Clearly, the first difficulty in such an instance lies in characterizing the nature of the influence. Charles Edelman suggests still another difficulty when, in reflecting on "which is the Jew that Shakespeare knew" and prudently warning against trying "to reconstruct somehow the first Shylock about whom there is no reliable contemporary information whatsoever,"[59] he challenges the erroneous assumption that Shylock "must have conformed to a particular theatrical tradition, or that he must have been played in a certain way."[60] Because influences range from cultural (e.g., attitudes of the time toward Jews)[61] to personal (e.g.,

Shakespeare's attitude toward Jews from his own experience, including what he had heard and seen on or off the stage and what he had read), emotional to intellectual, superficial to deeply psychological, tangible to intangible, and definable to indefinable, they are not always easy to categorize. Equally difficult to determine is the extent to which the writer is aware of the influence; an influence may be unknown, dimly known, or consciously known, in whole or in part, to the writer and, often, there is little one can do to decide among the possibilities.

King John is a case in point. Linguistic play there seems to indicate that Shakespeare has accepted as a sanction and model Marlowe's efforts in the *Tamburlaine* plays to astound his audiences with innovative language—particularly, as Bloom notes, in the "Marlovian declamations and lamentations."[62] But Russell Fraser feels that "In *King John* a restive Shakespeare seeks to exorcize Marlowe's spell."[63] Both perspectives suggest Shakespeare's awareness of Marlowe as an influence, but each characterizes a radically different attitude toward the absorption of the influence. Few would deny that the play seems to be in search of a level of comfort in its characterizations and use of language. To its detriment, it frequently relies on Marlovian artistic techniques in its employment of language as declamation, occasions for speechifying, and ornamental excess rather than on what come to be Shakespeare's own more controlled, less ostentatious linguistic devices. Even so, it is difficult to understand Shakespeare's attitude toward Marlowe's play with language, to know whether he accepts or rejects the influence of Marlowe or if, as I suspect, the play reflects an ambivalence about it. Whereas the influence of Marlowe's style on Shakespeare's in *King John* is relatively easy to identify, any influence on content is difficult to ascertain because Shakespeare had access to specific historical and dramatic conceptions of the king and his political and religious context, portrayals ranging from John as a martyred hero to a ruthless tyrant.[64] Most would agree that the portrayal of the Bastard Faulconbridge speaks loudest for Shakespeare's creative independence in the play. It is just such independence that intimates the playwright's ambivalence toward Marlowe's influence.

Sources can be easy to talk about unless they are confused with influences.[65] If sources have traditionally ranged from definite to probable, influences have ranged from definite to possible—in which case they may have been confused with analogues. According to Marvin Spevack, an example of such confusion occurs when J. Leeds Barroll[66] "mentions various authorities for the thematic link he sees among lechery, gluttony, and sloth in *Ant.*, though he does not distinguish influences [which Spevack himself does not distinguish from sources] from analogues." Spevack goes on to enumerate 12 "authorities" listed in Barroll's article, among them Marlowe's *Doctor Faustus*.[67] Whereas sources have knowingly created a sense of certainty, influences have often stood in the shadows of uncertainty. A source and an influence can be overlapping if the meaning of the influence in its new context is substantially the same as its meaning in the old—as, for example, when Shakespeare seriously adopts the Marlovian stylistic mode of "high astounding terms" in which the mode itself signifies epic grandeur, someone or something extraordinary in an ordinary world; an early example of this occurs in *Titus Andronicus*, II, i, 1–24, Aaron's first words in the play and a soliloquy.[68] Or a source and an influence can stand in opposition if the new context reworks the old, contradicting or undermining it (say, through parody).[69] In any case, to talk about influences with a full sense of the complications and difficulties involved is, understandably, too daunting for most of us to undertake, especially if we are interested in an approach that is not ultimately reductive. This may well be the chief reason why critics have not distinguished between sources and influences and why they have less frequently discussed the latter.

IV

I have already suggested that this study views the discussion of influence as a process that expands critical inquiry and raises new issues. If, however, we ask why it is worthwhile to undertake a discussion of the content of influences per se, one answer must be to establish the grounds of a comparison that will enable us to understand better the play of forces in both the influencing and influenced works. Wilbur Sanders asserts that the study of influences can be used "to crystallise the true spirit of the work."[70] Without discriminating between a source and an influence but, in effect, talking about both, A.P. Rossiter declares that "source-study informs us" "(1) What the author did to give form and direction to his matter by selection; and (2) What he altered, suppressed, or inserted."[71] Both critics' statements contain truth, their idealism notwithstanding. I would stress in addition that, because of its comparative nature, a study of influences illuminates both the influencing and the influenced work, not simply the latter and takes into consideration the differences as well as the similarities; at its most helpful, such a study can lead to the overall complex of intentions in each work. Even when it does not detect a clear and unmistakable relationship of cause and effect, it can tell something distinctive about the operations of commercial theater, the mechanics of composition, the artistic aims, and the substance of the paired works, as well as the psychological and cultural forces that shape them. Thus, the comparison increases our understanding of the complexity of the works' individual ties with an historical context even as it augments our awareness of their aims, their success in fulfilling them, and the play of forces that controls the process of constructing them.

Before I examine what is included under the umbrella of *influences*, it may be helpful to recall what we can verify of Shakespeare's knowledge of Marlowe. We can be sure from verbal echoes that Shakespeare knew Part 2 of *Tamburlaine*, *Doctor Faustus*, *The Jew of Malta*, *Hero and Leander*, and "The Passionate Shepherd to His Love."[72] It seems as likely that he was familiar with *Dido, Queen of Carthage*, Part 1 of *Tamburlaine*, and *Edward II*, but the proof is less concrete. He may well have viewed *The Massacre At Paris*, but it is difficult to prove conclusively.[73] Even so, what is definite is that Shakespeare *continued* to be influenced by Marlowe's works and that he was attentive to the poetry as well as the drama. He may also have read Marlowe's translations but little tangible evidence exists to indicate this. As an actor, writer, and investor in the theater, most likely he saw Marlowe's plays staged, maybe quite often, and perhaps, as I have already suggested, took part in them as an actor.

Thus, his activities in the theater, in combination with the absorption of Marlowe's works over a period of time, not only increase the likelihood of inescapable influence but influence that is broad and deep.

An influence can be reduced to a source when it is as straightforward as a quotation or an allusion that recalls a particular phrase. But, even so, to let it go as a source may unnecessarily limit its significance, especially when, through parody, the source and influence become antithetical. In *As You Like It* (III, v, 81), Phebe repeats from *Hero and Leander* (I.176)[74] the well-known phrase, "Who ever loved that loved not at first sight." She is, as usual, comic in her affected literariness. In context, the sentiment does little to advance characterization or plot. It does, however, call on Marlowe to lend his authority to a notion, not new to the play, that the initial promptings of romantic love are unstintingly physical; one need only recall, for example, Rosalind and Orlando's immediate physical attraction to one another when they first meet at the wrestling match (I, ii), later echoed in the equally instantaneous attraction between Celia and Oliver (V, ii, 1–41). During the course of the play, Shakespeare does not use this notion as Marlowe does, to explore the power of physical attraction in the human personality, but, instead, employs the idea to establish the contrast between love that is exclusively sexual and love that, in addition to being sensory, encompasses moral and emotional values. As we see in Rosalind-Ganymede's exchanges with Orlando in the Forest of Arden, these values are established through a balanced mixture of romantic fancy and commonsense realism. Shakespeare is well aware of the ability of sexual love to delude us into believing that it alone is enough to ensure permanency in a relationship—that is, into believing that romantic love can thrive without forming nonsexual bonds and without possessing a clear sense of the effects of passing time. In articulating this view, only in small part through the wit of his undisguised allusion to Marlowe, Shakespeare makes clear his independence from Marlowe's exclusive focus on sexual love and, implicitly, his criticism of the limitations in content and attitude of that focus. Less charitably perhaps, one could also understand the phrase as self-congratulatory in that it invites comparison between Marlowe's single-mindedness and Shakespeare's complexity in portraying romantic love. Such defensiveness may in part lie behind Shakespeare's parodying of the phrase from *Hero and Leander*. But if Marlowe's comic perspective on romantic love shades into a cynicism that Shakespeare rejects, Shakespeare's perspective, perhaps somewhat in reaction to the poem and in spite of the play's moments of commonsense realism, represents the very self-deluding idealization of romantic love that Marlowe's poem rejects.

Another Marlovian phrase, "Was this the face that launched a thousand ships" (*Doctor Faustus*, V, i, 89 [A-Text] and V, i, 93 [B-Text]), haunted Shakespeare and, as I mentioned already, first appears in *Richard II*:[75]

> Was this face the face
> That every day under his household roof
> Did keep ten thousand men? Was this the face
> That like the sun did make beholders wink?
> Is this the face that faced so many follies
> That was at last outfaced by Bolingbroke? (IV, i, 281–86)

Unless the locution of "face" was a commonplace or from another source that we do not know about, it appears that Shakespeare is again acknowledging undisguisedly his familiarity with a work of Marlowe's. Shakespeare's use of the line has little bearing on the content of the play as a whole, especially since it boldly calls up a frame of reference familiar to him and his audience but not to Richard and his. Even so, it acknowledges the impact and stature of Marlowe's legacy. Richard's repetition of the phrase becomes a parody of Faustus's wonder at the recreation of Helen of Troy, but to the detriment of himself. Although we do not have to go as far as Marjorie Garber in seeing in the echo "an implied parallel between the fall of Troy and the fall of Richard's England,"[76] we can agree with her that Marlowe's phrase "undercuts Richard's self-dramatization."[77] Similar to other moments in the play when the content of Richard's words is pointedly stylistic, the excessive repetition of the line and the puns on "face" (lines 285, 286) cause us to recoil from Richard's blatant self-pity and childish egotism. The reworked phrase also points—and not for the first time—to the King's uncontrollable penchant for verbal doodling, for self-indulgently asserting the superiority of style over content, in effect, for retreating from his public moral responsibilities into a private, non-moral sanctuary of aesthetic play.

In retreating through a play with language, Richard anticipates a tendency manifested with greater sophistication by Hamlet. This tendency also finds a parallel in Shakespeare the playwright, who, especially in some of the plays of the 1590s, at times indulges in a free play of language to the exclusion of demands for artistic integration made by the characterization, plot, and language.[78] Language that the playwright integrates into the play can also be self-indulgent and self-congratulatory; but, at the same time, it gives continuity to the dialogue and communicates the sense of a social bond—the characters with each other and, hence, the play with its audience. By using language that draws upon the best resources of both art and nature to communicate with others, characters rise above mere self-indulgence to become, as Mercutio points out to Romeo, ideally "sociable" (*Romeo and Juliet,* II, iv, 88). In *Love's Labour's Lost* Shakespeare first dramatizes characters who, to the exclusion of a seriousness of purpose, are "wantoning" with wit;[79] in doing so, he makes plain the same tendency in himself as playwright. As I shall demonstrate, this tendency can also be understood as a way of accounting at times for Shakespeare's strong, salutary response to Marlowe's free-wheeling, verbal pyrotechnics but indifference to or firm rejection of his content.

On the sliding scale of identifiable influences, likenesses, and possible likenesses, characterization and events follow quotations and allusions in degree of definiteness. Even so, exactly when definite influence occurs is often impossible to determine. Would Hotspur have tried to pluck bright honor from the pale-faced moon if Tamburlaine had not shown that the better part of valor is sometimes *in*discretion? Would Shakespeare have allowed Richard II to abdicate his responsibilities as king with such open, verbal self-indulgence had not Edward II set the precedent? Setting aside other possible influences such as Virgil, does the conflict of love and honor in *Antony and Cleopatra* owe anything to the similar conflict of similarly legendary figures in *Dido, Queen of Carthage*? Their historical sources apart, do the events of

Richard II owe something to the events of *Edward II*, because they are both plays about weak kings, men temperamentally wrong for the positions they hold?

These questions do not, of course, take into account the distinction between specific and generalized influences from Marlowe and the mixture of both within a single play. *The Merchant of Venice*, for example, contains what Nicholas Brooke calls a "general reminiscence of a specific play."[80] As I have already pointed out, the generalized Marlovian influence is from *The Jew of Malta* and, according to Brooke, resides in "the language of Shylock, and the use made of him to criticize the hypocrisy of a Christian society."[81] The specific Marlovian influence, which is revealed in the style and tone of the speeches of the Prince of Morocco, takes us back to *Tamburlaine*.[82] There are, to be sure, other plays in which a characteristic reminds us of specific works of Marlowe, even if not of specific passages. *Antony and Cleopatra* is an example; the norm of hyperbole there reminds us of Marlowe's use of hyperbole in *Dido, Queen of Carthage*, the *Tamburlaine* plays, and *Hero and Leander*. Such variations in influence point to Shakespeare's multiconsciousness in his absorption of Marlowe. When he is influenced by the style of Marlowe and rejects the ethos, we also realize how selective the process can be.

Stylistic influences can be even more elusive than the influences of characterization and events. What exactly does Shakespeare owe to Marlowe's mighty line, his high astounding terms, and his ubiquitous hyperbole? Do plays as late as the tragedies and *Antony and Cleopatra* bear an even stronger imprint of Marlowe's stylistic traits than earlier plays such as *Titus Andronicus*? J.B. Steane mentions "a similar 'feel' in the substance of the poetry" and points to the imagery of vastness in *Dido, Queen of Carthage* and *Antony and Cleopatra* as evidence.[83] Is this parallel too nebulous to give support to the general point?

Certainly nebulous and more complicated is the influence of Marlowe's system of values on Shakespeare. Naturally enough, a writer can react to another writer's values by accepting or rejecting them, in part or in full, and a rejection of values, whether in part or in full, can be as strong an influence as an acceptance of them. For example, as I have shown, Shakespeare has read *Hero and Leander*, and he agrees with Marlowe's view of the importance of sexual desire in romantic love. But he rejects Marlowe's focus on physical attraction as its only ingredient. Marlowe's sentiment that "Love is not full of pity (as men say) / But deaf and cruel where he means to prey" (*Hero and Leander*, 771–72) is echoed in the Sonnets when Shakespeare says: "… and, till action, lust / Is perjured, murd'rous, bloody, full of blame, / Savage, extreme, rude, cruel, not to trust" (Sonnet 129, lines 2–4). Thus, Shakespeare would seem to accept the realistic acuity of Marlowe's psychological focus. Neither writer tries to make the origins of sexual desire part of a moral universe. In fact, by the end of the sonnet, Shakespeare has demonstrated with considerable irony that sexual desire, fulfilled or unfulfilled, cannot be made a part of an ethical system: "lust" is irrepressible; it can be neither controlled nor ignored. But instead of Marlowe's mix of amusement and indignation, his comically impertinent, open defiance of the standard characterizations of unfulfilled sexual desire, and his moral view that such characterizations delude through sentimentality and a lack of realism, Shakespeare responds with detachment and a more purely aesthetic perspective by dramatizing the omnipotence of sexual desire. Cleverly, he uses morally connotative language and morally pejorative imagery to portray the fearful actions of lust as a murderer; but the language and imagery, while conveying the effects of sexual desire as debilitating, also suggest with mordant irony the hopelessness of a moral stand on this uncontrollable, wholly involuntary psychological phenomenon. Based on the evidence from the sonnet, the question of whether Shakespeare's view of sexual desire was, in fact, influenced by Marlowe's is impossible to answer. The similarity in their understanding of the mechanics of its behavior, including its ability to make us temporarily psychotic without our knowing it, presents a real possibility that Marlowe might have ignited something in Shakespeare and even helped him to crystallize his own thinking. But about a definite influence we cannot know, especially when we allow space for the ways in which Shakespeare's own personal experience may have influenced the act of composition.

At the end of the scale is the clearly nebulous or ambiguous influence. We know that Shakespeare had seen the second part of *Tamburlaine* played, and we assume the first part as well. But what impact did it have on him when he sat down to compose *Henry V*? A similar question of influence might be asked about: (1) *Dido, Queen of Carthage* and *Antony and Cleopatra* and, to a lesser extent, *Troilus and Cressida* and *Venus and Adonis*; (2) *Tamburlaine* and (in addition to *Henry V*, already mentioned) *Antony and Cleopatra*, and, to a lesser extent, *Richard III*, *The Taming of the Shrew*, and *Romeo and Juliet*; (3) *The Jew of Malta* and *The Merchant of Venice*, *Titus Andronicus*, *Richard III*, and *Romeo and Juliet*; (4) *The Massacre At Paris* and *Titus Andronicus*, *Richard III*, and *Julius Caesar*; (5) *Edward II* and *Richard II*; and (6) *Hero and Leander* and *Venus and Adonis*, *Romeo and Juliet*, and *Antony and Cleopatra*. In each case, even when the likelihood is strong, definite influence may well elude verification. One example may suffice to show how difficult it can be to verify a definite influence and, yet, how worthwhile the pursuit. In *The Jew of Malta*, II, iii, 176–203, Barabas adduces a catalogue of his crimes to portray himself to Ithamore. In *Titus Andronicus*, V, i, 124–44, Aaron similarly makes use of a catalogue of his crimes to characterize himself. The question is, "does Shakespeare's catalogue originate in Marlowe's?"[84] The two passages are finally interesting less because they are catalogues that may be linked than because their significant differences help us to characterize the distinctness of the imaginations of the two playwrights.

Finally, still at the end of the scale, are those attitudes which are similar in the two writers and produce parallels in their works but which do not constitute influences, because in origin, they are psycho-cultural. For an example, we need look only at the two writers' disenchantment with the sociopolitical state and the systems that govern it, Shakespeare's increasingly so as his works progress. Even if we assume that Shakespeare was aware of Marlowe's disgruntlement and cynicism, we have little assurance that they affected him (and much less that there was a specific time in his career when they might have). It is likely that Marlowe's own views were conditioned by his cynicism about humankind, arising, perhaps, from a profoundly disappointed idealism. He exalts very few characters in his works and endows almost no one with full-blooded humanity.[85] Moreover, when in *Edward*

II and *The Massacre At Paris* he appears to be supportive of the orthodox system of monarchy, he is, in fact, just the opposite. Even though the structure of each play favors monarchy, the texture undercuts this political view by presenting a thoroughly convincing account of the pervasive malevolence inherent in a monarchical system and a more convincing portrayal of the agents of corruption than of the few agents of good. What ideas Shakespeare may have gleaned from Marlowe's dramatizations of politics would be difficult to pinpoint. His understanding of humankind's corporate existence in society was initially more naïve and ultimately more complicated than Marlowe's—not surprisingly, given his longer life. Shakespeare took a stronger interest in the dramatic possibilities of the conflict between the individual and society, evincing a greater awareness of the frailties, complexities, and transitory nature of each, as well as society's capacity for snuffing out individual creative energies. Perhaps without knowing it, Marlowe presents the case for drastic sociopolitical change. Shakespeare dramatizes the forces that are both creating and undermining social stability and, even though he finds some satisfaction in people as individuals, conveys little hope for change in the political system. By the end of his career, his disillusionment echoes Marlowe's. From this brief look at a similarity that is probably not an influence, we can see that the significance of such a discussion lies in the more precise definition one is able to give to the perspective of each writer, including changes in attitude. Even though we do not need an influence to sustain the comparison, the possibility that one exists can be the impetus for an illuminating discussion.

V

I now turn to the question of what preconceptions about the works of Marlowe and Shakespeare a study of influence implies. First, it indicates that there is a link between their works, which gives legitimacy to the term "influence." Second, it suggests that elucidating the link contributes significantly to our understanding of the two writers' distinctive imaginative processes and theatrical habits and to the procedures by which we locate meaning in their works.[86] We have seen that, when a quotation or an allusion is the link, it may not indicate anything about a larger meaning of the work. It may do little more than clarify or sharpen the focus of a particular passage. But it may indicate something about the closeness and even the cooperation of the two writers and their routine in the workplace during the period from 1590–93. The word "influence" carries with it a suggestion that Shakespeare was influenced profoundly enough to change what he might otherwise have done as a writer and man of the theater, enough to have a bearing on an overall concept, intention, or meaning of the work. Thus, scrutinizing influence prompts such questions as whether Hotspur, Henry V, and Antony would have been the overreachers they are without Tamburlaine. As soon as we begin to think of influence in this deeper sense, we realize that, although the stronger the influence, the more important it becomes, paradoxically, the more difficult it can be to pin down, or even to rule out.

The study of influence also presupposes that we have decided what the influencing and influenced works are about—that we have some preliminary notion of what they set out to do and that we find their focus and purpose somehow similar. If we thought that *Hero and Leander* and *Venus and Adonis* did not belong to the same genre with similar literary conventions and purposes, there would be little point in pairing them for a study of potential influence.[87] By the same token, if we did not regard *Dido, Queen of Carthage* and *Antony and Cleopatra* as similar in the conflict and kinds of characters that they present, why would we consider examining them for influence? The study of influence suggests, too, that we have some critical sense of how effectively each of the works being paired accomplishes its aims. Without making such an assessment of the success of both the influencing and influenced works, we cannot sensibly come to terms with the relevance of the influence, much less establish its presence.

Barabas and Shylock can be used to illustrate the point. Critics have commonly noted that, although consistently an overreacher, Barabas appears in the first two acts to be a more developed character than the comic, often caricaturized figure of the last three acts.[88] Commentators suggest that this inconsistency reflects a shift in intention as Marlowe was writing the play. A similar shift occurs in *The Merchant of Venice*. We know that Shakespeare, like other of his contemporary fellow dramatists—Marlowe included—sometimes wrote to the moment, not adhering to the intention with which he had apparently set forth, whether in character or genre, and, as Ben Jonson and Samuel Johnson complained, not bothering to rectify inconsistencies by revising or rewriting. The gratuitous comic material in the first two acts of *Romeo and Juliet* is an example of a mood and genre that shift after the death of Mercutio in Act 3; a more drastic shift occurs in *Measure for Measure* when, after III, i, 151, the potentially tragic plot turns abruptly into a comedy of intrigue. The impulse to enlarge on or pull back from the original intention may have been a purely aesthetic impulse, for, to apply a truism, if variety is the spice of life, it is even more so the spice of art. As Shakespeare wrote *The Merchant of Venice*, he veered from making Shylock a comic character as single-dimensional as the Barabas of the last three acts. Three well-known instances in which this occurs come immediately to mind: The speech in which Shylock asks, "Hath not a Jew eyes? Hath not a Jew hands, organs, dimensions, senses, affections, passions" (III, i, 54–56); the statement about his ring a bit later in the scene: "It was my turquoise; I had it of Leah when I was a bachelor" (III, i, 111–13); and in his final speech as he exits from the play, the line "I am not well" (IV, i, 394) which resonates with indications of severe emotional distress. At times, Shakespeare seems to sense a momentary dramatic value in investing his caricaturized figure with human traits. In doing so, he reveals through the inconsistent enlargement of the characterization either an uncertain control or a purposeful ambiguity. At crucial moments, Shylock dominates the play simply by virtue of being too human for the lesser comic role he was initially intended to perform. Thus, whereas Barabas diminishes from a three-dimensional character into a caricature, Shylock reverses this trajectory, shifting from a caricature to a more fully developed character. Shakespeare has, in effect, turned away from the identical form of Marlowe's excesses in plot as well as characterization, but not without indulging in an excess himself, for, partly through his reconfiguration of Shylock, he has crossed the boundaries of comedy by raising issues too serious for the comic framework to bear. We can therefore account for differences between Barabas and Shylock not only because, as a precondition to ascertaining influence, we have understood the different intentions of *The Jew of Malta* and *The Merchant of Venice*, but because we also understand the natural limitations (i.e., imperfections) of each writer in executing his aims.

By first interpreting the aims of the influencing and influenced works, critics are able to prevent themselves from forging a link apart from a consideration of the two contexts of the works, and from overstating the possibility of a direct source and confusing it with an influence. For, in order for the attribution of an influence to be convincing, one needs to see the link between the works as not violating the context of either of them. This is not to say that, in studying influence, one's understanding of the context of either the influencing or influenced work may not be modified.

This brings me to a final point. It is obvious that the time has come to expand and deepen studies of influence generally and to make more open and inclusive comparisons of apparently similar works by Marlowe and Shakespeare. Criticism has already begun to look outward to the play of psycho-cultural forces on the works of each writer independently, as well as inward to their often obscure psychology and even to the ultimately obscure psychology of some of their superficially similar characters (e.g., Edward II and Richard II). In pursuing a more complex, intertextual course, the present study finds that Marlowe and Shakespeare's roles as self-conscious dramatists working within literary traditions and the pragmatic conditions of the Elizabethan (and, for Shakespeare, Jacobean) theater deserve greater prominence than they have heretofore received. The degree to which Shakespeare was involved with the everyday workings of the theater and attentive to such important concerns as an actor's ability to captivate his audience can be gauged by the following psychological reflection voiced by York in *Richard II*:

> As in a theatre the eyes of men,
> After a well-graced actor leaves the stage,
> Are idly bent on him that enters next,
> Thinking his prattle to be tedious,
> Even so, or with much more contempt, men's eyes
> Did scowl on gentle Richard. (*Richard II*, V, ii, 23–28)

That Marlowe was similarly engaged with successful dramaturgy is clear from, among other things, his Prologue to Part 1 of *Tamburlaine* and his decision to write a sequel. Emulation between the two playwrights as they worked out of the same theater could only have heightened their awareness of the strategies necessary to composing a play that was a commercial hit.

This study contends that Marlowe and Shakespeare regarded one another not as writers with great themes but chiefly as practicing dramatists and poets, and that this is where the influence begins and ends. Thus, a detailed comparison of apparently similar works by the two authors grants us not only a greater understanding of the multiplicity of Marlowe's influence on Shakespeare but also a deeper insight into the import of individual works—in particular, the ideologies and artistic practices of the two writers that comprise this import. In effect, a careful, intertextual comparison enables us to range more freely and with greater inclusiveness and complexity as we attempt to illuminate our understanding of the complicated and uncommonly powerful professional bond between Shakespeare and Marlowe.

Notes

1   Unless otherwise noted, all references to the plays and poems of William Shakespeare are from *William Shakespeare: The Complete Works*, gen. eds Stephen Orgel and A.R. Braunmuller (New York: Penguin Putnam, 2002).

2   Unless otherwise noted, all references to the plays of Christopher Marlowe are from *Christopher Marlowe: The Complete Plays*, ed. Mark Thornton Burnett (London: J.M. Dent, 1999).

3   James Shapiro, *Rival Playwrights: Marlowe, Jonson, Shakespeare* (New York: Columbia University Press, 1991), 123, mentions the possibility that Shakespeare acted in *The Massacre At Paris* during the time he was associated with Pembroke's Men. But there is no proof that Pembroke's Men ever held the rights to the play. Harold Bloom believes that the two men must have known one another, even if they were not friends (*The Anxiety of Influence*, revised edition [New York: Oxford University Press, 1997], xxi).

4   Brian Vickers, *Shakespeare as Co-Author: A Historical Study of Five Collaborative Plays* (Oxford: Oxford University Press, 2002), 140–41, argues that recent studies, based wholly on internal evidence (stylometrics), attribute the authorship of the pamphlet to Chettle, not Greene. I am not convinced as Vickers is that internal evidence is conclusive, especially since he presents it without the support of any external historical evidence.

5   For the quotations from Greene, see Alexander B. Grosart, *The Life and Complete Works in Prose and Verse of Robert Greene*, 15 vols (New York: Russell and Russell, 1881–86), 12: 144. For a summary of the debate about the meaning of Greene's attack on Shakespeare, see D. Allen Carroll, "Greene's 'Vpstart Crow' Passage: A Survey of Commentary," *Research Opportunities in Renaissance Drama* 28 (1985): 111–27. See also Vickers, who feels that "the whole thrust of the passage is clearly directed against the actors" (209) of whom Shakespeare was one.

6   The line is "O tiger's heart wrapped in a woman's hide" (I, iv, 138).

7   Shapiro, *Rival Playwrights*, 76. Grosart, 12:142.

8   This reference to Marlowe apart, Marlowe was another playwright of whom Greene was "openly resentful and emulous." See David Bevington and Eric Rasmussen, eds, *Doctor Faustus: A- and B-Texts (1604, 1616)* (New York: St Martin's Press, 1993), 1.

9   See Shapiro, 76–77, who concurs and quotes from Chettle to support his point.

10   *Henslowe's Diary*, ed. R.A. Foakes, 2nd edition (Cambridge: Cambridge University Press, 2002), 16–18.

11   The popularity of Marlowe's plays can be documented, as theater historians have done, through the records in the business diary of Philip Henslowe. For imitations of *Tamburlaine*, see Peter Berek, "Tamburlaine's Weak Sons: Imitation as Interpretation Before 1593," *Renaissance Drama* n.s., 13 (1982): 55–82. Berek states that "Of the 38 extant plays for the public theater first performed in England between 1587 and 1593, 10 show clear debts to *Tamburlaine*" (58); he then goes on to discuss the "debts."

12   In her biography of Marlowe, *Christopher Marlowe: A Renaissance Life* (Ithaca, NY: Cornell University Press, 2002), Constance Brown Kuriyama comes to a similar conclusion: "During the late 1580s and 1590s, Marlowe was the most admired, envied, and widely imitated playwright in London" (80).

13   The two known references to the *Henry VI* plays are Robert Greene's allusion to Part 3 of *Henry VI*, I, iv, 138 in *A Groatsworth of Wit* and Thomas Nashe's reference in *Pierce Peniless his Supplication to the Divell* (1592) to the Talbot scenes in 1 *Henry VI*, IV, ii–vii: R.B. McKerrow, ed., *The Works of Thomas Nashe*, 5 vols. (London, 1904–10; repr. 1958), 1: 212.

14   Foakes, ed., *Henslowe's Diary*, 16–18.

15   I am in full agreement with the argument by Hanspeter Born, "The Date of *2, 3 Henry VI*," *Shakespeare Quarterly* 25 (1974): 323–34, that the *Henry VI* play listed by Henslowe, beginning in March of 1592, refers to the first part of *Henry VI* and that the second and third parts were written in succession after the first part.

16   Roslyn Lander Knutson, *Playing Companies and Commerce in Shakespeare's Time* (Cambridge: Cambridge University Press, 2001), 125. Her full argument is on pp. 125–26.

17   Roslyn Knutson, speaking from the perspective of commercial competition among playing companies, gives support for the irrelevance of a hostile, personal rivalry between Marlowe and Shakespeare when she summarizes her thesis: "I have emphasized the cooperative strategies of players, companies, and dramatists, a cooperation similar to that of members in a guild. I have argued that, although there were personal quarrels, those quarrels did not determine business strategies" (*Playing Companies*, 76).

   Although we have accounts of some playwrights' "personal quarrels"—Marlowe among them—no documents have surfaced to suggest a feud between Marlowe and Shakespeare.

18   Jonathan Bate, *The Genius of Shakespeare* (New York: Oxford University Press, 1998), 105.

19   For a similar assumption of a rivalry between Marlowe and Shakespeare, see Thomas Cartelli, *Marlowe, Shakespeare, and the Economy of Theatrical Experience* (Philadelphia: University of Pennsylvania Press, 1991).

20   Shapiro, *Rival Playwrights*, 14. The opening six lines of Sonnet 86 are:

> Was it the proud full sail of his great verse
> Bound for the prize of all too precious you,
> That did my ripe thought in my brain inhearse,
> Making their tomb the womb wherein they grew?
> Was it his spirit, by spirit taught to write
> Above a mortal pitch, that struck me dead?

21   Bate, *Genius of Shakespeare*, 130–32. For three others who agree with Bate, see Richard Levin, "Another Possible Clue to the Identity of the Rival Poet," *Shakespeare Quarterly* 36 (1985): 213–14; Roy T. Eriksen, "Anxious Art: Shakespeare's Rivalry with Marlowe," in Ishrat Lindblad, ed., *Proceedings From the Third Nordic Conference for English Studies* (Stockholm: Almqvist and Wiksell International, 1987), 639–49; and James P. Bednarz, "Marlowe and the English Literary Scene" in *The Cambridge Companion to Christopher Marlowe*, ed. Patrick Cheney (Cambridge: Cambridge University Press, 2004), 103. See, too, Maurice Charney, "The Voice of Marlowe's Tamburlaine in Early Shakespeare," *Comparative Drama* 31:2 (Summer, 1997): 218–19, who hears the voice of Tamburlaine

in Sonnet 86 and understands the Rival Poet as Marlowe. The other candidate for the Rival Poet most frequently mentioned is George Chapman. Apparently, Chapman's supporters are reminded of his translations of Homer when Shakespeare employs the phrase "the proud full sail of his great verse" (Sonnet 86, line 1).

22   Harold Bloom, *The Anxiety of Influence* (New York: Oxford University Press, 1973). In the revised edition of 1997, which Bate evidently has not seen, a new Preface (xi–xlvii) reveals Bloom focusing on Shakespeare's response to the influence of Christopher Marlowe (pp. xx–xxii and xxx–xlvii). My principal reservations about Bloom's characterization of Marlowe's influence stem from the harshness with which he denigrates Marlowe as a playwright, the claim, overstated, that Shakespeare spends his early years *emancipating* himself from "the image of Marlowe" (xliii), and several shameless assertions of influence (e.g., "Shakespeare … was haunted enough by his acquaintance Christopher Marlowe to portray him, with marvelous ambivalence, as Edmund" [xlvi]).

23   Bate, *Genius of Shakespeare*, 104.

24   Ibid.

25   Ibid.

26   Ibid. Again, Bate refers exclusively to the 1973 edition of *The Anxiety of Influence*. In the Preface to the 1997 edition, Bloom details his understanding of Marlowe's influence on Shakespeare.

27   As I shall contend, the principle may be understood (arguably) as a motivating element in Shakespeare at times during the writing of *Richard II*, *The Merchant of Venice*, and *Henry IV*, Part 2.

28   Marjorie Garber, "Marlovian Vision/Shakespearean Revision," *Research Opportunities in Renaissance Drama* 22 (1979): 3, and Shapiro, 79.

29   Scott McMillin and Sally-Beth MacLean, *The Queen's Men and their Plays* (Cambridge: Cambridge University Press, 1998), 155–69.

30   Ibid., 167.

31   Ibid., 168.

32   Ibid., xv.

33   Ibid., 161.

34   Knutson, *Playing Companies*, 53–54.

35   Compare *Doctor Faustus*, V, i, 89 (A-Text) or V, i, 93 (B-Text) and *Richard II*, IV, i, 281–86.

36   That Shakespeare counted on his audience's familiarity with the content of *Woodstock* is quite possible, even if there seems to be no direct influence. *Richard II* is, in fact, something of a sequel to *Woodstock*. *Woodstock* gives a fuller characterization of Richard's attachments to his favorites, his degeneracy, and his claim of divine right than *Richard II* does. The text can be found in *Elizabethan History Plays*, ed. and intro. by William A. Armstrong (London: Oxford University Press, 1965), 167–260.

37   Vickers, 148–243, presents the evidence of Shakespeare and Peele as collaborators in considerable detail. But, again, the evidence is wholly internal.

38   In *Rival Playwrights*, Shapiro discusses the long-term effects of what he apparently understands as an unfriendly, competitive rivalry—that is, on Shakespeare and Jonson after Marlowe's death, including "how much the unusual working conditions of the Elizabethan theater shaped these rivalries and how much should be attributed to the habits of mind of the playwrights themselves" (vii). As I have been contending, broad and deep influence can occur more easily without the dynamic of an unfriendly rivalry.

39 In Chapter 2, I discuss the difficulties associated with the dates of composition of the two plays.

40 See Shapiro, *Rival Playwrights*, 84, 85, and 91–96, for a discussion of the possible influence of Shakespeare in his *Henry VI* plays on *Edward II*. For two other critics who also sense the influence, see Clifford Leech in *Christopher Marlowe: Poet For The Stage*, ed. Anne Lancashire (New York: AMS Press, 1986), 129–32, and Lisa Hopkins, *Christopher Marlowe: A Literary Life* (New York: Palgrave, 2000), 8–12. Although the date of composition of *Edward II* is by no means clear, I am of course assuming, as many do, that *Edward II* was written after the *Henry VI* plays and that the chronology of Marlowe's works goes something like this: *Dido, Queen of Carthage* (1586); *Tamburlaine*, Parts 1 and 2 (c. 1587–88); *Doctor Faustus* (1588); *The Jew of Malta* (1589); *The Massacre At Paris* (1592); and *Edward II* (1593). See Ian McAdam, *The Irony of Identity* (Newark: University of Delaware Press, 1999), 41–42, and Kuriyama, 79, for two recent arguments supporting this arrangement as a probable order of composition. *Hero and Leander* appears to have been written late as well.

41 Shapiro, *Rival Playwrights*, 91–96.

42 Ibid., 92–93.

43 Bloom, xxiii. Bloom accurately characterizes Shakespeare's understanding of influence as (1) "The flowing from the stars upon our fates and our personalities" (xii) and as (2) "inspiration" (xii).

44 "Shakespeare and the exorcists" in *Shakespeare and the Question of Theory*, ed. Patricia Parker and Geoffrey Hartman (New York: Methuen, 1985), 163. Greenblatt is arguing that for him literary works must be located in their historical context: "For me the study of the literary is the study of contingent, particular, intended, and historically embedded works" (163).

45 Richard Levin, "Another 'Source' for *The Alchemist* and another Look at Source Studies," *English Literary Renaissance* 28:2 (Spring, 1998), 226. Levin exemplifies his point by identifying three types of sources: (1) those which are of major importance to the playwright, such as Sir Thomas North's translation of Plutarch's *Life of Antonius* and Shakespeare's *Antony and Cleopatra*; (2) those which are of lesser importance because they are only used for part of a work or because they are used in combination with other sources; and (3) those which "would not make any difference to our understanding of the play because they do not involve a meaningful causal connection in the playwright's creative process" (227). Levin is making distinctions that all have to do with influence since his standard of measure is the effect his "sources" have on the creative process.

46 Stephen J. Lynch, *Shakespearean Intertextuality: Studies in Selected Plays and Sources* (Westport, CT: Greenwood Press, 1998), 1. For some additional comments on the significance of intertextuality, see Richard Hillman, *Shakespeare, Marlowe and the Politics of France* (New York: Palgrave, 2002), 1–2.

47 Lynch, 1.

48 Ibid.

49 Ibid., 2.

50 Ibid.

51 Ibid.

52 M.L. Stapleton, "Venus As Praeceptor: The *Ars Amatoria* in *Venus and Adonis*," in *"Venus and Adonis": Critical Essays*, ed. Philip Kolin (New York: Garland, 1997), 320, n. 12. Stapleton expands this point, saying, "Furthermore, what poststructuralists claim is a new way to look at texts is surely an ancient idea in both theory and practice. Julia Kristeva's

preference for 'transposition' over 'intertextuality' or 'source' as a term has its roots in Renaissance thinking: 'If one grants that every signifying practice is a field of transpositions of various signifying systems (an intertextuality), one then understands that its "place" of enunciation and its denoted "object" are never single, complete, and identical to themselves, but always plural, shattered, capable of being tabulated'" [*Revolution in Poetic Language*, trans. Margaret Walker (New York: Columbia University Press, 1984), 60]. Stapleton continues, making the point that "[Thomas] Greene [Thomas Greene, *The Light in Troy: Imitation and Discovery in Renaissance Poetry* (New Haven, CT: Yale University Press, 1982), 54–103] and George W. Pigman [George W. Pigman, "Versions of Imitation in the Renaissance," *Renaissance Quarterly* 33 (1980): 1–32] ... demonstrate conclusively that sixteenth-century theorists such as Erasmus and Ricci identify and advocate a similar polyvocality in poetic composition (minus the deconstructive semiotics). Or, to invoke [Jonathan] Bate again [Jonathan Bate, *Shakespeare and Ovid* (Oxford: Clarendon Press, 1993), 51]: 'the creative imitator interprets his source narrative partly by means of other narratives that lie both outside and inside, around and within [the text].'"

53   Compare Levin's "final point about the general problems of source studies, which is the obvious need for some method to differentiate the various kinds of sources and the kinds of understanding they can yield" (225).

54   Lynch, 4.

55   Maurice Charney, "Jessica's Turquoise Ring and Abigail's Porridge: Shakespeare and Marlowe as Rivals and Imitators," *Renaissance Drama* n.s. 10 (1979), n. 11 (p. 43).

56   Ibid.

57   Or, as Maurice Charney in "Marlowe's *Edward II* as Model for Shakespeare's *Richard II*," *Research Opportunities in Renaissance Drama* 33 (1994): 31–41, might ask, "In what sense is Marlowe a model, rather than simply a source, for Shakespeare?"

58   This does not mean that the use to which this source is put cannot be considered an influence. See the discussion of Shakespeare's use of Marlowe's lyric in Chapter 5: "'For A Tricksy Word / Defy The Matter': The Influence of *The Jew of Malta* on *The Merchant of Venice*."

59   Charles Edelman, "Which Is The Jew That Shakespeare Knew?: Shylock On The Elizabethan Stage," *Shakespeare Survey* 52 (1999): 99.

60   Ibid., 100.

61   Strictly speaking, all "cultural" influences are psycho-cultural because they are passed through the filter of one's psyche. But some psycho-cultural influences are more exactly reflective of cultural attitudes (for example, patriarchal attitudes) than others are. That is, the influence has not been transformed but is received directly.

62   Bloom, 1997 edition of *The Anxiety of Influence*, Preface, xli.

63   Russell Fraser, *Young Shakespeare* (New York: Columbia University Press, 1988), 155.

64   These sources include John Foxe's *Acts and Monuments*, as well as the chronicles of Richard Grafton and Raphael Holinshed which were based on Foxe, Matthew Paris's *Chronica Majora*, and such plays as John Bale's *King John* (1534, with revisions in 1538 and 1561) and *The Troublesome Reign of King John* (c. 1587–91).

65   Generally speaking, without distinguishing between sources and influence, scholars of early modern texts have sustained a remarkable enthusiasm for establishing in Shakespeare's works similarities to Marlowe's. There are, of course, exceptions. In his discussion in *Shakespeare 1971: Proceedings of the World Shakespeare Congress*, ed. Clifford Leech and J.M.R. Margeson (Toronto: University of Toronto Press, 1972), 123–32, Wolfgang Clemen asserts, "The notion of Marlowe as Shakespeare's forerunner has been abandoned

long ago" (123). He goes on to explain that it is the differences between the two writers that critics now discuss. In support of his argument, he cites Irving Ribner, "Marlowe and Shakespeare," *Shakespeare Quarterly* 15 (Spring, 1964): 41–53, whose position that Marlowe had no influence on Shakespeare is clearly extreme and too reductively categorical. Moreover, as the references in previous endnotes patently attest, the tendency to link the two writers has not only increased but deepened since the time when Clemen was writing. To the list of recent critics who link the two playwrights one might add Lawrence Danson, *Shakespeare's Dramatic Genres* (Oxford: Oxford University Press, 2000), especially pp. 44–45 and 117–18; Martin Wiggins, *Shakespeare and the Drama of his Time* (Oxford: Oxford University Press, 2000); and James P. Bednarz, "Marlowe and the English Literary Scene," 90–105.

66   J. Leeds Barroll, "Antony and Pleasure," *Journal of English and Germanic Philology* 57 (1958): 708–20.

67   Marvin Spevack, ed., *A New Variorum Edition of Shakespeare*: *"Antony and Cleopatra"* (New York: The Modern Language Association of America, 1990), 609.

68   See the discussion of this passage in the next chapter.

69   In *As You Like It*, the phrase from *Hero and Leander*, "whoever loved that loved not at first sight," as I discuss later in this chapter, exemplifies this tendency.

70   Wilbur Sanders, *The Dramatist and the Received Idea* (Cambridge: Cambridge University Press, 1968), 318.

71   A.P. Rossiter, ed., *"Woodstock": A Moral History* (London: Chatto and Windus, 1946), 17.

72   Part 2 of *Tamburlaine*, IV, iii, 1–2 is echoed in Part 2 of *Henry IV*, II, iv, 157–61, and "The Passionate Shepherd to His Love" in *The Merry Wives of Windsor*, III, i, 16–28; *The Jew of Malta*, II, i, 47–48 and 54 is echoed in *The Merchant of Venice*, II, viii, 15; *Hero and Leander* I.176 is echoed in *As You Like It*, III, v, 82, and *Doctor Faustus*, V, i, 99 in *Richard II*, IV, i, 281–86, *Troilus and Cressida*, II, ii, 81–83, and *King Lear*, IV, vii, 32–37.

73   The line, "Thus Caesar did go forth," from *The Massacre At Paris*, Sc. 22.67 is used by Shakespeare in *Julius Caesar*, II, ii, 28 unless it was the compilers of Marlowe's text that borrowed the line from *Julius Caesar*. This latter possibility is suggested in *Christopher Marlowe: The Plays and their Sources*, ed. Vivien Thomas and William Tydeman (New York: Routledge, 1994), 258–59. In their discussion of the sources of Marlowe's play, the editors also suggest that the line might have come from pamphlet material that Marlowe had access to and seems to have made use of (pp. 251–60).

74   Unless otherwise noted, all references to Marlowe's poems are from *Christopher Marlowe: The Complete Poems*, ed. Mark Thornton Burnett (London: J.M. Dent, 2000).

75   Because of the continued popularity and revivals of *Doctor Faustus*, the line may have acquired a general currency. As I mentioned in endnote 72, two additional echoes of the phrase occur in Shakespeare's plays, suggesting that he was so impressed by it that he was willing to take theatrical advantage of it. The first echo is in *Troilus and Cressida*, II, ii, 81–83:

> Is she worth keeping? Why, she is a pearl
> Whose price hath launched above a thousand ships
> And turned crowned kings to merchants.

If *Troilus and Cressida* was on stage in 1602–1603 when *Doctor Faustus* was also probably revived, then the echo is all the more understandable. The second echo is in *King Lear*, IV, vii, 32–37:

> Was this a face
> To be opposed against the jarring winds?
> [To stand against the deep dread-bolted thunder?
> In the most terrible and nimble stroke
> Of quick cross lightning to watch, poor perdu,
> With this thin helm?]

76   "Marlovian Vision/Shakespearean Revision," *Research Opportunities in Renaissance Literature* 22 (1979): 3. Perhaps Garber was thinking that some members of Shakespeare's audiences could plausibly have made the connection between Richard's demise and the fall of Troy; but it seems to me too much of a stretch. Another critic whose argument seems forced is Nicholas Brooke, "Marlowe As Provocative Agent In Shakespeare's Early Plays," *Shakespeare Survey* 14 (1961): 34–44. He contends, for example, that Richard II is to be identified with Faustus: "the Richard who identifies himself with Christ, identifies himself also with the damned Faustus; or rather, like Faustus in his last speech, his reflexions oscillate between the visions of Heaven and Hell, and the shadow of Helen stresses the sensuality in Richard's narcissism" (40). The argument of Irving Ribner in "Marlowe and Shakespeare" is also forced, even if less so, but in the opposite direction: he sees very little influence of Marlowe on Shakespeare and only some of Shakespeare on Marlowe (53).

77   Garber, 4.

78   I am thinking of such plays as *Richard III*, *Love's Labor's Lost*, *Richard II*, and *Romeo and Juliet* where the characters go out of character to play with the language. Two examples may suffice. In *Romeo and Juliet*, Capulet, who can either be crusty, blunt, and cantankerous or, when the world is going his way, generous and full of bonhomie, becomes positively lyrical and ecstatic:

> At my poor house look to behold this night
> Earth-treading stars that make dark heaven light.
> Such comfort as do lusty young men feel
> When well-appareled April on the heel
> Of limping winter treads, even such delight
> Among fresh fennel buds shall you this night
> Inherit at my house. (*Romeo and Juliet*, I, ii, 24–30)

Capulet's usually coldly practical, outspoken wife has a similar departure from the norm when, after asking Juliet if she can love Paris, she indulges in an elaborate conceit, saying

> Read o'er the volume of young Paris's face,
> And find delight writ there with beauty's pen;
> Examine every married lineament,
> And see how one another lends content;
> And what obscured in this fair volume lies
> Find written in the margent of his eyes.
> This precious book of love, this unbound lover,
> To beautify him only lacks a cover.
> The fish lives in the sea, and 'tis much pride
> For fair without the fair within to hide.
> That book in many's eyes doth share the glory,
> That in gold clasps locks in the golden story;

So shall you share all that he doth possess,
By having him making yourself no less (*Romeo and Juliet*, I, iv, 81–94).

79   See James L. Calderwood, "*Love's Labour's Lost*: A Wantoning with Words," *Studies in English Literature* 5 (1965): 317–32.
80   Brooke, 41.
81   Ibid. But see my comments on Brooke's observations in Chapter 4 below.
82   Brooke, 42. James Shapiro, 107, suggests, following Brooke, that the Prince of Arragon is even more surely a descendent of the Guise (in *The Massacre At Paris*) than Morocco is of Tamburlaine. He argues that these figures are parodies of their Marlovian ancestors intended to assert Shakespeare's "command over Marlowe's style" (107). Whether we agree with the certainty of the influence of the Guise on Arragon, the relation of this influence to that of Tamburlaine on Morocco, and the conclusion drawn from these parodic pairings, Shapiro's argument gives us another possibility of a specific influence in the play. See my comments on these possibilities of influence in Chapter 4.
83   J.B. Steane, *Marlowe: A Critical Study* (Cambridge: Cambridge University Press, 1964), 59.
84   Evidently, Emily C. Bartels, *Spectacles of Strangeness* (Philadelphia: University of Pennsylvania Press, 1993), 193, n. 47, thinks that it does. But saying so does not make it so.
85   One might argue, however, that at the end of *Doctor Faustus* Marlowe takes a giant step forward in rounding out a character when he portrays his protagonist with psychological density.
86   For a clear, illuminating discussion of the process of arriving at meanings in a work, see Robert B. Pierce, "Understanding *The Tempest*," *New Literary History: A Journal of Theory and Interpretation* 30:2 (Spring, 1999): 373–88.
87   This does not mean, of course, that a work of one genre—for instance, fiction—could not influence a work of another—for instance, drama. Nor does it rule out the possibility of one art form—painting, for example—influencing another—poetry, for example.
88   For a more detailed discussion of this point, see Chapter 4.

Chapter 2

"Unfelt Imaginations": Influence and Characterization in *The Massacre At Paris*, *Titus Andronicus*, and *Richard III*

I

In any serious consideration of Christopher Marlowe's influence on early Shakespearean drama, one question that inevitably comes up is, "What might there be in the truncated, memorially reconstructed text of *The Massacre At Paris* that would lead one to see the play as an important influence on *Titus Andronicus* and *Richard III*?" Two telling facts prompt the question: Shakespeare composed both of his plays close to the time that Marlowe wrote *Massacre*, a period during which he and Marlowe were known to be working side by side in London (1590–93); and the three plays contain some striking similarities in their apparently successful theatrical strategies. But, except for an occasional discussion of a parallel, such as F.P. Wilson's comparison of the Duke of Guise's soliloquy in the second scene of *Massacre* and Richard III's opening soliloquy,[1] critics have shied away from answering the question of influence and from attempting an intertextual examination of the plays. The chief reason may well be the maimed state of the text of *The Massacre At Paris*. Even so, such important parallels can be drawn between Marlowe's play and the two plays of Shakespeare that the question persists. Each play features a self-styled Machiavellian villain—canny, ambitious, and ruthless to the point of savagery—and each partakes of unspeakable atrocities and violence. All of the plays make use of a familiar historical setting, although Marlowe's play stands out in this respect because, unlike the histories of Shakespeare and other Elizabethan dramatists, it depicts events in contemporary European history, making the barbarism of those events all the more real. Finally, there are significant similarities in the high-pitched language and rhetoric of the three plays. Given these not inconsequential likenesses, the implication is that an analysis of this particular line of influence is overdue.

Unfortunately, the uncertainty of the dates of composition of the three plays makes such influence impossible to ascertain. *The Massacre At Paris* had to have been written after the death of Henry III on August 2, 1589 (and maybe after the death of Pope Sixtus V on August 27, 1590) but before its first recorded performance on January 26, 1593.[2] *Titus* was also composed before its first recorded performance in January of 1594 and perhaps as early as the late 1580s. *Richard III* appears to have been written sometime between 1591 and 1594. In the case of *Titus Andronicus*, there are, as well, questions of authorship that have recently drawn renewed critical attention.[3] But the degree to which Shakespeare and George Peele may each have contributed to *Titus* makes little difference in the matter of influence because the date of composition is so uncertain.

If this line of influence cannot be successfully pursued, other lines can be. They reveal more widely the imprint of Marlowe on *Titus Andronicus* and *Richard III*—as, for example, in the shaping of Aaron the Moor and Richard as villain-heroes.[4] Moreover, the definiteness of influences from Marlowe or Shakespeare apart, the very question of influence invites a three-way examination of the Guise, Aaron, and Richard III as diabolical figures. As we shall see, such an examination also illuminates the two writers' quite serious concern with the powers, functions, and abuses of the imagination and reveals a mutual understanding of the professional need for innovative uses of the imagination—especially for someone writing for the commercial theater of London in the early 1590s.

By the 1590s commercial theater was thriving. As theatergoing became a regular element in the culture and the business operations of London, changes in the demands on playwrights, theater owners, and actors took place quickly and constantly. More specifically, as Andrew Gurr states, "Regular attendances at a fixed venue required the impresarios to offer a constant supply of novelty. ... The result was constant, pressurised evolution in the players' repertoire of plays."[5] This phenomenon created a situation in which innovative uses of the imagination were in strong demand. It is clear from the entries in Henslowe's *Diary* alone that Marlowe and Shakespeare responded with alacrity and success to the call. It is also logical to assume that their consciousness of the need for novelty in their dramatic offerings spilled over into the content of their dramas, that their concern with their own imagination and its products encouraged them to make the powers, function, and abuses of the imagination an important subject of their dramas.

II

Before widening the scope of our discussion, we need to scrutinize a repeated verbal detail in *The Massacre At Paris*, because it links Marlowe's play most securely with Shakespeare. At the same time, I hope also to present a more complete understanding of the Duke of Guise than the fragmented text is usually thought to yield. The clearest and most definite parallel between *The Massacre At Paris* and Shakespeare's plays is a verbal echo, not with either *Titus Andronicus* or *Richard III*, but with *Julius Caesar*: "Yet Caesar shall go forth."[6] Near the end of *Massacre*, Marlowe employs a familiar dramaturgical device of Elizabethan and Jacobean drama: the introduction of a repentant murderer as a red herring to heighten the tension at the climax of the death of a major character—in this case, the Duke of Guise.[7] In a moment of sudden guilt brought on by pangs of conscience, the Third Murderer warns the Guise that he is about to be assassinated by his two fellow-murderers and should therefore not enter the next room. Disregarding the warning, the Duke responds with overweening arrogance, an arrogance that borders on dementia:

Yet Caesar shall go forth.
Let mean conceits and baser men fear death:
Tut, they are peasants; I am the Duke of Guise;
And princes with their looks engender fear. (xxi, 67–70)[8]

This last vain bubble of fantasy (70) instantly bursts when the Guise is stabbed to death by the murderers. Earlier, in his well-known soliloquy in the second scene of the play, the Duke also compares himself to Caesar, but, there, the analogy seems less startling and strained, more natural, and, perhaps because he has no audience but himself, the implicit self-adulation not so emphatic: "As Caesar to his soldiers, so say I: / Those that hate me will I learn to loathe" (ii, 95–96). The Duke frequently uses Roman analogies to elevate his stature while fashioning an identity for himself as a figure of absolute power.[9] For instance, thinking that he has duped Henry III, he blindly congratulates himself and, undoubtedly with a swagger, comments, "As ancient Romans over their captive lords, / So will I triumph over this wanton king" (xxi, 52–53). But his identity as an omnipotent force is as illusory as his triumph over Henry.

One might at first think that, when the Duke is responding to the Third Murderer, Marlowe makes him unduly offensive in accordance with the moralizing tradition of accentuating the ugliness of evil personalities just before their downfall, particularly since the braggadocio conveyed by his words seems, in retrospect, even more patently foolish and hollow a few minutes later when he is actually dying. But, after he has been stabbed, the Duke, just as vainly, continues to act superior, redirecting the misery he feels because he has not had the "power to stay … [his] life" (xxi, 79) into a bitter lament that he has "To die by peasants" (xxi, 81). He then calls upon the Pope to avenge his death, and, in an effort to create the impression that he has somehow acted nobly because of his strong religious beliefs, extols Catholicism and decries the Huguenots, thereby solidifying forever and with potent irony the hypocrisy of his pretense to genuine religious motives. One wonders what audience he imagines he is addressing here. His last words are, "Thus Caesar did go forth, and thus he died" (xxi, 87). This final bit of puffery and posturing, in recalling the earlier preposterous analogy with Caesar, appears to be a desperate attempt to assert control over a public image that he has never attained in the play and to give that image direction in the eyes of posterity—something that the Antony of *Antony and Cleopatra*, with full justification, attempts more successfully. It is also an indication of the Guise's capacity for profound self-deception, his most convincingly realistic psychological trait.

Viewed from Marlowe's perspective, it is quite possible that the Duke's overblown assertions just before and after he is stabbed actually show the playwright subverting the convention of moralizing the death of a villain. The scene does not characterize the Guise's show of pride as an attempt to assert his sense of dignity, stereotypically portrayed by remaining constant in his uncompromising attitude to the end. Instead, eschewing the convention of deathbed penitence, it dramatizes his unregenerateness one last time. Moreover, because he truly feels no compunction for the brutal murder of so many helpless and innocent victims and because he too is murdered rather than brought to justice through an honorable legal means, the lesson to be learned from his death has nothing to do with social (much less personal) ethical ideals but only with the unromantic reality of political power—its amorality and transitoriness, and the Machiavellian alertness and cunning needed by those who would wield it successfully. Further, the scene portrays a figure of evil seeking control through the affective power of grossly swollen expressions of a righteous defiance that we know is meaningless and a nobility and importance that we know are false. His "high astounding terms" do not have the solidity of Tamburlaine's. If the Guise's language can be viewed as self-parodying, and I think it can, then Marlowe has found a vehicle for conveying through irony a subversive assessment of moralizing traditions in both literature and life, traditions that he sees as platitudinous, unrealistic, and ineffective.[10] At the very least, the parallels with Caesar bespeak with savage irony the Duke's illusions of grandeur.[11]

In *Julius Caesar*, Calphurnia exhorts Caesar not to leave home lest some dire tragedy befall him. Intending to sound authoritative and imposing in his defiance, he replies assertively, addressing her with his customary, third-person loftiness, "Caesar shall forth" (II, ii, 10). Then, in an egotistical, self-important statement, remarkable in its similarity to the Guise's pronouncement that "princes [like himself] with their looks engender fear," he adds, "The things that threatened me / Ne'er looked but on my back. When they shall see / The face of Caesar, they are vanishèd" (II, ii, 10–12). Calphurnia proceeds, almost doggedly, to explain to her husband the origin of her fears, but Caesar responds assertively again, this time with a bluff fatalism, taking refuge in the generalized commonplace that there is no denying the fate planned by the gods: "What can be avoided / Whose end is purposed by the mighty gods" (II, ii, 26–27). He continues with his usual display of hubris, "Yet Caesar shall go forth" (II, ii, 28), and, 20 lines later, concludes with an even more emphatic display of hubris, "And Caesar shall go forth" (II, ii, 48). This statement, not to be found in Plutarch or any other identified source, appears to have originated with Marlowe's text. *The Massacre At Paris* was neither dated nor registered when it was first published. Thus, no one can be absolutely sure whether Marlowe or perhaps his revisers or compilers are echoing Shakespeare's play or Shakespeare Marlowe's play. But the evidence for the date of *Julius Caesar* makes it likely that Shakespeare was echoing Marlowe. Either way, the parallel attests the strong awareness that the playwrights had of each other's work. If one writer manifested such awareness, it is likely that the other one possessed it, too, and that the interconnections among the theatrical companies and the possibilities for influence were stronger than we have acknowledged heretofore.[12]

In speculating on who took material from whom, one might conceivably argue that it would have been easier for Marlowe or, more probably, his revisers or compilers at a date after Marlowe's death in 1593, to borrow from Shakespeare's play and incorporate the sentiment about the power of a look and the line, "Yet Caesar shall go forth," than for Shakespeare to have worked both the sentiment and the line into his more tightly integrated and unified psychological portrayal.[13] Adapting Coleridge's distinction between Fancy and the Imagination, the argument might declare—from internal evidence since external evidence cannot affirm that the one text we have is based on the January, 1593 performance of *Massacre*—that the line in Marlowe's play is mechanically affixed whereas in Shakespeare's drama it is organically fused with character and action. To extend the argument, one might suggest that *Massacre*'s generalization about the power of the look of princes could more easily be thought to emanate from the specificity of Caesar's remark than the other way around. But if, in fact, the influence were on Marlowe and not Shakespeare, it would mean a surprisingly earlier date of composition for *Julius Caesar* than is usually supposed—before January of 1593 if this first performance of the play in fact contained the sentiment and line—unless, again, as would be more plausible, the influence was on revisers or compilers after 1593. In this case, someone may have seen an opportunity to enhance the stature of the uncertain text we have, even if put together through memorial reconstruction, by alluding to London's most well-known rising playwright. To counter this hypothetical argument one might note that it is certainly characteristic of Marlowe to exploit the *power* of a look: he had used this motif to great advantage in *Tamburlaine*, Part 1, and also in *Massacre* at the end of the Guise's first extensive soliloquy (in ii, 97–103).[14] It would, however, be uncharacteristic of Marlowe to borrow a line from Shakespeare, marking only the second time he had done so.[15] Speculation apart, however, I see no reason to attribute the origin of the line to anyone other than Marlowe himself. The strongest bit of external evidence is the probability that *Julius Caesar* was the first play performed by the Lord Chamberlain's Men at the Globe Theater early in the summer of 1599.

III

Although *Titus Andronicus* and *Richard III* lack verbal echoes of *The Massacre At Paris*, similarities among the characters of the three plays would seem to suggest some possibilities of influence. If we use the Duke of Guise as the point of comparison with Aaron and Richard III, we can see almost immediately, however, that the reason for comparing these three as figures of evil is based on superficial likenesses. Consequently, any influence would be so broadly based or so transformed as to be unrecognizable. Even so, the comparison leads to some important distinctions. The malice of the Guise is utterly gratuitous and unmotivated and, unlike Richard's, not at all heroic.[16] In his deeds, Richard at times evokes from us the kind of awe that a hero evokes through superhuman feats. The Guise, although claiming to espouse the rights of Catholicism, never generates such a response; his relentless cruelty simply makes him repulsive. The early soliloquy of the Guise indicates that "peril is the chiefest way to happiness" (ii.35), and we may think that, like Aaron, he enjoys living on the edge and that he takes great delight in perpetrating acts of evil. But as the speech continues, we sense, as Ian McAdam puts it, that "the soliloquy … parodies the rhetoric of Marlowe's earlier aspiring heroes"[17] and that the Guise's motiveless malignity—devoid of interest and excitement even for him—is of less consequence to Marlowe than the high-flying style he uses in the paean to power that concludes the soliloquy:

Give me a look that when I bend the brows
Pale death may walk in furrows of my face;
A hand that with a grasp may gripe the world;
An ear to hear what my detractors say;
A royal seat, a sceptre, and a crown;
That those which do behold, they may become
As men that stand and gaze against the sun. (ii, 97–103)

As is so often the case with Marlowe, our immediate attention is drawn to the style of the speech rather than to the personality of the character speaking—a characteristic one might also often attribute to *Richard III*. But, unlike our estimation of Tamburlaine even at his worst or of Aaron or Richard III, our sense of the Guise, beyond his overwrought style, is of an empty vessel, someone without an animating spirit or enthusiasm, a figure who, remarkably, takes little ostensible pleasure in either the mechanics or the success of his evil machinations but who is, instead, concerned with his power to control what others think of him, beginning with his alertness in spying on others; without sensing how ineffectual he is, he portrays himself with inflated egotism as "An ear to hear what my detractors say." In short, he is a figure incapable of consistently internalizing or structuring his ideas, much less any ideals—religious ideals in particular.[18] The Duke's imagination lacks creative and synthesizing powers and, consequently, receives no consistent support from his rational faculties, common sense, and will. Instead, he has only blind resolve ("resolution"—ii, 105). This failure of the imagination may explain his surprise at his wife's infidelity and his vulnerability to the King who persuades him that he has his friendship and advocacy even as he is arranging for his murder.

The failure of the creative and synthesizing imagination also distinguishes the Guise from Aaron and Richard III. But, as we shall see, some sort of failure of the imagination in all three figures precipitates their downfall. Commentators have readily pointed out that Aaron is more like Barabas than the Guise[19] but, even so, there are major differences. Granted, both Barabas and Aaron boast in the manner of the conventional Vice figure:

Barabas: I walk abroad o' nights,
             And kill sick people groaning under walls;
             Sometimes I go about and poison wells;
             And now and then, to cherish Christian thieves,
             I am content to lose some of my crowns,
             That I may, walking in my gallery,
             See 'em go pinioned along by my door.
                             (*The Jew of Malta*, II, iii, 179–85)[20]

Aaron: Few come within the compass of my curse,
             Wherein I did not some notorious ill:
             As kill a man, or else devise his death;
             Ravish a maid, or plot the way to do it;
             Accuse some innocent, and forswear myself;

Set deadly enmity between two friends;
Make poor men's cattle break their necks;
Set fire on barns and haystacks in the night,
And bid the owners quench them with their tears.
Oft have I digged up dead men from their graves,
And set them upright at their dear friends' door,
Even when their sorrows almost was forgot,
And on their skins, as on the bark of trees,
Have with my knife carvèd in Roman letters,
'Let not your sorrow die, though I am dead.'
But I have done a thousand dreadful things
As willingly as one would kill a fly,
And nothing grieves me heartily indeed
But that I cannot do ten thousand more.

(*Titus Andronicus*, V, i, 126–44)

However, in the first speech, one suspects that Barabas is embellishing his evil deeds in order to impress Ithamore. Aaron, on the other hand, like the Duke of Guise during the scene of his murder, is attempting to give final definition to a brief life of unmitigated wickedness. Moreover, the two catalogues of crimes do not clearly indicate the major differences that exist in these two evil characters. Barabas is cynical and serious. In advising Ithamore, he lays out a formula for success in evil that Shakespeare pays little serious attention to until he comes to characterize Iago and, later, Lady Macbeth, as she unsexes herself (*Macbeth*, I, v, 39–53): "… be thou void of these affections, / Compassion, love, vain hope, and heartless fear; / Be mov'd at nothing, see thou pity none" (II, iii, 173–75). Barabas seems to take little joy in his machinations—not as little as the Guise, however—only a strongly egotistical satisfaction.[21] Aaron is quite different. Not as intellectually astute as Barabas, he is just as clever. The main difference lies in his strong emotional nature. He is thoroughly delighted by the machinations of evil, even gleeful, and, when it comes to his son, exhibits the very compassion, love, and vain hope that Barabas warns against. Aaron proves that Barabas's admonition has validity, for the identical emotions that Barabas eschews become the catalysts to Aaron's undoing. The irony is, of course, that, although these are qualities that we traditionally admire, as we do in this instance, they are, paradoxically, the qualities of a figure that we utterly reject.

Nicholas Brooke and Maurice Charney have examined Aaron's first speech, a soliloquy opening Act II of the play, for its specifically Marlovian characteristics:[22]

Now climbeth Tamora Olympus' top,
Safe out of fortune's shot, and sits aloft,
Secure of thunder's crack or lightning flash,
Advanced above pale envy's threat'ning reach.
As when the golden sun salutes the morn,
And having gilt the ocean with his beams,
Gallops the zodiac in his glistering coach
And overlooks the highest-peering hills,

So Tamora.
Upon her wit doth earthly honor wait,
And virtue stoops and trembles at her frown.
Then, Aaron, arm thy heart and fit thy thoughts
To mount aloft with thy imperial mistress,
And mount her pitch whom thou in triumph long
Hast prisoner held, fett'red in amorous chains,
And faster bound to Aaron's charming eyes
Than is Prometheus tied to Caucasus.
Away with slavish weeds and servile thoughts!
I will be bright and shine in pearl and gold,
To wait upon this new-made empress
To wait, said I? to wanton with this queen,
This goddess, this Semiramis, this nymph,
This siren that will charm Rome's Saturnine
And see his shipwrack and his commonweal's. (II, i, 1–24)

Charney sees in the final four lines of the speech an imitation of Tamburlaine's ability to top himself and a similar rhetorical "rise to a brilliant climax."[23] Brooke finds that the Tamburlainian excesses in hyperbole and detail give the speech Marlowe's most genuine stamp, but that in the context of the play as a whole

> Shakespeare is committed to a total rejection of this imaginative force whose identity he establishes not only by a Marlovian figure, but by a fully Marlovian utterance. What is remarkable is that the moral rejection accompanies an imaginative recognition so strong as to generate a fully original creation, of words and character, in Marlowe's mode.[24]

This stance needs to be qualified, for Aaron is less Marlovian than Brooke indicates. What Brooke does not say is that a joyful enthusiasm and near ecstasy animate the speech, and they are not Marlowe's. Shakespeare's consciousness here as well as elsewhere is such that he can embrace the soaring style of Marlowe—including its extravagance and vitality, its grandiloquence and climactic intensity, and its emphatic rhythms—and still remain unwilling to imitate the substance and overall tone of the Marlovian passage(s) he carries in his mind. By the same token and as we are about to see, Shakespeare can hold himself aloof from the ethos found in the worlds of Marlowe's plays and poetry even when this ethos is an integral part of the influencing passages.

If through the portrayal of the death of the Guise in *The Massacre At Paris* Marlowe is ridiculing didactic literary conventions and the notion of an orthodox morality, Shakespeare at the end of *Titus Andronicus* clearly is not. In much of what takes place *before* the end of the play, however, Shakespeare is considerably less conventional. A major reason lies in the portrayal of Aaron. In spite of our inevitable disapproval of the Moor as a figure of heinous immorality, in large part we respond to him with considerable delight. We do so because we are fascinated by someone who overturns our ingrained moral expectations and takes such an exuberant enjoyment in the mechanics of his own evil. Shakespeare evidently sensed that his audiences would find pleasure in experiencing contradictory moral and aesthetic responses and that he could further complicate and, hence, heighten their pleasure by making Aaron's protective compassion for his son attractively human. Brooke is undoubtedly correct in suggesting that, because of Marlowe, Aaron is "a fully original creation."[25] He assumes that Shakespeare had a knowledge of Tamburlaine, Barabas, Faustus, and even the Guise. Whether the playwright was actually familiar with all four, he saw from Marlowe's eliciting of simultaneous contradictory responses in portraying his villain-heroes the dramaturgical and commercial advantages of making his creation "original." Once again, what is most striking is that Shakespeare could so single-mindedly focus on Marlowe's artistic uniqueness without also actively responding to his ethos. But perhaps this limited perspective should be considered a rebuff by implication, one graciously indirect and non-confrontational.

Richard III is less a Marlovian figure than Aaron, but one would nevertheless be hard pressed to deny the presence of a Marlovian influence on his characterization.[26] The same cannot be said of other elements of the play. For example, although the possibility of a link exists, I am not as willing as Brooke to assert that Queen Margaret's warning, "O Buckingham, take heed of yonder dog! / Look when he fawns he bites" (*Richard III*, I, iii, 289–90) is an explicit echo of Barabas's "We Jews can fawn like spaniels when we please; / And when we grin we bite" (*The Jew of Malta*, II, iii, 20–21).[27] As Barabas's analogy suggests, the idea seems to be a commonplace. Nor am I as persuaded as G. Blakemore Evans that Queen Margaret's venomous words about Richard III to the Duchess of York and Queen Elizabeth owe something to the scene of Doctor Faustus's death.[28] Margaret exclaims, "Earth gapes, hell burns, fiends roar, saints pray, / To have him [Richard III] conveyed from hence. / Cancel his bond of life, dear God, I pray" [IV, iv, 75–77]). The *Faustus* texts say, "Earth, gape!" (A-Text, V, ii, 88) and "Gape, earth!" (B-Text, V, ii, 164). All three passages make use of some form of "gape" and "earth" but so also does the apostrophe of Zabina in Part 1 of *Tamburlaine*, "Gape, earth, and let the fiends infernal view / A hell as hopeless and as full of fear / As are the blasted banks of Erebus" (V, i, 242–44), and Evans makes no mention of this passage. In any case, Shakespeare's "Earth gapes" need not have an origin in Marlowe's texts. If it did, it would only go to show what we already know, that Shakespeare had an intimate familiarity with the language of some of Marlowe's plays. Both Brooke and Evans imply that Shakespeare's knowledge of Marlowe came from a reader's acquaintance with Marlowe's texts. But the evidence for such a conclusion is missing. Given his daily involvement with the operations of a theater such as the Rose, it is more likely that Shakespeare saw the plays acted than that he had access to written versions of them and that they registered in his auditory imagination.

We have more to work with when we become aware that Richard III is an irrepressible overreacher in the Tamburlainian sense; he, too, finds "an earthly crown" "the ripest fruit of all" (1 *Tamburlaine*, II, vii, 29 and 27). Moreover, he continually reaches for the seemingly impossible and often attains it, beginning with the infamous wooing of Lady Anne (I, ii). Like the Duke of Guise, his credo seems to be, "That like I best that flies beyond my reach" (*The Massacre At Paris*, ii, 39).

Unlike Tamburlaine and the Guise, however, Richard admits to deformities, both physical and moral, and these deformities color his perception of the world, especially after the visitation of the ghosts. From the beginning, Richard is very much aware of his moral position in the scheme of what he acknowledges is a universal moral order. Shakespeare has him assess that position with a psychological complexity and density that neither Tamburlaine nor Aaron ever projects, whereas the Duke of Guise blindly follows the dictates of his "resolution" (ii, 105). Richard, too, follows the dictates of his "resolution" but never blindly. Moreover, Richard is canny whereas the Duke is single-mindedly forceful, recklessly and ruthlessly butchering his victims with a sadistic bludgeoning power. Although we may enjoy in varying degrees the relentlessness of Tamburlaine, the Guise, Aaron, and Richard III, partly because it gives them a defiantly larger-than-life quality, this relentlessness does not add moral points to their score cards. Brooke feels that in the character of Aaron Shakespeare deliberately creates a "Marlovian figure in the tragic complex"[29] in order to see exactly what use he might make of such a figure. By contrast, he argues that, both in *Richard III* and in *3 Henry VI* before it, Marlowe's influence is pushed into the background, particularly in *Richard III* because, there, Richard's voice is so distinctive as to be quite independent from the voices of Marlowe's protagonists. I am more inclined to agree with Brooke's conclusion about *Richard* and *Henry* than with that about *Titus*, for, as I already indicated, I do not find Aaron as Marlovian as Brooke does. Indeed, the case for Marlowe's influence could be more easily made if one considers some of Shakespeare's later figures—for example, Henry V and the Antony of *Antony and Cleopatra*—where it is apparent that Shakespeare has taken a careful measure of Marlowe's protagonists and, over time, decided how best to make dramaturgical use of his findings. Like those of Marlowe's Tamburlaine and Faustus, Aaron's aspirations and his fulfillment of them are beyond the ken of ordinary folk to imagine, let alone accomplish. But Aaron lacks the intellectual power of a Tamburlaine or a Faustus and has a more fully developed emotional and sensual nature.

Brooke makes the point that in *3 Henry VI*, "there was a much wider Marlovian absorption implied"[30] than that in *Titus Andronicus* and certainly in *Richard III*. His evidence is solid, beginning with Richard's lines:

> And, father do but think
> How sweet a thing it is to wear a crown,
> Within whose circuit is Elysium
> And all that poets feign of bliss and joy. (*3 Henry VI*, I, ii, 28–31)

This passage is reminiscent of Tamburlaine's well-known speech, glanced at above, which ends with the warrior's desire to "reach the ripest fruit of all, / That perfect bliss and sole felicity, / The sweet fruition of an earthly crown" (*1 Tamburlaine*, II, vii, 27–29). Richard's exclamation suggests the content of Tamburlaine's without explicitly echoing either his high-pitched style or hyperbolic tone. Moreover, the verve in Tamburlaine's words results in part from the intensity of the declamatory verse. In Richard's speech, the verve contains a more personal form of intensity. This parallel and the others Brooke mentions[31] illustrate that Shakespeare was to some extent aware of the influence of Marlowe by the time he composed *Richard III*. The parallel also helps to characterize the development of Shakespeare's control in his conscious response to Marlowe: his willingness to absorb influence from Marlowe in expressing a similar sentiment while still maintaining his own artistic individuality through his manner of expression, an individuality that, as we shall see, is remarkably flexible and fluid. Marlowe's learned, formal style and philosophical tone and scope in Tamburlaine's speech become a simpler, more straightforward, individualized exclamation in Richard's.

The language and tone of *Richard III* are often Marlovian in their intensity and verve if not in their specific tonal quality, but the amount of rhetorical language exceeds anything we ever see in Marlowe, even in the *Tamburlaine* plays. In *Richard III* Shakespeare is most Marlovian not when Richard is overreaching but when he is emotionally wrought up after the full realization of the consequences of his villainy (V, iii, 178–207). In this, he is like Faustus just before he is taken to Hell (A-Text: V, ii, 66–122; B-Text: V, ii, 143–96); both men have looked inward and now, with a strong awareness of a universal ethical scheme, see that they are irretrievably damned. Their intensely emotional self-reflections and agony are apparent:

Richard: O coward conscience, how doest thou afflict me.
              The lights burn blue. It is now dead midnight.
              Cold fearful drops stand on my trembling flesh.

              My conscience hath a thousand several tongues,
              And every tongue brings in a several tale,
              And every tale condemns me for a villain.
              Perjury, perjury, in the highest degree,
              Murder, stern murder, in the direst degree,
              All several sins, all used in each degree,
              Throng to the bar, crying all, 'Guilty! guilty!'
              I shall despair. There is no creature loves me;
              And if I die, no soul will pity me. (*Richard III*, V, iii, 180–82; 194–202)

Faustus: Let Faustus live in hell a thousand years,
              A hundred thousand, and at last be saved.
              O, no end is limited to damnèd souls.
              Why wert thou not a creature wanting soul?
              Or why is this immortal that thou hast?
              Ah, Pythagoras' *metempsychosis*, were that true,
              This soul should fly from me, and I be changed
              Unto some brutish beast.
              All beasts are happy, for, when they die,
              Their souls are soon dissolved in elements,
              But mine must live still to be plagued in hell.

Although the contexts of the excerpts are very different, the two protagonists both articulate with tremendous force their suffering on a psychological torture rack.

Each passage reflects a desire to internalize the portrayal of its speaker. This focus, in turn, produces a similarity in the desperation, the vehemence of expression, the self-dramatizing tendency, and the vital energy of the speeches. It is commonly said that Richard "is Shakespeare's first character to possess a 'voice' of his own."[32] One wonders how distinctive a voice Richard would have had if Marlowe had not first written *Doctor Faustus.*

In both *Titus Andronicus* and *Richard III,* Shakespeare presents a world in which conventional morality still prevails. This world differs from the amoral one portrayed in *The Massacre At Paris.* Marlowe's association of Catholicism with the Guise and evil and Protestantism with Navarre and good, which some critics and scholars have seen as propagandistic, suggests a more arbitrary sense of political morality than Shakespeare depicts.[33] But, beyond that, no principles of right and wrong appear to be imprinted on this Marlovian world. Power and the control that attends it dominate, and, invariably, they prove to be transitory and unstable. Most significantly, they exist apart from and in spite of any idealized moral framework. Navarre, whose character we are meant to admire, keeps sending the question of morality upstairs to God, sometimes (as in the second passage below) with an irony he does not intend:

> He that sits and rules above the clouds
> Doth hear and see the prayers of the just,
> And will revenge the blood of innocents ... (i, 41–43)

> [to Charles] Comfort yourself, my lord, and have no doubt
> But God will sure restore you to your health. (xiii, 6–7)

> whilst that these broils do last,
> My opportunity may serve me fit
> To steal from France and hie me to my home,
> For here's no safety in the realm for me,
> And now that Henry is call'd from Poland,
> It is my due by just succession;
> And therefore, as speedily as I can perform,
> I'll muster up an army secretly,
> For fear that Guise, join'd with the King of Spain,
> Might seem to cross me in mine enterprise.
> But God that always doth defend the right,
> Will show his mercy and preserve us still. (xiii, 30–41)

> The duke [Joyeux] is slain and all his power dispers'd
> And we are grac'd with wreaths of victory.
> Thus God, we see, doth ever guide the right,
> To make his glory great upon the earth. (xviii, 1–4)

> But God, we know, will always put them down
> That lift themselves against the perfect truth,
> Which I'll maintain so long as life doth last,
> And with the Queen of England join my force

To beat the papal monarch from our lands … (xviii, 12–16)

> But if that God do prosper mine attempts
> And send us safely to arrive in France,
> We'll beat him [the Guise] back and drive him to his death
> That basely seeks the ruin of his realm. (xx, 26–29)

Navarre is wise enough to know that the assumption of royal authority must appear to come unforced and through the tacit agreement of those whom he would govern. At the beginning of the third passage quoted above, he makes clear his aspirations for the throne and his political savvy, using, as the last two lines of the speech indicate, his customary myth of godly righteousness to legitimize and affirm his position. Well aware that the power of the monarchy is itself a myth arrived at through a deception that must appear to be natural and legitimate, Marlowe makes his political figures transparent to the world that they are shaping, a world that, at the same time, is shaping them.

When Navarre hears that Henry is about to send an army "To march against the rebellious king Navarre" (xvii, 3), he employs outsized metaphors which, at the very least, are intended to sound commanding and authoritative,

> The power of vengeance now encamps itself
> Upon the haughty mountains of my breast—
> Plays with her gory colours of revenge,
> Whom I respect as leaves of boasting green
> That change their colour when the winter comes,
> When I shall vaunt as victor in revenge. (xvi, 20–25)

The passage is confused and metaphorically obscure,[34] but the intensity of Navarre's desire for revenge and his trust in "the power of vengeance" nevertheless emerge. The final words of Navarre, which conclude the play, indicate with clarity that little hope exists for a stable sociopolitical morality in the future:

> Come, lords, take up the body of the king,
> That we may see it honourably interr'd;
> *And then I vow for to revenge his death*
> As Rome and all those popish prelates there
> Shall curse the time that e'er Navarre was king
> And rul'd in France by Henry's fatal death! (xxiv, 106–11; my italics)

Now that Navarre is in an official position of power he will become actively aggressive, something he has not always been in the past.[35] Moreover, he will perpetuate the hostility and ill will that Henry was seeking to quell. At the end of *Titus* and *Richard III*, by contrast, we have a sense that, whatever disruptions the future may hold, conventional moral standards are intact and there is a reasonable hope that these standards may now possibly be attained. This contrast between Marlowe's cynical perspective[36] and Shakespeare's optimistic one considerably lessens by the time Shakespeare writes *Troilus and Cressida, Antony and Cleopatra*, and *Coriolanus*. In these later plays, the behavior of political figures engaged in power politics engulfs ethical principles and the resulting conditions produce an amoral world similar to the one that Marlowe depicted.

IV

If the Marlowe of *Massacre* and the Shakespeare of *Titus* and *Richard III* are worlds apart in their affirmation of conventional public values, they are less so in their depiction of private values. McAdam observes about Marlowe that "the relative power, or powerlessness of the human imagination is a major theme of his writing" (21). Surely the same could be said of Shakespeare. It is no surprise that both Marlowe and Shakespeare would be especially sensitive to the powers and effects of the imagination in the human personality. After all, their own imaginations defined their distinctiveness as writers, especially during the early 1590s as they responded to the expanding theatrical demands for new, innovative dramas and became increasingly well known. Moreover, from the outset of their careers, both dramatists portrayed the power of the imagination in evil and good characters alike, delineating the imagination as a force of destruction as well as creation. The role of the imagination in the Guise, Aaron, and Richard in establishing the uniqueness of their identities and in giving further definition to their characters bear important similarities. The imaginations of these three figures enable them to create fantasies of power which, in turn, fuel their wills as the chief means of initiating a process whereby they are able to acquire that power. Yet, in all three characters, an unruly imagination, utterly deleterious in its power to undermine its possessor, can be said to contribute to their demise.

Like Macbeth, the Guise uses his imagination to dream of the highest reaches of power, "our possession to the crown" (ii, 94), and to give impetus to his evil acts. But, as we have already seen, his imagination, defective and impoverished, does him a disservice when, in subverting his rational powers and common sense, it enables him to shroud himself in self-deception. His wife and Henry III betray him, because, in yielding to the self-deception brought on by the desires of satisfying an enormous ego, he is unable to use his imagination to see from another person's perspective. Just before his death he has illusions of grandeur, elevating himself to the stature of Caesar, while viewing himself as invulnerable, impervious to attack. Because he lacks control over his imagination and is not able to give it direction, he becomes a victim of it, and potential use is supplanted by inadvertent abuse.

Nor is Aaron able to control his imagination once his newborn son is brought to him. As soon as he puts his son's welfare first, his imagination—always fertile, witty, and energetic—instead of waiting to be called into service, takes charge and blocks out his rational hardheadedness. He uses his imagination to give protection to his son, but the idea of protection is based on a wholly fabricated myth of the duties and rites of fatherhood—one that, given his personality and circumstances, seems absurdly paradoxical. Clearly, Shakespeare constructs such paradoxes in his characterization of Aaron in order to compel the audience's attention. Aaron has an imagination that we cannot help admiring, even as it is used for evil purposes that we cannot help condemning. Also a product of his imagination, Aaron's humanity—meager though it is—addresses our moral sensibilities and evokes our admiration; yet, it leads to horrendous crimes (beginning with the murder of the Nurse and Cornelia the midwife) and to his own death. Through Aaron, the play appears to suggest the paradoxes that are embedded in the very nature of the imagination itself—its power to create and destroy and its ability to be channeled at times but not at other times.

Richard III's fertile imagination serves his evil purposes well until it impairs his will. We see this begin to happen in the scene in which Buckingham balks at murdering "Young Edward" (IV, ii, 10). In this scene Richard first begins to acknowledge the enormity of his crimes but suddenly and unaccountably, without his usual detachment. He says to himself :

> I must be married to my brother's daughter,
> Or else my kingdom stands on brittle glass:
> Murder her brothers, and then marry her—
> Uncertain way of gain! But I am in
> So far in blood that sin will pluck on sin.
> Tear-falling pity dwells not in this eye. (IV, ii, 59–64)

Later in the same scene, he recalls the prophecy of Henry VI "that Richmond should be king" (IV, ii, 94) and the prediction of the "bard of Ireland" who told him that he should not live long after he saw Richmond (IV, ii, 104–5). At Bosworth Field, Richard's imagination erupts, and he sees the ghosts of his victims (V, iii, 119–77). Following this trauma, he becomes stricken with guilt at his villainy (V, iii, 178–207), and then becomes fearful and terror-ridden. He nevertheless manages to rouse the troops and in the battle to enact "more wonders than a man, / Daring an opposite to every danger" (V, 14, 2–3). But to no avail. With his downfall, the uncertainty and, to him, dangers of the imagination are unmasked. After the scene with Buckingham (IV, ii) and apart from the energy expended in battle heroics, Richard's imagination seems to rob him of will—like that of the Second Murderer earlier in the play (I, iv) and the Third Murderer in *Massacre* (xxi, 59–67). In each case, the essentially amoral imagination has been inexplicably besieged by a potent sense of guilt. Under such strong moral governance, the imagination is denatured of its ability to inspire the will. Thus, as with the Guise and Aaron, Richard experiences the imagination as a faculty that can blur the vision as well as enhance it.

In their imaginings, the Guise, Aaron, and Richard III, like Tamburlaine, dream of opportunities and successes that are not subject to traditionally accepted laws, much less to the conventional moral principles of the political state. At times, their imaginations also enable them to deny the absolute dictatory powers of Nature and Fortune, thereby leaving them out of touch with ultimate reality. In a brief monologue in *Richard III*, Brackenbury employs the phrase "unfelt imaginations" (I, iv, 80) to characterize the delusions of princes who fail to experience the imagined glories associated with their titles; instead, by ironic contrast, these ruling figures "often feel a world of restless cares" (I, iv, 81). Using the term "unfelt imaginations" more inclusively, we can see, without trying to assign Marlovian or Shakespearian influence, that it accurately describes a similar psychological pattern in the Guise, Aaron, and Richard III at crucial points in their lives. Because they cannot ultimately make their "unfelt imaginations" felt, and in the Guise's case cannot always recognize the disparity between unfelt and felt imaginations, the senseless violence at the ends of the three plays intensifies even as the plays lay claim to a kind of poetic justice resulting from the deaths of the evil figures. The Guise cannot attain the sovereign power he so desires, and he never understands that some of the most fundamental causes lie within himself. Aaron never achieves his fantasy of fatherhood, and Richard cannot sustain his villainy to achieve peace, either in the land or within himself. Their "unfelt imaginations" render all three powerless.

That Shakespeare introduces the phrase "unfelt imaginations" in a context that does not necessitate it suggests that the functions, powers, and abuses of the imagination are concerns pressing strongly on his consciousness. From a metadramatic perspective, the phrase "unfelt imaginations" can be useful in discussing the two dramatists' foremost responsibility: their obligation to captivate and please their audiences. To fulfill this obligation they need to transform the elements of their own unrealized imaginings into felt experience—to turn "things unknown" "to shapes" and give to "airy nothing / A local habitation and a name" (*A Midsummer Night's Dream*, V, i, 15–17). An obvious difference between the two playwrights and their evil characters is that the writers understand the functions and powers of the imagination, including how to make use of the imagination to realize their aims, whereas, as their demises make clear, the villains do not. Looked at pragmatically, the writers use their imaginations to satisfy their ambition of gaining mastery as dramatists. As a result, they establish a professional identity that successfully enables them to come to terms with their world, something the villains can never do. The contrast between the playwrights and their characters in their control over their imaginations reveals a greater significance than this, however.

Before discussing this significance, we would do well to recall an important distinction between theatergoers and readers in their response to a play and, by means of this distinction, explain how one is able to arrive at an understanding of the writer's perspective. Controlled by the unbroken pace of the performance, theatergoers tend to look from the perspective of someone within the world of the play; they are frequently but not invariably limited to the characters' perspective. Moreover, although they can respond with immediacy through their senses and emotions, they have little time to reflect upon what they are viewing. Readers, who are able to control the rate at which they experience the play, as well as the quantity and quality of their reflections on the text, can, like the theatergoers, look from the perspective of someone within the world of the play and respond with immediacy through their senses and emotions. But they can also pause to reflect and view with detachment that world from the godlike perspective of the writer. No matter what the extent of awareness of the viewing or reading audience, the contrast between a character's limited, human viewpoint and the writer's omniscient, godly perspective is always present. In the case of the three plays before us, this contrast helps us to construe the immediate causes of the "unfelt imaginations" of the characters within the world of the plays and to understand the artistic causes of the *felt* imaginings created by their authors and, hence, the attributes that make them superior dramatists.

Marlowe and Shakespeare encourage us to take stock of this contrast at those moments in their plays when the artifice of the language or an action draws attention to itself. I am thinking of such passages in *The Massacre At Paris* as the Guise's first words in ii, 1–8, which accentuate their own metaphorical profusion, and his soliloquy in Scene ii, especially lines 45–62, with their rhetorical repetition of "for this," and lines 95–105, already cited, which are too lavish in their use of metaphors for us not to attribute their potency to their creator. One example of the patent artifice of an action that indicates Marlowe the artist trying to achieve a sensationalized dramatic effect is Henry's vindictive desire to see the initial reactions of the Guise's son and Catherine to the Duke's death (xxi, 117–61). In *Titus Andronicus*, the elaborate imagery of Aaron's opening soliloquy typifies a number of speeches that foreground the style rather than the personality behind it. The first action of the play that may strike us as Shakespeare striving for a strong dramatic effect is Titus's slaying of his son Mutius (I, i, 294), which some commentators have seen as Shakespeare echoing Tamburlaine's killing of his son Calyphas. In *Richard III*, the frequently commented-upon rhetoric of several of the characters' speeches calls attention to the playwright's linguistic skills, as does the scene in which Richard tries to convince Queen Elizabeth that her daughter Elizabeth should be his next bride (IV, iv, 200–430); Richard's action, with all the stops out in order to awe us and, in so doing, to lead us to acknowledge the author's artistic powers, is enhanced by the stichomythia in lines 343–67.

At such moments, we sense the puppeteer behind the puppets pulling the strings. In effect, this response—at least momentarily—causes us to break with the reality of the world of the play where we willingly have as realistic an engagement with the characters as we can and to move into the reality of the world of the writer where, in a detached and reflective state, we can more properly view the mechanics of dramaturgical technique and even their rationale. In addition, this state allows us to define the individual identities of Marlowe and Shakespeare as writers, and, because their linguistic cleverness is often unabashedly self-advertising, it also encourages us to bestow a proper importance on their efforts. As the Prologue to Part 1 of *Tamburlaine* and Duke Theseus's discussion of the imagination in *A Midsummer Night's Dream* (V, i, 2–22) suggest, both writers are intensely aware of the shaping powers of their own imaginations. But such self-consciousness within their own, private artistic worlds does not signify the full extent of their awareness of the functions and powers of the imagination. Each writer relies on his larger professional context to find the truest measure of his imaginative achievements, ultimately gauged by his success in drawing audiences to the theater. One can only imagine the pressures for novelty from audiences and from the need to make dramatic productions commercially viable—in 1592, say—that caused Marlowe and Shakespeare to feel the intensity of their own imaginative resources and to reflect on the potency of the imagination. The urge to fit successfully into this context of theatrical artistry and commercial canniness undoubtedly led each to familiarize himself with the other's imagination—in the long run, Shakespeare obviously more than Marlowe—and, in so doing, to open himself up to the possibilities of influence. Whatever the truth about the influence of Marlowe on Shakespeare or Shakespeare on Marlowe during the composition of *The Massacre At Paris*, *Titus Andronicus*, and *Richard III*, the exchange of influence that was taking place must have encouraged Marlowe to become as remarkably innovative a dramatist as his short life would allow; and it must have inspired Shakespeare to be bolder and more inventive than he would otherwise have been. Given Marlowe's strong consciousness of linguistic and dramaturgical technique, Shakespeare must certainly have been alerted to devices of artistry and, since he was not a slavish imitator, to have become more resourceful in his employment of them.

In characterizing the influence of Marlowe on the early plays of Shakespeare, Nicholas Brooke declares that Shakespeare regarded his "rival" as an "inescapable imaginative creator of something initially alien which he could only assimilate with difficulty,"[37] and Maurice Charney tells us, "The more we probe Shakespeare's hypothetical debt to Marlowe, the more we discover matter of uneasiness and skittishness."[38] Beginning with the notion of Marlowe as a rival, both of these comments demand more evidence than they receive. Nevertheless, such comments as these return us to the crucial general question this chapter asks: How do we determine and characterize the debt to Marlowe of early Shakespeare? Was Shakespeare so awed by *Tamburlaine*, *Doctor Faustus*, and *The Jew of Malta*, both as remarkable dramatic pieces unlike anything he had ever come across before in native theatrical tradition and as uncommonly popular commercial successes, that he became wary of the power his fellow playwright's influence might have on him; and was he, consequently, made uncomfortable about his own efforts at composing plays, perhaps even intimidated by Marlowe? Without excluding any of these possibilities, did he feel the need to extricate himself from what he sensed could become the pervasiveness of Marlowe's influence, from a fear of becoming a mere imitator? Did Shakespeare detect in Marlowe's plays the sources of excitement for an audience and did he find them so forceful and effective that he tried to incorporate some of these sources in his plays? If so, is that what led him into the quirky inconsistency of language and characterization in his portrayals of Aaron and Richard III? As we have seen, the figure in Aaron's initial soliloquy makes a slight bow toward Tamburlaine before moving on to a style of language and behavior quite unlike those of the shepherd warrior—very likely an example of Shakespeare trying to find himself as a playwright through the creative output of his fellow playwright. The inconsistency is more complicated in *Richard III*. The brutal, ruthless Richard who opens the play eventually does an about-face to become a guilt-ridden, stricken, Macbeth-like figure, moving, in effect, from displaying some of Tamburlaine's bold characteristics as a villain-hero to something akin to the internalized agonies of Faustus. Was Shakespeare so drawn to Marlowe's amazingly successful, defiant innovations in language, character, and genre that he felt about these new artistic innovations an infatuation—an enraptured state analogous to having fallen in love; and, as a result, could he not help but utilize them in some form, even when the concepts ran against the natural grain of his talent and impeded his own individuality? Did he find Marlowe's creations overblown and worthy of parody?

Overriding all the claims that Marlowe made on the psychology of composition in Shakespeare, did Shakespeare have a determination to better his fellow playwright and stake his claim of individuality?

There is of course no sure way to give authoritative answers to these questions. But probably, in some form, all of these questions and their answers, plus others, passed through Shakespeare's consciousness as he set about writing the *Henry VI* plays, *Titus Andronicus*, and *Richard III*. This much is clear: Early Shakespeare appears determined to find his own true dramatic and poetic sensibility. Among his many influences, the most immediate, a model for him to react to, is Marlowe. Shakespeare could readily measure his endeavors against Marlowe's works and commercial success while, at the same time, absorbing some of the features of those works. Early in his career especially, everything is grist for Shakespeare's mill, even those elements in his contemporary's works that he chooses to reject and parody. Thus, we come to consider Marlowe's body of works as a prime testing ground for the development of Shakespeare's own creativity. No doubt Shakespeare's genius would have flourished without Marlowe but probably not as quickly or with as much daring.

I have attributed Shakespeare's alertness to multiple possibilities in his response to Marlowe and his works to an enhanced multiconsciousness. In a letter to Richard Woodhouse almost as familiar to Shakespeareans as the related notion of "negative capability" (in a letter to George and Thomas Keats), Keats helps to clarify why such multiplicity is possible. He explains that the poet has no identity but a phenomenal imaginative ability to shift from perspective to perspective:

> As to the poetical Character itself, … it is not itself—it has no self—it is in every thing and nothing—It has no character—it enjoys light and shade; it lives in gusto, be it foul or fair, high or low, rich or poor, mean or elevated—It has as much delight in conceiving an Iago as an Imogen…. A Poet is the most unpoetical of any thing in existence; because he has no Identity—he is continually in for[ming]—and filling some other Body—The Sun, the Moon, the Sea and Men and Women who are creatures of impulse are poetical and have about them an unchangeable attribute—the poet has none; no identity—he is certainly the most unpoetical of all God's Creatures.[39]

Leaving aside what the passage says about Shakespeare's ability to conceive figures as dissimilar as an Iago or an Imogen, the characteristic described here can be said to account for the diversity and inclusiveness of Shakespeare's multiconsciousness in his response to the Marlovian imagination. Brooke and Charney are justified in seeing the influence of Marlowe on early Shakespeare as a complex matter, for, under scrutiny, the early plays manifest a potent creative sensibility that is less controlled and at ease than it will become, a sensibility eager to subject itself to Marlowe's output. Very likely, Shakespeare reacted to Marlowe's work and its consequences with responses that range from an inducement of fear to an exhortation to achieve his own glory as a thriving commercial dramatist.

This chapter attempts to suggest the complicated beginnings of Marlowe's influence on early Shakespeare, delineating the absorption of a Marlovian complex rather than a single play in the composition of *Titus Andronicus* and *Richard III*.

In addition, the question of influence that began the chapter has led us to consider Marlowe's part in generating Shakespeare's early struggle to balance convention with unconventionality, and it has enabled us to understand sooner rather than later what was to become his lifelong preoccupation with the functions, powers, and abuses of the imagination. Like Marlowe, early Shakespeare writes more about the destructive than the creative powers of the imagination in humankind and, also like Marlowe, he preserves the sanctity of the creative imagination as it applies to his own creativity. Shakespeare's perception of the imagination as a subject in Marlowe's works, as well as in the writer himself, at the very least gives him a license to portray his own fascination with the topic.

In commenting on "Marlowe's rapid, direct route to tragedy"[40] as opposed to Shakespeare's "far more complex development,"[41] C.L. Barber asserts that Marlowe

> commanded properly artistic powers almost equal to Shakespeare's. He had a greater range of scholarly learning, and equal or perhaps greater executive intelligence, though not equal intelligence of still more important kinds. The greatness of the very greatest artists depends on the human resources they bring to their art as well as on their genius for artistic innovation. Marlowe's humanity limits his art at the same time that it motivates his breakthroughs.[42]

Barber does not particularize Marlowe's limitations in his humanity, but certainly the writer's tendency in both his plays and poetry to intellectualize feeling must be included. Barber suggests at the end of the passage that Marlowe's limitations enabled him to concentrate more wholeheartedly on artistic innovations than, say, on what we might understand as emotional elements of psychological realism in the behavior of his characters. I fully agree and would add that a major force in what made Shakespeare the superior playwright he became developed out of the inescapable wealth of accomplished Marlovian innovations that lay before him as he first began to write. When he composed *Titus Andronicus* and *Richard III*, he had probably seen (maybe several times) the *Tamburlaine* plays, *The Jew of Malta*, and *Doctor Faustus*; although it is possible that he had seen *The Massacre At Paris* before he wrote *Richard*, it is more likely that he saw it before writing *Titus* which, according to Henslowe, first opened a year after *Massacre* did.[43] In the final analysis, it was not so much the specifics of Marlowe's texts that at this stage motivated Shakespeare but the artistic daring of the mind behind those texts. Marlowe eschewed the dearth of imagination that he detected in contemporary English drama and cleared a pathway for his own and others' felt imagination. Shakespeare was the first to step onto the pathway and take the journey.

Notes

1   F. P. Wilson, "*The Massacre At Paris* and *Edward II*," in *Marlowe: A Collection of Critical Essays*, ed. Clifford Leech (Englewood Cliffs, NJ: Prentice-Hall, 1964), 129–30.

2   According to Henslowe who described the play as new ("ne"): *Henslowe's Diary*, ed. R.A. Foakes, 2nd edition (Cambridge: Cambridge University Press, 2002), 20. For a thorough

discussion of the evidence of the first recorded production of *The Massacre At Paris* and the date of composition, see *"Dido, Queen of Carthage" and "The Massacre At Paris" Christopher Marlowe*, ed. H.J. Oliver (Cambridge, MA: Harvard University Press, 1968), xlvii–lii. Oliver's conclusion is that the play was likely to have been written in 1592: "Proof of a 1592 date is impossible; the presumption is strong" (lii). David Potter, "Marlowe's *Massacre At Paris* and the Reputation of Henri III of France," in *Christopher Marlowe and English Renaissance Culture*, ed. Darryll Grantley and Peter Roberts (Burlington, VT: Ashgate, 1996), 70–71 and nn. 4, 5, and 6 (90–91), concurs with Oliver's conclusions about the date of composition and the first performance of the play. More recently, Clare Harraway in *Re-citing Marlowe: Approaches to the Drama* (Burlington, VT: Ashgate, 2000), 143–45, surveys the evidence and comes to conclusions similar to those of Oliver and Potter.

3   The complicated arguments for the date of composition and the authorship of *Titus Andronicus* are neatly summarized by Frank Kermode in the preface to the Riverside edition of the play: *The Riverside Shakespeare*, gen. ed. G. Blakemore Evans, 2nd edition (Boston: Houghton Mifflin, 1997), 1065–66. See also Thomas Merriam, "Influence Alone? More on the Authorship of *Titus Andronicus*," *Notes and Queries* 45:3 (September, 1998): 304–8, who concludes that the "balance of evidence would favour a degree of divided authorship of *Titus Andronicus*, within the context of the influence of Marlowe and the university wits" (308). More recently, Brian Vickers in Shakespeare, *Co-Author: A Historical Study of Five Collaborative Plays* (Oxford: Oxford University Press, 2002) has argued for a date of composition and a first performance that are "wide open" (149), although Henslowe first records a "ne" (new) performance of it on January 23 of 1594 [Foakes, ed., *Henslowe's Diary*, 21]. Vickers posits exclusively through internal evidence that Shakespeare and Peele are responsible for the dual authorship of the play (pp. 148–243).

4   The pioneering study of the villain-hero is Clarence Valentine Boyer's *The Villain As Hero In Elizabethan Tragedy* (New York: Russell and Russell, 1914; reissued in 1964). Boyer discusses the Guise, Aaron, and Richard III as villain-heroes. He characterizes as far as possible the origins of their particular idiosyncrasies within the developing tradition of the villain-hero as a type.

5   Andrew Gurr, *Playgoing in Shakespeare's London*, 2nd edition (Cambridge: Cambridge University Press, 1996), 119.

6   See Oliver, ed., *"Dido, Queen of Carthage,"* lvii–lviii, for a discussion of the phrase, "Yet Caesar shall go forth," found in both *The Massacre At Paris* and *Julius Caesar*. He does not come to a conclusion about the priority of the text of either play, although he does consider *Massacre* the product of "memorial reconstruction" (lix). In addition, he raises some doubt about a connection between Marlowe and Shakespeare when he says, "Kocher and others have shown that Guise was often compared to Caesar in the pamphlets that probably gave Marlowe his material ..." (lvii). Even so, he does not cite a parallel as exact as that in the playtexts of Marlowe and Shakespeare. James Shapiro, *Rival Playwrights: Marlowe, Jonson, Shakespeare* (New York: Columbia University Press, 1991), 122–26, assumes that Shakespeare borrowed the line from Marlowe and that it reveals "the slipperiness with which history is reconstructed through theatrical representation" (125) and helps to bring to the surface the unsavory aspects of Caesar's character. Shapiro bases his assumption on the findings of Fredson Bowers who, in his two-volume edition of *The Complete Works of Christopher Marlowe* (Cambridge: Cambridge University Press, 1975), 1: 357, gives late 1593–early 1594 as a probable date for the quarto, thereby disagreeing with Oliver's probable date of 1602. Although I find Bowers's arguments sound, even if not definitive,

I nevertheless think that Shapiro's assumption is based ultimately on speculation; and I am less willing than he is to build a case for influence on speculation. Jonathan Bate, *The Genius of Shakespeare* (Oxford: Oxford University Press, 1998), 123–24, sees a similarity between Shakespeare's *Julius Caesar* and *The Massacre*, but he does not mention the verbal parallel. He believes that "the murdered Clerk in *The First Part of the Contention* was Shakespeare's first portrait of the artist as a young man" (123) and that Marlowe made the idea "more explicit" (123) with the murder of Peter Ramus. Then, "The figure of the murdered writer is reclaimed by Shakespeare in *Julius Caesar*. And this time it is explicitly a poet" (124). Overall, Bate seems more interested in establishing identifications than in considering influence.

7   In *Richard III*, the Second Murderer, who with his cohort is about to kill Clarence, is a part of this tradition (I, iv, 84–278). He has "certain dregs of conscience" (I, iv, 121) before killing Clarence which create tension; his show of conscience after the murder is indicative of a world in which a system of ethics is in place, whether or not it is adhered to. All references to this play and others by Shakespeare are from *William Shakespeare: The Complete Works*, gen. eds Stephen Orgel and A.R. Braunmuller (New York: Penguin Putnam, 2002).

8   All references to *The Massacre At Paris* are from the edition by Oliver with his scene and line numbers included in parentheses in the body of the text.

9   Marlowe's knowledge of the Romans and of Caesar as an overreacher has firm scholarly roots stemming at the very least from his translation of "Lucan's First Book" of *De Bello Civili* in *Christopher Marlowe: The Complete Poems*, ed. Mark Thornton Burnett (London, J.M. Dent, 2000). There, in his rant, Caesar "out-herods Herod" (e.g., ll. 300–52).

10   Like Rick Bowers in "*The Massacre At Paris*: Marlowe's Messy Consensus Narrative" in *Marlowe, History, and Sexuality. New Critical Essays on Christopher Marlowe*, ed. Paul Whitfield White (New York: AMS Press, 1998), 133 and 139–40, I do not believe that the play can be reduced to crude Protestant propaganda. Bowers is particularly illuminating on the subversive ironies of the play that prevent an oversimplified understanding of its politics. See, too, Julia Briggs, "Marlowe's *Massacre At Paris*: A Reconsideration," *Review of English Studies* 34 (1983): 257–78. Like Bowers, Briggs argues that the play is not Protestant propaganda. Briggs is particularly astute on the relationship of the play to historical fact; where I am in disagreement with her is in her view of the Guise to whom she attributes "personal courage" (266) in the face of death. I am closer to Ian McAdam's views in *The Irony of Identity: Self and Imagination in the Drama of Christopher Marlowe* (Newark: University of Delaware Press, 1999), 183–86, even though I find the Guise in his dying moments more unhinged than "stupid or blind" (184).

11   See Alan Shepard's discussion of the Duke as a "despot rhetorically constructing himself" (158) in his book *Marlowe's Soldiers: Rhetorics of Masculinity in the Age of the Armada* (Burlington, VT: Ashgate, 2002), 157–60.

12   Although he is dealing with a few years later in Shakespeare's career, David Farley-Hills in *Shakespeare and the Rival Playwrights 1600–1606* (London: Routledge, 1990) gives a convincing account of "constant contact between playwrights, of shifting rivalries and alliances" (1), asserting that "There is plenty of evidence of constant communication between the playwrights and of interest in each other's work" (2). That the awareness of competing marketing practices extends back to Shakespeare's earlier career is suggested by such remarks as the following: "… it is acknowledged as more than coincidental that Shakespeare's *Jew of Venice* appeared in the repertory of the Chamberlain's Men, while the rival firm of Henslowe's Admiral's Men were doing such successful business with the *Jew*

of Malta" (4). See also Roslyn L. Knutson, "Marlowe Reruns: Repertorial Commerce and Marlowe's Plays in Revival" in *Marlowe's Empery: Expanding His Critical Contexts*, ed. Sara Munson Deats and Robert A. Logan (Newark: University of Delaware Press, 2002), 25–42, for an account of a similar industry-wide marketing strategy by which theatrical companies used competing yet complementary revivals to attract larger audiences.

13   Robert A.H. Smith, "*Julius Caesar* and *The Massacre At Paris*," *Notes and Queries* 44:4 (December 1997): 496–97, comes to this same "reasonable conclusion" (497).

14   Two examples from Part 1 of *Tamburlaine* may suffice: When Argier says to Bajazeth, "… all flesh quakes at your magnificence," Bajazeth answers, "True, Argier, and tremble at my looks" (1 *Tamburlaine*, III, i, 49–50); a Messenger tells the Soldan of Egypt that "The frowning looks of fiery Tamburline" "…with his terror and imperious eyes / Commands the hearts of his associates" (1 *Tamburlaine*, IV, i, 13–15). I quote the relevant lines of the Guise's soliloquy (ii, 101–7) in the next paragraph of the text. See also McAdam, *Irony of Identity*, 182–84, who talks about the use of the "blindness-sight motif" throughout *The Massacre At Paris*.

15   As we saw in the first chapter in the discussion of the influence of the *Henry VI* plays on *Edward II*, Marlowe at least echoes lines from 2 *Henry VI*. For details, see Shapiro, *Rival Playwrights*, 91–94.

16   McAdam, *Irony of Identity*, 178, points out that there are critics who have considered the Guise heroic, although he clearly is not one of them. Oliver, too, feels that it is as much of a mistake to to elevate the Guise to the stature of a hero as it is to denigrate Navarre ("*Dido, Queen of Carthage*," lxiv–lxvii).

17   McAdam, Ibid, 179. McAdam gives a fine, full analysis of the soliloquy (178–82), arguing that "The speech … communicates more a sense of uncontrolled restlessness than of steady purpose" (180).

18   McAdam, Ibid, 185, comes to much the same conclusion about the Duke's inability to internalize. Of course, it is always possible that in the complete text this is not the case.

19   For example, see Shapiro, *Rival Playwrights*, 120–21, who feels that Shakespeare was trying to outdo the hyperbolic language and sentiments of Barabas through the language and characterization of Aaron. See also Bate, *Genius of Shakespeare*, 116, and M.C. Bradbrook's "Shakespeare's Recollections of Marlowe" in *Shakespeare's Styles: Essays in honour of Kenneth Muir*, ed. Philip Edwards, Inga-Stina Ewbank, and G.K. Hunter (Cambridge: Cambridge University Press, 1980), 192–95. Bradbrook is careful to notice the differences as well as the similarities between Marlowe and Shakespeare in portraying Barabas and Aaron; she is influenced in her views of the relationship between the two dramatists by Nicholas Brooke ("Marlowe as Provocative Agent in Shakespeare's Early Plays," *Shakespeare Survey* 14 [1961]: 34–44) whose thesis she paraphrases and accepts: "It is as if recalling Marlowe pushed Shakespeare into a further degree of inventiveness" (195).

20   All citations from and references to *Tamburlaine*, *Doctor Faustus*, and *The Jew of Malta* are from *Christopher Marlowe: The Complete Plays*, ed. Mark Thornton Burnett (London: J.M. Dent, 1999).

21   Although, compared to Aaron, I do not find Barabas "exultant" (284) as do Sara Munson Deats and Lisa S. Starks, "'So neatly plotted, and so well perform'd': Villain as Playwright in Marlowe's *The Jew of Malta*," *Theatre Journal* 44 (1992): 375–89, I do find that his irrepressible will to play is further evidence to support the central analogy of their argument.

22 Brooke, 35–36. Maurice Charney, "The Voice of Marlowe's Tamburlaine in Early Shakespeare," *Comparative Drama* 31:2 (Summer, 1997): 214–16.

23 Charney, "Voice of Marlowe's Tamburlaine," 215.

24 Brooke, 36. Like Brooke, Charney focuses on style, noting that "the soaring amplitudinous imagery and the music of the long period pushing on to its triumphant conclusion is familiar from Marlowe" (214).

25 Brooke, 36.

26 See Bate, *Genius of Shakespeare*, 116–20, who sees evidences of Tamburlaine, Barabas, and Faustus in Richard III. Bate also sees some differences and makes some statements that are questionable. Examples of the latter occur when he is talking about Tamburlaine and remarks: "It is Mahomet, not the Christian God, who seems to strike down the self-styled scourge of God" (117) and when, in talking about Richard III's sense of guilt after the appearance of the ghosts, he asserts: "This final emphasis upon guilt is the pragmatic Shakespeare's correction of the blasphemous Marlowe toward religious and moral orthodoxy" (119). See also Bradbrook, *Shakespeare's Recollections*, 195–96, who finds that Richard "betters the Marlovian villain-heroes" (196).

27 Brooke, 37.

28 G. Blakemore Evans in his edition of *The Tragedy of King Richard III* in the Pelican edition of *William Shakespeare: The Complete Works*, gen. ed. Alfred Harbage (New York: Viking Press, 1969), has a footnote to IV, iv, 75–77 (p. 585) in which he indicates that there is a parallel between these lines of Queen Margaret and the "conclusion" of *Doctor Faustus*.

29 Brooke, 37.

30 Ibid., 38.

31 Ibid.

32 Evans, ed., Introduction to *The Tragedy of King Richard III*, 552, is a representative example.

33 See Rick Bowers, 131–41, who is particularly strong on this aspect of *Massacre*.

34 In his edition of *"Dido, Queen of Carthage" and "The Massacre At Paris"* (p. 135n), Oliver identifies some of the difficulties of the passage and bravely tries to paraphrase it.

35 See Harraway, 162–63, who has a sense similar to mine that Navarre is something of an iron fist in the velvet glove patiently waiting to spring into action.

36 Marlowe's cynicism would undoubtedly have deepened had he known that "in July 1593 Navarre became a member of the Church of Rome" (Oliver, ed., *"Dido Queen of Carthage,"* lxiii).

37 Brooke, 44.

38 Charney, "Voice of Marlowe's Tamburlaine," 221.

39 From a letter to Richard Woodhouse, dated October 27, 1818, in *John Keats: Selected Poems and Letters*, ed. Douglas Bush (Boston: Riverside Press, 1959), 279.

40 C.L. Barber, *Creating Elizabethan Tragedy: The Theater of Marlowe and Kyd* (Chicago: University of Chicago Press, 1988), 49.

41 Ibid.

42 Ibid.

43 Foakes, ed., *Henslowe's Diary*, 20 and 21.

Chapter 3

Hero and Leander and *Venus and Adonis*: Artistic Individuality and the Ideology of Containment

I

Marlowe's influence on Shakespeare begins with the plays, not the poetry. There are several reasons for concluding this. We saw in the preceding chapter that *Titus Andronicus* and *Richard III* show clear signs of a familiarity with Marlovian drama. But when we look at *Venus and Adonis*, we do not find a similar familiarity with Marlowe's poetry—*Hero and Leander*, in particular.[1] In the 1960s, however, when F.T. Prince published the Arden edition of Shakespeare's poems,[2] scholars and critics commonly viewed *Hero and Leander* as an important influence on Shakespeare in his composition of *Venus and Adonis*. Support for this position came from such formidable authorities as W.B.C. Watkins, Muriel C. Bradbrook, Douglas Bush, and Kenneth Muir.[3] But, unfortunately, these scholar-critics based their stance on two unverifiable assumptions: first, that Marlowe wrote his poem before Shakespeare composed his and, second, that Shakespeare read Marlowe's poem and allowed it to influence him. Perhaps because of an increased awareness of the uncertainty of the dates of composition of the two poems and perhaps because of a tacit skepticism among scholars about the eight parallels recorded as sources in the footnotes to Prince's edition, most contemporary critics and editors have retreated from the earlier position.[4]

Even so, among the most recent critics to write about the relationship of the two poems, Maurice Charney reaffirms the view prevalent in the 1960s, slightly modifying it by arguing that Marlowe's poem served as a model rather than as a source for Shakespeare.[5] Charney asserts, "Shakespeare obviously knew Marlowe's poem."[6] He cites Douglas Bush to support his position and invokes *As You Like It* as conclusive evidence. Although the play confirms that Shakespeare knew the poem,[7] it does not verify that he knew it before he wrote *Venus and Adonis*. Charney also speculates that both poems were written in 1592 when the plague had closed down the theaters in London. But this speculation, probable as it is, still does not make one poem the model for the other.

Scholars believe, largely on stylistic grounds, that Marlowe wrote his epyllion in 1592–93, toward the end of his brief career. It was entered into the Stationers' Register in September of 1593, four months after he died, but no published editions of it survive before 1598. Shakespeare's *Venus and Adonis* was entered into the Stationers' Register in April of 1593 and was published that same year. Surprisingly, those who have tried to see in Marlowe's poem a source for *Venus and Adonis* have not argued that the roughly equivalent dates of composition make the reverse just as possible.[8] Whether one looks at Marlowe's poem or Shakespeare's for the origins of the other's, the suggestion of a link through sources remains unconvincing.[9] My guess is that neither writer had read the other's epyllion when he wrote his poem; if either had, he rejected it outright as a model for his own epyllion. The uncertainty concerning who might have read whose poem when indicates why a traditional source study that tries to trace the direct influence of *Hero and Leander* on *Venus and Adonis* or vice versa would have little value.

Having read this far, a reader might well ask why a book about influences contains a chapter on two poems that show no influence from one another. If the sole purpose of this study were to discuss the effects of definite influence, then, indeed, this chapter might conclude at this point. But the process of answering the question of whether influence exists necessitates an intertextual examination of the two poems and from this emerges significant perceptions about their composition and aims. It is these perceptions that give impetus to the following discussion.

The putative Marlovian sources of *Venus and Adonis* listed in the footnotes of Prince's edition consist of similarities in phrasing and like details—resemblances, I contend, that are common to the epyllion and to other poems written in the Ovidian tradition.[10] Both writers use the epithet "rose-cheeked" to describe Adonis (*Hero and Leander*, 93 and *Ven.*, 3); both refer to the mythological figure of Narcissus (*Hero and Leander*, 73–76 and *Ven.*, 161–62); both link an unruly horse with the behavior of a lover (*Hero and Leander*, 625–29 and *Ven.*, 263–75 and 385–408); both mention a beloved's sweet-smelling breath (*Hero and Leander*, 21–24 and *Ven.*, 443–44); as in *Romeo and Juliet* (III, ii, 1–25), both associate the night with love-making: "(dark night is Cupid's day)" (*Hero and Leander*, 191) and "'In night,' quoth she [Venus], 'desire sees best of all'" (*Ven.*, 720); both introduce the familiar *carpe diem* argument that physical beauty is enhanced by use (*Hero and Leander*, 232–36 and *Ven.*, 768); both make an analogy between fearful lovers and soldiers afraid of death (*Hero and Leander*, 119–21 and *Ven.*, 893–94); and both touch upon the credulousness of a lover (*Hero and Leander*, 705–6 and *Ven.*, 986). The looseness[11] and inconsequentiality[12] of the eight parallels in this list argue against any strong, sustained, or significant influence. Moreover, little about these parallels seems other than commonplace or standard for a Renaissance love poem. The indefiniteness of these parallels creates serious doubts about their usefulness in attempting a source study, as well as problematizing their validity as evidence of influence. In addition, although the similarities between Leander and Adonis, at first glance, appear to be more far-reaching and deeper, I will argue that the traits the youths have in common originate in the independent demands of each epyllion and in the controlling perspective of each writer—certainly not in Marlowe's influence on Shakespeare or Shakespeare's on Marlowe.

In considering similarities between the two poems, I have found it helpful to keep in mind that, although Marlowe had translated Ovid's *Amores*, as far as anyone knows, neither author had written an epyllion before. Both writers are therefore experimenting with content and devices of artistry they have seen used by Ovid and by others, like themselves, writing in the Ovidian tradition. Consequently, rather than narrowly trying to attribute similarities in details of expression in the poems to Marlowe's influence on Shakespeare or even the other way around, we can with greater justification attribute such resemblances to a like understanding of the same literary traditions. Assuming some such degree of understanding, I would posit that one of the benefits of a comparative study of the two poems is that it reveals specifically how the writers draw from a single stockpile of Ovidian ideas and literary devices and yet fulfill their own aesthetic aims, affirming their individuality as poets.[13]

Consequently, in presenting an unrestricted, intertextual examination of the two poems, I hope, in part, to explain why Marlowe would *not* have been influenced by Shakespeare or Shakespeare by Marlowe even if either had had the opportunity to be. Neither reductive nor didactic, an intertextual study enables us to clarify the divergent artistic aims of the two writers and the discrete import of their poems.[14] In the latter case, it helps us to see that a chief source of tension in each poem grows out of a conflict indigenous to amatory poems, especially epyllia: the struggle between containment and lack of restraint. But significant differences manifest themselves in the two writers' handling of the conflict and in the value each assigns to its two components—ultimately, differences that help to individualize each writer's artistic habits of mind. In both poems forces that restrain, whether psychological or external (i.e., fate, the actions of gods, the "law and process of great nature" [*The Winter's Tale*, II, ii, 260]), are set in opposition to forces that enable unrestrained behavior, both human and extra-human, moral and non-moral. But just as the writers' temperaments differ, so too do their aesthetic perspectives on the consequences of these contending forces—as, for example, in the Marlowe text's approval of Neptune's and (ultimately) Hero's exertion of will as a lack of restraint and the Shakespeare text's approval of the exertion of Adonis's will as an act of containment. As we shall see, one of the ironies of living with flux in a timed universe is that such freeing forces as sexual desire, once active, may transform themselves into forces of containment.[15] Finally, by juxtaposing Marlowe's and Shakespeare's portrayal of an opposition between containment and lack of restraint, we can come to some understanding of the ideology of each narrative—that is, each writer's sense of the political and social needs of the culture from which his poem takes its origin.

II

Before discussing the opposition and its ideological implications, let us examine in the two poems important similarities that arise out of the genre of the epyllion. At the beginning of her discussion of the differences between *Venus and Adonis* and contemporary epyllia, Heather Dubrow remarks: "To understand how Shakespeare's approach to the epyllion differs from that of his contemporaries one must, of course, delineate the contours the genre normally assumes, an apparently straightforward task that proves surprisingly complex."[16] Dubrow goes on to list some of the difficulties and to show how they reflect the "ambiguous nature"[17] of the genre. William Keach similarly comments on the epyllion's "ambiguous status as a classical literary category"[18] but decides that, on the whole, epyllion is a useful term. There are nine recorded instances of the term in classical writing. They speak only to the relative shortness of the form. The term next emerges in early nineteenth-century European scholarship where it is used to describe a genre of classical poetry. In the twentieth century, this application was much disputed. But "epyllion" became popular as a term for a type of poem, loosely Ovidian, written in England between 1589–1618—that is, from *Scylla's Metamorphosis* by Thomas Lodge to *Narcissus, or, The Self-lover* by James Shirley.

Although too amorphous to be rigidly categorized, the epyllion can be loosely defined as an Ovidian narrative poem about mythological and human figures in situations of frustrated love, usually unrequited or unfulfilled. The plots are negligible, frequently trite, and the characterizations thin. Often rhetorical and formal, the language is plied with undisguised artifice, prolixity, and ostentation—a style in whose effects Renaissance readers evidently luxuriated. In the epyllion the emphasis is on experimenting with devices of style to produce an expansiveness—embroidery, filigree, embellishment carried to the furthest reach. Troni Grande, a recent critic writing about one form of expansiveness—dilation—focuses her study on Marlowe's works, but, in effect, she describes a device of artistry familiar in the works of many other Renaissance writers. Grande demonstrates that Marlowe was well versed in the rhetorical technique of dilation (*dilatatio* or *copia* or *amplificatio*)[19] and that "At both the diegetic and extradiegetic levels, the conflict in *Hero and Leander* depends upon the deferral of expectation."[20] This same principle of deferral could of course be applied with equal validity to *Venus and Adonis*.

Such sententiousness as the following lines contain exemplifies still another type of expansiveness, moralizing the obvious, a common device of the epyllion. Characteristically, Marlowe mocks the tradition itself by exaggerating the moralisms and the solemnity.[21] In the following passage, with the comically incongruous words "*deeply*" and "True love," the mocking irony becomes pointed; Marlowe plays off the specificity and concreteness of the physical attraction between Hero and Leander against the vagueness of an idealized, stereotypical notion of a richer love:

> He [Leander] touched her [Hero's] hand; in touching it she trembled:
> Love deeply grounded hardly is dissembled.
> These lovers parlèd by the touch of hands;
> True love is mute, and oft amazèd stands. (*Hero and Leander*, 183–86)

The comic confusion of erotic feeling and "true love" ridicules the idea (let alone the realistic attainment) of the latter; the moralizing mode, in its pretentiousness and puffery, only heightens the comedy. Shakespeare too senses the comic silliness of inflated moralizing, but, unlike Marlowe, he creates effects of humor without ridiculing the tradition itself. With an excess that is comic, Venus responds to the pouting Adonis who is angry at her because his horse has broken loose and run off:

Thy palfrey as he should,
Welcomes the warm approach of sweet desire.
Affection is a coal that must be cool'd;
Else, suffer'd, it will set the heart on fire.
    The sea hath bounds, but deep desire hath none;
    Therefore no marvel though thy horse be gone. (*Ven.*, 385–90)

Venus continues with additional moralizing, but her message tells us less about her ethics than her psychology:

'Who sees his true-love in her naked bed,
Teaching the sheets a whiter hue than white,
But when his glutton eye so full hath fed,
His other agents aim at like delight?
    Who is so faint that dares not be so bold
    To touch the fire, the weather being cold? (*Ven.*, 397–402)

Venus's expansive arguments produce comic incongruity because, while they are couched in an impersonal, authoritative moralizing mode, they are, in fact, utterly personal—although to judge from their effect on Adonis, anything but authoritative. Moreover, the leisurely development of her argument runs counter to the intensity of her desires and demands, thus providing an additional irony. Another, less favorable interpretation of this contrast is that Shakespeare's natural impulse to portray Venus's psychology with a fast-paced dramatic intensity struggles against the epyllion's demand for a slow, relaxed, even playful development.

The seduction arguments of Leander and Venus to their respective objects of adoration appear on the surface to be similarly aphoristic and turgid. In the passages cited below, each lover is presenting perhaps the most familiar argument of all love poetry, *carpe diem*:

But this fair gem [Hero's chastity], sweet in the loss alone,
When you fleet hence, can be bequeathed to none.
Or if it could, down from th' enamelled sky
All heaven would come to claim this legacy,
And with intestine broils the world destroy,
And quite confound nature's sweet harmony. (*Hero and Leander*, 247–52)

The tender spring upon thy tempting lip
Shows thee unripe; yet mayst thou well be tasted.
Make use of time, let not advantage slip;
Beauty within itself should not be wasted.
    Fair flowers that are not gather'd in their prime
    Rot, and consume themselves in little time. (*Ven.*, 127–32)

I cite four more lines of *Hero and Leander* than are necessary in order to show the contrast between Marlowe's distinctive, unconventional use of the *carpe diem* motif and Shakespeare's equally distinctive but conventional use of it. Marlowe reveals much less interest in *carpe diem* than in the power of physical attraction. Conversely, with sensory detail and emotional suggestiveness, Shakespeare centers his focus on the hastily fleeting nature of time. Clearly, the notion of adhering to a standard expression of the motif is alien to Marlowe's perspective, just as it is not to Shakespeare's. This difference alone gives us one strong indication why Shakespeare would not have imitated Marlowe's poem, even though, like Marlowe, he made use of the device of expansiveness common to all epyllia.

One related feature that both writers liberally employ is the looseness of the form. In an epyllion, a writer can expand or contract his material at will without impairing the structure of the poem. Thus, in addition to a dawdling pace, the digressions in both poems give clear evidence of an overall structural looseness. In *Hero and Leander*, as Hero struggles simultaneously to accept and reject her attraction to Leander, Marlowe initiates a series of digressions that pokes fun at the unruliness of the form itself. He begins with a dissertation on Cupid and the Destinies (369) and moves from that digression with a mirthful "Hearken awhile, and I will tell you why" (385) to discuss Mercury and a country maid; and, later, he again breaks away from his immediate focus to explain etiologically why "to this day is every scholar poor" (471).[22] Shakespeare, as usual, is less ironic about the literary technique and more stolidly traditional in his use of it. His digression on the breeding jennet exemplifies the point (259–324). Here, he uses the interruption to present an ironic contrast to the unrequited love in the main plot (Venus herself points out this contrast in 403–08); yet, he also employs it to give credibility to the overwhelming power of Venus's sexual desire and, more generally, to dramatize the superiority of natural instinct—that is, to assert the force of nature, *natura naturans*, as a norm. In effect, he overturns an imposed commonplace standard of ethics by portraying the indomitability of nature and by indicating that it is the chief agent of measure in the poem's system of values. Shakespeare's digression contains a richness in meaning and emotional suggestion absent from Marlowe's but, in being included almost as a set piece, it misses the naturalness of being easily integrated into the poem. Its chief source of delight for many readers lies in the genuineness of its sentiment and its descriptive intensity. One feels an imaginative commitment to the sexual tension portrayed here that much of the rest of the poem lacks. Ironically, although the digression acknowledges the supremacy of instinct over a prefabricated scheme of values, Shakespeare has not yet found a felt way to put this perceived idea into practice in his artistic structuring of the poem.

Perhaps the most obvious similarity between the two poems emerges in the mutual characterization of love as less than an ideal state. Although they inherit this perspective from Ovid, Marlowe and Shakespeare both manage to make it their own. Both writers depict the all-consuming, aggressive character of sexual passion, its frustrations, lack of tenderness, pain, and cruelty. Neither one goes beyond the manifestations of love as physical desire, although, largely through Venus's persistent aggressiveness and Adonis's (unwarranted) denouncement of the goddess for a history of lust under the pretense of love (788–804), Shakespeare does invoke a sense of deeper love and with it a moral frame of reference. This frame of reference suggests not only that love can be more encompassing than purely physical gratification but hints that it can be linked to a system of values that governs one's life as a whole. Marlowe's stamp of individuality shows in his focus on the *power* of physical love—its ability to overpower people, to control their behavior, and its ruthlessness in doing so. Shakespeare, on the other hand, portrays the psychology of physical love as it encounters an insurmountable barrier. We know that for Marlowe physical love is all-powerful and hard-edged, "deaf and cruel where he means to prey" (II, 288). Shakespeare dramatizes the same trait through his portrayal of Venus's behavior. In her intensity toward Adonis and her unrelenting assault on him, "… she murders with a kiss" (54):

> Even as an empty eagle, sharp by fast,
> Tires with her beak on feathers, flesh and bone,
> Shaking her wings, devouring all in haste,
> Till either gorge be stuff'd or prey be gone:
>> Even so she kiss'd his brow, his cheek, his chin,
>> And where she ends she doth anew begin. (55–60)

Having summoned our faculties of judgment in portraying this unpleasant side of Venus, Shakespeare then complicates our moral response with psychological understanding: "Look how he can, she cannot choose but love" (79). Shakespeare's compassion reveals an emotional awareness and depth that Marlowe lacks. The absence of both traits helps to make *Hero and Leander* more tonally unified, more truly Ovidian, and a better poem; but it indicates as well what eventually will make Shakespeare the superior writer.

From this comparison of representative features common to the epyllion as manifested by Marlowe and Shakespeare, let us now turn to an examination of aspects of tone and characterization of less certain origin—specifically, to the comedy in the two poems and to the characterization of the male protagonists. Even if these aspects bear a superficial similarity in the two poems and can be said to somehow derive from the epyllion, when scrutinized closely, they reveal some distinct differences in Marlowe and Shakespeare. Let us take as our first example wit and humor.[23] Whereas most writers of an epyllion would probably argue for the necessity of wit, Marlowe and Shakespeare stand out as writers who also find humor an important ingredient. The chief element of Marlowe's humor is a subversive mocking irony, an irony with a clear cutting edge, used primarily to debunk everything from lofty notions of the origins of historical events (e.g., the love-kindled Trojan war—154) to the epyllion itself. Accompanied by abruptness, surprise, or slyness, it finds its origin in the incongruity of overstatement, inconsistency (e.g., Hero as Venus's nun—320), and outrageousness (e.g., the description of Venus's glass in 142–56), and in the jolting contrast between idealistic notions and hardheaded truths. Examples of this latter effect have a wide range: there is the shock that the resistance of a country maid to Mercury's sexual advances can cause upheavals in the political order of Olympus and in human society, and there is the unconventional, anti-romantic notion that "Love is not full of pity, (as men say) / But deaf and cruel where he means to prey" (771–72).[24] Marlowe's view that the origins of political, social, and psychological events are the result of an exertion of power rather than of something more idealistic and noble provides ample opportunity for comic surprise and irony; it also bespeaks a realism that Shakespeare later comes to embrace in *Antony and Cleopatra*, although he views historical events there less with an eye to power than to star-crossed psychologies acting upon each other purely by chance.

Brian Morris has pointed out that the comedy of *Hero and Leander* "resides in the narrator's odd manipulation of the story."[25] Whether the comedy has the lightness and merriment of the farcical elements in the episode of Neptune and Leander or the ironic seriousness of the view that "Midas' brood shall sit in honour's chair, / To which the Muses' sons are only heir" (475–76), the narrator is for Marlowe a major comic device. Readers rely on the narrator of a poem as a strong figure of authority. Marlowe's narrator is no exception, even though he is unconventionally inconsistent in the extent of his knowledge and in his ability to interpret characters and events. Because of the inconsistency of his perspective, he becomes the poet's chief means for conveying through humor the anti-romantic attitude that pervades the poem. As I have discussed elsewhere, Marlowe also employs humor as a device for detaching readers so that they may understand rationally just how naïve romantic or idealistic illusions are.[26]

Another potent source of humor, as Elizabeth Bieman has demonstrated,[27] lies in Marlowe's handling of comic rhyme. Bieman amply shows how Marlowe wrenches rhymes comically and makes use of multisyllabic rhymes in an "openly deflationary"[28] manner that anticipates Byron's use of comic rhymes in *Don Juan*. She also rightly concludes that Shakespeare seldom avails himself of this comic technique, preferring instead to produce comedy in *Venus and Adonis* through "image and event."[29] Moreover, Shakespeare's stanzaic form enables him to create ironies through a leisurely development of his material—the opposite of the quick, satiric thrusts facilitated by the verve and energy that Marlowe's couplet form creates. These differences affirm once again the individuality of the two writers in the tools they use to give mood and shape to their epyllia.

Shakespeare's humor tends to be more droll, more playful, and more carefree than Marlowe's—clearly without the emphatic mockery of his fellow poet. Also, as W.B.C. Watkins points out, it is "sporadic and incidental rather than interfused throughout."[30] Watkins finds that "Shakespeare wavers between taking himself too seriously and not seriously enough" and that such "wavering is symptomatic of his lack of perfect control."[31] However, "his lack of perfect control" means that he can give free rein to his desire to experiment, and he can also develop his proclivity for creating dramatic situations involving recognizable tensions in both characters and external nature rather than dutifully weaving artifice into descriptions of the fantastic behavior of mythological figures. In addition, the same "lack" reveals Shakespeare's inability to find a comfortable, detached Ovidian perspective, one not undermined by his natural tendency to infuse more emotion and remain less impersonal than either Ovid or Marlowe. Also unlike Ovid and Marlowe, Shakespeare makes relatively little use of the narrator as an intermediary or authority figure whose detachment and moral imprint cannot help but be imposing.[32] He chooses instead to allow the psychological interplay between Venus and Adonis to dominate. By this means, he creates comedy, especially irony, through the language and situations of the characters. The chief irony of the poem lies usually in an Ovidian reversal of roles or of situation—for example, Venus, not Adonis, is the "bold-fac'd suitor" (6) and thus she is the one "to pluck him from his horse" (30):

> Over one arm the lusty courser's rein,
> Under her other was the tender boy,
> Who blush'd and pouted in a dull disdain,
> With leaden appetite, unapt to toy:
>> She red and hot as coals of glowing fire,
>> He red for shame, but frosty in desire. (*Ven.*, 31–36)

Although irony is the major comic effect in the poem, the irony is not always as lightly humorous as it is in this passage, nor is the farcical nature of the first two lines characteristic of the humor in the poem as a whole. At his most humorous, Shakespeare uses comic hyperbole as Marlowe does: "... the star-gazers, having writ on death, / May say, the plague is banish'd by thy breath" (509–10). But, overall, there is less out-and-out humor and more wit in *Venus and Adonis* than in *Hero and Leander*. This tendency makes Shakespeare the more conventional writer of epyllia, except at those times when, as some readers have complained, the excess of wit appears overdone and self-indulgent. Examples of Shakespearean wit appropriate to an epyllion may be found in the cleverness of Venus' remarks to Adonis, in her banquet of sense (427–50), and in such Sidneyesque passages as the one in which the narrator characterizes the goddess's despair when she thinks that Adonis might have been killed by the boar:

> O how her eyes and tears did lend and borrow!
> Her eye seen in the tears, tears in her eye:
> Both crystals where they view'd each other's sorrow,
> Sorrow that friendly sighs sought still to dry;
>> But like a stormy day, now wind, now rain,
>> Sighs dry her cheeks, tears make them wet again. (961–66)

The language of the "new" *Arcadia* is used here, complete with the personifications that to modern ears seem cloying.[33] It is conceivable that Shakespeare's excessiveness here may be tinged with comedy, but it is more likely that he is adopting the Sidneyesque mode experimentally as he does off and on during the course of the poem. The "tears" and the "sighs" are specifically reminiscent of Petrarchan poetry where they are major staples. John Donne alludes to these same two, familiar Petrarchan ingredients when, in "A Valediction Forbidding Mourning," the speaker warns his beloved against "teare-floods"(6) and "sigh-tempests"(6)[34] during his absence; unlike Shakespeare, Donne clearly intends the references satirically—as comic exaggerations. Marlowe would not have been able to write the passage as it appears in Shakespeare. He would have turned it into comic mockery and used it to undermine the narrator by portraying his propensity for self-deception.

I have already mentioned that the parallels between Leander and Adonis can, on the surface, suggest a source where none exists. As they are portrayed, the youths share characteristics that might lead one to assume that Shakespeare was influenced by Marlowe—in particular, the emphasis on the two youths' physical charms (stressed more than those of Hero or Venus), on their feminine qualities, and on their naïveté and inconsistency. But such an assumption would be erroneous. In addition to the thinness of characterization that the epyllion encourages, Marlowe focuses on the physical beauty of Leander to the exclusion of much else because he is interested in dramatizing the *power* of physical beauty; he does the same with Hero, although the spotlight is more often on Leander. Shakespeare, on the other hand, is chiefly interested in Venus as a character, in her psychology as well as her beauty, and he is interested in the drama of a conflict impossible to resolve. Thus, he makes Adonis younger than he is in Ovid's tale, thereby enabling the youth to resist the goddess, and he endows him with considerable physical beauty; but, so as not to detract from Venus's actions and reactions, he gives him very little personality.[35]

Leander's feminine traits have more to do with Marlowe's brash defiance of conventional heterosexual stereotypes and clichéd romantic illusions than they do with the psychology of Leander.[36] Moreover, lines such as "Some swore he was a maid in man's attire, / For in his looks were all that men desire" (83–84) and Leander's reply to Neptune's advances, "'You are deceived, I am no woman, I'" (676) are intended to provide comic amusement, apart from any desire to jolt us into a reconsideration of our standard views of gender types and the literary and sociopolitical forces that undergird them. Adonis's feminine traits—he is "thrice fairer" than Venus (7), a "stain to all nymphs, more lovely than a man" (9), his cheek is "tend'rer" (353) than Venus's hand, and he has a "mermaid's voice" (429)—constitute part of the irony that Shakespeare playfully creates in reversing the suitor's roles.[37] The clearest effect of this ironic reversal of roles is that it provides opportunities for dramatizing with attention-getting forcefulness the relationship between the goddess and the youth rather than merely describing it.

The feminine features also help to suggest Adonis's boyishness: puberty has yet to take up residence. If we ask if the irony of Adonis's looks leads to much beyond itself, we must either respond with a "no" or turn to speculation to find an answer.[38] In speculating, I prefer to move in the direction of the artistic context and suggest that the poem stylizes the language and characters so heavily throughout that the portrayal of Adonis's feminine characteristics is partly a direct consequence of stylization, a stylization able to make use of the commonplace observation that it can sometimes be difficult to distinguish between the facial features and voices of young (English) males and females, especially those on the edge of puberty. Shakespeare wittily exploits this difficulty in the Sonnets when he describes the Young Man, "the master-mistress" of his "passion" (Sonnet 20, line 2), as having "A woman's face" (Sonnet 20, line 1). Moreover, as a dramatist in a theater culture that used young men to play the roles of women, Shakespeare, like Marlowe, undoubtedly had more than an average awareness of such physical characteristics.

Leander's sexual naïveté and much-commented-upon inconsistency form part of Marlowe's plan to upset expectation, whether it be literary or psychological, and thereby bring his audience to a perspective of hardheaded realism in which they understand how completely the forces of cultural control govern their attitudes. Otherwise, these two characteristics do not elicit anything deeper than the platitudes that youth tends to be naïve and that those caught up in passion tend to behave inconsistently. Conversely, we understand Adonis's naïveté. He is unlearned in the ways of the world. Thus, when Venus pretends to faint, Adonis thinks she has died and tries to revive her with exaggerated means that evoke a comic response (463–80). We understand Adonis's inconsistency less. Much like one of Shakespeare's precocious children with a wisdom beyond his years, he tells Venus, "Before I know myself, seek not to know me" (525); however accurate his point, one is startled to hear him utter it. Later, he sermonizes about love and lust with a knowledge, simplistic as it is, that his actions and words have suggested he does not have (768–810). If Shakespeare wishes to suggest that Adonis is maturing, then he has failed; the turnabout takes place too abruptly. More likely, Adonis serves primarily as a functional figure, fulfilling Shakespeare's immediate ends without ever becoming a fully formed character in his own right. I would guess, too, that Shakespeare is writing to the moment, that he is satisfying a desire to experiment with a mode of expression he has not yet tried. As we shall see, this is an instance of his lack of stylistic restraint—in contradistinction to the text's favoring of containment, an attitude conveyed through the basic situation of the poem.

The differences in the perspectives conveyed by Marlowe and Shakespeare as they write their poems are most telling. Marlowe tries to debunk and shock, to strip away illusion in order to see how personal, social, and political events result from power struggles. He assumes a stance of *realpolitik*: power is all that matters; everything is in a state of flux and struggle and—whether by rejecting established modes of personal behavior, accepted social and political systems, or literary traditions—an assertion of power can seem to bring flux under momentary control. In the expenditure of energy, such an assertion also carries with it a sense of exhilaration. Because he tends to ridicule and tear down standard notions rather than to criticize them constructively, we understand his perspective as negative—angry, subversive, and cynical, not simply realistic. One might well ask what there is about the poem that prevents us from feeling its gloomy outlook. The answer is its energy and its comedy and the poet's wonder at the vibrancy and forcefulness of struggles for power. Moreover, anticipating a major technique of a known admirer, Bertolt Brecht, Marlowe deploys stylistic forces of detachment to prevent us, as well as himself, from responding to the content of the poem with purely emotional engagement.

He expresses a similar attitude toward erotic experience—an attitude detached and cerebral, perceived but not felt. In the consummation scene, the spotlight shines on the power of sexual desire, illuminating the way in which it controls the two lovers and their feelings. After a sexual struggle, Leander asserts his power and the sexual consummation takes place but with a comic anticlimax that suddenly supplants the intense heightening eroticism of the scene:

Leander now, like Theban Hercules,
Entered the orchard of th' Hesperides,

> Whose fruit none rightly can describe but he
> That pulls or shakes it from the golden tree. (781–84)

The clever tease, the suggestiveness of the myth, and the detachment are Ovidian in spirit.[39] Like Ovid, Marlowe has little interest in analyzing the essential quality of the eroticism he is portraying.

For Shakespeare, the perspective appears to be more traditional but, ultimately, it is ambiguous. By "traditional" I mean that it contains a conventional sense of moral justice and of the power and capriciousness of fate. We are at times called upon to disapprove of Venus's aggressiveness and persistence; and, in direct contrast to Marlowe's sexual pursuer, she does not prevail in her efforts to seduce her love object. Moreover, Adonis's demise is the result of an impersonal fate, just as it is in Ovid's *Metamorphoses* (X.705–28); the only difference is that Ovid's Venus has the power to change Adonis into an anemone. In his account, Shakespeare does not name the agent of change. In fact, Venus's powers as a goddess seem limited to a prophecy of the unhappy effects of loving (1135–64) and to having herself drawn through the skies in a chariot by silver doves (1189–94).

The ambiguity in Shakespeare's perspective stems from a confusion of moral and aesthetic impulses. On the one hand, he raises the question of the morality of Venus' behavior—for example, by characterizing her passion again and again with the inflammatory term "lust."[40] On the other, by deciding to write an epyllion in the Ovidian manner, he accepts the given that moral assessments of the characters' behavior are irrelevant even if moralizing as an expressive mode is not. Complicating these contradictory perspectives is Shakespeare's occasional tendency to give psychological depth to the characterization of the goddess. When we become involved with Venus psychologically, moral considerations of her behavior seem oversimplified and superficial. Moreover, the uncertainty of Shakespeare's perspective, taken as a whole, is augmented by the passages in which he suspends a sense of a unified purpose to experiment stylistically or to dramatize something that he feels comfortable with (e.g., the passage on the hare, "poor Wat"—673–708). The truth is that, much as he was attracted to Ovid throughout his career, Shakespeare finds the Ovidian spirit, with its detachment and immunity from feeling human concerns, alien to his natural inclinations. *Venus and Adonis* shows him caught in a crossfire between those inclinations and the tradition he tries to adopt. Marlowe, on the other hand, accepted Ovidian detachment and moral neutrality as characteristics of the epyllion and thereby avoided Shakespeare's confusions of feeling and judgment in his characterizations.

Shakespeare presents a view of art in the digression on the breeding jennet that helps to account for his lack of a fixed perspective. He gives license to his tendency to move above the commonplace in both substance and manner when, with considerable poise and authority, he says:

> Look when a painter would surpass the life
> In limning out a well-proportion'd steed,
> His art with nature's workmanship at strife,

As if the dead the living should exceed:
    So did this horse excel a common one,
    In shape, in courage, colour, pace and bone. (289–94)

Art is able to present ideal images instead of reality at its most ordinary. In doing so, it may, by contrast, evoke one's sense of reality and the disparity between the ideal and the real. Once we sense that disparity, our faculties of moral judgment are energized and set in motion. On the other hand, ideal images may invite us to fantasize, to escape into the world of the ideal. Unlike Shakespeare, Marlowe tries, by deliberately exaggerating the idealizations, to bring us sharply to our senses about commonsense reality and our tendency to obscure or ignore it through self-styled illusions. Like Shakespeare, however, he revels in an expression of the liberated imagination which idealizing provides. For Shakespeare, this freedom means including material with which he is thoroughly at home: passages such as those on the "blue-vein'd violets" (125), the breeding jennet (259–324), the hare (673–709), and the snail (1033–36). But, in their strong imaginative involvement, such passages clash tonally with the detached artifice and formality of the poem, creating a conflict between what the poet thinks he has committed himself to write and what he desires to write. This conflict, in part, results in an ambiguity of perspective.[41]

Like Marlowe, Shakespeare can be witty in his depiction of love. But there is a difference:

The studded bridle on a ragged bough
Nimbly she [Venus] fastens—O how quick is love!—
The steed is stalled up, and even now
To tie the rider [Adonis] she begins to prove:
    Backward she push'd him, as she would be thrust,
    And govern'd him in strength, though not in lust. (37–42)

The wit detaches us but the mechanics of the situation and the interaction of the two figures, especially the psychology of Venus, engage us. The same is true of the perspective on erotic experience: Shakespeare is more emotional than Marlowe—we are more absorbed and we participate in the experience with a greater density of engaged feeling; yet, in being attracted to the style, we are also disengaged. The well-known passage of Venus as a deer park is a case in point (229–40). So too are the following lines spoken by the narrator:

Now quick desire hath caught the yielding prey,
And glutton-like she feeds, yet never filleth.
Her lips are conquerors, his lips obey,
Paying what ransom the insulter willeth;
    Whose vulture thought doth pitch the price so high
    That she will draw his lips' rich treasure dry. (547–52)

We are caught up by the potential eroticism of the passage and by the violence of Venus's uncontrollable desire to feed voraciously. But, at the same time, we are conscious of the high-pitched style, mannered and overdone to the point of parody, and this awareness counters our emotional involvement.

If in his narrative focus Marlowe highlights sensation, spectacle, and event, Shakespeare emphasizes psychology, conflict and tension, and exalted feeling. Each poem articulates a contrast between a focus on external events and one on inward human states. In *Hero and Leander* the external focus predominates; in *Venus and Adonis* the opposite is true. Moreover, if *Hero and Leander* can be said to concentrate on *causes*—usually, the sources of power (especially, the widespread potency of physical attraction)—*Venus and Adonis* can be said to concentrate on *effects*—usually, the psychological consequences of frustrated love. What facilitates the narrative focus of each poem is Marlowe's extremely flexible use of a narrator and Shakespeare's extensive use of a dialogue that, at times, has the appearance of a monologue.

We have seen that the epyllion as a form is elastic, enabling rapid action and quick movement as well as a leisurely pace. Both Marlowe and Shakespeare take advantage of this structural flexibility; yet, distinct differences mark the way in which they do. Whether or not one assumes that Marlowe completed *Hero and Leander*, the poem is more structured, more noticeably blocked out than *Venus and Adonis*. This may be in part because of the structure Marlowe found in the poem written by his source, Museaus. But one notices that even Marlowe's digressions seem firmly under control—a clear demonstration of his power as a poet. *Venus and Adonis*, on the other hand, is more casual, intuitive, and spontaneous, more ready to relax or tighten the reins of the narrative without wanting to make evident the presence of authorial control—perhaps in part because the stanzaic form encourages greater leisureliness. Shakespeare feels less compelled to take Marlovian critical stances than to complete the drama. However, he disrupts the organic coherence that this artistic principle involuntarily affirms by introducing elements that he thinks an epyllion should contain. What gives Marlowe's poem a structural unity and helps to clarify the difference in his perspective and Shakespeare's is his single-mindedness. Conversely, Shakespeare appears less settled in his mind. This uncertainty is revealed in those elements of structure which seem merely tacked on—for example, Venus's speech on Adonis and her five senses (427–50), her prophecy (1135–64), and Adonis's lecture on love and lust (769–810). Because there exists no clear, overriding unified perspective, the poem as a whole adds up to less than the sum of its parts.

III

One of the strongest determinants shaping the narrative perspectives in the poems of Marlowe and Shakespeare at any given moment is the attitude conveyed toward containment and restraint and toward the forces that challenge them. Understood psychologically, this opposition is binary. The very act of containment implies as its motive a fear of a lack of control, including the consequences, just as unrestrained behavior implies a desire for freedom from the oppression of containment or, more aggressively, an act of willful transgression against an imposed limitation. The latter could also express an urgency to exert power, whether or not it leads to a specific form of control. The hostility between these opposed forces provides much of the tension in each poem: in *Hero and Leander* in the struggles for power, especially the sexual struggles, and in *Venus and Adonis* in the psychological conflicts between the two protagonists and within Venus herself.

In *Hero and Leander*, containment and restraint mean abiding by orthodoxy, convention, and tradition; and, as we shall see, Marlowe applies this definition to the writer of literature as well as to the participants of the world of the poem. During the course of the poem, he presents us with multiple figures (e.g., Leander, the shepherd maid, Neptune) whose natural *élan vital* suggests through implicit contrast that restraint encourages passivity and inhibits action. As soon as Hero becomes sexually attracted to Leander, she struggles between her conventional understanding of proper behavior and her instinctual drives, allowing the latter finally to surface. By focusing chiefly on the controlling force of sexual feelings and on their unsentimental nature, Marlowe protests the artificiality of conventions of amatory behavior in literature and life. He also challenges his readers' preconditioned responses to idealized romantic love and, in effect, prevents them from succumbing passively to two related dangers of containment: the suppression of the imagination and the denial of one's independence and individuality. In Marlowe's characters surges of natural energy, usually employed to attain power through rebellion, defy the manifestations of containment. The poem champions such forces by suggesting that ultimate reality and happiness reside in the assertion of power, even if only briefly.

This notion of a sweet fruition also encompasses the writer who, in controlling time and events, has the power of a god. Such power is essentially psychological and self-gratifying—again, even if only briefly. Two additional consequences of the writer's power stand out, but they are less tightly under his control—his immediate influence on the audience and his long-term influence on the subsequent course of literature. As the Prologue to *Tamburlaine* makes clear, Marlowe is well aware of both of these effects of his power as a writer. There, he promises that "high astounding terms" (5) will be used in the play to awe the audience. By breaking away from the traditional, impoverished poetic standards in drama (1–2), he will introduce through a forceful language new to English theater the majestic expansiveness of the epic tradition. In *Hero and Leander*, he demonstrates his awareness of immediate and long-term influence (respectively) in his attempts to make his readers know how easily they can deceive themselves with romantic notions and in his attempts to use standard characteristics of the epyllion such as digressions and the reliable narrator against themselves.

Marlowe may well think that through his iconoclasm the poem rejects containment. To be sure—especially through the actions of his chief protagonist, Leander—it often does. But it also demonstrates that, given the inevitable passing of time, the characters find it virtually impossible to move permanently away from restraint. However much they are repelled by containment, especially if it entails suppressing their sexual feelings or restraining their attempts to assert power, the characters cannot help participating in it. In effect, they valorize containment. Hero's contradictory feelings about yielding to her sexual impulses make the point most clearly. She feels impelled to restrain herself and yet she resists this restraint. At the end of the poem, after abandoning herself to erotic pleasure, she attempts to steal away (791–96)—a return to containment. Only those of godlike stature seem able to act wholly without restraint—for example, the deities depicted in "Venus' glass"—but only some of the deities and only some of the time. Both Mercury and Cupid find that the Destinies finally restrain their unbridled behavior (460–84), and Neptune learns to his chagrin that in his pursuit of Leander he is fated to be restrained (which, significantly, means that he is unsuccessful). Thus, Marlowe reveals in his characterizations that, much as he might like it to be otherwise, the coin is unalterably two-sided.

In *Hero and Leander*, the protagonists, the gods in Venus's glass, Mercury, the country maid, and Neptune all find containment of their desires inimical. Consequently, they become defiant. As one critic has noticed, in Marlowe's characters "external restraints ... serve only to rouse and heighten desire."[42] Measured in terms of power, the characters' degree of success in defying containment varies. From those who do achieve success, Marlowe draws no moral lesson, partly because he knows that such success is subject to flux. Moreover, he understands that an assertion of power often invites challenges to usurp that power. Even so, we are meant to admire the characters' displays of vigor and their reach toward power, especially if it appears to exceed their grasp.

We have seen that, although Marlowe is primarily interested in depicting struggles for control as efforts to escape constraints, he also depicts the necessity of containment. Sexual passion is a perfect vehicle to portray the tension between these contradictory tendencies because, paradoxically, the more his two protagonists give themselves over to unrestrained sexual expression, the more they move—obliviously, to be sure—back toward the containment which inevitably ensues after they have achieved a momentary state of equilibrium through consummation. Hero's embarrassment as she attempts covertly to slide out of bed (791–800) suggests an impulse to regain containment just as Leander's response to the sight of her nakedness (807–10) suggests the opposite—that in his present state of containment he has a further desire for sexual abandon. The movement from containment to a lack of restraint, back to a form of containment, can be likened to ceaseless travel along a Mobius strip with a constant alternation between the two states. Such travel accurately suggests the poem's overriding sense of realism about the power and instability of flux even as it exalts the exhilaration of unrestraint. Leander's "vows and promises" (580) to Hero and his single-mindedness as he tries to bypass Neptune suggest a form of containment that Marlowe may or may not have sensed undermines his celebration of the freedom from restraint that enables it. Missing, however, from his dramatization even if not from his perception is an awareness that, as a form of self-control, containment can itself be an expression of power.

A view of containment opposite to that of Marlowe's appears to be the narrative stance informing *Venus and Adonis*. The goddess's lack of restraint is made to seem unattractive—psychologically destructive for both her and Adonis. This does not mean that Venus would have succeeded in enticing Adonis into her bed had she been more restrained; nor does Shakespeare retreat into a simple moral dichotomy to extol the virtues of restraint. We understand by implication that Venus's restraint might have meant less emotional *sturm und drang* for her and less hostility from Adonis, but, in matters of passion, as in matters of stylistic indulgence during the writing of an epyllion, no formula of right and wrong, however apt, can be applied. Self-control is not readily possible, even if it were desirable; inevitably, one's psychology dominates. With this last generalization, Marlowe would probably agree. What distinguishes the two writers' portrayals of the dialectic is Shakespeare's reluctance to shift from his position of psychological ambiguity to a Marlovian position of moral clarity. Marlowe sides with those who defy constraints because it energizes them and that, he feels, is when they most completely fulfill themselves as human beings and know their humanity. This position is one that Shakespeare comes to celebrate in *Antony and Cleopatra*. But in *Venus and Adonis* he is attracted to the impossibility of resolving the conflict of values and to the opportunities for drama and tension that it provides. In that sense, he is more the aesthete and less the moralist than Marlowe is. Yet, paradoxically, it is probably from Marlowe that he learned the most about the aesthetics of ambiguity.

In *Venus and Adonis*, the conflict between restraint and abandon is central to Venus's psychology, the primary focus of the poem. Of course Venus *is* love and cannot act other than herself. Thus, she chaffs against the containment of her desires, and it causes her psychological pain and defeat. As we have just seen, there is never any guarantee that containment will lead to infinite riches in a little room, but, even when we understand and sympathize with the goddess's aggressive behavior, we are not invited to admire it. Shakespeare appears to be exposing the dangers of a lack of restraint, not only in Venus's uncontrollable sexual passion but in Adonis's unquenchable thirst to hunt the boar. On the other hand, if we are to judge by the behavior of Adonis, containment is no answer either. The imagery of containment and excess in the poem, its descriptive function apart, reveals the compassion of a psychological perspective, not merely the harsh criticism of a moral one. The following passage refers to Venus and typifies the narrator's sympathy with the goddess:

> An oven that is stopp'd, or river stay'd,
> Burneth more hotly, swelleth with more rage:
> So of concealed sorrow may be said
> Free vent of words love's fire doth assuage;
>   But when the heart's attorney once is mute,
>   The client breaks, as desperate in his suit. (331–36)

Our overall estimation of Venus's aggressiveness and persistence may not be as sympathetic as the narrator's is here, but even when we criticize the goddess's behavior, we understand that she is trapped by uncontrollable feelings.[43]

In *Venus and Adonis*, the implication is that containment means self-control and that some measure of self-control constitutes a mature perspective because it enables continuance—ultimately, the only defense against the ruinous effects of time. For Marlowe, it is the defiance of containment that leads, through power, to control, but control of a more precarious sort. One might plausibly argue that his perspective lacks maturity because such defiance results in mere venting and, since the control cannot be secured, it cannot guarantee continuance. Because he portrays an unruly defiance rather than a planned expansiveness, he conveys an attitude destructive of continuance. Moreover, he reveals little concern for the moral and social responsibilities that are part of the consequences of defiance. Hence, one senses that his portrayals express negative feelings; certainly they do not promote a creative independence that binds or is constructive, one that, in effect, secures continuance.

Viewed from within the world of each poem as something affirmative, containment may be considered a reasonable modus operandi in the lives of the characters, as it apparently has been for Hero and is for Adonis. Viewed as something negative, it is a condition imposed upon the characters by cultural forces of which they may well be unaware, forces harmful to their own desires and creative independence. This is particularly true of Leander and of Venus. Marlowe puts the case well in describing his hero:

> For as a hot proud horse highly disdains
> To have his head controlled, but breaks the reins,
> Spits forth the ringled bit, and with his hooves
> Checks the submissive ground, so he that loves,
> The more he is restrained, the worse he fares. (625–29)

In theory, the characters can liberate themselves from containment by asserting their wills, whether through sexual passion or some other means. But it may be to ill rather than good effect, as both writers seem to recognize.

Both writers are strongly aware that sexual desire itself is imposed upon the characters by nature, even if cultural forces determine the value attached to its forms of expression. Marlowe's narrator says, "It lies not in our power to love or hate, / For will in us is overruled by fate" (167–68) and Shakespeare's Venus (as we have seen) "cannot choose but love" (79). Paradoxically, such desire partakes of containment in its concentrated focus while it evinces a lack of restraint in its operation. As a force that overturns other kinds of containment and restraint, sexual aggressiveness is marveled at in Marlowe's poem and viewed skeptically, even disparagingly, in Shakespeare's.

Whether either writer thought consciously about his poem in such terms, the treatment of containment and freedom can be used to understand the poetic form and stylistic means of each. We see first that modulating the containment and excess of form and style constitutes a modus operandi for the writer. Containment in form and style suggests knowledge of one's poetic craft, a firm control over it. Regarded affirmatively, such containment can be a means of stability through which writers can both establish and validate their authorial identity. Further, writing with containment in form and style can provide a temporary sense of control over change in a life which is by nature broken into disconnected segments and which is forever evanescent. In writing their poems, Marlowe and Shakespeare can be said to have provided such psychological control for themselves. Looked at in the same affirmative light as containment, expressive freedom that is not merely disruptive can be viewed as the healthy expression of a liberated imagination; as such, it helps to establish the chief characteristics that individualize the writer.

In *Hero and Leander*, form and content appear to be mutually supportive in their disregard of the containment of orthodoxy and tradition but, knowingly or not, Marlowe also supports containment. The form of the epyllion liberates Marlowe's imagination as we have already seen, both in his use of digressions and in the slowness with which he builds up to the sexual consummation at the end of the poem. Yet, for all its brash antics, the love story and its ambling development follow a conventional pattern. To this extent, Marlowe participates in containment. He thereby reinforces the tension between orthodoxy and heterodoxy established in the content of the poem. Stylistically, his sense of containment is best reflected in his use of heroic couplets. This device serves to highlight by contrast his defiance, just as the energy and stressed rhyme of the couplets serve to accentuate it.

If in the content of his poem Shakespeare often appears to support containment, in the looseness of the form and the indulgences of his style, he at times gives vent to those aspects of his aesthetic personality which cannot be contained, his fatal Cleopatras. We understand that Shakespeare himself is alert to indulgences of style when Lorenzo in *The Merchant of Venice* describes those verbal gymnasts who "for a tricksy word / Defy the matter" (*MV*, III, v, 62–63). In *Venus and Adonis*, the poet's lack of restraint is expressed in verbal inventiveness (e.g., "Full gently now she takes him by the hand / A lily prison'd in a goal of snow, / Or ivory in an alablaster band" [361–63]), excess (e.g., the description of Adonis's dimples [241–52]), and in those passages in which the narrator speaks familiarly of nature as if it were from a first-hand account (the divedapper, violet, lark, jennet, hare, and snail). One senses the lack of restraint—that is, the liberated imagination—in passages of imaginative commitment, such as those just listed, whereas in the more cold-fingered and perfunctory passages, such as Venus's banquet of sense (426–450), one senses restraint, the author trying to adhere to established Ovidian techniques. This conflict between the personal desires and dutiful obligations of a neophyte writer of epyllia may be one reason why the poem does not uniformly succeed and why Shakespeare never went back to write another epyllion. Ultimately, he is at odds with himself because the rational, morally responsible, trained self is fighting with the irrational, amorally aesthetic, instinctual self. Marlowe's zestful celebration of sexual liberation is contained within a well-structured poem following the conventional pattern of the epyllion, whereas Shakespeare's affirmation of restraint is expressed through a meandering form and stylistic excess that belies the restraint affirmed in the poem. Thus form and content jar in both poems but in opposite ways.

In both *Hero and Leander* and *Venus and Adonis*, the polarity between containment and lack of restraint can be understood ideologically. By logical analogy, the polarity suggests the two writers' sense of sociopolitical needs within their culture, as well as its aspirations. The political implications of the defiance of containment in Marlowe include moving in the specific direction of greater individual freedom but with a purpose that substitutes immediate gratification in the release of angry feelings for a long-range sociopolitical vision; this view correlates better with a system of individual enterprise than it does with the values of a medieval comitatus band or a rigid Renaissance class structure. Marlowe appears to believe that defiance of political and social systems is healthy, that yielding to them—a form of containment—can only bring about injustice and hypocrisy. At the end of the sustained series of digressions, the narrator gives an etiological account of why poverty will forever accompany learning (470–72). The complaint turns political as he goes on to observe that financial support and moral worth are not linked:

> Midas' brood shall sit in honour's chair,
> To which the Muses' sons are only heir;
> And fruitful wits that inaspiring are
> Shall discontent run into regions far.
> And few great lords in virtuous deeds shall joy,
> But be surprised with every garish toy;
> And still enrich the lofty servile clown,
> Who with encroaching guile keeps learning down. (475–82)

In describing the overturning of the political system on Olympus (451–64), Marlowe suggests that political situations evolve out of capricious, even trivial occurrences and, like the cause of the Trojan War, are in origin more irrational than rational. The mingling of the gods and humankind throughout the poem and the focus on individual psychology (proving, for example, that physical attraction knows no social barriers) and not on the characters as social or political beings suggest that Marlowe has little respect for traditional ideas of social barriers and class structure. The proud shepherd maid who bargains with Mercury when he makes advances toward her prompts the following comment:

> Her breath as fragrant as the morning rose,
> Her mind pure, and her tongue untaught to glose,
> Yet proud she was (for lofty Pride that dwells
> In towered courts is oft in shepherds' cells). (391–94)

The description becomes generalized and, hence, more authoritative as Marlowe focuses moralistically on an unfortunate likeness rather than on a difference between the court and the country. The proud shepherd maid perhaps reminds us of the shepherd Tamburlaine who also disregarded traditional notions of a hierarchical social order in the quest for control and power. For Marlowe here, as well as in his plays, all social order is the result of endless struggles for power—energy expended and suppressed. Everything is constantly in a state of flux. Taken as a whole, the social and political attitudes throughout the poem suggest the need for a new ideology and, consequently, new social and political systems. But the stance is so fragmented and so negative that one hesitates to draw such a definite inference.

The implications of the ideology of containment in *Venus and Adonis* are more complex. The content of the poem suggests that Shakespeare holds some respect for containment and, consequently, a system of values that reflects the containment of the status quo. The logical extension of this implication is that he is socially and politically conservative, that he supports a traditional social order and the orthodox sources of social and political stability. What undercuts this all-too-pat view is that the poem reveals an author being pulled in two directions at once—by self-created obligations to write an epyllion and by unrestrained impulses that lead him to give free expression to his own inclinations. Put another way, he is torn between acting responsibly with control and acting self-indulgently without control. In political terms, this could be considered logically analogous to the pattern that gives rise to the dichotomy between what Terry Eagleton sees as the conditions of "traditional feudal social order"[44] and "bourgeois individualism."[45] Shakespeare focuses critically on the lack of containment in Venus, a sign of where his interest lies, and, yet, he himself defies containment through an indulgence in free-wheeling stylistics.[46] Again by logical extension, this conflict has a cultural parallel in that adherence to social and political responsibility means a loss of individual creative independence. That this conflict later dominates such plays as *Antony and Cleopatra* makes it that much less surprising that it crops up in *Venus and Adonis*.

One can take this analogy one step further by noting, again speculatively, that Marlowe and Shakespeare reflect an uncertainty about the well-being of their culture although they express this uncertainty in different ways. We have seen that both writers equate containment with maintaining the social status quo of society—for Marlowe, such containment includes—odiously, to be sure—not reaching beyond the boundaries of traditional class structure. Both writers would agree that sociopolitical containment exists at the expense of sacrificing one's individuality. The notion of containment grows out of an older order of feudal values in which the well-being of the social unit came first. What undermines this notion is any view in which the desires of the individual come first. The two writers very likely understand that, at best, unrestrained, vigorously self-aggrandizing action can lead to the success of the individual, especially when measured in terms of power and material gain. In making the shepherd lass of *Hero and Leander* successful, Marlowe idealizes his understanding of this principle. In *Venus and Adonis*, this form of success would seem to be measured in terms of Venus's power in controlling Adonis, with sexual favors the equivalent of material gain. Although Venus is vigorously self-aggrandizing, she does not meet with success because her methods antagonize rather than entice Adonis, and, given the ending of the poem, antagonize Shakespeare as well—especially since they foster neither creative independence nor bonds of human mutuality. If Venus's methods, like those of the shepherdess, can be said to reflect a newer order of values, one in which bourgeois individualism is firmly established, then not only are the conflicting perspectives of the two orders not easily reconciled but Marlowe and Shakespeare are both expressing chagrin about the results of the behavioral changes taking place. Marlowe's view in *Hero and Leander* is that the older order of values is not working, and so, with perhaps not enough regard for the consequences, he defiantly favors a newer order, although he has mixed feelings about the one in place. Shakespeare, on the other hand, is attracted to some aspects of the newer order, represented by

Venus, and at times enjoys personally the verbal anarchy which it seems to sanction; but he also gives ambiguous support to the older order of values—"ambiguous" because the loss of individuality and creative independence seems a very high price to pay for social stability. If *Venus and Adonis* suggests in the impossibility of the amatory situation that the newer order of values will create permanent problems, it also suggests that by no means is it possible to find salvation in the older order. It is clear that both writers are trying to be realistic about the fortunes of the individual in the face of the changes taking place in their culture, including the tendency of individuals to disenfranchise themselves from society. It is just as clear that, because of the internal and external problems that afflict individuals, they are a long way from finding workable solutions.

Notes

1   If, in fact, there was an influence from Marlowe, it comes from *Dido, Queen of Carthage*. There, Dido is as aggressive and manly in her courtship of Aeneas as Venus is in wooing Adonis.

2   F.T. Prince, ed., *The Arden Edition of the Works of William Shakespeare: The Poems*, 3rd edition (Cambridge, MA: Harvard University Press, 1960). All references to *Venus and Adonis* are taken from this edition.

3   W.B.C. Watkins, *Shakespeare and Spenser* (Princeton, NJ: Princeton University Press, 1950), 6–7. M.C. Bradbrook, *Shakespeare and Elizabethan Poetry* (London: Chatto and Windus, 1951), 61–66, but especially 65–66. Douglas Bush: *Mythology and the Renaissance Tradition in English Poetry* (New York: Norton, 1963; revised edition, first published in 1932), 137–48, but especially 142, 144, 148; "The Influence of Marlowe's *Hero and Leander* on Early Mythological Poems," *Modern Language Notes* 42 (1927): 211–17; and "Notes on Marlowe's *Hero and Leander*," *Publications of the Modern Language Association* 44 (1929): 760–64. Kenneth Muir, "*Venus and Adonis*: Comedy or Tragedy," in *Shakespearean Essays*, ed. Alwin Thaler and Norman Sanders (Knoxville: University of Tennessee Press, 1964), 3 and 12.

4   The hesitation among critics to name *Hero and Leander* as a source for *Venus and Adonis* appears in Hallett Smith, *Elizabethan Poetry* (Cambridge, MA: Harvard University Press, 1952), 77–90; William Keach, *Elizabethan Erotic Narratives* (New Brunswick, NJ: Rutgers University Press, 1977); Clark Hulse, *Metamorphic Verse: The Elizabethan Minor Epic* (Princeton, NJ: Princeton University Press, 1981), 146; Clifford Leech, *Christopher Marlowe: Poet for the Stage*, ed. Anne Lancashire (New York: AMS Press, 1986), 190–98, finds "many links" (190) between *Hero and Leander* and *Venus and Adonis* and states that "debt one way or the other seems at least likely" (190). But he backs away from a firm assertion of either writer's influence on the other, because, as he argues, "the total effects of the poems differ widely" (192). The following critics from standard editions of Shakespeare also do not perpetuate the claim that *Venus and Adonis* was influenced by *Hero and Leander*: Richard Wilbur in his introduction to *Venus and Adonis* in the Pelican Shakespeare, *William Shakespeare: The Complete Works*, 2nd edition, rev. (New York: Viking Press, 1969), 1401–05; William Empson in *The Complete Signet Classic Shakespeare* (New York: Harcourt Brace Jovanovich, 1972), 1667–69; David Bevington in *The Complete Works of Shakespeare*, 4th edition, rev. (New York: Addison Wesley

Longman, 1997), 1608–9 and Appendix 2, A-58; Katharine Eisaman Maus in *The Norton Shakespeare* (New York: W.W. Norton, 1997), 601–6; and Hallett Smith in *The Riverside Shakespeare* (Boston: Houghton Mifflin, 1997), 1798, who does express an uncertainty about whether Shakespeare knew Marlowe's poem before he wrote his own but then, in contrast to his view in 1952 in his book, goes on to speculate that *Venus and Adonis* could have been "written in imitation of or competition with *Hero and Leander*."

5   Maurice Charney, "Marlowe's *Hero and Leander* Shows Shakespeare, in *Venus and Adonis*, How to Write an Ovidian Verse Epyllion" in *Marlowe's Empery: Expanding His Critical Contexts*, ed. Sara Munson Deats and Robert A. Logan (Newark: University of Delaware Press, 2002), 85–94. See also James P. Bednarz, "Marlowe and the English Literary Scene" in *The Cambridge Companion to Christopher Marlowe*, ed. Patrick Cheney (Cambridge: Cambridge University Press, 2004), 90–105, who is more tentative about the link between the two poems but nevertheless indicates that there is one: "Marlowe and Shakespeare's final literary exchange appears to have occurred in the context of poetic patronage … It is possible that he [Shakespeare] saw Marlowe's poem in manuscript and posed Venus's failed enticement of Adonis against Leander's successful seduction of Hero as a kind of literary diptych, creating contrasting variations on the theme of tragic desire" (102; 102–03). Such speculation has the virtue of tidiness, but, ultimately, only makes one more wary of scholarship that presses to forge a link between the poems.

6   Charney, "Marlowe's *Hero and Leander*," 6.

7   See Chapter 1 for a discussion of the links between *Hero and Leander* and *As You Like It*.

8   The depiction of the tension between Venus and Adonis on Hero's "wide sleeves green," is so different from Ovid's portrayal (in *Metamorphoses* X) and so much like Shakespeare's that one might wish to argue that Marlowe had read *Venus and Adonis* and that there was an influence from Shakespeare on Marlowe:

> Her wide sleeves green, and bordered with a grove,
> Where Venus in her naked glory strove
> To please the careless and disdainful eyes
> Of proud Adonis that before her lies. (11–14)

The trouble with such an argument is, of course, that there is no other evidence in the poem to support it and, as David Bevington remarks in his edition of *The Complete Works of Shakespeare*, Adonis's disdain "had evidently become a commonplace in the 1590s" (Appendix 2, p. A–58). See also Clark Hulse, 146, who believes that in these lines, Marlowe is alluding to Shakespeare's poem. About *Venus and Adonis*, Hulse says, "the most sensible conclusion … seems to be that Shakespeare had no particular source, and actually thought of the idea himself" (146). All references to *Hero and Leander* are from Mark Thornton Burnett, ed., *Christopher Marlowe: The Complete Poems* (London: J.M. Dent, 2000).

9   Charney, "Marlowe's *Hero and Leander*," presents instances in *The Two Gentlemen of Verona*, *A Midsummer Night's Dream*, and *Much Ado About Nothing* that suggest Shakespeare's familiarity with the story of Hero and Leander. In addition, he discusses Marlowe and Shakespeare's use of Ovid, and he comments on similarities in language and detail. But, ultimately, his argument for Marlowe's poem as a model for Shakespeare's remains theoretical and speculative.

10   For a valuable discussion of what "Ovidian" means—especially to Marlowe and Shakespeare but also to other writers of epyllia, see William Keach, *Elizabethan Erotic*

Narratives (New Brunswick, NJ: Rutgers University Press, 1977), 3–35. Keach examines three aspects of Ovid's poetry that Elizabethan writers of epyllia responded to: (1) Ovid's thoroughly literary attitude toward ancient myth; (2) Ovid's ambivalent view of erotic experience, its pleasures and its sorrows; and (3) Ovid's "stylistic virtuosity" (5). Keach concludes "that the alternative to an orthodox 'Elizabethan Ovid,' an Ovid made safe for the Christian reader, is not necessarily a frivolous, indulgently decorative decadently 'Italianate Ovid'" (35), but a much more complicated, ambivalent Ovid, one capable of capturing the grotesqueness and misery of love as well as its comedy and joy. For a comparative examination of the story of Venus and Adonis and its implications in Ovid and Shakespeare, see Jonathan Bate, *Shakespeare and Ovid* (Oxford: Clarendon Press, 1993), 48–67. Bate demonstrates that the Ovidian context of Shakespeare's poem is "distinctly unwholesome" (51); as we shall see, the spirit of *Venus and Adonis* at most pays only lip service to this context. Bate also discusses *Hero and Leander* (e.g., pp. 38, 48–50), not as a source for *Venus and Adonis*, but only in relationship to the Renaissance portrayals of Ovid and the epyllion.

11   For example, the link between an unruly horse and the behavior of the lover and the analogy between fearful lovers and soldiers afraid of death are only loosely parallel in the two poems.

12   For example, note the epithet "rose-cheeked" to describe Adonis and the reference to Narcissus in both poems. These details are also stock-in-trade for poems written in the Ovidian tradition.

13   In saying this, I am reminded of the following remarks of Janet Adelman in *The Common Liar: An Essay on "Antony and Cleopatra"* (New Haven, CT: Yale University Press, 1973): "In general, the study of sources is, I think, too often restricted to the attempt to explain the genesis of a work. ... It seems to me more useful to consider sources affectively rather than genetically: that is, as the context of tradition to which Shakespeare could appeal in shaping his play and the attitudes of the audience toward it. ... The meaning of any play is partly defined by the traditions in which it asks to be seen" (53–54). The same is usually truer of a poem which demands even more strongly than a play an audience's familiarity with traditions and its consciousness of them as part of the experience of reaching an understanding of the poem.

14   Like Georgia E. Brown in her essay, "Gender and Voice in 'Hero and Leander,'" in *Constructing Christopher Marlowe*, ed. J.A. Downie and J.T. Parnell (Cambridge: Cambridge University Press, 2000), 148–63, I find that *Hero and Leander* can be viewed through the eyes of New Criticism as well as New Historicism and Cultural Materialism if the former takes into account the literary context of the 1590s (see pp. 149–50). Also like Brown's essay, my essay concentrates more on aesthetics and the text than on sociopolitical considerations, although it does indicate how the latter can be adduced.

15   One of the chief tenets of Stephen Greenblatt in *Shakespearean Negotiations* (Berkeley: University of California Press, 1988) is that dominant political power produces and contains within it the forces of revolt and subversion, forces which at first affirm the power but which may eventually unseat it.

16   In *Captive Victors* (Ithaca, NY: Cornell University Press, 1987), 49.

17   Ibid.

18   *Elizabethan Erotic Narratives*, xvii.

19   See Troni Y. Grande, *Marlovian Tragedy: The Play of Dilation* (Lewisburg, PA: Bucknell University Press, 1999), 15–16 for a discussion of the training Renaissance writers received as school children in the technique of amplification.

20 Ibid., 27 (from Grande's chapter on *Hero and Leander*, pp. 25–43).

21 Georgia E. Brown observes that *"Hero and Leander*'s inconclusive and contradictory sententiae undermine the existence of a shared perspective. Moreover, as our choices are not determined by the exercise of morality or reason, we may legitimately wonder whether there is any point to didacticism" (153). Her points are well taken, although not without invoking considerable irony since the poem is itself strongly didactic in its defiant undermining of prevailing aesthetic tendencies and, as we shall see, in its denunciation of some dominant cultural and political attitudes.

22 See Judith Haber, "'True-loves Blood': Narrative and Desire in *Hero and Leander*," *English Literary Renaissance* 28:3 (Autumn, 1998): 372–86 but especially 377–78. Haber discusses Marlowe's purposeful "disruption of narrative sequence" (377).

23 Wit and humor can of course each be classified as a species of comedy. Those personae responsible for creating wit knowingly display a verbal ingenuity. However, those who create humor, with its broader range of reference, do not depend exclusively upon verbal means and may well not have an awareness that they have produced humor.

24 In his essay *"Hero and Leander*: the Arbitrariness of Desire" in *Constructing Christopher Marlowe*, 133–47, Claude J. Summers says that "Marlowe's deconstruction of his age's received ideas about same-sex relationships … is but one piece of the poem's larger elaborately orchestrated strategy to interrogate conventional ideas about and idealisations of love" (137). Although he does not pursue the point, Summers is rightly noticing Marlowe's tendency to reshape contemporary aesthetic tendencies by applying a dose of Ovidian realism.

25 "Comic Method in Marlowe's *Hero and Leander*" in *Christopher Marlowe*, ed. Brian Morris (New York: Hill and Wang, 1968), 118. Cf. Nancy Lindheim, "The Shakespearean *Venus and Adonis*," *Shakespeare Quarterly* 37 (Summer, 1986): 192, and Judith Haber, especially 381–86.

26 Robert A. Logan, "Perspective in Marlowe's *Hero and Leander*: Engaging Our Detachment" in *"A Poet and a Filthy Play-maker": New Essays on Christopher Marlowe*, ed. Kenneth Friedenreich, Roma Gill, and Constance B. Kuriyama (New York: AMS Press, 1988), 279–91.

27 Elizabeth Bieman, "Comic Rhyme in Marlowe's *Hero and Leander*," *English Literary Renaissance* 9 (Winter, 1979): 69–77.

28 Ibid., 76.

29 Ibid., 76, n. 15.

30 W.B.C. Watkins, 12.

31 Ibid.

32 For a summary of the views of various critics on the narrative voice of *Venus and Adonis*, see Philip C. Kolin's introductory chapter, "Venus and/or Adonis Among the Critics," in *"Venus and Adonis": Critical Essays*, ed. Philip C. Kolin (New York: Garland, 1997), 50–52.

33 Near the beginning of the "new" or Countess of Pembroke's *Arcadia*, Strephon is describing to Claius the departure of Urania: "There she sate, vouchsafing my cloake (then most gorgeous) under her: at yonder rising of the ground she turned her selfe, looking back toward her woonted abode, and because of her parting bearing much sorrow in hir eyes, the lightsomnes whereof had yet so naturall a cherefulnesse, as it made even sorrow seeme to smile; at that turning she spake unto us all, opening the cherrie of hir lips, & Lord how greedily mine eares did feed upon the sweete words she uttered? And here she laide her hand over thine eyes, when shee saw the teares springing in them, as if she would conceale

them from other, and yet her selfe feele some of thy sorrow" (*The Prose Works of Sir Philip Sidney*, ed. Albert Feuillerat, 4 vols [Cambridge: Cambridge University Press, 1912; reprinted with corrections, 1962], 1, 6.). The passage exemplifies the personification and exalted feeling that find a parallel in the passage from *Venus and Adonis*. The attention to the eyes and the personification of sorrow in both passages only augment the affinities in stylistic elevation.

34   John T. Shawcross, ed., *The Complete Poetry of John Donne* (New York: Doubleday, 1967), p. 87.

35   For a summary of the critical discourse on the ambivalence and contradictoriness present in the characterizations of Venus and Adonis, see Kolin, ed., 30–37 (for Venus) and 38–44 (for Adonis).

36   For a stimulating discussion of the ways in which *Hero and Leander* both defies sociopolitical norms and, yet, verifies the reality of sociopolitical power, see Gregory W. Bredbeck, *Sodomy and Interpretation* (Ithaca, NY: Cornell University Press, 1991), 108–39.

37   In attempting to explain the emphasis on Adonis's "soft, effeminate beauty" (*Elizabethan Erotic Narratives*, 66), William Keach discusses both "the homoerotic overtones of Shakespeare's presentation of Adonis" (67) and "the ambivalence with which Shakespeare treats the ideality of Adonis's beauty" (68). But neither explanation, astute as each is, dispels our perplexity about the portrayal of Adonis.

38   One standard speculation is that the irony reveals something of Shakespeare's psychology and, possibly, in conjunction with Venus's aggressiveness, a fear of women which smacks of homosexuality. I am not able to follow this line of reasoning because of two assumptions which have always seemed to me dubious: (1) the too simple view that the writer's portrayals exactly mirror the writer's personal beliefs and, consequently, have nothing to do with the less subjective, purely artistic demands of the poem and (2) the (stereotypical—?) notion that homosexuality necessarily carries with it a fear of women.

39   For a psychological sense of why Marlowe is temperamentally able to adopt the Ovidian spirit whereas Shakespeare is not, see Watkins, 6–7. Although Watkins's credibility is shaky when he does not explain the basis for his view that Shakespeare read Marlowe and felt "admiration" "for Marlowe's recapture of the Ovidian spirit in *Hero and Leander*" (6), he is astute on how the psychologies of the two writers differ.

40   Specifically, in lines 42, 47, 556, 792, 794, 800, 802, 803, and 804. See also Catherine Belsey, "Love As Trompe-L'oeil: Taxonomies of Desire," in *"Venus and Adonis": Critical Essays*, ed. Philip C. Kolin, 261–85, but especially 271–77. (First published in *Shakespeare Quarterly* 46 [Fall, 1995]: 257–76.)

41   Well after writing his epyllion, Shakespeare's interest in idealizing becomes a source for dramatic tension. It reveals itself in such plays as *Timon of Athens* and *Antony and Cleopatra*; in both, the playwright is clearly pleased that "art with nature's workmanship" is "at strife." See, for example, *The Life of Timon of Athens*, I, i, 37–38 and *Antony and Cleopatra*, II, ii, 210–11 and V, ii, 98–101 in *William Shakespeare: The Complete Works*, gen. eds. Stephen Orgel and A.R. Braunmuller (New York: Penguin Putnam, 2002). By the time of these plays, Shakespeare is able to objectify the conflict between art and nature that we feel manifested within the poet of *Venus and Adonis*. He, in fact, makes the conflict a part of the fabric of the drama.

42   Jane Adamson, "Marlowe, *Hero and Leander*, and the Art of Leaping in Poetry," *Critical Review* 17 (1974): 64.

43 Other lines that contain imagery of restraint and excess are 71–72, 217–22, 264–70, 289–94, 389, 547–64, 793–804 (Adonis's characterization of lust), 955–60, and 1007–8.

44 In *William Shakespeare* (Oxford: Blackwell, 1986), 98.

45 Ibid., 4–6 and 98–100.

46 For a feminist reading of the poem that claims that Venus "responds to the transition from a late-Medieval feudal order to a pre-capitalist society by adjusting her personal economy to a new set of contingencies" (253), see Nona Fienberg, "Thematics of Value in *Venus and Adonis*," *Criticism* 31 (Winter, 1989): 21–32.

Chapter 4

Edward II, *Richard II*, the Will to Play, and an Aesthetic of Ambiguity

I

During the second half of the twentieth century, critics vigorously expressed differing views on the debt Shakespeare's *Richard II* owed to Marlowe's *Edward II*. Not surprisingly, they reached no consensus. To exemplify: Nicholas Brooke found that the first scene of Shakespeare's play parodied Marlovian rhetoric, that, in effect, Shakespeare criticized Marlowe's dismissive attitude toward the conflict between the individual and the state in *Edward II*, and that *Richard II* registered a stronger reaction to Marlowe's plays overall than to *Edward II* specifically.[1] Wolfgang Clemen went a step further toward loosening the connection between the two plays; in examining their dramatic technique and form and their impact on the audience, he concluded that Shakespeare deliberately departed from Marlowe's artistic strategies and, hence, showed little influence.[2] Marjorie Garber moved in a contrary direction, finding similarities in the deposition scenes of the two plays; traveling along the same course, Robert P. Merrix and Carole Levin discovered that likenesses in the deposition scenes led to conclusions about more encompassing likenesses—in dramatic structuring and in the psychology of role-playing.[3] More inclusively, Muriel Bradbrook noted both parallels and differences between the two plays.[4] James Shapiro invoked his characterization of the continuing rivalry between the two playwrights to explain in brief why Shakespeare's earliest histories influenced *Edward II* and why Marlowe's play, in turn, influenced *Richard II*.[5] Citing several parallels between the plays, Maurice Charney suggested that *Edward II* was a "model" rather than a source for Shakespeare.[6] Meredith Skura, adopting the notion of a model but assuming a psychological approach, discussed aspects of *Edward II* that "might fill in the missing gaps of *Richard II*."[7] Taken as a whole, these examples reveal, as one might expect, differences in focus and perspective. But they also record a strong disagreement among the critics about the specific value of *Edward II* as an influence on *Richard II*.

One would think that the similarities in the psychologies and situations of the two weak kings and in their unhappy political consequences as they are deposed and murdered would override enough of the discordances among the critics to provide a sufficient basis for drawing significant parallels. In theory, the parallels could then be used as definite signs of Marlowe's influence, ultimately providing some general agreement. But, in spite of clear similarities in the personalities and political contexts of Edward and Richard, ambiguities in the characters and actions of both plays have presented such severe problems of interpretation that they have prevented agreement on all but the most superficial of the likenesses. Instead of trying to resolve the ambiguities to establish links, I suggest that we regard them as an especially effective artistic device—one that Shakespeare perceived as a chief reason for the success of Marlowe's play and subsequently developed for himself as he wrote *Richard II*. It is in the development of an aesthetic of ambiguity that a similarity and, most likely, an influence of major importance lie.

Without actually saying so, the critics sampled above indicate that *Edward II* was not an especially meaningful source for *Richard II* in the way that traditional source studies assume—that is, in echoing particular details of characterization, plot, and language. In spite of the strong tradition in criticism of ferreting out likenesses between the works of Marlowe and Shakespeare, only to a limited extent has this approach proved worthwhile in studies on these two plays.[8] Moreover, a close, contextualized examination of the behavior of each king reveals that the two monarchs are even less alike than is commonly supposed. The same is true of the plays in their entirety. Ironically, although Marlowe and Shakespeare were born into the same moral, political, and aesthetic milieu, their dramatizations of the conflict between the kings' royal obligations and their disregard of those obligations only deepen our understanding of the *differences* in the characterization, content, and focus of the two plays and augment our sense of what individualizes each writer. One plausible reason for the differences, paradoxically, is Shakespeare's familiarity with Marlowe's play. It takes little imagination to see that he made use of his knowledge of the reception of *Edward II* to promote the artistic and commercial success of his own play.

The influence of *Edward II* appears to work on Shakespeare in the following manner: it motivates him to build upon the dramaturgical advances in the genre of the history play put forth by his fellow playwright. Together, the two playwrights forged anew the genre of the history play, investing it with a unified, serious focus. Thus, Shakespeare establishes enough parallels with *Edward II* so that his audiences can become immediately engrossed in a chronicle that again dramatizes the downfall of a weak king and the rise of a strong one. That the playwright could count on his audiences' familiarity with Marlowe's plays is of course clear in *Richard II* from the parody in the Deposition Scene (IV, i, 281–91) of Faustus's words of wonder as he gazes on the spirit of Helen of Troy: "Was this the face that launch'd a thousand ships" (*Doctor Faustus*, V, i, 89 [A-Text] and V, i, 93 [B-Text]).

The process of being influenced by *Edward II* must have begun when Shakespeare first saw a production of the play. From the audience's reaction, he undoubtedly learned what to do to make his play successful. He saw, for example, how Marlowe generated sympathy for each of the contending sides of a controversy, the nobles and the king, at the same time that he created disapprobation for each. Moreover, he must have been impressed by Marlowe's strategy of continually unsettling a secure response of moral certainty in the audience as the events of history unfolded, forcing audience members to keep revising their views. Knowing this, we cannot say simply (with Clemen) that Shakespeare rejected *Edward II*, deliberately or not, and that the play did not significantly influence him. We can agree, however, with those critics who have stated that the Marlovian influence on *Richard II* ranges beyond influence from a single play (e.g., Brooke, Bradbrook, Skura). As a bourgeoning playwright and practical man of the theater, Shakespeare must have been keenly aware of the productions of all of Marlowe's plays and, especially, what enabled their continuing popularity. As I hope to show, Marlowe's influence on Shakespeare in *Richard II* indicates an absorption that is both wide-ranging and particular. For this reason, the argument in the following sections may seem to sprawl somewhat as it tries to fashion a representative multiplicity of the ideas and topics that an intertextual approach to not only *Edward II* and *Richard II* can adduce, but to other works by Marlowe as well.

II

Throughout their works, Marlowe and Shakespeare portray figures who are incapable of meeting the moral and amoral demands of the roles they find themselves cast in, especially the demands of their sociopolitical roles. Often, this inability and its consequences severely impinge upon the characters' private lives. In general, this type of behavior dominates a greater number of major characters in Marlowe's works than in Shakespeare's and is more pervasive in the actions of these characters. But the psychology of such behavior registered forcefully enough on Shakespeare to sustain itself in portrayals throughout his works. For both writers, the origins of this behavior would seem to lie in the characters' irrepressible will to play, a compulsion that dominates their psychology.[9] Edward II and Richard II stand out as the best examples of characters who seem dominated by such an urge. Their ingrained narcissism only encourages their will to play, deepening their alienation from the sociopolitical reality that envelops them and over which, ironically, they are meant to preside. Because both kings have been born into a political role for which they are by temperament eminently unsuited, each is doomed to a life of continual strife and frustration and, eventually, to deposition and murder.

Ever since Stephen Greenblatt first made the term "will to play" familiar in his book *Renaissance Self-Fashioning*,[10] it has lacked clarity and, hence, become controversial. Greenblatt entitles his fifth chapter "Marlowe and the Will to Absolute Play," but what he means by "the Will to Absolute Play" and how he distinguishes it from "the will to play" are never entirely clear.[11] Greenblatt sees the playfulness in Marlowe's characters as a reflection, though less self-aware, of the playfulness of Marlowe himself:

> The will to play flaunts society's cherished orthodoxies, embraces what the culture finds loathsome or frightening, transforms the serious into the joke and then unsettles the category of the joke by taking it seriously, courts self-destruction in the interest of the anarchic discharge of its energy. This is play on the brink of an abyss, absolute play.[12]

This passage contains a confusing shift from "the will to play" to "the will to *absolute* play." Apparently, "play" is "absolute" when the player risks self-destruction. In Edward II's case, there is no single point at which the will to play becomes "*absolute* play" because, like Richard II, he is always risking self-destruction. If Greenblatt is thinking of "the will to absolute play" as roughly equivalent to the phrase "living on the edge," then, although the risk-taking element in both phrases is clear, the latter phrase frequently suggests a self-awareness and voluntarism that are not evident in Marlowe's characters, even if they might have been in Marlowe himself. Moreover, what remains unclear and even questionable about the use of "the will to absolute play," as well as "the will to play," is the confusion of cause and effect—the amoral, essentially aesthetic context in which the psychological trait originates (the cause), and the social-moral context in which its manifestations must eventually be judged (the effect).[13]

Criticizing Greenblatt's shift from "the will to play" to "the will to absolute play," Howard Felperin states, "In unqualifying the play-motive in Marlowe, in revising the terms in which it is cast from those of a 'will to play' to those of a 'will to absolute play,' Greenblatt seems to move into an altogether more modern, decentred, and ungrounded realm than that of the Renaissance carnivalesque."[14] Felperin takes Greenblatt to task for "the displacement of Marlovian play from the matrix of Elizabethan culture."[15] In doing so, he shifts the focus from the will to play in an individual to society's control over humankind's potentially subversive desire for playfulness, a trait which he may or may not take to mean the same as the will to play. He nevertheless acknowledges that, "properly understood, the will to play is in no way a misrepresentation of that peculiar dynamic of Marlovian tragedy which underlies and motivates the more particular wills to power, pleasure, wealth, and knowledge that respectively characterize the careers of Tamburlaine, Edward II, The Jew of Malta, and Dr. Faustus."[16] In spite of this statement, Felperin reproves Greenblatt for pretentiously assuming a perspective that is less historical than that of "old historicism," for privileging that perspective, although he stands against the notion of privileging, and for indulging himself in an exercise that says more about his own will to play than about that of Marlowe or his characters. Set against Greenblatt's self-defined, new-historicist theoretical perspective,[17] these objections may seem to have validity. One's estimation of Felperin's accuracy in condemning Greenblatt's perspective, however—the first criticism in particular—would be made easier if he had accounted for some troubling elements in his own perspective. First, Felperin does not pinpoint the simple lack of expressive clarity in Greenblatt's shift from "play" to "*absolute* play." Second, he does not distinguish between the *will* to play and the *desire* for play; although overlapping, they differ in potency and tenacity. Third, like Greenblatt, he does not often enough distinguish between the amoral origins of the will to play and the inevitable social context of their moral consequences; in contrast to Greenblatt, he largely discounts the former in favor of the latter. Fourth, scholars and critics have neither the data nor the means to recapture as much of "the matrix of Elizabethan culture" as Felperin advocates, even if "the idea of play, in an anthropological and a metatheatrical sense that are pre-eminently Elizabethan, seems a highly promising point of departure for a new-historicist understanding of the Marlovian project."[18] Felperin's idealism, implicit in urging Greenblatt to recapture "the Renaissance carnivalesque," seems a bit hollow since he offers no practical means to achieve it. Fifth, the will to play is a clearly recognizable trait in Marlowe's characters and in Marlowe himself, as Felperin himself acknowledges,[19] and is, consequently, no less a part of Elizabethan culture than ours;[20] the difference is in our heightened awareness of it as part of a branch of knowledge we now call psychology. One is left to wonder (*reductio ad absurdum*—?) whether Felperin is positing that for a characteristic of a culture to have validity, the culture must show itself aware of that characteristic.

The will to play, as I am using the notion, involves two steps: the first is the initial, involuntary compulsion to play that sets the will in motion;[21] the second is the action of the will itself, the driving force that propels the compulsion to fulfillment. If the will is usually thought of as a zealously active faculty, one that chooses its own desires and then functions as the driving force to see them satisfied, in this case its powers are reduced, because the desires have been decreed in advance. The will, no less conscious of its purpose and no less determined than when it chooses its own desires, here acts solely as the agent that controls the process of fulfillment. Thus, the will can be involuntarily ignited, as it is when one becomes enamored (e.g., Edward II, Leander) and when one cannot resist turning events into dramatizations and word games, to the exclusion of their moral or political significance (e.g., Richard II, Falstaff). I am using the word "play" (anachronistically) in a psychological sense to indicate an activity defined solely by what a character finds pleasurable and thoroughly engaging. Like the actions of an infant, it is neither moral nor immoral at its inception. Consequently, the phrase overall suggests a compulsive, unrelenting pursuit of pleasure, an eagerness to disregard the constraints of passing time and to live for the moment, and a refusal to take any moral responsibility for the consequences of playing. At root, the will to play is as pure as a basic aesthetic impulse—unrestrained and amoral, emanating from a reserve of senses and emotions. Once it takes charge, it becomes all-consuming, "deaf and cruel where he means to prey" (*Hero and Leander*, 772).

Like any critical point of entry, this one has its limitations, especially if the notion of the will to play is employed reductively and if one does not also take into account other psychological influences on the characters and their differing milieux. Moreover, I have some mild reservations about an historical application of the term. Nevertheless, as a doorway into an intertextual examination of *Edward II* and *Richard II*, I have found the term quite helpful. Not only does it assist in illuminating complex patterns of uncontrollable willfulness in the protagonists of both plays, but it helps to move us outward into some of the cultural issues that the plays enfold and leads us to consider complex crosscurrents in the influence of Marlowe on Shakespeare. Thus, I am making use of the term for the new directions in which it can take us, not as a way of closing down discussion or, much less, of writing off the characters of Edward and Richard by too simply categorizing them.

III

In Marlowe's works, there are remarkably few characters who assume the moral responsibilities their roles imply. The exceptions are Aeneas, Zenocrate, Olympia, Abigail, Edward III, Faustus's Good Angel and the Old Man (Mercy), and Navarre. Of these, Edward III is the most impressive; not only does he defeat Mortimer, a force of evil both political and personal, but, in sending his mother off to prison, he overcomes strong filial feelings to attain political justice. Olympia is runner-up, because her suicide, although a personal triumph, is not, like Edward III's, also a political one. The only major character in the group is Aeneas and he is not a self-starter; he needs to be nudged into moral action by the gods (Hermes, in a dream, makes clear the wishes of Jove and Venus [IV, iii]). One major reason for so few conventionally moral role-players is that Marlowe's predominant interest is in those who, by giving themselves over to play (leading, sometimes, to mayhem!), deny the conventional moral limitations of their roles—either by acting amorally, as in the case of Edward II, who often conducts himself as if there were no such thing as a moral frame of reference, or immorally, as in the case of Barabas, whose evil is predicated by society, however hypocritically, upon an acknowledged moral frame of reference.[22] Although probably the strongest continuing interest in Marlowe's works is the exploration of restrictions on human power, the works do not suggest that such figures as he portrays will succeed, whether they be called underachievers (as in the case of Edward II) or overachievers (as in the case of Barabas), or even if one figure, Tamburlaine, for the most part does succeed; nor do they ever suggest prescriptively that the protagonists should adjust their perspective to correspond to that of a conventional social-moral norm. Throughout Marlowe's works, the norm comes into strong conflict with those characters who are out of bounds, frequently to create dramatic tension, even though an audience's mix of disdain and sympathy toward the norm may vary and even though the norm may only be implicit. With much less direct or indirect reference to the norm, the playwright's explicitly moral role-players undercut an audience's conventional expectations by providing a chiefly aesthetic function. They are striking because they evoke slight response as realistic individuals, and they seem to represent little in the way of real, attainable moral value. Edward III and Olympia, for instance, are so idealized that one understands that they serve aims having more to do with immediate dramaturgical needs than with the portrayal of achievable values.[23]

Shakespeare's employment of idealized moral role-players is more steady and pervasive than Marlowe's and his figures considerably more developed. But, then, Shakespeare is essentially hopeful, not the idealist-turned-cynic that Marlowe often appears to be. Moreover, whereas Shakespeare promotes a traditional value system that genuinely holds meaning for him, Marlowe, less optimistic, points up the disparities between illusions and realities in the present system. Throughout Shakespeare's works, characters who live up to the ethical standards of their roles abound—both males and females who are idealized in such roles as rulers (e.g., Theseus), heroes (e.g., Prince Hal), soldiers (e.g., Bates, Scarus), lovers (e.g., Perdita and Florizel), wives (e.g.,

Hermione, Desdemona), daughters (e.g., Cordelia), sons (e.g., Edgar, Ferdinand), and friends (e.g., Celia and Rosalind). Even so, Shakespeare is as aware as Marlowe that disruptive forces exist in the form of amoral and immoral figures (e.g., Falstaff and Richard III respectively), and that they are only a part of the constantly changing circumstances that flux brings in its wake. The most impressive moral role-players, like Horatio, are not a pipe for Fortune's finger to sound what stop she please.

Throughout Marlowe's works, an almost obsessive determination to assert power of one sort or another functions as an essential ingredient in the psychological makeup of both the amoral and immoral role-players. Those whose will is chiefly to play make up the strongest subcategory of the group. That many in the group are protagonists suggests that Marlowe's chief interest is in exploring the limits to which such figures can go. Any list would include Dido, Tamburlaine, Barabas, Ferneze and most of the rest of the dramatis personae of *The Jew of Malta*, Edward II, the younger Mortimer, Doctor Faustus, the Duke of Guise, Hero, and Leander. For most of the protagonists in the plays, the assertion of power, whether in the form of the will to play, leads to misery and death rather than to sustained happiness. It manifests itself differently in Tamburlaine who at first is portrayed as a hero, the Duke of Guise who is portrayed as a villain, and in those characters who are portrayed as neither hero nor villain and, yet, contain elements of both—as, for example, Edward II and Faustus. For all of Marlowe's fascination with characters who energetically test the limits of human power, whatever their circumstances and intentions, not one comes to a happy conclusion. The chief cause is the impersonal force of flux which destroys all assertions of power and fixity but its own. The character who, in his amoral role-playing, comes closest to imitating flux is Tamburlaine and he is, understandably, the most successful.

For Shakespeare, the amoral and immoral role-players are figures with a heightened aesthetic sense and a disregard for the well-being of humankind's sociopolitical corporate existence, prime ingredients in his portrayals of the will to play. Many examples can be readily cited but Falstaff is a clear, early example of an amoral role-player. He has an aesthetic sensibility that turns the base metals of any situation into gold, as, invariably, he manipulates words and the elements of his surroundings into entertaining play. This sensibility is never more apparent than when, with great relish and irony, he plays the role of the sermonizing or catechizing cleric (e.g., 1 *Henry IV*, I, ii, 147–52 and V, i, 127–40, respectively).[24] His comrade in misrule, Prince Hal, is a special case. He makes use of his experience as an amoral role-player to become a hero. However little we may admire what his political canniness reveals about his humanity, his awareness of his amoral role-playing (1 *Henry IV*, I, ii, 188–210) enables him to use it to help integrate himself sociopolitically—ultimately, to bind the political state into a unified whole. If Shakespeare asks us to admire the Prince for helping to unify the state, then Richard III in his role as villain is to be denounced, chiefly because he throws the political state into chaos. Whether we turn the spotlight on Falstaff and Richard III or on such amoral figures as Richard II and Cleopatra and such immoral figures as Iago and Macbeth, all of them at one time or another reveal a heightened aesthetic sensibility, especially when they enclose themselves in a fortress of words.

This refuge can provide temporary relief from the oppressive sense of an all-powerful external reality, one that redefines the character's relation to the sociopolitical world to include a humbling of the ego and a loss of independence, creativity, and autonomy. But the verbal fortress cannot withstand the powerful necessity of the sociopolitical world to vanquish utterly those who do not conform to its demands.

IV

Both Edward II and Richard II were apparently born with an aesthetic sense so strong that, triggered by the will to play, it easily obliterates whatever moral sense they have or might develop. Had their will to play been conscious initially—that is, voluntary, deliberate, or controlled in its original impulse—then they might have been accused of being thoroughly cynical about life and, given their roles as kings, even masochistic and self-annihilating.[25] But, in both cases, the will to play began involuntarily and firmly controls their behavior in their personal and professional lives.

This trait in Edward manifests itself most immediately and most powerfully in his obsession with Gaveston. Concern with securing his ties to Gaveston never fails to unleash his will to play. Through not very subtle manipulation, Gaveston himself encourages this tendency in Edward. Before the King first appears, the minion tells us of Edward's strongly sensual aesthetic sense and how he intends to excite that sense:

> Music and poetry is his delight,
> Therefore I'll have Italian masques by night,
> Sweet speeches, comedies, and pleasing shows;
> And in the day, when he shall walk abroad,
> Like sylvan nymphs my pages shall be clad;
> My men, like satyrs grazing on the lawns,
> Shall with their goat-feet dance an antic hay;
> Sometime a lovely boy in Dian's shape,
> With hair that gilds the water as it glides,
> Crownets of pearl about his naked arms,
> And in his sportful hands an olive tree
> To hide those parts which men delight to see,
> Shall bathe him in a spring; and there, hard by,
> One like Actaeon, peeping through the grove,
> Shall by the angry goddess be transform'd,
> And running in the likeness of a hart,
> By yelping hounds pulled down, and seem to die.
> Such things as these best please his majesty. (I, i, 53–70)[26]

If Edward were characterized as the creator of these events rather than as a responder to them, one might view his will to play as assertive rather than reactive. Clearly, Gaveston is the active force here. From the beginning of the play, it becomes increasingly clear, as the younger Mortimer bitterly asserts, that "the King is love-sick for his minion" (I, iv, 87) and is unable to restrain himself. We see this in the opening scene when Edward heaps titles on Gaveston, refusing to rein himself in, even after Gaveston himself demurs, "My lord, these titles far exceed my worth" (I, i, 156), and Kent adds crisply, "Brother, the least of these [titles] may well suffice / For one of greater birth than Gaveston" (I, i, 157–58). Edward replies defiantly:

Cease, brother, for I cannot brook these words.
Thy worth, sweet friend [Gaveston], is far above my gifts,
Therefore, to equal it, receive my heart.
If for these dignities thou be envied
I'll give thee more, for but to honour thee
Is Edward pleased with kingly regiment. (I, i, 159–64)

This response is the will to play run rampant and prepares us for the ensuing onslaught of foolish acts by the King. One way to account for these acts is by locating their origins in Edward's will to play. But, first, it is necessary to clarify the confusion that has long surrounded the portrayal of Edward's "wanton humour" (I, iv, 199; I, iv, 401) by ridding ourselves of some unwarranted assumptions and by alerting ourselves to the dangers of superimposing postmodern stereotypical notions of homosexuality on instances of early modern homoeroticism. The discussion of *Edward II* that follows attempts to encompass both aims.

The consensus among contemporary critics and cultural historians is that, during the early modern period, however much same-sex activity took place, neither a concept of homosexuality nor the identity it characterizes existed.[27] James I could write an unmistakably homoerotic letter to his favorite, Buckingham, and, without our postmodern sense of contradiction, also write to his son condemning "sodomie."[28] Probably the most developed early expressions of postmodern notions of homosexuality occur in Marlowe's works, and, most extensively, in *Edward II*, which may be the first text to dramatize, as one critic-historian puts it, "the beginnings of a specifically homosexual subjectivity."[29]

Yet the harder one looks at the playtext, the less clear the specific attributes of Edward's homosexuality become. To be sure, the king is "love-sick" (I, iv, 87). Emotionally excessive, willful, and reckless, Edward's generosity to Gaveston knows no bounds. Ultimately, he is self-destructive, because, in addition to being thoroughly self-absorbed, self-pitying, pliant, and weak, he dotes on his favorite to the exclusion of all else. He clearly allows his uninhibited personal desires to push aside his obligations as king, even though he fears the power of the nobles who, with considerable envy, keep remonstrating with him, not about his sexual activities but about his devotion to a social inferior.[30] Edward's unrelenting preoccupation is abetted by a simple, childlike, wholly emotional perspective that enables him to remain remarkably unreflective. When Mortimer asks him about Gaveston, "Why should you love him whom the world hates so" (I, iv, 76), Edward replies, "Because he loves me more than all the world" (I, iv, 77). A moralizing provocation, the question suggests that Edward, because he is king, is not free to act independently, that he can only show open allegiance to those who are politically acceptable to the nobles—that is, to those who allow the nobles to feel empowered. Edward's answer, although not entirely clear,[31] says more about him than it says about Gaveston who has at least as much love for the "world" of the king as he has for Edward.[32] Apart from a muddling attempt to play on the word "world," Edward is defiantly emotional and personal, suggesting that the affairs of state are well lost for a private bond of intense devotion. In its lack of royal impersonality, the answer also indicates the shallowness and narcissism with which he makes judgments and decisions; it further indicates that the will to play can promote a dangerous assertion of independence in its disregard for the body politic and in its subversion of it.

After Gaveston's death, in a frantic desire to reestablish another close bond, Edward turns to Spencer—the only route to emotional security for Edward, dominated as he is by the will to play. It is the desire itself, however, not a specific attraction to Spencer that motivates him. It is not clear from the text that Edward dotes on Spencer as a minion to the degree that he doted on Gaveston.[33] Nor does Edward express the passionate feeling for Spencer that he did for Gaveston. Even so, his will to play, almost a reflex action, is unstoppable. In his pain and grief over what has happened to Gaveston, it expresses itself as a compensatory need. In his portrayal of Edward, Marlowe's emphasis is on the action of the will rather than on the object of the will.[34] Typically, Marlowe appears to be interested in the will to play as an instrument of power, including the forces that restrict it.[35]

It is not until Edward's abdication that he gains in sustained stature and respect.[36] He is still self-pitying, but the imagery in his words gives him some dignity (e.g., V, i, 5–37). The lengthiness of his speeches in the abdication scene and until his death also helps to enhance his stature as a tragic figure. In them, he has the leisure to be reflective and, in being so, indicates that he is more gracious, more humane, and more capable of self-control than he has shown himself to be earlier. Later, having just been humiliated by being washed with puddle water and then shaved, Edward expresses his appreciation of Gaveston and the Spencers and his sustained devotion to them:

> O Gaveston, it is for thee that I am wrong'd;
> For me, both thou and both the Spencers died,
> And for your sakes a thousand wrongs I'll take.
> The Spencers' ghosts, wherever they remain,
> Wish well to mine; then tush, for them I'll die. (V, iii, 41–45)

The myth of self-ennoblement, which he creates here in order to find a way of accepting his approaching death, and his stoic bravery in facing that death are generated from a new strength, not from the weakness of the past. Indeed, throughout his torturous imprisonment, he is heroic in his stamina and, at his death, more perceptive than he has been before. At the same time, his role has changed to that of a deposed king utterly without power, a long-suffering political prisoner. Thus, he can afford to omit consideration of his failed political responsibility and can turn his attention exclusively to his personal relationship with those who have, in what he perceives as their loyalty to him, given up their lives. It is not necessary to conclude moralistically that his unremitting will to play has dissipated and that a true, mature ethical sense has finally asserted itself. It is simply that for us to be reminded of his will to play and former playground at this point would diminish his stature just when Marlowe needs to augment it to establish a tragic climax. If the shift from obsessiveness to heroic martyrdom strains psychological credulity, it nevertheless gives us a sense of Marlowe's artistry as he struggles to make the play successful structurally. In his attempt to fuse story and character, uppermost in the playwright's mind at this moment is structure, not realistic characterization.[37]

Marlowe's difficulties are understandable if we take a hard look at his focus in the play, for we see that it is neither steady nor clear. At the beginning of the play, the two Mortimers give assessments of Edward's fondness for Gaveston that seem reasonable and forbearing. The elder Mortimer says that the King is "by nature" "mild and calm" (I, iv, 387). But if Edward is "mild and calm" "by nature," it is a side of him we seldom see; we usually see him wrought up by the conflict between the role he wants to play and the role he must play. Speaking from a perspective well within the orthodox conception of manly behavior, Mortimer Senior continues:

> seeing his [Edward's] mind so dotes on Gaveston,
> Let him without controlment have his will.
> The mightiest kings have had their minions:
> Great Alexander loved Hephaestion,
> The conquering Hercules for Hylas wept
> And for Patroclus stern Achilles drooped.
> And not kings only, but the wisest men:
> The Roman Tully loved Octavius,
> Grave Socrates, wild Alcibiades.
> Then let his grace, whose youth is flexible,
> And promiseth as much as we can wish,
> Freely enjoy that vain, light-headed earl,
> For riper years will wean him from such toys. (I, iv, 388–400)

This lengthy defense of Edward's penchant for a minion appears to tell us that Mortimer Senior's attitude toward Edward and his minion is well under control, that he is, in fact, unruffled. His sentiments would seem to indicate an understanding, a generosity, and an unbounded optimism—not the harshness we usually hear when he is discussing Edward with the other nobles. But the reversal in Mortimer Senior's usual reaction to Edward makes it difficult to know just how to take this speech. Moreover, in contradistinction to the evidence of the play, it reduces homoerotic liaisons to "toys," a perspective that, ironically, could be understood as an early modern form of homophobia.

Further, according to this speech, Mortimer thinks that Edward's doting can be largely attributed to his youth. Later in the play, however, Kent refers to his brother as "aged Edward" (V, ii, 118), and a bit later the King says about himself: "Thus lives old Edward" (V, iii, 23). Even allowing for a telescoping of time by the playwright, the unprepared for shift in age indicates that Marlowe is writing to the dramaturgical needs of the moment, without concern for verifying or contradicting the truth of Mortimer's assessment or for showing coherence in the development of Edward's psychology. This shift suggests, then, that a unified conception of the protagonist is not Marlowe's primary interest, that the character serves the immediate purpose of the dramatist in helping to create pathos, thereby making impossible a credible psychological characterization. If so, what can we conclude about the writer's purpose—that he wants to focus on the workings of history? Or perhaps on the power of fate to inevitably bring about some semblance of justice? Both of these possibilities seem forced. The shift in our attitude toward Edward as the play progresses, not to mention that toward Mortimer and Isabella as they become evil, suggests that Marlowe's focus changes from a sense of the true unhappiness and messy complexities in life to the satisfactions of poetic justice and clarity in art.

Ultimately, the aptness of Mortimer Senior's comments and his manly perspective are called into question because the accomplishments of the historical figures he cites bear little relevance to the Edward of the play. Mortimer describes well-known figures whose relationships with minions did not prevent them from achieving professional success. But this is certainly not Edward's case or even his interest. In fact, his only ostensible interest in the kingship is in the power it affords him to secure his relationship with Gaveston: "… for but to honour thee / Is Edward pleased with kingly regiment" (I, i, 163–64). Unlike the "mightiest kings" and the "wisest men," Edward appears obsessed, driven only by his personal desire to bind himself to his minion.

As I noted above, in the elder Mortimer's speech, the masculine perspective is well within the boundaries of traditional patriarchal theory, especially with regard to the ideology of manliness from which, as Simon Shepherd points out, the "assumed values of sex roles [were] derived."[38] Conventional wisdom—again, strongly patriarchal—held that women were more passionate and less rational than men; "a manly man expresses his emotion in social intervention,"[39] not in an all-consuming private desire. Edward could therefore be labeled unmanly; he is so controlled by emotion that he abandons his political responsibilities. Given his obsessive behavior, his unmanliness cannot be considered solely the result of a specific sexual predilection or activity but of a more psychologically encompassing and dominant emotionalism. Interestingly, the play invites us to view Edward's emotionalism from a less orthodox perspective, in part because it does not dwell overtly on his lack of manliness. We continually sense the mysteriousness of the origins and yet the power of the emotional force in Edward. Ultimately, this response has the effect of making the conventional equation of uncontrolled passion with unmanliness seem facile and even suspect.

The younger Mortimer does not contradict or gainsay his uncle's assessment of Edward. He responds to him with the envy that has characterized his complaints from the outset, couching it as an objection to Gaveston's lowly social status:

> Uncle, his [Edward's] wanton humour grieves not me
> But this I scorn, that one so basely born
> Should by his sovereign's favour grow so pert
> And riot it with the treasure of the realm

While soldiers mutiny for want of pay,
He wears a lord's revenue on his back,
And Midas-like, he jets it in the court
With base outlandish cullions at his heels,
Whose proud fantastic liveries make such show
As if that Proteus, god of shapes, appeared.
I have not seen a dapper jack so brisk;
He wears a short Italian hooded cloak
Larded with pearl, and in his Tuscan cap
A jewel of more value than the crown.
Whiles other walk below, the king and he
From out a window laugh at such as we,
And flout our train and jest at our attire.
Uncle, 'tis this that makes me impatient. (I, iv, 401–18)

From neither Mortimer do we hear any objection to Edward's homoeroticism; in fact, the younger Mortimer claims indifference to Edward's "wanton humour." Nor do we hear any objection from anyone else in the play against Edward on purely sexual grounds. Even Isabella's objections do not pinpoint a homoerotic sexual preference in her husband. Her ego is bruised at being brushed aside: "For now my lord the King regards me not, / But dotes upon the love of Gaveston" (I, ii, 49–50). Apparently, she would not be so upset had there not once been something of a romantic bond of love between them. Edward himself hints at this bond when, in complaining to Lightborn about his prison conditions, he says:

Tell Isabel, the Queen, I looked not thus
When for her sake I ran at tilt in France
And there unhorsed the Duke of Cleremont. (V, v, 67–69)

If the focus of the text were as strongly on Edward's homoerotic feelings toward Gaveston as recent productions of the play would have us believe, one would think that Marlowe might have left out the marriage between Lady Margaret and Gaveston in order not to cloud the issue—especially since it is clear that Margaret believes that Gaveston loves her (II, i, 57–82). Margaret's response to Gaveston's romantic letter ("'when I forsake thee, death seize on my heart'"—II, i, 64) indicates that he has spent time persuading her that his feelings were genuinely amorous.[40] Nothing in the play undercuts the sentiments in the letter and Margaret's response.

Further, it has become a commonplace in criticism on the play to say that the manner of Edward's death suggests just retribution for his acts of sodomy.[41] But, to begin with, there is no evidence in the play (or in Holinshed's *Chronicles* from which the episode was taken) that anal sex was a part of Edward and Gaveston's relationship, any more than there is that anal sex is an inevitable ingredient of all homosexual liaisons. Furthermore, since no one in the play seems bothered by the specific sexual nature of Edward's relationship with Gaveston or with Spencer (supposing that a sexual relationship existed between Edward and Spencer), why would Marlowe be? And why would the playwright suddenly narrow the focus at the climax of the play to moralize? Moreover, as Stephen Orgel shrewdly points out,[42] there is nothing in the text or the stage directions to indicate that the spit is brought on stage during the death scene. That of course does not prevent directors from introducing it (*has* not prevented them, in fact). Consequently, one has to ask what basis there is for assuming that the climax of the play is a moral commentary on Edward's supposed acts of sodomy?[43] In Holinshed's *Chronicles*, what is stressed about the "hot spit" is that it should not reveal outwardly any wound or hurt;[44] in the play as well Lightborn tells Matrevis and Gurney to "lay the table down, and stamp on it, / But not too hard, lest that you bruise his body" (V, v, 111–12). Nothing is mentioned to suggest that the punishment fits a sexual crime. The emphasis is on the *protocol* of such a murderous act—the aim being to neutralize the manner of death so that there would be no clues leading to a particular murderer or a particular murderer's style.[45] Given Marlowe's tendency to end his plays with a spectacle that as forcefully as possible engages his audiences' senses and emotions, it is not surprising to see that at first he seems to have retained the three deadly instruments of torture mentioned by Holinshed. Lightborn tells Matrevis and Gurney to prepare a red-hot spit and to have ready a table and featherbed (V, v, 27–36); but, finally, he only makes use of the table. In killing Edward, Lightborn is solely responsible for the means. In his initial demand for three means, he is as vehement as he is excessive, perhaps Marlowe's way of investing the fatal assault on Edward with a sensationalism that he felt would have been difficult to portray. In any case, the success of Lightborn's willfulness dislodges any final illusions in the play about the absoluteness of a just, controlling, political and moral order. The manner and fact of Edward's death suggest a crazed world of anarchic evil, one in which the firm control of Edward III seems all the more powerfully attractive and, yet, because it is so idealized, all the more unattainable. In dispelling any conventional illusions of a firmly fixed political and moral order, the play appears to support the need for such an order even as it instills in us a heavy skepticism about achieving it.

Given the early modern interest in promoting the conventional ideal of manliness and, in *Edward II*, the portrayal of homoerotic feeling as a symptom of a mysteriously motivated obsession, one that leads to unmanly acts, we are ready to consider the interrogation this ideal is subjected to. In particular, we are ready to understand how the politics of homoeroticism, not only in *Edward II*, but in *Dido, Queen of Carthage* and *Hero and Leander*, subverts the ideal, including the forces promoting it. Through the dramatization of unrestrained homoerotic desire, the three texts, in direct proportion to their ability to shock their audiences, indicate the extent of the control and power of patriarchal forces. In treating homoerotic feeling as an unremarkable, wholly natural expression of one's personality, the texts raise questions about the validity of conventionally constructed sexual differences and gender roles. By implication, they also cast aspersions on the artificiality of the entire moral and political order empowered through the acceptance of conventional ideas. Put differently, not only do the texts question the truth of what people are made to see but also the validity of the strategies by which they are made to see it. The irony is that Marlowe could be said to be trying to exercise a similar control through the strategies of his texts, but, of course, for an opposite purpose, to move his audiences away from a blind acceptance of orthodoxy. The problem here is that, in moving them away from a blind acceptance of orthodoxy, he does not move them clearly toward anything. In *Edward II*, the idealized actions of Edward III serve the function of restoring the political balance through a myth of orthodoxy, but this shift into fantasy only produces more skepticism about a realistic acceptance of orthodoxy.

Shepherd argues convincingly that Marlowe's playtexts recognize that manliness is learned rather than natural behavior; manliness begins as "an argument, a rhetorical construction, to be learnt."[46] Although wholly self-validating, manliness is essentially a patriarchal social ideal that encourages a strengthening of the political order: "…manliness lies in a mode of acting, particularly in the relationship between the inner person and public action."[47] More pagan than Christian in origin, the "mode" is neither right nor wrong, just politically effective or ineffective, an assertion of power that lasts, relatively speaking, for only a moment. If we take Tamburlaine as the clearest example in Marlowe's writings, we see that his manliness comes about through actions that lead to politicized displays of empowerment. Because manliness cannot exist as a permanent state of being, Tamburlaine has to act continually to reinscribe it.

The strongest contrast between manliness and unmanliness in Marlowe's works appears in *Tamburlaine*, Part 2, when Tamburlaine kills his unmanly son Calyphas (IV, i, 122). Even as the play presents this dramatic conflict, it undermines uncomplicated, conventional notions of manliness and unmanliness. First, we are offended by Tamburlaine's excessive display of manliness in stabbing his son, because it is an act that, instead of arising rationally from a principle, is too merely personal, too egotistical.[48] Second, the play encourages us to feel some sympathy for the unmanly Calyphas because he dares to defy the patriarchy that his father so absolutely represents. Moreover, the play makes clear that Calyphas's decision not to subscribe to manliness has nothing to do with his sexuality, which is firmly, even lecherously established as heteroerotic (Part 2, IV, i, 61–75). But the undermining is even more radical. Articulate and self-aware, Calyphas *chooses* not to fulfill the manly gender role that his father has selected for him and his brothers (Part 2, IV, i, 27–30). He thereby not only calls into question the ideology of manliness but presents a challenge to the authority that promotes it. That he is brutally killed—and by his own father—for scorning manliness only makes an audience more skeptical about the ideal and cynical about the forces supporting it. According to his father, Calyphas, while alive, was an "effeminate brat" (Part 2, IV, i, 164) who never strove to acquire power; he was without energy, the "Image of sloth" (Part 2, IV, i, 93). Tamburlaine is so outraged at the defiance of his own (exaggerated) manly ideal and of his power that he justifies stabbing his son because of the latter's unmanliness. After killing Calyphas, he issues an order that Turkish concubines be employed to bury him, "For not a common soldier shall defile / His *manly* fingers with so faint a boy" (Part 2, IV, i, 165–66; my emphasis). In summary, then, this part of the play undermines the conventional ideal of manliness, partly because it makes a figure of excessive manliness repugnant and an unmanly figure somewhat sympathetic, but chiefly because it portrays a figure who *chooses* to see the ideal as irrelevant.[49]

Edward II can be called unmanly not only because he asserts the superiority of his private desires over his public responsibilities, even though he is king, but, also, because, like Calyphas, he chooses to.[50] In making this choice, Edward calls attention to his rejection of the political dangers of his situation, including what politics, in the form of the lords' hostility, is trying to do to control his way of perceiving and thinking. Edward's homoeroticism is symptomatic of what I have suggested above is an uncontrollable will to play. The power of his will to play is portrayed as more real than either the conception or the fact of manliness. As such, it undercuts both the notion of manliness and the political and moral order it supports. In effect, it presents a challenge both to authority and to the principles on which authority is based. Portrayed as a figure of justice, understandably harboring feelings of revenge, Edward III is the strongest example of manliness in the play. But, as we have seen, he is so idealized that the credibility of the ideal is undermined. He does prove, however, that the test of manliness has less to do with age and sexuality than with power—specifically, with manifesting control of the political state.[51] By this criterion Edward II achieves manliness only once, at his political high point, when he has Warwick and Lancaster decapitated and sends Mortimer to prison (III, iii). But, significantly, it occurs because of advice from his favorite, the younger Spencer, not because he is compelled by a standard of manliness from without. It could perhaps be argued that Edward's decision not to complete his revenge by also executing Mortimer, a decision that leads to his downfall, fails to achieve the ideal of manliness promulgated by his society. If so, this decision shows once again how unaffected Edward is by current notions of manliness. In addition, it affirms a patriarchal source of absolute power, for the play dramatizes with ominousness that the penalty for departing from the norm can be death. Edward is emblematically at his most unmanly when he appears on the battlefield dressed not in armor but in "garish" apparel (II, ii, 181–86). This strong expression of the will to play is yet another outward sign of the psychology of emotionalism in which his being is so firmly centered. By portraying not just a minor character but a protagonist who, despite the cost, chooses to see manliness as irrelevant, whose modes of perception are what they are because of internal rather than external forces, the play defies an unthinking, blind acceptance of both the conventional ideal of manliness and the forces that perpetuate it.

The pattern of defiance in *Edward II* is echoed in *Dido* and *Hero and Leander*, only at a higher level. In *Dido*, Jupiter, chief of the gods, chooses to view manliness as irrelevant by giving in to his passion and dallying with Ganymede. Not only does Jupiter undermine the conventional notion that men are by nature more rational than women but also that women are more prone than men to succumb to unruly desires. That this episode occurs in the first scene of the play is especially significant, because it prepares us for the subversively unconventional portrayals that follow—in particular, Aeneas's disregard for manliness and Dido's manly mode of behavior—even if her manly mode is for purely personal desires.[52] Like Jupiter, *Hero and Leander*'s Neptune reveals that he is indifferent to any notion of manliness when, by catering to his personal desires, he tries to seduce Leander. The context is a leisurely narrative of erotic and comic delight, calculated to vex a reader interested in portrayals that uphold prescribed gender roles. In the portrayals of Edward, Jupiter, and Neptune, the texts manage not only to unsettle their audiences' complacent notion of manliness but to undermine the equally complacent strategies of restricting one's choice to accepting or rejecting the ideal and to being judged by how successfully one meets the ideal. In the case of Edward, the undermining also complicates any hasty blanket judgment of the monarch as utterly irresponsible. In all three instances, the result is that playgoers and readers are led to understand the strategies working to make them accept a conventional ideology of manliness. In associating with homoerotic activity personal pleasure over public responsibility and, consequently, unmanliness over manliness, Marlowe—brashly, impudently, even outrageously—makes his audience confront a disruptive piece of reality, one that brings into conflict the unnatural construction of illusory, high-minded sociomoral ideals and the natural existence of same-sex activity.

Asking an audience controlled by orthodox ideas to confront unmanliness as a deliberate choice and as a sign of indifference to the ideology of manliness feeds an even larger anxiety: the fear of a breakdown of conventional constructions of gender and sexual difference. Marlowe's description of Leander is a comically irreverent passage that confounds conventional notions of gender and sexual difference:

Had wild Hippolytus Leander seen,
Enamoured of his beauty had he been;
His presence made the rudest peasant melt,
That in the vast uplandish country dwelt.
The barbarous Thracian soldier, moved with nought,
Was moved with him, and for his favour sought.
Some swore he was a maid in man's attire,
For in his looks were all that men desire,
A pleasant smiling cheek, a speaking eye,
A brow for love to banquet royally;
And such as knew he was a man would say,
"Leander, thou art made for amorous play." (77–88)

Leander's "beauty" crosses sexual barriers and the response to it ("in his looks were all that men desire"), gender barriers. Moreover, the implications in the description are that, naturally enough, homoerotic response is widespread and cuts across social classes. The activities of the gods portrayed in "Venus' glass" (142) give additional support to the assertion of unconventional notions of sexual and gender difference (143–56). Both genders (not just women, stereotypically) succumb to free-wheeling desire, and sexual behavior (incest, pederasty, homoeroticism) abides by no prescribed rules. In addition to subversively asserting the dominance of irrational over rational behavior, this passage asserts the superiority of private desires over public responsibilities. Both this passage and the description of Leander depict moral and political orders being overturned as easily as the Destinies usurp Jove (451–59), and the actions of Hero, Leander, Mercury, the country maid, Cupid, and Neptune all lend additional credence to the idea.

In *Edward II*, there is a similar assertion of the superiority of private desires over public responsibilities. Edward's conduct makes his private desires the center and essence of his existence, even though they threaten the political order, functionally creating a version of civil war. Nor does he ever consider an action as responsible as abdicating. The reason, of course, is obvious: childlike, he wants to eat his cake and have it, too.

What we see in *Edward II*, *Dido*, and *Hero and Leander* is that independent interaction between the texts and dominant cultural ideas is not hampered by Marlowe's own "wanton humour," whatever that specifically was. We can understand from his texts that, ultimately, the portrayal of homoerotic feeling, valorized as natural, is never an end in itself. Whether the results are comic or tragic, uncontrolled homoerotic behavior is characteristic of a psychology that disregards the firmly fixed, conventional ideology of manliness and, thereby, undermines the power of the controlling forces of orthodox thinking in late sixteenth-century England.

In *Edward II*, Marlowe's own will to play shows itself most frequently in bringing into opposition an independent amoral perspective and a conventional social-moral perspective and not credibly resolving the conflict. This conflict is generated by Edward's disagreement with Mortimer and the other nobles. Part of the difficulty of resolving the conflict comes from Marlowe's inability to move beyond his portrayal of the inveteracy of Edward's psychology on the one hand and the hypocrisy of the political state on the other. With the appearance of Edward III, he drops this conflict, substituting one that is more standard and commonplace, for he pits ideal good, in the form of Edward III, against evil, the machinations of Mortimer and Isabella. The abruptness of the shift reveals not only a structural dislocation, as we have already seen, but the suppression of Marlowe's own will to play.

V

However similar Edward II and Richard II are in having a will to play that ill equips them for the role of king that has been thrust upon them, they are also very different.[53] Three major differences stand out. First, Richard has a more complex personality. Part of what makes him more complicated comes clear when one measures Edward's shallowness, emotionalism, and obsessiveness against Richard's intellectual powers, his constantly proliferating imagination, his remarkable variety in linguistic inventiveness, his detachment from others and concomitant self-absorption, and his mercurial shifts in mood. Richard's complexity also partly derives from Shakespeare's invocation of two frames of reference—political and personal. The playwright gives us a sense of Richard's interconnected place in both; but he never allows Richard to see them as two different worlds, let alone act as if there were a distinction between them. Further, as Gaunt and York make clear, Shakespeare sets the public and private worlds in opposition, allowing us to see conflict and tension where Richard does not. The same opposition exists in *Edward II* but with two differences. First, in his wariness of the nobles and in his hostility towards the Queen, Edward appears to sense that the political context requires a role different from the one he assumes in his private life. But of course his will to play brushes aside his dim understanding and drives him foolishly onward into self-destruction. Second, in *Edward II*, the king's personal life dominates the action. In fact, Edward spends most of his time trying to make his personal life his only life. With greater defensiveness, Richard sees himself as a vital part of what for him is a single, seamless context. Thus, he expresses his will to play without any realization of a political context that may require a mental state less purely instinctive, one more rational and detached.

It follows that Richard's will to play dominates him at every moment, both in public and in private, and that he never shows any inclination to rein it in in accordance with the demands of the conditions of his milieu. At the beginning of the play, he, as king, publicly asks Bolingbroke and Mowbray to settle their dispute through combat and then, even though he has already determined that the fight will not ensue, his indomitable will to play insists on his viewing the ritualized drama that brings the antagonists to the point of combat. The immediate consequence is that, in calling off the duel, he divests the ceremonious proceedings of any meaning. A later consequence of this action occurs when he returns from Ireland and finds that he is unable to invest the ceremony attendant upon his kingship with enough meaning to save himself from being deposed. His will to play has supplanted his ability to furnish rituals with symbolic meaning. In his private life, he is "basely led / By flatterers" (II, i, 241–42) and, in squandering the treasury on private pleasures, has been forced to tax the commoners and to fine the nobility. Thus, like Edward, his will to play in his private life helps to strangle him in his professional life. But, unlike Edward, who often expresses a childish defiance in the face of political pressures, Richard never acknowledges a difference between his personal desires and public responsibilities and, therefore, between the two contexts, never has to perceive the causal relationship of the will to play.

The second major difference is that the will to play in Edward and Richard is endemic in dissimilar ways. In psychological terms, Edward's will to play appears to be a function of instinct, a pleasure principle that must be fulfilled at any expense, or a "death instinct" that must be lived through in terms of the pleasure principle. In Richard's case, the will to play seems more of an ego function, a version of ego defense.[54] Richard's will to play automatically defends him from knowing himself. On a nonconscious level, the will to play blocks out aspects of his behavior that would enable him to define himself and, hence, come to know himself morally, including an acknowledgment of the burdens of royal responsibility. Moreover, whereas Edward's will to play is social in the sense that it has to have another human being present to express itself, Richard's is solitary. Edward needs another person to react to just to set his will to play in motion, but Richard needs only his own fertile imagination.

This difference suggests that Edward sees his environment as part of himself, whereas Richard separates himself from his environment, perhaps because on some level he cannot bear the shame of not being able to control it. Richard is on a quest for a human identity that shields him from his failures as a king and his loss of his royal identity. If Richard's can be called an identity problem, Edward's cannot.

Edward has not yet reached that stage of development. Like an infant, he sees his surroundings as extensions of himself and can only respond with tantrumy shrieking when they fail to satisfy him.

The third major difference is that Richard is forceful and active, whereas Edward is usually weak and passive. I realize that, next to Bolingbroke, Richard seems to be only talk. Whereas Bolingbroke consistently appears to be a man of action, Richard often substitutes words for action—for example, when he surrenders to Bolingbroke without a fight. At other times, he takes action but it is irresponsible and wantonly destructive—as, for example, when he orchestrates the murder of his uncle, the Duke of Gloucester, or when he stages the tournament and banishes Bolingbroke and Mowbray, or when he confiscates John of Gaunt's estate, or even when he makes a stagy performance of his deposition. We have little knowledge of his actions offstage, but in his soliloquy (V, v, 1–66), virtually the only time we see him alone, he still shows himself performing. Considered as a substitute for responsible actions, Richard's performances may, in fact, not seem to be actions at all but merely a retreat from moral obligations. Even so, his constant exertion of energy and continuous outpouring of inventiveness mark him as a much more forceful and active figure than Edward II. Edward II has his moments of defiance and pettishness, but, overall, he reacts to others' actions rather than initiating his own. This means that Richard's will to play is more radical, more absolute, more fixed, and less susceptible to manipulation through external circumstances.

With his strongly self-dramatizing personality, Richard is never without resources. Even when alone, he plays with language with an inventiveness and forcefulness never seen in Edward. The impersonality of his only soliloquy (V, v, 1–66) differs very little from that of his public speeches in which, because of his irrepressible will to play with words, he is detached from his content and, consequently, his audience. Richard is utterly dominated by his aesthetic sense, by his eager interest in the mechanics of verbal contrivance. He concentrates on the play with language without making significant content his first priority. He is indeed one who will "for a tricksy word / Defy the matter,"[55] both in public—as in the Deposition Scene (IV, i, 162–318)—and in private—either alone, as in his soliloquy, or in his final parting with the Queen where our interest in the style of the language distracts us from the unhappiness of the Queen and, presumably, that of Richard (V, i, 35–50 and 91–96). R.F. Hill suggests that Richard "endeavours to elude the immediate experience by enclosing it in a cage of words."[56] But that is not quite it. Richard is quintessentially aesthetic in his responses, and, in an odd way, innocent. Just as a snail crawls and a bird flies, Richard responds to events and to language, his own and others', with an aesthetic eye and ear. Rather than merely trying to dodge reality, he expresses with absolute consistency the only reality he knows or wants to know, and he does so with an energy, imagination, and intelligence that awe us. The soliloquy prevents us from responding with emotional engagement to Richard's tragic situation, briefly identified but not deeply felt when he says, "I wasted time, and now doth time waste me" (V, v, 49). Even this statement, his most direct, self-aware, and self-critical in the soliloquy (and in the play), one apparently meant to evoke from us pathos, distracts us from the content by playfully entrapping us through the word play and rhythmic affectiveness of the line. The soliloquy is 66 lines long and, at its conclusion, one is most struck by how ingenious Richard and, behind him, Shakespeare, are.[57] Their ingeniousness signifies their detachment from the content—in this case, Richard's tragic feelings; and, if Richard and Shakespeare are emotionally detached from the tragedy, then, inescapably, so are we. The fact is that we will continue to be as long as in the use of language the means are more important than the ends. That is, we will continue to be whenever the will to play dominates, either Richard's or Shakespeare's.

One might well ask at this point wherein the "tragedy" of *Richard II* lies. From the play's perspective, it is probably embedded in the irony that a man of such considerable talent could not parlay that talent into a sociopolitical usefulness as a king. Since the contention between private and public desires, so prominent in this play, is a major dichotomy running throughout Shakespeare's work, it is certainly no surprise that it crops up here. In part, the text's glances at an idealized nationalism were probably intended to magnify the tragedy resulting from this dichotomy. That we acknowledge the tragedy rationally rather than feelingly, in contrast to our response in later plays, simply means that other, more urgent interests such as the play with language governed Shakespeare's writing as he composed the play.

I have discussed the differences between the two plays and psychological and political similarities in the two kings. Still left to demonstrate is how significant, shared character traits can be used to suggest both Shakespeare's inheritance and departure from Marlowe. Taken as a whole, such traits seem by design meant to recall Marlowe's characterization of Edward II and, also, to invite comparison with Richard II. Both rulers are extremely self-involved and self-indulgent. Neither has much of a moral sense, political or personal. We may feel that Edward is malleable enough to develop a momentary political moral sense; and, by the end of the play, when, to the detriment of consistent characterization, Marlowe has shifted the focus, the king does say, as we have seen, that his personal moral convictions enable him to die with dignity (V, iii, 41–45). But we do not feel the same about Richard. In expanding Marlowe's less full characterization of Edward's susceptibility to aesthetic delights, Shakespeare portrays a Richard who regularly conveys an active, thoroughly absorbed aesthetic response to people and events. When we first see him, he is about to listen to Bolingbroke's accusations of treason against Mowbray. Before Bolingbroke begins, Richard turns up the volume and directs the ensuing verbal battle to be played as high drama:

> Face to face,
> And frowning brow to brow, ourselves will hear
> The accuser and the accusèd freely speak.
> High-stomached are they both and full of ire,
> In rage deaf as the sea, hasty as fire. (I, i, 15–19)

When Bolingbroke makes his accusations, Richard exclaims, "How high a pitch his resolution soars" (I, i, 109). It can be argued that Richard responds to Bolingbroke's style rather than his content because he is trying to divert attention from his own participation in the Duke of Gloucester's death. But the theatrical manner in which he responds is itself significant. It is perfectly consistent with the personality that the rest of the play dramatizes. In retrospect, we might well ask, "Is it at all likely that Richard would have responded less theatrically—say, with a just, moral assessment of the charges—had he *not* been involved in the murder of his uncle?" When the dying Gaunt plays on his name (II, i, 73–83), Richard discards the moral implications of the speech to ask, "Can sick men play so nicely with their names" (II, i, 84). The content of Gaunt's next lengthy speech becomes pointedly moral and accusatory, and Richard grows angry and imperious (II, i, 115–23), but, significantly, without invoking a moral frame of reference of his own. In this tendency, he resembles Edward.

Marlowe and Shakespeare's kings resemble each other in yet another way: they both have considerable stamina, but we tend not to admire it until their death scenes where they become vigorous and staunchly stoical. Another similarity, too lightly characterized by both dramatists, manifests itself in the devotion of each Queen Isabella for her royal husband: we are no clearer on why Richard's queen expresses such strong love for him than we are on why Edward's wife is so enamored of her husband (at least initially). Finally, because of their unalterable will to play, both men are self-destructive—Edward, passively, and Richard actively.[58] When Bolingbroke returns from exile and first encounters Richard, the King all too quickly turns himself over to Bolingbroke and without any prompting (III, iii, 72–175). Then, when Northumberland asks Richard to come down to "the base court" (III, iii, 176), Richard, understanding the political reality of his situation, replies with grand theatrical posturing, a gesture of self-dignity:

> Down, down I come, like glist'ring Phaethon,
> Wanting the manage of unruly jades.
> In the base court? Base court, where kings grow base,
> To come at traitors' calls and do them grace!
> In the base court come down? Down court! down king!
> For night owls shriek where mounting larks should sing. (III, iii, 178–83)

One senses that it is the drama of the situation and the chance to play with words, not the moral turpitude of the usurper, that chiefly impel Richard. Thus, he destroys himself through self-victimization, clearly the most deleterious effect of a sustained will to play.

From the perspective of the structure of their chronicle histories, Marlowe and Shakespeare share a similarity in turning their kings, victimized by what might be called their natural disposition in a hostile environment, into heroic martyrs at the ends of their lives. Whether Shakespeare was specifically influenced by *Edward II*, two facts stand out: *Richard II* is very different in structure from the four or five histories of Shakespeare that precede it (the *Henry VI* plays, *Richard III*, and, depending upon when it was written, also *King John*)—less episodic and, as a principle of unity, more realistically and deeply characterological. But it is quite similar to *Edward II* in its focus on the demise of the king. One need only think of the episodic nature and cartoonlike protagonist of the *Tamburlaine* plays in contrast to the more unified plot and more realistic, in-depth protagonist of *Edward II*. The same progression exists in the plays preceding *Richard II*, even if *Richard III* can be considered an intermediate step between the *Henry VI* plays and *Richard II*. *Richard III* is structurally different from the *Henry VI* plays in its focus on a dominant evil figure, just as *Richard II* is different from *Richard III* in making Richard's nemesis, Bolingbroke, so prominent and in making it difficult throughout for us to come to final judgments on either Richard or Bolingbroke and to categorize them. Secondly, the complicated, interwoven political and personal (psychological) sources of unhappiness for a ruler, explored in *Edward II* and *Richard II*, become a strong element in Shakespeare's next three Henry plays. Clearly, Shakespeare is experimenting. How much of his initiative is due to Marlowe is uncertain, but the parallels are striking enough to seem more than coincidental. Although Shakespeare does not return to the situation of a king weakened by an unruly will to play, he does develop the notion of ruling figures whose psychology impedes their ability to function effectively as kings.

Ultimately, *Richard II* affirms the political well-being of the state above the well-being of the individual.[59] That is because the play stands behind effective power, tainted though it may be. This position is pragmatic and realistic, even if not moral, and it clearly asserts the necessity of a public perspective over a private one. Superficially, *Edward II* appears to accept the same perspective. But, as we have seen, the wrenching of the focus needed to make this come about calls into doubt the genuineness with which Marlowe undertakes it. In comparing the two dramatists, what seems clear is that Shakespeare is the more successful at integrating substance and form because, having weighed the issues with more detachment, he has a more settled grasp of content. My guess is that he owes this advancement—at least, in part—to his understanding of Marlowe's dramaturgical struggle. Marlowe, interestingly, seems caught in a crossfire between content and form, because he tends to engulf the issues, subsuming them into the recesses of his own consciousness where they are hidden from our view. In bringing about a final resolution that smacks of poetic justice, for example, he pulls back unexpectedly from the tough, almost defiant realism of character and events that begins the play to arrive at a conclusion that, from the perspective of *Hero and Leander*, he might have scorned.

VI

If a parallel between the two plays' final political stance seems tenuous, a likeness in the use of ambiguity seems solid and strong.[60] Once again, we find that examining influence leads us into a discussion of dramaturgical technique where Marlowe's strongest influence seems to reside. The plays' similar employment of ambiguity suggests that Shakespeare took note of the effectiveness of the technique in *Edward II* and incorporated it into his own historical drama. Shakespeare had surely observed ambiguity in Marlowe's other plays but that in *Edward II* was particularly fitting for a history, because it allowed Marlowe the freedom to stimulate and tease his audience by playing with their preconceived notions of historical figures and events. Both writers knew that ambiguity generates a desire for clarification in an audience; it challenges the audience to be attentive to a resolution of a mystery even if the resolution never materializes. It also stimulates the audience's imagination and reflective powers, securing their engagement with the drama as they become willing participants in fathoming the ambiguities.

I have already recounted several instances of ambiguity in *Edward II*, some of which grow out of contradictions: the older Mortimer's contradictory attitude toward Edward and his minionizing; the true nature of Gaveston's feelings toward Edward;[61] the strength of Isabella's love for Edward early on in the play; the indications of a romantic liaison between Margaret and Gaveston (II, i, 57–82) and Edward and Isabella (V, v, 67–69); the reason Edward gives for loving Gaveston (I, iv, 77) and the depth of his feelings toward Spencer; the shift in Edward from obsessiveness to heroic martyrdom; and the sudden aging of Edward. In *Richard II*, ambiguities also abound in the characterizations and events: the truth of Mowbray's and Bolingbroke's accusations; the basis of Isabella's ardent love for and devotion to Richard, especially given his inexplicable detachment from her; the rationale behind Bolingbroke's desire to usurp the throne; the reason for Aumerle's devotion to Richard and the role of Aumerle in the Duke of Gloucester's murder; the shadier aspects of Richard's behavior—his part in the Duke of Gloucester's death, the "divorce betwixt his queen and him" (III, i, 12), how exactly he is "basely led / By flatterers" (II, i, 241–42); Richard's sexual proclivities; Mowbray's guilt or innocence in Gloucester's death and his lament that his worst punishment in being banished will be that he must "forgo" his "native English" (I, iii, 160); the legitimacy of the grievances that are aired and the accusations hurled—especially those hurled at Richard—which, although crippling if true, are never clearly affirmed or denied. Part of the ambiguity in *Richard II* may derive from Shakespeare's own will to play, his interest in playing with language at the expense of dramatizations of political events that might have clarified the truth of the grievances and accusations. But another part derives from the aesthetic soundness of creating mysteries that will hold an audience's attention—as, for example, when both writers dramatize the inexplicable strength of love that the two queens have for their husbands.

Two other elements help to contextualize this aesthetic. The first: Before experiencing the plays, the original audiences of Marlowe and Shakespeare would have possessed some common knowledge of the history of Edward, Richard, and their times. We can readily see that the two playwrights made frequent use of this knowledge to overturn their audiences' expectations and thereby increase their pleasure. In doing so, they muddied with ambiguity historical waters thought to be clear and, as a consequence, found an effective way to create and sustain interest in the chronicle histories their dramas portray. For instance, Gaveston's social rank was actually higher than the nobles in the play take it to be. In lowering it, Marlowe creates a difference between fact and fiction that introduces an intriguing ambiguity about Gaveston's motives in assuming the role of Edward's minion. In *Richard II*, the role of Aumerle has more prominence than it has in historical accounts, but Shakespeare does not make clear why Aumerle is so fond of the king; nor is it clear why he fares so well during the course of the play, given his offensiveness (I, iv) and his offenses (IV, i, 1–106 and V, ii and V, iii). Perhaps the most one can say is that Aumerle seems intended to fulfill various momentary artistic needs in the play rather than functioning as a character in his own right. Even so, the ambiguity of his motives and actions helps to keep an audience attentive throughout.

Both dramatists understand that an arsenal of previous historical knowledge can also be useful in creating ambiguities that call into question standard notions of kings and kingship. In his portrayal of Edward's uncontrollable will to play, Marlowe creates a psychological ambiguity that, in complicating an audience's knowledge of history, subverts any notion that achieving success as a king derives from other than raw power. In *Richard II*, the ambiguity is more than psychological. Richard, for instance, leans heavily on the inviolability of the divine right of kings. This belief is given support by Gaunt's reluctance to avenge his brother Gloucester's murder; as he asserts moralistically to Gloucester's widow:

> God's is the quarrel; for God's substitute,
> His deputy anointed in his sight
> Hath caused his death; the which if wrongfully,
> Let heaven revenge; for I may never lift
> An angry arm against his minister. (I, ii, 37–41)

Bolingbroke's show of guilt after Richard's death (V, vi, 45–52) also seems to give some credence to the belief in the divine right of kings. But the turn of events in the play does not. Thus, for most of the play, Shakespeare encloses in ambiguity the impact of this belief—in part to produce suspense about how the test of its validity will conclude and in part to characterize the utter lack of pragmatism in Richard's invoking it. At the end of the play, the dramatist leaves open the possibility of future retribution for Richard's usurpation and death. So the notion remains cloaked in ambiguity but ready for use in Shakespeare's next history, Part 1 of *Henry the Fourth*.

The second element: From their frequent interaction with religious symbols and iconography and their acquaintance with representational painting and sculpture, early modern audiences, like the two playwrights themselves, were as familiar with signifiers as they were with literal realism. As a result, they appear to be more accepting than we are of the lack of realism that comes with a partial knowledge of characters and events and any ambiguity that surrounds them—that is, with characters and events that are less realistic and more ambiguous than what they signify. Thus, it is of less consequence that Mortimer and Bolingbroke's psychologies be portrayed realistically and without ambiguity than that we understand at any given moment what they represent.

There is of course always the possibility that some of the ambiguity in the two plays was unintended. But both playwrights must have known that some amount of ambiguity keeps audiences involved, just as it provides an opportunity for interpretive freshness in each new production of the plays. The sixteenth- and seventeenth-century fascination with Tamburlaine (and, ours—at least among scholars) and, to this day, our fascination with Hamlet demonstrate conclusively how powerful aesthetic ambiguity can be. In his decision to dramatize the history of Richard II, Shakespeare chose a figure who at least superficially, in personality and political situation, resembled Edward II—in part, I suspect, because of the effectiveness of a figure whose will to play created such an engrossing ambiguity. In addition, Shakespeare may also have wanted to link himself to the tradition of higher aesthetic standards in historical drama that Marlowe sought to achieve. Whatever his specific reasons, in choosing, as Marlowe had chosen before him, to make ambiguity a major artistic device, Shakespeare created characters who would readily come alive in audiences' imaginations, not just for an age but for centuries to come.

In attempting to gauge the will to play in *Edward II* and *Richard II*, only one of many approaches that help us to come to an understanding of these works, we have found a telling way to account for significant differences as well as likenesses between the two contemporary plays and their creators. Moreover, in both plays, the tension born of the conflict between the private desires of the will to play and the public demands of professional responsibility may well enable us to become aware of the analogous shift in our own perspective as we move from a psychological understanding of causes of actions to a judgmental perspective on their social-moral effects. If it also means that we reexamine the complex relationship between psychological understanding and moral assessments, then so much the better.

What is the final attitude of *Edward II* and *Richard II* toward the will to play? Both texts regard this governing tendency in the personality of the king fatalistically, as a sure road to self-destruction. Marlowe and Shakespeare each employ the trait as a major means for keeping an audience absorbed. The will to play constantly creates surprise, for the audience does not know where or how it will manifest itself next. It also intrigues an audience through the mysteriousness of its origins. This mysteriousness, like other ambiguities in the two plays, releases rather than restricts an audience's imagination. Thus, the will to play becomes a device for successful dramaturgy, even if, as an uncontrolled, predominant characteristic in human personalities that are unavoidably thrust into a sociopolitical setting, it is regarded as inescapably debilitating. In contrast to the two plays' sociomoral denigration of the will to play, Marlowe and Shakespeare as playwrights are able to make admirable creative use of their own will to play, although, as we have seen, Marlowe retreats from it, wary of its emotionalism, as he attempts to invest the play finally with a coherent structure.

One final dramatic device that links Marlowe and Shakespeare through their chronicle histories needs to be mentioned. We have discovered that *Richard II*'s evocation of aesthetic and moral viewpoints as opposed categories of consciousness is put to use to create conflict, thereby commanding interest and instilling engagement in audiences. The aesthetic viewpoint allows a suspension of the desire to make moral judgments and a freedom and eagerness to be awed through the responses of our senses and emotions, whereas the moral viewpoint requires a need to reason, judge, and become reductive. Our attitude toward Richard at any given moment depends upon whether we view him from an aesthetic or from a moral perspective—as a powerfully creative figure or as a king saddled with responsibilities;[62] we know that both perspectives exist, often simultaneously, and we are less troubled than intrigued as a result. This double perspective does not exist in *Edward II* where the dominant perspective on Edward is emphatically moral, but it does in the *Tamburlaine* plays where our attitude toward the warrior hero fluctuates between awe and disapproval. If Shakespeare shows himself at ease in *Richard II* in employing this contradictory perspective, it may well be that his equanimity comes from his understanding of the difference between the single and double perspectives in Marlowe's plays. We can see that in adopting different perspectives for their plays, both authors are engaged in a process of honing their dramaturgical tools, Marlowe's interest perhaps stimulating Shakespeare's.

How influential Marlowe's play with perspectives may have been on Shakespeare is as difficult to ascertain as the degree to which Edward's will to play marked Shakespeare's conception of Richard II's. However, Edward's unrestrained behavior could only have increased Shakespeare's awareness of the possibilities for portraying Richard's unruly actions and, very likely, heightened his awareness of the will to play in his own artistic self. It may well be that Shakespeare is registering something of his indebtedness to Marlowe when in the Deposition Scene (IV, i, 281–91) he parodies Doctor Faustus's well-known words of wonder as Faustus looks in awe on the spirit of Helen of Troy, "Was this the face that launch'd a thousand ships" (*Doctor Faustus*, V, ii, 99). Although the passage has been considered a belittlement of Marlowe's extravagance and intensity of language, it nevertheless stands as a strong tribute. It comes undisguisedly at a climactic moment, one in which Richard's will to play is at its most intense and the audience's response at its most engaged. As such, the allusion overtly acknowledges that Shakespeare is writing in the immediate wake of a potent dramatist and that he recognizes, implicitly at least, the importance of certain linguistic elements of Marlowe's legacy in achieving his own professional success. Furthermore, in the patent directness of the reference, Shakespeare for the first time openly embraces a part of what he will eventually come to accept wholeheartedly, his full dramaturgical inheritance from Marlowe. One would like to think that, as Shakespeare is asserting his own individuality in fashioning the language of this scene and in contributing to the genre of the history play, even if, as some would consider it, in a backhanded way, he is also tipping his hat in thanks to the most impressive of his contemporary English playwrights.

Notes

1   Nicholas Brooke, "Marlowe as Provocative Agent in Shakespeare's Early Plays," *Shakespeare Survey* 14 (1961): 34–44, but especially 39–41.

2   Wolfgang Clemen, "Shakespeare and Marlowe," in *Shakespeare 1971*, ed. Clifford Leech and J.M.R. Margeson (Toronto: University of Toronto Press, 1972), 123–32.

3   Marjorie Garber, "Marlovian Vision/Shakespearean Revision," *Research Opportunities in Renaissance Drama* 22 (1979): 3–9, but especially 3–4, and Robert P. Merrix and Carole

Levin, "*Richard II* and *Edward II*: The Structure of Deposition," *The Shakespeare Yearbook* 1 (1990): 1–13.

4　M.C. Bradbrook, "Shakespeare's Recollections of Marlowe," *Shakespeare's Styles: Essays in honour of Kenneth Muir*, ed. Philip Edwards, Inga-Stina Ewbank, and G.K. Hunter (Cambridge: Cambridge University Press, 1980), 191–204, but especially 196. See also Bradbrook's essay, "Shakespeare's Debt to Marlowe," in her book, *Aspects of Dramatic Form in the English and Irish Renaissance* (Sussex, UK: Harvester Press, 1983), 17–31. Here, in discussing *Edward II*, she calls *Richard II* "Shakespeare's counter-play" (32).

5　James Shapiro, *Rival Playwrights: Marlowe, Jonson, Shakespeare* (New York: Columbia University Press, 1991), 75–96. Although on these pages Shapiro discusses Marlowe and Shakespeare as rivals, he spends relatively little time discussing *Edward II* and *Richard II*.

6　Maurice Charney, "Marlowe's *Edward II* as Model for Shakespeare's *Richard II*," *Research Opportunities in Renaissance Drama* 33 (1994): 31–41. Charney distinguishes between a model and a source and claims that *Edward II* acted as the former but not the latter for Shakespeare. In his comparison of *Edward II* and *Richard II*, Charney discusses seven elements in the two plays which suggest that Shakespeare may have made use of Marlowe's play as a model: "the theme of sodomy" (32); a parallel between underlings—Bushy, Bagot, and Green play a role "analogous" (34) to that of Spencer and Baldock; similar "details of frivolity and self-indulgence" (34); the unhappiness of the two queens: "both Isabellas are represented as melancholy and discontented with their lot" (35); similar deposition scenes (36–38); likenesses in the psychologies of Edward and Richard (38); a stylistic influence: "some of Richard's rhetoric sounds strikingly Marlovian" (39). However persuaded we may or may not be about these elements as indicating that Shakespeare used Marlowe's play as a model, one salutary consequence of Charney's examination is that it provides the opportunity for seeing complex relationships and strong differences between the protagonists and the plays.

7　Meredith Skura, "Marlowe's *Edward II*: Penetrating Language in Shakespeare's *Richard II*," *Shakespeare Survey* 50 (1997): 42. During the course of the article (41–55), Skura also discusses the relationship of *Edward II* to other plays by Shakespeare and how Shakespeare's response to Marlowe's play "may help us understand new dimensions of dramatic collaboration on the early modern stage" (42).

8　Charles R. Forker summarizes the parallels and differences between the two plays as they have been recorded by scholars and critics, including himself: "Marlowe's *Edward II* and its Shakespearean Relatives: The Emergence of a Genre," in *Shakespeare's English Histories: A Quest for Form and Genre*, ed. John W. Velz, 55–90, but especially 80–88. In describing the relationship between *Edward II* and Shakespeare's early history plays, Forker sees a "symbiosis" (90). However much one may agree or disagree with individual points, Forker's intertextual approach provides additional support for the subtlety and complexity of the relationship between the two dramatists.

9　In Marlowe's plays, the will to play can be seen in Jupiter, Dido, Tamburlaine, Doctor Faustus, Barabas, and Edward II, although, in the case of Tamburlaine, the sense of "play" becomes more and more disagreeable to us. In Shakespeare's plays, the will to play can be viewed, for example, in Aaron the Moor, Richard III, Richard II, Berowne, Mercutio, Launcelot Gobbo, Falstaff, Touchstone, Lucio, Iago, Edmund, Antony (intermittently) and Cleopatra, and Autolycus. One might also include Rosalind who maintains her disguise as Ganymede from a will to play that abets her desire to tutor Orlando.

10 *Renaissance Self-Fashioning: From More to Shakespeare* (Chicago: The University of Chicago Press, 1980).

11 Greenblatt summarizes the will to play in Marlowe's characters at the close of the chapter but without distinguishing play from *absolute* play: "This playfulness in Marlowe's works manifests itself as cruel humor, murderous practical jokes, a penchant for the outlandish and absurd, delight in role-playing, entire absorption in the game at hand and consequent indifference to what lies outside the boundaries of the game, radical insensitivity to human complexity and suffering, extreme but disciplined aggression, hostility to transcendence" (*Renaissance Self-Fashioning*, 220).

12 Ibid.

13 In his essay, "'Writ in Blood': Marlowe and the New Historicists," in *Constructing Christopher Marlowe*, ed. J.A. Downie and J.T. Parnell (Cambridge: Cambridge University Press, 2000), 116–32, Richard Wilson asks what Greenblatt means by the phrase "the will to play" (122–23; 127) even as he questions the value of New Historicism as an approach to Marlowe's texts.

14 Howard Felperin, *The Uses of the Canon: Elizabethan Literature and Contemporary Theory* (Oxford: Oxford University Press, 1990), 119. Renaissance "carnival" was one of the forms of play sanctioned by society as a holiday ritual.

15 Ibid.

16 Ibid., 115. One might add to this list Dido and, in the form of parody, the Nurse; the Duke of Guise; and the gods depicted in "Venus'glass" (*Hero and Leander*, 142). All references to Christopher Marlowe's poems are from *Christopher Marlowe: The Complete Poems*, ed. Mark Thornton Burnett (London: J.M. Dent, 2000).

17 Greenblatt, *Renaissance Self-Fashioning*, "Introduction," 3–6.

18 Felperin, 116.

19 Ibid., 115–16.

20 Both Greenblatt and Felperin understand that, as a potentially subversive element in society, "play" can be used by society to reinforce its norms, whether through direct suppression or holiday rituals.

21 Felperin seems to be getting at this same psychological feature when, as we have just seen, he identifies "that peculiar dynamic of Marlovian tragedy which underlies and motivates the more particular wills to power, pleasure, wealth, and knowledge that respectively characterize the careers of Tamburlaine, Edward II, The Jew of Malta, and Dr. Faustus" (115). Greenblatt seems to blur the crucial distinction between the voluntary and involuntary motivating forces that activate the will; he focuses instead on the force of the will and its effects.

22 Put a bit differently, Gregory W. Bredbeck in *Sodomy and Interpretation: Marlowe To Milton* (Ithaca, NY: Cornell University Press, 1991), 50–77, makes a similar point about Edward II when he says that the king, although a participant in the monarch's natural body, which is temporal, and the monarch's political body, which is eternal, is a rebel against his own body politic, because he promotes his passion in disregard for the demands of the political state.

23 Michael Hattaway provides an example which supports this generalization when, in an article on "Marlowe and Brecht" in *Christopher Marlowe*, ed. Brian Morris (New York: Hill and Wang, 1968), 106, he says, "The Olympia episode derives from Ariosto, and the chivalric ideals of the family, and death before dishonour, show up the harsh politics and theology of the scourge of God." For a summary of the controversial interpretations of Edward III, see Sara Munson Deats, *Sex, Gender, and Desire in the Plays of Christopher*

Marlowe (Newark: University of Delaware Press, 1997], 254, n. 28. My contribution to these interpretations appears further along in the text.

24   All references to Shakespeare's works are from *William Shakespeare: The Complete Works*, gen. eds. Stephen Orgel and A.R. Braunmuller (New York: Penguin Putnam, 2002).

25   This is not to say that they cannot be accused of being *unconsciously* masochistic and self-annihilating.

26   All references to Marlowe's plays are from *Christopher Marlowe: The Complete Plays*, ed. Mark Thornton Burnett (London: J.M. Dent, 1999).

27   To name only a handful of critics and historians in chronological order: Michel Foucault, *The History of Sexuality*, Vol. 1 (New York: Pantheon, 1978), 43; Alan Bray, *Homosexuality in Renaissance England* (London: Gay Men's Press, 1982), 13–32 and 58–70; Bruce Smith, *Homosexual Desire in Shakespeare's England: A Cultural Poetics* (Chicago: The University of Chicago Press, 1991), 9–13; Gregory Bredbeck, 5–13; Viviana Comensoli, "Homophobia and the Regulation of Desire: A Psychoanalytic Reading of Marlowe's *Edward II*," *Journal of the History of Sexuality* 4:2 (1993): 175, n. 1; Emily Bartels, *Spectacles of Strangeness: Imperialism, Alienation, and Marlowe* (Philadelphia: University of Pennsylvania Press, 1993), 143–47; Stephen Orgel, *Impersonations* (Cambridge: Cambridge University Press, 1996), 39–40 and 59; Deats, 81–86 and 194–200; Mario Di Gangi, *The Homoerotics of Early Modern Drama* (Cambridge: Cambridge University Press, 1997), 1–28 and 107–15; and Ian McAdam, *The Irony of Identity: Self and Imagination in the Drama of Christopher Marlowe* (Newark: University of Delaware Press, 1999), 33–41 and 199–202. For an illuminating discussion of how homoeroticism was considered a natural part of amity in the early modern period, see Steve Patterson, "The Bankruptcy of Homoerotic Amity in Shakespeare's *Merchant of Venice*," *Shakespeare Quarterly* 50:1 (1999): 9–32.

28   Here used in the limited sense of anal penetration, not as the early modern period's standard catch-all term for the disapprobation of religious, political, and sexual transgressions against nature, real or imagined. See Smith, *Homosexual Desires*, 14, for evidence of the influence that context ("who is speaking to whom, and under what circumstances") has on James I's views of sodomy. See Bredbeck, 1–30, and Deats, *Sex, Gender, and Desire*, Chapter 5, Section 4, for discussions of the early modern meanings of "sodomy."

29   Smith, *Homosexual Desire*, 23. Emily Bartels, 147, agrees with Smith, commenting that homosexuality "was beginning to have a place, however nameless, formless, and faint, in Renaissance discourse." Perhaps the strongest statement of the position shared by Smith and Bartels, that "the Renaissance had a definite recognition of a distinct homosexuality" (9), is that of Joseph Cady, "'Masculine Love,' Renaissance Writing, and the 'New Invention' of Homosexuality" in *Homosexuality in Renaissance and Enlightenment England: Literary Representations in Historical Context*, ed. Claude J. Summers (Binghamton, NY: Haworth Press, 1992), 9–41.

30   The words of the Earl of Pembroke are typical: "Can kingly lions fawn on creeping ants" (I, iv, 15).

31   Does he mean "because he loves me more than all the world loves me" or "because he loves me more than he loves all the world?"

32   Compare McAdam, *Irony of Identity*, 203–4, who ends his discussion of Edward's reply by denying the love of Gaveston and by expanding this view into a more general conclusion: "It is in fact the absence of spiritual wholeness that lies at the heart of the play" (204).

33   Greenblatt observes that "when Gaveston is killed, Edward has within seconds adopted someone else: the will exists but the object of the will is little more than an illusion" (*Renaissance Self-Fashioning*, 218–19). (Simon Shepherd, *Marlowe and the Politics*

of Elizabethan Theatre [New York: St Martin's Press, 1986], 205, expresses a similar sentiment: "Not so much a 'toy', the desire is more permanent than its object.") Greenblatt seems to mean that, in Edward's mind, Spencer has been substituted for Gaveston, that the exercising of Edward's will takes primacy, and, thus, that "the object of the will" is of less significance, even illusory. It is perhaps easier to agree with the second half of Greenblatt's statement than with the first.

34 Compare Greenblatt, 217.

35 Greenblatt says that: "for Marlowe ... all objects of desire are fictions, theatrical illusions shaped by human subjects. And those subjects are themselves fictions, fashioned in reiterated acts of self-naming" (218–19). Greenblatt is talking about Marlowe's portrayals of the self-validation of "heroes" (by which he seems to mean "protagonists"). But, again typically, Marlowe dramatizes such acts as successful assertions of power. We can see that, much to the chagrin of his wife and the nobles, Edward validates the obsessiveness of his will to play through those repeated actions in which, in order to center his life in his favorites, he abandons his role as king but retains enough of its power to give momentary success to his assertions.

36 See Charney, "Marlowe's *Edward II*," 36–38, who discusses parallels in the "archetypal victims" (38) of the deposition scenes in *Edward II* and *Richard II*.

37 For a well-explained description of the differences between our perception of apparent inconsistencies in characterization and Elizabethan conceptions, see Madeline Doran, *Endeavors of Art: A Study of Form in Elizabethan Drama* (Madison: University of Wisconsin Press, 1954), 216–58.

38 Shepherd, 197.

39 Ibid.

40 Marlowe's changes in historical fact throughout the play are so frequent that he could easily have deleted this episode. He did delete the marriage between Spencer and Margaret's sister. Some of the other facts of history that he changed were: (1) that Edward's brother Kent was only six years old at the time the play begins—in 1307; (2) that Isabella did not marry Edward until 1308, after Gaveston had been recalled and, consequently, that Edward III was not born until 1312; (3) that Lancaster, not the Mortimers, strongly opposed Gaveston, the Spencers, and Edward II. The Mortimers had no actual part in the opposition to Gaveston. Warwick was, historically, the most persistent foe of Gaveston and Edward II; (4) that the Spencers virtually governed the country from the time of Gaveston's death until 1327; they were clearly the power behind the throne.

I agree with Stephen Orgel's comment on the union of Lady Margaret and Gaveston, that "marriage here is fully complicit with homoeroticism" (*Impersonations*, 46) and that such a marriage is inescapably political. But these insights do not account for the focus of the scene (II, i, 57–82). Margaret expresses her joy as she reads from Gaveston's letter to her. There is nothing in the scene or elsewhere in the play to detract from the genuineness of Gaveston's romantic sentiments and Margaret's reaction. Evidently, in the culture of Marlowe's audience what we would call a homoerotic relationship between two men was not considered a threat to what we understand as romantic heterosexuality.

41 In discussing how the action of *Edward II* "is given both thematic unity and wider relevance by the play's emblematic technique" ("Marlowe and the 'Comic Distance,'" in *Christopher Marlowe*, ed. Morris, 57), J.R. Mulryne and Stephen Fender observe that "Edward's death, the nature of which is suggested by Lightborn's prescription for a hot spit, recalls Edward's life" (58). They continue by quoting from an introduction by Professor Moelwyn Merchant: "'That suffering and death should bear an appropriate

relation to sins committed is a commonplace of medieval thought, theological, literary or aesthetic' (p.xxi)." The assumption in all three critics is that Marlowe, following his source, suggests that the punishment (graphically) fits the crime. See also the comments by Stephen Guy-Bray, "Homophobia and the Depoliticizing of *Edward* II," *English Studies in Canada* 17:2 (June 1991): 126–30.

42   Orgel, *Impersonations*, 47–48.

43   Although two critics, William Empson, in "Two Proper Crimes," *The Nation* 163 (1946): 444–45, and Stephen Guy-Bray, 125–33, assume the insertion of the poker and see it as a "parody" of sodomy, neither is clear on what function such a parody serves. Empson sees it as playing to the audience's idea of just retribution for Edward's supposed sexual activity with Gaveston, but not necessarily to Marlowe's idea. Empson assumes the existence of sodomy and then assumes that Marlowe would play to the audience's idea of just retribution even if he did not himself believe in it. But an argument built on unwarranted assumptions is not a convincing argument. Guy-Bray says cryptically, "Marlowe dramatizes the historical account of Edward's murder in order to analyze the way in which society controls sexuality" (126). What leads this critic to see the second method used to kill Edward as a parody of sodomy is not clear. By reading the ending as an analysis of the way in which society controls sexuality, he may mean that he thinks Lightborn links sodomy, a transgression against nature and therefore a crime, to Edward and punishes him to show that society sanctions and thereby controls only traditional ideas of sexual behavior. This argument seems forced, however, because it assumes that the evil executioner Lightborn, whose idea the insertion of the poker was, is to be understood as the voice of society. Even in Holinshed, where the executioning force is an unspecified "they," the idea of the insertion of the poker seems to be the sole invention of the executioners.

In trying to account for the ending of the play, both Empson and Guy-Bray are looking outward to the politics of sexual behavior rather than exclusively inward to the obscure psychology of either Edward or Marlowe. This same focus can be applied to the issue of homoeroticism in *Edward II*. Although we are limited in how far we can psychoanalyze and even characterize Edward's homoerotic words and actions, we can see why in late sixteenth-century England the portrayal of homoerotic feeling in the play, for all its ambiguity, might well be considered politically significant.

44   Raphaell Holinshed, *The Third Volume of Chronicles, Beginning At Duke William The Norman, Commonlie Called the Conqueror; and Descending By Degrees of Yeeres to all the Kings And Queenes of England in their Orderlie Successions ... 1586* (New York: AMS Press, 1965), 587, says: "Wherevpon when they [Edward's "keepers"] sawe that such practises would not serue their turne, they came suddenlie one night into the chamber where he laie in bed fast asleepe, and with heauie featherbeds or a table (as some write) being cast vpon him, they kept him down and withall put into his fundament an horne, and through the same they thrust vp into his bodie an hot spit, or (as other have) through the pipe of a trumpet a plumbers instrument of iron made verie hot, the which passing vp into his intrailes, and being rolled to and fro, burnt the same, but *so as no appearance of any wound or hurt outwardlie might be once perceived*" [my emphasis].

45   Interestingly, in his section on Richard II, Holinshed describes the death of the Duke of Gloucester, using the same detail of the featherbed: "... he [Mowbray] caused his seruants to cast featherbeds vpon him [Gloucester], and so smoother him to death, or otherwise to strangle him with towels (as some write)" (837). Whether featherbeds or towels, the emphasis is also clearly on protocol.

46   Shepherd, 207.

47 Ibid., 197.

48 Nina Taunton in *1590s Drama and Militarism: Portrayals of War in Marlowe, Chapman, and Shakespeare's* Henry V (Burlington, VT: Ashgate, 2001) claims that there is some justification for Tamburlaine's killing of Calyphas but that he has applied a military doctrine "*ad extremum*" (59). For another balanced perspective on Calyphas as a dissident in a military context, see Alan Shepard, *Marlowe's Soldiers: Rhetorics of Masculinity in the Age of the Armada* (Burlington, VT: Ashgate, 2002), 25 and 43–47.

49 For an extensive treatment of Calyphas as an interrogation of Tamburlaine's credo of "manliness," see Deats, *Sex, Gender, and Desire*, 152–55.

50 Simon Shepherd describes in effect the cause of Edward's unmanliness when he says, "The ideology of manliness, or masculinity, inscribes the individual within interpersonal competition and denigrates emotion without action" (198).

51 Simon Shepherd sees Edward III as a mix of manly and unmanly behavior, citing his judgments on Mortimer and Isabella as manly and his tears "of grief and innocency" (V, vi, 102) as unmanly (205–6). The problem is that Edward III is a child. For a manly adult, tears would be unmanly and innocence simply would not exist. But is it not plausible that, because Edward III is a child, his show of manliness is all the more striking? The portrayal would seem to have more to do with dramatic effectiveness than with the desire to present a clear-cut figure of manliness.

52 For a comprehensive treatment of the gender role reversals of Dido and Aeneas, see Deats, 92–98. For a discussion of the Jupiter/Ganymede episode as subversively undercutting patriarchal values, see Joyce Green McDonald, "Marlowe's Ganymede," in *Enacting Gender on the English Renaissance Stage*, ed. Viviana Comensoli and Anne Russell (Urbana: University of Illinois Press, 1999), 93–113.

53 Although James Shapiro writes about the connections between the works of Marlowe and Shakespeare, the relative little that he has to say about *Edward II* and *Richard II* indicates that there are more differences than similarities. He does suggest that, whereas *Edward II* is a response to the presentation of history in the *Henry VI* plays, *Richard II* is a response to the presentation of history in *Edward II*. See *Rival Playwrights*, 84, 85, 91–96. Charles Forker states that "comparison of the two dramas has tended, justly enough, to stress differences rather than similarities" (83).

54 Unlike the will to play in the two kings, Barabas's will to play is socially engendered; what is antisocial in him is a function, paradoxically, of the society that plays *on* him.

55 *The Merchant of Venice*, III, v, 62–63.

56 R.F. Hill, "Dramatic Techniques and Interpretation in 'Richard II'" (in *Early Shakespeare* [volume 3 of the Stratford-Upon-Avon Studies], ed. John Russell Brown and Bernard Harris (London: Edward Arnold, 1961), 117.

57 For other passages in which we recognize a playwright who is bursting with inventiveness, both unabashedly pleased with and proud of his linguistic achievements, one might point to the Duchess of Gloucester's elaborate conceit in I, ii, 11–21; Mowbray's response to Richard's sentence of exile in I, iii, 154–73; Bolingbroke's to his father's attempts to comfort him after Richard has pronounced his sentence in I, iii, 294–303; Gaunt's death speech in II, i, 31–68; Richard's speeches when he returns to England in III, ii, 4–26 and 144–77; the Gardener in III, iv; Richard in the Deposition Scene, IV, i, 162–318; and Richard as he takes leave of his wife in V, i.

58 Edward's passivity does not mean that he is not at times aggressive in his defiance of the nobles; since his defiance is wholly emotional, he does not see, as we do, that the

consequences will sooner or later destroy him. (See "Edward's Perils," 167–90, in Matthew N. Proser's *The Gift of Fire: Aggression and the Plays of Christopher Marlowe* [New York: Peter Lang Publishing, 1995] for a subtle and complex discussion of Edward's underlying aggressiveness.) Richard's self-destructiveness is more direct, more baldly egotistical and self-dramatizing.

59   This position represents that of early Shakespeare. By the time he comes to write *Antony and Cleopatra*, he appears to have reversed this stance.

60   Although critics have long accepted ambiguity as a chief characteristic of Shakespeare's works, they have not understood it as part of his aesthetic. One of the first essays to focus on it as a significant aspect of Marlowe's aesthetic is Sara Munson Deats' "Marlowe's Interrogative Drama: *Dido, Tamburlaine, Doctor Faustus*, and *Edward II*" in *Marlowe's Empery: Expanding His Critical Contexts*, ed. Sara Munson Deats and Robert A. Logan (Newark: University of Delaware Press, 2002), 107–30. As far as I am aware, no one has previously commented on the degree to which Marlowe influenced Shakespeare in this aspect of his artistry.

61   As Lawrence Danson says, "Gaveston is a character about whom we cannot make up our mind" (*Shakespeare's Dramatic Genres* [Oxford: Oxford University Press, 2000], 44).

62   Norman Rabkin in *Shakespeare and the Problem of Meaning* (Chicago: University of Chicago Press, 1981), 34–35, quotes E.H. Gombrich whose well-known discussion of viewing a picture as a rabbit or a duck captures the essence of the dramatic technique that I am discussing here (and Rabkin is using in his discussion of the technique employed in Shakespeare's *Henry V*). Both Shakespeare and Marlowe tempt us to choose a single perspective and not always the same one, but we know that as soon as we do, we are falsifying the truth.

Chapter 5

"For a Tricksy Word / Defy the Matter": The Influence of *The Jew of Malta* on *The Merchant of Venice*

I

Despite Geoffrey Bullough's declaration in 1957 that *The Jew of Malta* was "one of Shakespeare's major sources in developing the character of the Jew in *The Merchant of Venice*,"[1] with a single exception, the influence of Marlowe's play on Shakespeare's has never been obvious. For the most part, Bullough's description of the sources contains examples of neither correspondences nor parallels but vague, generalized similarities[2] and forced links.[3] Consequently, like many other source hunters eager to validate their efforts, Bullough is left to assert rather than demonstrate that the "sources" he discusses are crucial to the connections between the two plays.[4] At the conclusion of his observations, Bullough's vagueness,[5] apart from reinforcing the tenuousness of his claims, underlines the difficulties all scholars and critics have had establishing definite sources and clear lines of influence between the two plays.

The origin of these difficulties is clear. Like other scholars, Bullough focuses primarily on the connection between *The Jew of Malta* and Shylock. But establishing this connection is seriously impeded by the absence of any evidence that could tell us how Shakespeare's initial audiences responded to Shylock. As a stage Jew, was Shylock understood as a type or an antitype? To what degree was he played seriously and to what degree for laughs? I pointed out in the introductory chapter that Charles Edelman has demonstrated that "there is no reliable contemporary information whatsoever"[6] about the first Shylock. Consequently, no means exist to determine that "Shylock must have conformed to a particular theatrical tradition, or that he must have been played in a certain way."[7] As I shall argue, the differences between Barabas and Shylock as Jews give additional support to this view.

The one parallel that seems indisputable and confirms Shakespeare's familiarity with *The Jew of Malta* is registered in Bullough's account when he states, "Shakespeare has taken over from Marlowe the Jew's confusion between love for money and of his daughter": [8]

> O my girl,
> My gold, my fortune, my felicity,
> Strength to my soul, death to mine enemy;

> Welcome, the first beginner of my bliss!
> O Abigail, Abigail, that I had thee here too,
> Then my desires were fully satisfied.
> But I will practise thy enlargement thence:
> O girl! O gold! O beauty! O my bliss! *Hugs his bags.* (*The Jew of Malta*, II, i, 47–54)

> My daughter! O my ducats! O my daughter!
> Fled with a Christian! O my Christian ducats!
> Justice! The law! My ducats and my daughter! (*MV*, II, viii, 15–17)[9]

Always keenly attuned to verbal and situational ironies, Shakespeare apparently found the ironic confusion of values in Barabas's exclamations too effective to pass up. Thus, when he has Solanio mimic Shylock's reaction to Jessica's romantic flight with a portion of her father's money, he echoes Barabas's confusion. For the theatrical in-crowd that identified the Marlovian origins of Shylock's exclamations, Solanio's mimicry must have provided the pleasure of recognition and strengthened their sense of the connection between the two dramatists.

For Shakespeare, the echo seems to have been a way of undisguisedly establishing a link with a popular play without diminishing his own talents or belittling Marlowe's. Written in the wake of the deceased Marlowe, Shakespeare's allusion could be taken ideally as an acknowledgment of the comradeship among dramatists dedicated to advancing the quality of the plays being produced within a swiftly evolving Elizabethan dramatic tradition. But probably the chief reason was more practical. If Shakespeare's play was composed in 1594, the year that the Queen's Jewish doctor Roderigo Lopez was brought to trial and executed, then it may have been written to capitalize on that sensationalized event as well as on the continuing popularity of *The Jew of Malta* which was being revived also in 1594. *The Merchant of Venice*'s ties with Marlowe could only have enhanced its chances for becoming popular and, thus, commercially successful. Certainly Shakespeare knew that any reminder of Marlowe would hold some commercial value in attracting audiences, beginning with the parallelism of the titles. Given Marlowe's known excellence as a dramatist and the continuing popularity of his plays, Shakespeare would be seen as a playwright who consciously linked himself with high standards in dramaturgy and with a sure source of entertainment. As scholars and critics have long acknowledged, Shakespeare's business sense and aesthetic concerns as a playwright blended harmoniously. Less frequently realized is Marlowe's role in providing his fellow dramatist with the inspiration for promoting these dual interests.

Lawrence Danson remarks that the difference between the two plays' confusion of love for money and love for a daughter points up the two playwrights' essentially different artistic aims. In Barabas's speech the satire is aimed directly at the speaker, who is a Jew; in Solanio's speech

> the satire is also aimed at the speaker—but he is a Christian acting (better perhaps than he intends) the part of a merciless Jew. The relative crudeness of Solanio's mimicry … cuts in two directions, forcing us toward a complicated response simultaneously to the Jew and to the Christian mediator.[10]

Shylock's phrase, "My ducats and my daughter" evokes the following comment from A.R. Braunmuller: "By inserting 'and' into the alliterative series, Shakespeare moves from Marlowe's equation of daughter and money to a more complicated sense of the money-lender's loss: daughter *and* money rather than daughter *as* money."[11] Whether we agree with the details of Danson and Braunmuller's interpretations, we can concur with their implication that Shakespeare's situational complexity is thicker. Thus, in recognizing how Shakespeare's lines were in fact influenced by Marlowe, we understand that the echo reveals itself not as simple imitation or parody but as a catalyst in the heightening of Shakespeare's creative sensibility to a complex use of situation and language, including the latter's comic possibilities: "Fled with a Christian! O my Christian ducats!" The self-denigrating, ironic confusion of values in Barabas becomes in Shakespeare's play an equally self-denigrating, ironic commentary but on both Solanio's unfeeling harshness in his hatred of Shylock and Shylock's unfeeling harshness in his anger toward his daughter's departure. Like Barabas, neither Solanio nor Shylock possesses the ability to see from someone else's perspective and, hence, feel any sympathy. If Barabas's confusion of values contains less serious irony, it is because the situation is more agreeable and contains little tension: Abigail has just retrieved her father's money; as a result, Barabas exults in his good fortune and in her success as its chief instrument. But, also, Barabas demonstrates what we have already come to understand about him: he does not prize that which is non-material, human, and emotional—in this instance, Abigail's devotion. Instead, he champions material possessions, arrived at through a clever, rational means—that is, his gold regained through cunning. In fact, throughout the play, he revels in his means even more than in his gains.

In trying to account for the difficulties in determining the influence of Marlowe's play on Shakespeare's, Maurice Charney has suggested the following psychological schematic:

> It is as if Shakespeare were trying to conceal the intensity of his own indebtedness to Marlowe, as if he were trying to prove that, although he could not rival Marlowe on his own ground, he could explore areas of dramatic awareness in which Marlowe would never dare to venture.[12]

The speculative nature of this scenario makes its content difficult either to confirm or deny. It is certainly true that Marlowe did not inhibit Shakespeare's creative individuality but, rather, provided sparks to set it ablaze. Unlike Bullough, Charney senses the strong differences between the two plays and, to his credit, tries to account for them. More recently, James Shapiro has affirmed what, as he acknowledges, other critics before him have noticed: that the influence of Marlowe on Shakespeare in *The Merchant of Venice* is not restricted to *The Jew of Malta* but includes *Tamburlaine* as well.[13] This more complicated view of influence not only tells us that there are at least two Marlovian sources for *The Merchant of Venice*, but, more important, it forces us to acknowledge that there are differences in the *kinds* of influence from Marlowe. Consequently, in attempting to define relationships between the two plays, we need first to understand the complexity of Marlowe's influence on the play. We can do this by examining the self-imposed restrictions of Shakespeare's focus on the Marlovian texts, regardless of whether the restrictions appear voluntary or involuntary, and by taking stock of the differences in the types of Marlovian influence revealed in *The Merchant of Venice*.

I have already demonstrated that Marlowe's influence on Shakespeare could manifest itself in a focus exclusively on style rather than on content or on a combination of style and content. There is no set pattern that describes how Marlowe's influence characteristically took hold of Shakespeare's imagination—that is, what elements he accepted and rejected and how many types of influence would reveal themselves in a single work. Nor is there a guarantee that once an influence took hold, especially a stylistic influence, it would remain fixed and not be developed or transformed, ultimately to incorporate Shakespeare's own individuality. As I have demonstrated in the discussions of other plays, Shakespeare shows himself primarily interested in the theatrical and literary techniques of Marlowe that made him a successful commercial playwright, and not in Marlowe, the Cambridge intellectual reflecting and moralizing on serious issues. Also, as I suggested in the introductory chapter, the impression a Marlovian production makes on Shakespeare can range from specific to general, emotional to intellectual, superficial to deep, tangible to intangible, and from an influence dimly known to one consciously realized. *The Merchant of Venice* demonstrates both a focus on Marlowe's style that is definable and a generalized impression of *The Jew of Malta* that is only partially so.

II

Critics have pointed out that the language of the Prince of Morocco is identifiably Marlovian (in II, i, 24–38 and II, vii, 38–47), although the influence is from *Tamburlaine*, not from *The Jew of Malta*. To define this influence more specifically, let us examine some of Morocco's statements:

> Morocco: By this scimitar,
> That slew the Sophy and a Persian prince
> That won three fields of Sultan Solyman,
> I would o'erstare the sternest eyes that look,
> Outbrave the heart most daring on the earth,
> Pluck the young sucking cubs from the she-bear,
> Yea, mock the lion when 'a roars for prey,
> To win thee, lady [Portia]. (*MV*, II, i, 24–31)

In this passage, Shakespeare captures the norm of hyperbolic intensity (27–28), the childlike boastfulness (25–30), and the proud name-dropping of exotic persons, titles, and places (25–26) typical of the assertions of Marlowe's warrior leader.[14] The phrase "By this scimitar, / That slew ..." is reminiscent of Tamburlaine's "By this my sword that conquered Persia" and the line that follows, "Thy fall [Bajazeth's] shall make me famous through the world" (1 *Tamburlaine*, III, iii, 82–83), a declaration no less vain than Morocco's vaunting. In addition, the parallel periodic phrasing (25–26), the regular, hard stresses and absence of caesuras (27–28), and the use of repeated word sounds (25–26) and onomatopoeia (29) all recall Marlowe's attempts to strengthen the forcefulness of his verse. The exaggerated portrayal of a savage nature red in tooth and claw (29–30), although less cosmological than Tamburlaine's usual declamations and pronouncements involving nature, nevertheless energizes the poetic lines in a fashion similar to that of Marlowe. It is easy to imagine that the playgoing audiences of the late sixteenth century, eagerly receptive to oral language, thrilled to Shakespeare's poetic lines of heightened energy much as they thrilled to Marlowe's.

The following two passages illustrate the influence on Shakespeare of Marlowe's hyperbolic norm in an ecstatic vein. The speakers are praising the extraordinary power of two remarkable women—"divine Zenocrate" and "this mortal breathing saint," Portia—to convey their intense, religious-like admiration of them. Whereas Zenocrate is able to command the forces of nature in the cosmos, Portia holds sway over human admirers from the furthest reaches of the earth:

Tamburlaine: Apollo, Cynthia, and the ceaseless lamps
That gently looked upon this loathsome earth,
Shine downwards now no more, but deck the heavens
To entertain divine Zenocrate.
The crystal springs whose taste illuminates
Refinèd eyes with an eternal sight,
Like trièd silver runs through Paradise
To entertain divine Zenocrate. (2 *Tamburlaine*, II, iv, 18–25)

Morocco: From the four corners of the earth they come
To kiss this shrine, this mortal breathing saint.
The Hyrcanian deserts and the vasty wilds
Of wide Arabia are as throughfares now
For princes to come view fair Portia.
The watery kingdom, whose ambitious head
Spits in the face of heaven, is no bar
To stop the foreign spirits, but they come
As o'er a brook to see fair Portia. (*MV*, II, vii, 39–47)

The two passages demonstrate that, without using the same details (apart from a metaphor of water), Shakespeare has caught the lofty, ornate style and tone of Marlowe—the emphatic rhythms, rhetorical repetitions, and elevated language; and the formal grandeur with its awesome spatial sweep. As usual, Shakespeare's individuality shows itself in creating action and intensity through dramatic situations ("kiss, "view," "spits," and "come") and Marlowe's in the awe he creates through generalized description. Even so, the Shakespearean passage reveals Marlowe's influence at its flattering best.

In Morocco's verbal out-Tamburlaining of Tamburlaine, the second passage also reveals Shakespeare injecting an element of comic exaggeration.[15] The dramatist gives us a royal lover whose immodest, effusive manner of speaking seems always to be mirthfully over the top. I believe that the comedy here resides in the way Morocco expresses himself rather than in his actions as a suitor and, as such, is not intended as mockery of Tamburlaine's behavior as a warrior hero. The Prince's extravagance serves Shakespeare's need for the character to seem less attractive than Bassanio and, at the same time, different from the other suitors. Moreover, to give Morocco's language a humorous edge well suits the genre of romantic comedy within which Shakespeare is working. The difference between viewing the Prince as a figure of comedy and a figure of parody comes clear if we look at *The Alchemist* and briefly compare Ben Jonson's portrayal of Sir Epicure Mammon with Shakespeare's of Morocco. Sir Epicure has the oversized heroic proportions of a Tamburlaine and the same image of himself as a titan out to transform the world. Morocco has no such grandiose heroic hopes; he is simply a lover who, in the manner of Tamburlaine, uses high astounding terms immoderately and incongruously in an effort to impress Portia. Jonson is able to make Sir Epicure into a parody of Tamburlaine because he adopts the Marlovian figure's strongest characteristic, an all-encompassing ambition, thereby creating an unmistakable behavioral similarity. The effectiveness of the parody depends upon the familiarity of Jonson's audiences with the superhuman actions of Marlowe's Scythian warlord and the exaggerated behavior of those in the many imitations that followed.[16]

In order to clarify further the distinction between imitation and parody, it might be helpful to address the functions of parody more generally in Shakespeare. What we see in *The Merchant of Venice* is an imitation of Tamburlaine's style and tone tinged with humor, not a parody of them. I say this because, even as we smile at Morocco's comic extremes, we are awed by Shakespeare's imaginative fireworks in portraying them. Parody is usually less benign. In fact, we normally associate it with an imitation that deflates the original, a lowering in our estimation of something or someone by a person out to show his or her superiority. We know, too, that almost everything and everyone can be parodied and that the effect ranges from lighthearted silliness to serious vitriol. Shakespeare tends to be lightly comic in his parodies. In *As You Like It*, there are many instances of parody, all lightly comic—for example, in the songs (in II, v, 1–7 and 34–40 where the idealization of the pastoral life is subverted by Jaques's "ducdame" spoof) and in Touchstone's response (III, ii, 97–109) to Orlando's verses to Rosalind (III, ii, 85–92). I have already mentioned in the introductory chapter that Shakespeare parodies Tamburlaine's "Holla, ye pampered jades of Asia! / What, can ye draw but twenty miles a day" (2 *Tamburlaine*, IV, iii, 1–2) when, in 2 *Henry IV*, Pistol says, "Shall pack-horses / And hollow pampered jades of Asia, / Which cannot go but thirty mile a-day, / Compare with Caesars ..." (II, iv, 148–51). This is the purest instance of Shakespeare's parodying of Marlowe throughout his works. Here, Shakespeare exaggerates Tamburlaine's already exaggerated sentiment. The effect is a comic undercutting of Marlovian hyperbole, and, at the same time, paradoxically, an affirmation of the popularity of Marlowe's Scythian conqueror. Linda Hutcheon points out that parody "both legitimizes and subverts that which it parodies."[17] Indeed, parody affirms the widespread familiarity and even popularity of its subject at the same time that it undercuts the subject. This is certainly true of the example cited from 2 *Henry IV*. Oddly enough, parody has much the same *effect* as the language of Philo at the beginning of *Antony and Cleopatra* (I, i, 1–13) where the majesty of the language establishes Antony's stature as the "triple pillar" (I, i, 12) of the world and a hero even as the content of it criticizes and tries to diminish him.

In *The Merry Wives of Windsor*, Evans in effect parodies Marlowe's lyric "Come Live With Me And Be My Love" when he sings,

> "To shallow rivers, to whose falls
> Melodious birds sing madrigals;
> There will we make our peds of roses.
> And a thousand fragrant posies.
> To shallow—"
> Mercy on me, I have a great disposition to cry.
> "Melodious birds sing madrigals,—
> Whenas I sat in Pabylon,—
> And a thousand vagram posies.
> To shallow—" (III, i, 16–25)

Here is an instance of parody in which the comic butt is more Evans than Marlowe. But, as in the case of the previous example of parody, it affirms the popularity of the original work rather than simply making it an object of ridicule.[18] Even at his most egotistical, Shakespeare never declines into mean-spiritedness. In echoing or in parodying Marlowe, he acknowledges candidly the imaginative impact of his contemporary's art. In addition, by providing reminders of Marlowe's works, he effectively calls them to mind as a standard of measurement. He thereby induces his audience to take stock of his own inventiveness, distinctiveness, and excellence as a writer.

Evidently, by the time of *The Merchant of Venice*, Shakespeare found a way to link himself openly and without anxiety with England's best known playwright. The characterization of Morocco allows Shakespeare to suggest that he feels able to match Marlowe's achievement and, yet, by virtue of the very different genre, manifest his artistic individuality—all the while tacitly acknowledging the continuing impact of the two *Tamburlaine* plays as an influence. The truth is that Shakespeare did not have to invoke Marlowe specifically in creating Morocco. That he did so tells us, among other things, that he is not ungrateful for the association.

In illustrating with Morocco that he has the ability to transform a popular Marlovian figure to suit his own purposes, Shakespeare anticipates his similar, focused emulation of a contemporary's major dramatic achievement in *The Winter's Tale*. There, he acknowledges that he is writing a type of play that is not currently in fashion (*WT*, IV, i, 9–14); in particular, he is not writing plays such as the "glistering" (*WT*, IV, i, 14) city comedies of Ben Jonson—"the freshest things now reigning" (*WT*, 4, i, 13). But, by creating Autolycus, his version of the rogue figure found in Jonsonian city comedies, he proves that he can portray this type of character and vie with Jonson's achievement. The parallel between Shakespeare's adaptation of a popular dramatic figure of Marlowe and Jonson prompts three observations that bear on the workings of influence: first, Shakespeare understands clearly the degree of control he has in absorbing influence from Marlowe and Jonson; second, he is fully conscious of both writers as major forces in shaping the course of drama—especially, the standards of popular innovation that each manifests; third, he is strongly aware of his own image as a major dramatist contributing to the course of drama because, in adapting the figures of Morocco and Autolycus, he not only reminds his audiences of what his fellow playwrights have done but also alerts them to what he is doing that is different. Rather than denigrating either Marlowe or Jonson as a rival, Shakespeare admits each as a potential model (to be sure, marking the boundaries more sharply in *The Winter's Tale* than in *The Merchant of Venice*). In the process, he undergoes a self-definition and self-fashioning that, early and late in his career, provide valuable insight into the mechanics of his assimilation of influence.

Both Nicholas Brooke[19] and (after him) Shapiro[20] suggest the possibility of still another instance of Marlovian stylistic influence when they posit the arrogance of the Guise in *The Massacre At Paris* as the forerunner of the Prince of Arragon's braggadocio. With this claim, however, the lines of influence for me begin to blur. I am not as convinced as Brooke and Shapiro that Shakespeare required a specific source for the Prince's overbearing, superior manner. Arrogance is not a characteristic that of necessity lends itself to reliance on a source. The well-established literary tradition of the *miles gloriosus* would have provided either writer with sufficient models had he needed one. Moreover, if one were to assume that Marlowe did influence Shakespeare in his conception of the Prince's braggadocio, Shakespeare need not have gone to the Guise to find an example. Barabas's contempt for his fellow Jews conveys a similar attitude:

> See the simplicity of these base slaves,
> Who for the villains have no wit themselves,
> Think me to be a senseless lump of clay.
> That will with every water wash to dirt!
> No, Barabas is born to better chance,
> And framed of finer mould than common men,
> That measure naught but by the present time. (I, ii, 218–24)

With the final three lines of this passage, one might compare Arragon's:

> I will not choose what many men desire
> Because I will not jump with common spirits
> And rank me with the barbarous multitudes. (II, ix, 30–32)

Because of the similar context of the word "common" in each passage, I would be less hard pressed to claim Barabas as a source for Arragon than I am to assent to the Guise as a source. Even so, Arragon's moralizing mode (II, ix, 36–48), a major element in characterizing the Prince as pompous and overbearing, is not a trait found in either Barabas or the Guise. This example reveals the difficulties of the outer limits of stylistic influence—in particular, the inability to forge a conclusion with scholarly confidence, because, finally, the trait resists analytical examination and the establishment of a definite causal relationship.

Shapiro feels, too, that, because the "voices of Morocco and Arragon are exposed and dismissed,"[21] Shakespeare is asserting through parody "his command over Marlowe's style, confirming his power to pluck out the heart of its mystery, to subdue it to his own artistic design."[22] But, even if we were to include Arragon with Morocco, no *necessary* connection exists between the exposure and dismissal of the two princes and Shakespeare's employment of Marlovian language. I would go even further: the plot details and the language used in portraying Arragon and Morocco evolve from two distinct categories of aesthetic consideration—the one, standard elements of a romance plot and the other, elevated language appropriate to the rank and different personalities of the suitors. As a result and as I observed above, the Marlovian language of Morocco can be understood as salutary in its imaginative reach and not simply denigrating to its progenitor because of its comic dimension. From this affirmative perspective, Morocco's Marlovian language reveals the degree to which Shakespeare was captivated not only by his fellow playwright's style and tone but by his overall sanctioning of bold linguistic inventiveness. Given Shakespeare's own keen interest in experimenting with language and his self-consciousness about his style, especially in the plays of the early and middle 1590s, it is certainly no surprise that in *The Merchant of Venice* Marlowe's style inspires him both in a particular way—in fashioning the language and thus the character of Morocco—and in a general way—in granting him a license to create for himself fresh opportunities for playing with language. Surely, one of Shakespeare's delights throughout *The Merchant of Venice*, speaker and action apart, is with the sheer variety of language he finds himself able to display and the distinctness of the many types—whether it be language of metaphorical excess (e.g., Salerio in I, i, 8–14); comic, dramatizing language (e.g., Gratiano in I, i, 79–102); sententious, moralizing language (e.g., as Bassanio is deliberating which casket to choose in III, ii, 73–107); easy, sassy wit (e.g., Portia in I, ii); language of prolix literalness and plodding rationality (e.g., Shylock in I, iii, 15–26); comic garbling (e.g., by the Gobbos in II, ii); or antiphonal lyricism (e.g., Lorenzo and Jessica in V, i, 1–68).

To summarize: once we understand that Marlowe's influence is both particular and general, then Morocco's language and tone can be considered the undisguised results of both the playwright's infatuation with Marlowe's style and the declaration of imaginative freedom it signifies to him, whereas Morocco's exposure and dismissal can be considered a function of the workings of the romance plot.[23] If for Shakespeare the Prince's language and tone belong to a different frame of reference from his exposure and dismissal, his words may be understood as a tacit tribute to Marlowe's distinctiveness and effectiveness, not simply a parodic diminishment or burlesque of them. By the same token, if in using Marlovian language Shakespeare demonstrates "his command over Marlowe's style," as Shapiro asserts, it may well be that, spurred on by Marlowe's linguistic inventiveness, he is exulting in his own creative powers, not vindictively (and pointlessly) thumbing his nose at the style of a now dead rival. To be sure, the two desires are not mutually exclusive; or they can at least be perceived as not being so. But since in Shakespeare's works I find no indication of a harshness or severity in his reaction to Marlowe, much less any personal enmity, I have the strong sense that his colleague's influence was generally salubrious.

The verbal echo from *The Jew of Malta* discussed in the previous section and the style of Morocco are not the only manifestations in the play of Shakespeare's linguistic sources of inspiration from Marlowe. Marlowe undoubtedly played a crucial role throughout *The Merchant of Venice* in unleashing Shakespeare's remarkably strong awareness of language, both its uses and abuses. The eminently functional Solanio reveals the playwright's level of consciousness about his own linguistic means when, animatedly to Salerio, he exclaims: "But it is true, without any slips of prolixity or crossing the plain highway of talk, that the good Antonio, the honest Antonio—O that I had a title good enough to keep his name company" (III, i, 10–13). Other examples collectively suggest the degree to which Shakespeare sustains an awareness of language beyond that of his characters: Portia says to Nerissa, "Good sentences, and well pronounced" (I, ii, 10), and, soon after, about her English suitor Falconbridge, "He hath neither Latin, French, nor Italian; and you will come into the court and swear that I have a poor pennyworth in the English. He is a proper man's picture, but alas! who can converse with a dumb show" (I, ii, 65–69)? Later, she tells Bassanio: "I speak too long, but 'tis to peize the time, / To eke it and to draw it out in length, / To stay you from election" (III, ii, 22–24). Bassanio warns Gratiano:

> Thou art too wild, too rude, and bold of voice—
> Parts that become thee happily enough
> And in such eyes as ours appear not faults;
> But where thou art not known, why there they show
> Something too liberal. Pray thee take pain
> To allay with some cold drops of modesty
> Thy skipping spirit, lest through thy wild behavior
> I be misconstered in the place I go to,
> And lose my hopes.

Gratiano: Signior Bassanio, hear me:
> If I do not put on a sober habit,
> Talk with respect, and swear but now and then,
> Wear prayer books in my pocket, look demurely—
> Nay more, while grace is saying hood mine eyes
> Thus with my hat, and sigh and say 'amen,'
> Use all the observance of civility
> Like one well studied in a sad ostent
> To please his grandam, never trust me more. (II, ii, 169–85)

Having chosen the right casket and having been given a ring as an assurance that he is loved in return, Bassanio speaks ecstatically to Portia:

> Madam, you have bereft me of all words.
> Only my blood speaks to you in my veins,
> And there is such confusion in my powers

> As, after some oration fairly spoke
> By a belovèd prince, there doth appear
> Among the buzzing pleasèd multitude,
> Where every something being blent together
> Turns to a wild of nothing, save of joy
> Expressed and not expressed. (III, ii, 175–83)

In an exchange with Lancelot, Lorenzo tells him:

> How every fool can play upon the word! I think the best grace of wit will shortly turn into silence, and discourse grow commendable in none only but parrots. Go in, sirrah; Bid them prepare dinner.

Launcelot: That is done, sir. They have all stomachs.

Lorenzo: Goodly Lord, what a wit-snapper are you! Then bid them prepare for dinner.

Launcelot: That is done too, sir. Only 'cover' is the word.

Lorenzo: Will you cover then, sir?

Launcelot: Not so, sir, neither! I know my duty.

Lorenzo: Yet more quarrelling with occasion! Wilt thou show the whole wealth of thy wit in an instant? I pray thee understand a plain man in his plain meaning: go to thy fellows, bid them cover the table, serve in the meat, and we will come to dinner.

Launcelot: For the table, sir, it shall be served in; for the meat sir, it shall be covered; for your coming in to dinner, sir, why let it be as humor and conceits shall govern. *Exit Clown [Lancelot]*

Lorenzo: O dear discretion, how his words are suited!
> The fool hath planted in his memory
> An army of good words; and I do know
> A many fools that stand in better place,
> Garnished like him, that for a tricksy word
> Defy the matter. (III, v, 39–63)

The sensitivity to language as style rather than as content begins with Gratiano's language gag in the opening scene (I, i, 86–118) and continues throughout the play. So also does the sense that language creates true as well as illusory realities. Clearly, Shakespeare has not only taken notice of Marlowe's statement about language in the Prologue to *Tamburlaine* and the inventiveness evident in his plays and poetry, but he has also successfully run with the ball that he feels Marlowe has tossed to him. I hasten to add that word play in Shakespeare is not exclusively a Marlovian influence; it is everywhere apparent in Shakespeare's literary and theatrical environment. But Marlowe has certainly provided a strong sanction, one Shakespeare could not have overlooked.

Lorenzo's statement to Jessica that Lancelot Gobbo will "for a tricksy word / Defy the matter" (III, v, 62–63) can be applied metadramatically to Shakespeare in *The Merchant of Venice* when he indulges in a play with language. It would be difficult to imagine that Shakespeare was not aware that Lorenzo's words could be used to describe himself. Moreover, he well demonstrates the psychological elements of impulsive abandon and intense engagement which characterize such moments of unrestrained pleasure, and not only in *The Merchant of Venice*. Lorenzo's profile of linguistic self-indulgence also helps us to understand how Shakespeare could become caught up in the stylistics of language to the exclusion of matters of character, action, and content and how he could therefore become engrossed in Marlowe's style without, at the same time, wanting to parody it. We have just seen that the Marlovian language of the Prince of Morocco can signify both the joy of a particular discovery and, in the context of the other styles of language in the play, one strong source of inspiration and support for Shakespeare's own irrepressible linguistic inventiveness. Beginning with the second speech of the play, the inventiveness of the language throughout the drama draws attention to itself. Salerio is trying to understand Antonio's melancholy:

> Your mind is tossing on the ocean,
> There where your argosies with portly sail—
> Like signiors and rich burghers on the flood,
> Or as it were, the pageants of the sea—
> Do overpeer the petty traffickers
> That cursy to them, do them reverence,
> As they fly by them with their woven wings. (I, i, 8–14)

The imagery of the mind as a ship, though it may strike us now as being overwrought, is meant to be noticed and admired, as is the creator of it. In using Marlowe so undisguisedly as his model for Morocco, in playing with several different modes of language throughout the play, and in having characters show their awareness of the power of language, Shakespeare draws attention to his own creative powers and, by an implication perhaps more ours than his, his advances over Marlowe—even in death his chief contemporary standard of measurement.

III

The general influence of *The Jew of Malta* on *The Merchant of Venice* is, understandably, more difficult to discuss. As I indicated in the opening chapter, Shakespeare's play contains what Nicholas Brooke has called a "general reminiscence of a specific play [*The Jew of Malta*]."[24] Brooke gives as his only illustration "the language of Shylock, and the use made of him to criticize the hypocrisy of a Christian society."[25] I do not know what Brooke means by "the language of Shylock." Although some sententiousness is to be found in the words of both Barabas and Shylock and although both characters know how to call into service material from the Old Testament to support a point, no identifiable similarities in their manner of expression stand out.[26] Barabas indignantly asks a knight, "What? Bring you Scripture to confirm your wrongs" (I, ii, 113)? Yet, later, when a Jew tells Barabas to "remember Job" (I, ii, 182) and be patient in the face of the Christians' ruthlessness in demanding half of the Jews' wealth, with considerable irony on the part of Marlowe, Barabas denounces the Jew's admonition by invoking details of the story of Job to give biblical support (like the knight) to *his* position—one of defiance and protest (I, ii, 183–93). Shylock uses the story of Jacob and his uncle Laban's sheep from *Genesis* xxvii and xxx, 25–43, to justify lending money at interest, but, here as elsewhere, he uses details of the Bible in surroundings more public and with more impersonality and less self-consciousness than Barabas:

Shylock: A Daniel come to judgment! Yea, a Daniel!
                  O wise young judge, how I do honor thee! (IV, i, 221–22)

Barabas (to himself):
                  O thou, that with a fiery pillar led'st
                  The sons of Israel through the dismal shades,
                  Light Abraham's offspring, and direct the hand
                  Of Abigail this night; ... (II, i, 12–15)

In calling up particulars from the Old Testament, each figure associates himself with a trait common to the stereotype of the Jew. Evidently, for both writers the trait provided increased linguistic possibilities. No doubt Shakespeare was impressed by Marlowe's fashioning of this trait in Barabas and was either prompted to take artistic advantage of it or supported in his own movements in that direction. The more one examines the context of each character's use of biblical detail, the more certain one becomes of general rather than specific influence and the more divergent appear the artistic needs of the two plays, beginning with the differences in genre.

In addition, the content of the characters' language is dependent upon their situations and psychologies (insofar as they are dramatized) which, despite their common status as alien Jews, are very different. Barabas seeks power within society, whereas Shylock, less inclusively and less impersonally, seeks power over one person, Antonio.[27] Nor am I convinced that Shylock's criticism of "the hypocrisy of a Christian society" necessarily descended from Barabas's; it may just as well be that there is no influence, that, simply, the specifics of each character's immediate predicament triggered such criticism. It is nevertheless true that Shakespeare was familiar with Marlowe's play when he formulated the design of his own drama and that, consequently, Marlowe's criticism of Christian hypocrisy may have colored his own. But it is also true that he chose to make Shylock very different from Marlowe's conceptions of Barabas. I pluralize "conceptions" because, as critics have commonly noted, the Barabas of the first two acts of the play appears to be a more developed character than the comic, often caricaturized figure of the last three acts.[28] Neither conception is close to the more consistent conception of Shylock. But, if Marlowe did in fact exert an influence, from the first two acts Shakespeare may have learned generally or reaffirmed his understanding of how possible it is to invest a stock character with individualizing human traits, and from the last three how possible it is to invest a character with comic traits even when the seriousness of the context does not make it easy. Again, to extend the speculation and with an eye toward general rather than specific influence, I would suggest that Marlowe gave Shakespeare a precedent and thus a sense of ease about indulging his own desires for artistic flexibility and variation.

The following intertextual discussion of *The Jew of Malta* as an influence on

The Merchant of Venice is speculative, as all such discussions must be—but, I hope, probable rather than merely possible. It attempts to suggest some of what Shakespeare may have responded to as the play took hold of his imagination. In the Prologue to *The Jew of Malta*, Machevill suggests, as the play does not, that Barabas has acquired his money through Machiavellian means ("Which money was not got without my means"—Prologue, 32). In combination with the biblical suggestiveness of Barabas's name as an anti-Christ (specifically, a political revolutionary and a murderer), the Prologue prepares us to view the Jew as a stock villain capable of clever underhandedness and treachery. What we get is a more complicated, less stereotypical personality, a character whose true motives in shifting and remaining obscure prefigure Iago's.[29] In his second soliloquy, just after the merchants report to him the success of his ships, Barabas reveals the keen, wholly materialistic nature of a man thoroughly self-interested, devoid of emotional, moral, and spiritual values. He revels in his good fortune, confidently exclaiming, "What more may heaven do for earthly man / Than thus to pour out plenty in their [wealthy Jews'] laps" (I, i, 105–06). He then exults in the power over natural forces that "heaven" demonstrates in bestowing good fortune on wealthy Jewish merchants like himself:

> Ripping the bowels of the earth for them,
> Making the seas their servants, and the winds
> To drive their substance with successful blasts? (I, i, 107–9)

A twenty-first-century playgoer might feel that these lines are excessive, merely a superfluous expression of glee. But in their focus on effective power, they reflect a central interest of the play. Barabas goes on to ask cynically, "Who hateth me but for my happiness? / Or who is honour'd now but for his wealth" (I, i, 110–11)? The latter, more generalized sentiment corresponds to the bitingly ironic pronouncement in *Hero and Leander* "That Midas' brood shall sit in honour's chair" (474). In this shrewdly candid frame of mind, Barabas easily moves next into a criticism of Christian hypocrisy:

> Rather had I, a Jew, be hated thus,
> Than pitied in a Christian poverty;
> For I can see no fruits in all their faith,
> But malice, falsehood, and excessive pride,
> Which methinks fits not their profession. (I, i, 112–16)

Like Iago in his denial of the worth of the non-rational aspects of the human personality and his affirmation of the prudence and power of material wealth, Barabas adopts a perspective more single-mindedly rational than Shylock's. Barabas's surprising, fateful countertwist at the end of the play when he offers Ferneze his and Malta's freedom in exchange for money and the governorship (V, ii) bespeaks the ultimate impulse of irrationality that drives him, as well as Shylock and, for all his surface pragmatism and rationality, Iago. Barabas tells Ithamore:

First be thou void of these affections:
Compassion, love, vain hope, and heartless fear;
Be mov'd at nothing, see thou pity none. (II, iii, 171–73)

Clearly, Barabas lives by this extreme credo. Whereas Shylock can also be unrelentingly void of affections—say, about adhering to the details of the bond with Antonio—he does give us glimpses of a more sensitive nature. Shylock evokes a domestic picture in explaining the origin of the turquoise ring: "I had it of Leah when I was a bachelor" (III, i, 112–13), but immediately undermines it comically with the quantitative judgment, "I would not have given it for a wilderness of monkeys" (III, i, 113–14). The wit of the comment helps to undercut the sentimentality of his mention of the ring and Leah, for it plays upon Tubal's previous remark, "One of them [Antonio's creditors] showed me a ring that he had of your daughter for a monkey" (III, i, 109–10). At the end of the trial scene, Shylock says to Portia/Balthasar, "I pray you give me leave to go from hence. / I am not well" (IV, i, 393–94). In giving us a sense of the emotional defeat of the man, Shakespeare shows that Shylock is not utterly insensitive, indicating that his bitterness throughout the play ultimately bespeaks the lack of human mutuality in his life and is not derived from the frustrations of obtaining power through money. Significantly, he never presents to those who, like Antonio, are angry at his charging interest for loans, the argument that, as a Jew, he is excluded from owning property and, hence, limited in the means open to him for achieving economic well-being.[30] Thus, the playwright has called upon his audience to respond with some sympathy, however slight.

Barabas goes on to list other Jews who, internationally, have accumulated "more wealth by far than those that brag of faith" (I, i, 121), presenting an abbreviated catalogue of exotic names reminiscent of similar, extended catalogues in 1 *Tamburlaine*. Setting the wealth of Jews against the lack of wealth of Christians, he implies that money is the only source of power for Jews and that acquiring it is less hypocritical than a profession of faith by Christians who are, in reality, as much interested in establishing power through wealth as he is. He moves on to the subject of power as it is demonstrated by those Christians who, because they outnumber the Jews, inevitably become kings (I, i, 127–31). Implicit in his argument is the notion that the desire for power is indigenous to all human beings and that Jews are more open than Christians in acknowledging both their desire for and means of obtaining such power through material possessions. Barabas tells us that only Christians gain ultimate power as kings, either as a result of succession or by force. About the latter method, he moralizes realistically, "… nothing violent, / Oft have I heard tell, can be permanent" (I, i, 130–31). The play goes on to demonstrate the truth of this declaration and, ironically, Barabas himself becomes part of the very machinery of the coupling of violence and instability. He closes this section of the speech by approving the status quo ("make Christians kings, / That thirst so much for principality"—I, i, 132–33) if it allows "a peaceful rule" (I, i, 132). He then concludes the soliloquy by affirming his bond with his daughter. But, as commentators have pointed out, he undermines this fatherly sentiment by using an analogy to Agamemnon and his daughter Iphigen that, unfortunately, turns out to be prophetic; Agamemnon's bond consisted not of affection but of a willingness to sacrifice Iphigen for his own ends, and Barabas demonstrates the same willingness. Thus, even before he sacrifices his daughter, the analogy works ironically to suggest that his moral stature is no better than that of the Christians he has just been criticizing.

To complicate matters, Barabas is an alien among the Christians and for more reasons than simply a difference in religion. For a moment, one might be inclined to be sympathetic to him because, in the face of Ferneze's unjust demands, he seems an underdog and a valid spokesman for the mightily abused. But we soon see that he is also an alien among the Jews as his defiance of them (I, ii, 161–214) and scorn for them (I, ii, 214–21) make clear. Thus, what at first seems the result of cultural conditions and evil political machinations imposed on him, later comes to seem an ingrained psychological trait. Barabas is vehement in his spite, especially toward the Christians in the first two acts of the play, and we are made to feel some sympathy for him, because the Christians, the governor Ferneze in particular, are utterly ruthless in their self-serving materialism. But when his cunning turns unheroically diabolical and he uses his daughter, first, to secure his money and, then, unwittingly, to help arrange for the deaths of her true love, Don Mathias, and his rival in love, Lodowick, fascinated as we are by his cleverness, we disapprove of him morally. In our aesthetic approval of his means and our ethical disapproval of his ends, our attitude toward him is complexly ambivalent. Shakespeare must have also sensed the doubleness of this response and yet the degree of engagement it produced in an audience. In taking notice of it, he may have felt he had been given a license as playwright to make Shylock a mix of both sympathetic and unsympathetic characteristics, a figure, as it turns out, who has been controversial and not easily pigeonholed for the past four centuries. More generally, Marlowe's display of artistic freedom set before Shakespeare a model that encouraged and supported his desire to write a romantic comedy that would not fit snugly into that category, a play that firmly denies the limitations of generic designation.[31] Like Marlowe, then, on the face of it Shakespeare seems to accept traditions in characterization and genre but, in actuality, breaks the mold of traditional expectations to establish and sustain his audience's engagement.

Perhaps the most general and, yet, in its dramatic emphasis, the strongest influence of *The Jew of Malta* on *The Merchant of Venice* is in the portrayal of a Jew as an alien in a predominantly Christian culture.[32] What makes the influence general rather than specific are the important differences in the two figures' alien status. Whereas Barabas proves himself an alien among Christians, Jews, and Turks alike and set apart from, as he says, "common men" (I, ii, 220), almost as a hero might be,[33] Shylock seems an alien only among Christians and certainly no self-styled hero, inverted or otherwise. In his role as alien, he comes into conflict with a romantic tradition first embodied in Antonio's desire to aid Bassanio in winning the hand of Portia and then in the flight of his daughter. Through Shylock's differences with the Christians, Shakespeare creates a tension with deeper, more disturbing resonances than those produced by Barabas's experiences as an alien. Shylock stands in opposition to the non-material values affirmed by Elizabethan romantic conventions and to the non-rational consciousness that fosters them. This is not to say that these conventions do not encompass material values; witness Bassanio's awareness that Portia "is a lady richly left"(I, i, 161) and Jessica's departure with a "casket" (II, vi, 33) of "gold and jewels" (II, iv, 31) and some "ducats" (II, vi, 50). But these standard pragmatic accoutrements are not the essence of the romantic experience.[34] Barabas enhances his alien status through his words and evil machinations but, in fact, acts out and represents power through materialism, the chief value of the very society he claims to be alienated from. Perhaps Barabas's self-characterization as an alien is most strongly supported by his displays of motiveless malignity; it creates an ambiguity about his actions that makes him appear different from everyone else in the play.

The same is not true of Shylock. Shylock is an antagonist more than an alien, a foil to the conventions of romance in the play. He knows how to needle and rile people, and he knows how to slide off a hook. Even his daughter is disdainful of his "manners" (II, iii, 19); she tells Lancelot: "Our house is hell, and thou a merry devil / Didst rob it of some taste of tediousness" (II, iii, 3–4). In his animus toward Antonio, Shylock tells Solanio and Salerio:

He hath disgraced me and hindered me half a million, laughed at my losses, mocked at my gains, scorned my nation, thwarted my bargains, cooled my friends, heated mine enemies—and what's his reason? I am a Jew. (III, i, 50–54)

But that is not his reason. Beginning with a stream of exaggerations that builds to a climax of illogic, Shylock takes refuge in a generalization, a non sequitur, thereby diverting attention from the major conflict between the materialistic mode of existence which he stands for and which Antonio, merchant though he be, stands against. What makes the speech affecting is its emotional unity—an anguished cry of pain, anger, and frustration. But if it is the cry of one who objects to the identity society has given him—an identity even more readily recognized in modern rather than early modern times, it is not the identity the society of this play has given Shylock. When, for example, does anyone in the play scorn his nation? In effect, Shylock has shown that he too can "For a tricksy word / Defy the matter" (III, v, 62–63). In this case, the words are so deceptively tricksy that they seem, in changing the frame of reference, to have hit upon more important "matter," the woes of the victimized alien. To be sure, there are actors and directors that have understood the speech as seriously, even solemnly authoritative and, with it, have attempted to make Shylock into a figure of sympathy. But, in doing so, they have had to close their eyes to the ironies that an Elizabethan audience, more accustomed to shifting modes of language than we are, was attuned to.[35] The speech continues as if Shylock were uttering an impassioned cry for tolerance, incorporating, not without tremendous irony and hypocrisy, the standard argument that human beings have so much in common, although they differ in superficial ways, that it is hard to see how they can persecute one another. But it ends up as mere speechifying. After asserting that we all have good qualities in common (54–63), Shylock adds that we all have bad qualities in common as well, and he is going to prove it by persecuting Antonio (63–67). The words reveal a Shylock who, with clever and amusing illogic, is deliberately invoking a familiar perception of the victimized alien to attempt to draw pity toward himself and to justify any vengeance he might take. He tries to create an emotional smoke screen in order to legitimize his role as antagonist. But, as his daughter has already made clear, it is less his alien status as a Jew than his "manners" as a difficult human being that set him apart. The speech is called into service in post-Holocaust productions of *The Merchant of Venice* to help make Shylock the protagonist of the play—even though he appears in only five scenes and has fewer than four hundred lines of dialogue—and to make him into a figure of pity rather than, more detachedly, one of illogic. But, as we have seen, the speech, like the text as a whole, could just as well be understood as less sentimental than the superimposition of contemporary pro-Semitic feelings on it would suggest.[36]

That Shakespeare has Antonio stipulate at the close of the trial scene that Shylock become a Christian (IV, i, 384–85) has been taken as an act of mean-spiritedness. But such an interpretation, as I see it, runs counter to the genre of romantic comedy that the play has adopted. I read the act as an attempt to remove any stigma by the end of the play of Shylock's remaining, even superficially, an alien. In the mid 1590s, when the play was presumably written, there was, as everyone knows, little of what we understand as religious tolerance in Italy and England and only one road to heaven and salvation. So, by making Shylock take that road, Antonio is being merciful and, at the same time, promoting a sense of the thoroughly integrated society that the conventions of comedy and romance support. This resolution probably tells us more about the literary and theatrical traditions that are pressing on Shakespeare's consciousness than about his religious or political views, although critics certainly have not shown a consensus in their view of the goodness of Antonio's request.[37] By the same token, Marlowe's ironic portrayal of Barabas being hoisted with his own petar smacks of the literary notion of poetic justice rather than of a political statement, even if the success of Ferneze may strike us as an ugly political reality. In both cases, the playwrights have relied on literary conventions to achieve a superficial social harmony. Whether one can claim direct influence, this reliance on literary convention rather than on the conditions of life, not surprisingly, marks Shakespeare as a member of Christopher Marlowe's literary fraternity.

Marlowe's use of ambiguity to characterize Barabas's motives may or may not have specifically encouraged Shakespeare to shroud in ambiguity the causes of Antonio's melancholy. At the very least, however, Marlowe reinforced Shakespeare's lifelong interest in ambiguity as a major artistic device. Iago of course better represents than Antonio the line of descent from Barabas's ambiguous motivations. But, as we are sometimes able to conclude, Marlowe's immediate influence on Shakespeare can look less like Marlowe than influence that is more distant in time. And not only in the case of ambiguity. The language and tone of *Antony and Cleopatra* are more like those of *Tamburlaine* than are the language and tone of, say, *Henry V*, a play that bears the influence of the *Tamburlaine* plays and is written closer to the time that Marlowe's plays were composed. What this example reveals is how deep and abiding Marlowe's influence was and how willing, as he gained confidence in his work, Shakespeare was to build openly on the foundations of his predecessor.

One has the sense that Barabas's alien status as a Jew is regularly governed by theatrical artistic needs rather than by specifically didactic intentions. In calling up that status to serve those needs, Marlowe makes it neither an integral part of the Jew's psychology nor the pressures of his culture on him—especially as we move into the last three acts of the play. There, the focus of interest seems to be the machinations of Barabas as he goes from committing one unbelievable, heinous act of villainy to the next, beginning with the poisoning of his daughter and the convent of nuns and ending in his plot with Ferneze to destroy the Turks. More credibly, Shylock's alien nature is psychological in origin, for it has more to do with his self-dehumanization through his materialistic obsession than with his Jewishness—that is, than with his profession as usurer or his religion. One could argue that the obsession with acquiring and maintaining stability through concrete possessions is forced upon Shylock because of his alien status as a Jew. But the play does not present such an argument. In fact, given the values of the world of the play, we are led to understand that Shylock alienates himself by proving to be incapable of genuine, sustained human mutuality. He confuses his love for his daughter with his love for money (II, viii, 15–22), and he treats Tubal more as a servant than a friend (III, i, 73–122). We do not have enough information about his relationship with Leah to characterize that relationship. But our lack of information also tells us something about Shylock's sensibility. Neither Shylock nor Shakespeare seems much interested in the Jew's alienation as a social agent of power. The opposite is true of Marlowe who uses Barabas's alienation to explore the limits of power in the political workings of Malta. Thus, if Shakespeare were led to write a play about a Jew in an alien culture because of Marlowe's play, it must have been because of the popularity of a tale about an uncommon foreign figure and not because of an interest in the specific causes of the figure's alienation.

But *The Merchant of Venice* is not chiefly about an uncommon foreign figure. It is more centrally about Bassanio's fortunes as a romantic hero and about the merchant who puts his life in jeopardy to help advance those fortunes. Consequently, unlike Barabas, Shylock is not the protagonist of the play, although he is called into service as the chief antagonist to its romanticism to ensure the audience's engagement. Like Barabas, he is employed as an alien figure because of artistic needs rather than for didactic purposes or to enhance the realism of the play. This means, for example, that Shylock's spitefulness toward Antonio is necessary for the creation of tension, apart from how well motivated it may or may not be psychologically. That this principle dominates is revealed when an action is less well motivated psychologically—for instance, Shylock's change of mind in his decision to have a meal with the Christians.[38] Shakespeare needs to have Shylock out of the way so that Jessica can escape with Lorenzo and thereby promote one more romantic element in the play. He chooses this means instead of another because, presumably, it also enables him to provide the Jew with an opportunity for denouncing the "masques" (II, v, 28) and music of the Christians, both elements of romance. Here, to the death of romanticism, Shylock manages to widen the gap between himself and the Christians, emphatically demonstrating that he possesses a dour personality and is devoid of any sense of fun (II, v, 28–37).

In sum, I am suggesting that the influence of Marlowe's protagonist on Shakespeare's relates primarily to the artistic process that created Barabas as an alien rather than to the specific results of that process (the particular dramatic context and the individual characteristics and actions of Barabas). Dramatic necessity largely governs the status of both Barabas and Shylock as figures in contention with a predominantly Christian culture. Each playwright realizes the possibilities such figures offer for generating conflict and tension, and neither writer eliminates opportunities for complications by absolving the Christians of wrongdoing. Both playwrights also appear to recognize that the figure of a Jew in a hostile environment will encourage an audience to consider the ethics of social forces even as it becomes engrossed in the powerful elements of the exchanges of enmity between individuals. Moreover, each dramatist makes use of a father-daughter relationship to suggest defects in the sensibilities of figures overly enmeshed in the politics of materialism. We are in effect called upon to look at each figure publicly, as part of a social context, and, privately, as an individual, although Shakespeare draws a figure who is more psychologically compelling and Marlowe one who is grander, more "astounding" (1 *Tamburlaine*, Prologue, 5). Finally, if Marlowe's use of ambiguity in characterizing Barabas seems less extensive than Shakespeare's use of it in characterizing Shylock, as well as Antonio, they are both refining it as a theatrical device. As we saw in the last chapter, like Marlowe, Shakespeare is intent upon exploring the possibilities of ambiguity as a means for engaging and holding our attention. Both dramatists sense that ambiguity complicates our responses by stretching the limits of our multiconsciousness, our capacity for entertaining multiple perspectives at the same time, during the course of the play as well as later, upon reflection.

From an intertextual study of *The Jew of Malta* and *The Merchant of Venice* what is visible and, at the same time, not so visible is that Marlowe's chief influence on Shakespeare lay in emboldening him to discover and develop creative resources in himself, especially those responsible for the artistry of his play. That these resources set him on a path very different from that of Marlowe does not diminish the latter's impact. As we have seen, Shakespeare did not borrow from Marlowe's play the particulars of either character or action. Instead, in combination with the accumulation of influences that he felt from other of Marlowe's writings, both the specific and the general influences, he allowed Marlowe's free play of imagination in *The Jew of Malta* to inspire his own in *The Merchant of Venice*. This is perhaps nowhere more apparent than in Shakespeare's innovations in the genre of romantic comedy. He saw that Marlowe stretched the boundaries of tragedy by incorporating elements of farce into the plot; he followed suit by introducing dark elements into his romantic comedy. In effect, Marlowe became for him the prototype of the artistic imagination in healthy operation. As such, Shakespeare better understood how to exercise and give form and definition to his own strong, individual talent.

In experiencing the *The Jew of Malta*, Shakespeare was alerted to aspects of dramatic writing that he then had to decide whether to accept or reject—as, for example, Marlowe's rhetorically engaging but psychologically unrealistic characterizations, which he rejected. There is no way of knowing how Marlowe's classical university training affected Shakespeare—whether he felt any of Ben Jonson's inferiority and defensiveness in the face of university learning and, consequently, compensated for his lack of advanced schooling by strutting his talent for playing with language. In any case, Shakespeare's awareness that one might "for a tricksy word / Defy the matter" (*MV*, III, v, 62–63) has to be credited in part to the influence of Marlowe's strong interest in the powers of language, an interest undoubtedly nourished by his reading at Cambridge and his translating of Ovid and Lucan. To be sure, Shakespeare did not try to imitate his fellow playwright, but he did perceive and absorb Marlowe's freedom of invention. It is difficult not to conclude that he was thereby made more aware of his own artistic choices and, as we have consistently seen in our previous discussions, was thereby better able to raise his own talent and commercial success to greater heights.

Notes

1   Geoffrey Bullough, *Narrative and Dramatic Sources of Shakespeare*, Vol. I (New York: Columbia University Press, 1957), 454. More recently, Stephen Greenblatt made a similar claim, also without offering evidence to support it: "… in creating the usurer Shylock, Shakespeare borrowed heavily from Marlowe" ("Shakespeare's Leap," *The New York Times Magazine*, September 12, 2004, 53). The article is an adaptation of Greenblatt's chapter "Laughter At The Scaffold" (256–87) from his book *Will in the World: How Shakespeare Became Shakespeare* (New York: W.W. Norton, 2004).

2   "The presentation of Shylock by Shakespeare as a villain with a point of view, not just a monster, owes much to Marlowe's Jew" (Bullough, 454).

3   "Barabas's 'Sufferance breeds ease' in hope of an occasion for vengeance, becomes Shylock's sinister 'patient shrug / For suff'rance is the badge of all our tribe' [I, iii, 108–9]" (Bullough, 455).

4   Bullough, 454–56.

5   "For much of the atmosphere of his Jewish theme Shakespeare was thus indebted to Marlowe" (Bullough, 456).

6   Charles Edelman, "Which Is The Jew That Shakespeare Knew? Shylock On The Elizabethan Stage," *Shakespeare Survey* 52 (1999): 99.

7   Ibid., 100. Edelman explains that "In the twelve years leading up to *The Merchant of Venice* there are exactly three Jews in extant plays" (100)—Abraham in Greene's *Selimus*, Barabas in *The Jew of Malta*, and Gerontus in Wilson's *Three Ladies of London*. Whereas Abraham (in a very small role) and Barabas have villainous characteristics, Gerontus is a man of honor.

8   Bullough, 456.

9   See M.C. Bradbrook, "Shakespeare's Recollections of Marlowe," in *Shakespeare's Styles: Essays in honour of Kenneth Muir*, ed. Philip Edwards, Inga-Stina Ewbank, and G.K. Hunter (Cambridge: Cambridge University Press, 1980), 192–93, who very briefly recapitulates Bullough's parallels and supports his position. More recently, in the Introduction to a new edition of the Pelican Shakespeare's *The Merchant of Venice* (New York: Penguin Putnam, 2000), A.R. Braunmuller both supports and departs from the tenets of this position. Braunmuller admits the strong differences between the two plays (xxxiv, xxxv) but nevertheless mentions ways in which Shakespeare's play may have been

influenced by Marlowe's (xxxiv–xxxviii): in Barabas's attack on "Christian hypocrisy, sanctimony, and lack of charity" (xxxiv); in presenting a relationship between a father and a daughter; in the pride Barabas and Shylock take in being Jewish; in "the vaunting egomania that equates an act of filial impiety with the 'curse … upon our nation'" (xxxvi); and in raising the question of how human beings are to be valued—in *The Jew of Malta*, through the purchase of a slave and in *The Merchant of Venice*, through the bargain of a pound of human flesh. Braunmuller does not examine the parallels to determine their significance or worth, much less arrive at an overall conclusion about Marlowe's influence.

10 *The Harmonies of "The Merchant of Venice"*(New Haven, CT: Yale University Press, 1978), 182.

11 Braunmuller, xxxvi.

12 Maurice Charney, "Jessica's Turquoise Ring and Abigail's Poisoned Porridge: Shakespeare and Marlowe as Rivals and Imitators," *Renaissance Drama* n.s. 10 (1979): 35. Charney restates this point later in the article: "*The Merchant of Venice* is so radically different from *The Jew of Malta* because Shakespeare was so intensely aware of his powerful rival. Without directly imitating Marlowe, he is attempting to surpass him in writing a tragic-comic play about an overweening Jew" (44). James Shapiro, *Rival Playwrights: Marlowe, Jonson, Shakespeare* (New York: Columbia University Press, 1991), 108, makes a similar point and then goes one step further when he says, "We find in Shakespeare's rendering of Shylock the most realized expression of the repeated pattern in which he tries to recall, outdo, and then reject Marlowe." What weakens this assertion, apart from the lack of support for it, is the absence of any discussion of how Barabas in his personality or conditions is a model for Shylock.

13 Shapiro, *Rival Playwrights*, 106–8. Some of Shapiro's arguments about the connections between *The Jew* and *The Merchant* seem to me rather forced and tenuous, partly because they do not take into account the conventions of romantic comedy. For example, he asserts that in *The Merchant of Venice* "communal harmony is achieved by the exclusion of the alien (and Marlovian) Morocco, Arragon, and Shylock" (108). Shapiro feels that Morocco and Arragon are "Marlovian" by virtue of the style of their language, but I am not clear on what basis Shylock is assumed to be Marlovian; moreover, all the suitors but Bassanio are rejected, as we knew from the outset they would be, less because they are aliens than because Bassanio has been set up as the romantic hero and, given the conventions of romantic comedy, we know this means that he will win Portia. Portia's satirical descriptions of her suitors (in I, ii) are rooted in Elizabethan stereotypes and include the English (I, ii, 62–72) and Scottish, as well as those who would have been considered foreigners. My point is that the overriding consideration for Shakespeare does not seem to be so much the alien status of the stereotypes as their comic possibilities.

14 Examples of these typical characteristics can be found in *Tamburlaine*, Part 1: II, iii, 6–24; III, iii, 44–54; III, iii, 244–60; IV, ii, 30–55; IV, ii, 95–110; IV, iv, 81–88; V, i, 446–79; and in *Tamburlaine*, Part 2: II, iv, 1–33.

15 Maurice Charney, "The Voice of Marlowe's Tamburlaine in Early Shakespeare," *Comparative Drama* 31:2 (Summer 1997): 213–23, finds in the first speech of Morocco quoted in the text (*MV*, II, i, 24–31) "something mock-heroic about Morocco's proposed feats" (218).

16 As I noted in Chapter 1, these imitations just during Marlowe's lifetime have been listed and discussed by Peter Berek, "Tamburlaine's Weak Sons: Imitation as Interpretation before 1593," *Renaissance Drama* n.s. 13 (1982): 55–82.

17 From Hutcheon's chapter, "The Politics of Parody," in *The Politics of Postmodernism* (London: Routledge, 1989), 101.

18 As we saw in the first chapter, there is a similarity in Shakespeare's use of Marlowe's well-known line from *Doctor Faustus* (V, i, 99), "Was this the face that launch'd a thousand ships." The echoes in *Richard II*, IV, i, 281–86, *Troilus and Cressida*, II, ii, 81–83, and *King Lear*, IV, vii, 32–36 attest the popularity of the words in *Doctor Faustus* and, in the latter two plays, without diminishing them through parody.

19 Nicholas Brooke, "Marlowe as Provocative Agent in Shakespeare's Early Plays," *Shakespeare Survey* 14 (1961): 42.

20 Shapiro, *Rival Playwrights*, 107.

21 Ibid. Charney also feels that Morocco is rejected on grounds other than those framed by the romantic plot: "By making Morocco so much like Tamburlaine, and therefore so remote, Shakespeare is guaranteeing that he will be rejected" ("Voice of Marlowe's Tamburlaine," 218).

22 Shapiro, 107.

23 With or without his comic dimensions, Morocco had no chance of succeeding as a suitor. We know that because Bassanio has already been introduced.

24 Brooke, 41.

25 Ibid.

26 Stephen Greenblatt in *Renaissance Self-Fashioning* (Chicago: University of Chicago Press, 1980) mentions that whereas Barabas and his society of Christians speak the same language ("Proverbs in *The Jew of Malta* are a kind of currency, the compressed ideological wealth of society, the money of the mind"—207), "Shylock is differentiated from the Christians even in his use of the common language" (207).

27 Greenblatt points out, interestingly, that Barabas's use of proverbs puts him "at the center of the society of the play, a society whose speech is a tissue of aphorisms" (*Renaissance Self-Fashioning*, 207) and helps to "*de-individualize*" him" (208). In his antisocial contempt and in his role as religious and political alien, Barabas is, paradoxically, actually the voice of a ruthlessly materialistic society, a society whose materialism is presided over and promoted by Christians.

28 See as recent examples of the changes in Barabas's character the comments of Emily C. Bartels, *Spectacles of Strangeness: Imperialism, Alienation, and Marlowe* (Philadelphia: University of Pennsylvania Press, 1993), 99–100, and Matthew N. Proser, *The Gift of Fire* (New York: Peter Lang, 1995), 114–15.

29 For a discussion of the obscurity of Barabas's motives throughout the play, see Emily C. Bartels, 98–100. From an opposite perspective, an argument that sees the motives through Marlowe's eyes as a dramatist, see Sara Munson Deats and Lisa S. Starks who, in their article "'So neatly plotted, and so well perform'd': Villain as Playwright in Marlowe's *The Jew of Malta*," *Theatre Journal* 44 (1992): 375–89, try to account for Barabas's lack of credible motivation by viewing him: realistically as "an inveterate role-player" (380); emblematically as "a rhetorical construct of the anti-theatrical debate" (379), "the surrogate playwright through whom Marlowe communicates with his audience" (381); and symbolically as a representation of "the power of dramatic art to construct reality" (379).

30 See Bartels, 99, who, in a different context, reminds us that, historically, Jews could not own land. Shakespeare's failure to advance this argument for Shylock may reveal his lack of interest in the social causes of Shylock's behavior and his desire to focus on Shylock as a theatrical device. This intention is of course waylaid when the figure erupts into a humanized character.

31   Shapiro talks about the "generic slipperiness" (*Rival Playwrights*, 104) of the play and refers "to the critical view that *The Merchant* is a 'problem play'" (104).

32   For a characterization of Barabas and Shylock as aliens in a Christian culture, see James Shapiro, *Shakespeare and the Jews* (New York: Columbia University Press, 1996), 180–89.

33   Whether one agrees with Ian McAdam, "Carnal Identity in *The Jew of Malta*," *English Literary Renaissance* 26 (Winter, 1966:1), 46–74, that "Barabas' role as the Jewish alien in Malta becomes a kind of metaphor in the play for the homosexual in society" (54–55), Barabas's alienation seems absolute, at times almost a mannerism; when he sets himself apart from "common men," the alienation seems willful and social, not cultural—almost Tamburlainian.

34   Lars Engle in "'Thrift is Blessing': Exchange and Explanation in *The Merchant of Venice*," *Shakespeare Quarterly* 37 (1986): 20–37, sees the materialism of the play as more integral to the actions of the characters, especially Portia's, than I see it. In his somber and even cynical reading of the play, he maintains, for example, that Antonio suppresses the truth when, in the opening scene, he tells Salerio and Solanio that his "ventures are not in one bottom trusted, / Nor to one place; nor is my whole estate / Upon the fortune of this present year" (I, i, 42–44), for, soon after, Antonio tells Bassanio that "all" his "fortunes are at sea" (I, i, 177). I agree that this is a contradiction, but I'm not convinced it is because Antonio is not telling Salerio and Solanio the truth. It may well be the result of the artistic needs of the two different moments. Another contradiction, not mentioned by Engle, occurs at the end of the play when Antonio appears jubilant at the news that three of his argosies have "richly come to harbor suddenly" (V, i, 277). He tells Portia, "Sweet lady, you have given me life and living! / For here I read for certain that my ships / Are safely come to road" (V, i, 286–88). This reaction seems to me to be more the result of Shakespeare's immediate need to make the final scene of his comedy as sunny as possible rather than some revelation of Antonio's deep-seated materialistic desires or a transference of his homoerotic desires for Bassanio to his argosies. In short, I think Shakespeare's contradictions chiefly signal artistic decisions of the moment rather than complexities in characterization, although, in theory, the two are not mutually exclusive. A useful corrective to Engle's reading of *The Merchant of Venice* is Karen Newman, "Portia's Ring: Unruly Women and Structures of Exchange in *The Merchant of Venice*," *Shakespeare Quarterly* 38 (1987): 19–33, who shows how the play "interrogates the Elizabethan sex/gender system" (33). Although Newman's essay does not set out to do so, it shows how Shakespeare plays with conventional notions and expectations of romantic comedy to create dramatic tension, some of it subliminal, but a tension that nevertheless forcefully engages an audience.

35   The tendency to take Shylock seriously is certainly not a twentieth-century phenomenon. As John Gross points out in *Shylock: A Legend and Its Legacy* (London: Chatto and Windus, 1992), 110, Nicholas Rowe in 1709, in the first critical edition of Shakespeare's plays, put forth a much more serious reading, acknowledging that, although the tradition has been to use a comedian in the role of Shylock and to make the role comic, the play has in it "such a deadly spirit of revenge, such a savage fierceness and fellness and such a bloody designation of cruelty and mischief, as cannot agree either with the style or characters of comedy." Gross goes on to point out that the first *known* performance of a Shylock who was not a comic character took place in 1741 with Charles Macklin in the role (111–15).

36   An outstanding essay on the ambivalences, ambiguities, and complexities of our responses to *The Merchant of Venice* is the first chapter ("Meaning and *The Merchant of Venice*") of

Norman Rabkin's book *Shakespeare and the Problem of Meaning* (Chicago: University of Chicago Press, 1981), 1–32. Rabkin warns against reductiveness in criticism and provides us with examples of our shifting, complex, and sometimes contradictory responses to the characters of the play as support for his argument.

37   Most recently, for example, in his discussion of "uncircumcision" (128–30), Shapiro, *Shakespeare and the Jews*, makes reference to "Antonio's consummate revenge upon his circumcised adversary" (130). But, see Rabkin as well, pp. 13–15 and 17–18, who feels that our response is more complicated, that it allows not only for what might be called a cultural response but a personal response.

38   In the first instance, the context is as follows:

Shylock: May I speak with Antonio?
Bassanio: If it please you to dine with us.
Shylock: Yes, to smell pork, to eat of the habitation which your prophet the Nazarite conjured the devil into! I will buy with you, sell with you, talk with you, walk with you, and so following; but I will not eat with you, drink with you, nor pray with you. (I, iii, 29–35)

In the second context, Shylock says to his daughter,

I am bid forth to supper, Jessica.
There are my keys. But wherefore should I go?
I am not bid for love, they flatter me;
But yet I'll go in hate to feed upon
The prodigal Christian. ... (II, v, 11–15)

Clearly, he has been inconsistent, as Barabas is, or has changed his mind. Either way, the reasons are obscure. That he would mention that he is "not bid for love" may be meant to reveal his desire for fellowship; the statement is otherwise a bit silly since, given the circumstances of the business arrangement and his and Antonio's mutual antipathy toward one another, there is no reason for him to even consider the possibility of being "bid for love." The obscurity is reinforced when he says soon after: "By Jacob's staff I swear / I have no mind of feasting forth to-night; / But I will go" (II, v, 36–38). Again, one is left to wonder if by this remark Shylock is not revealing a half-submerged desire for fellowship.

Chapter 6

Marlowe's *Tamburlaine* Plays, Shakespeare's *Henry V*, and the Primacy of an Artistic Consciousness

I

At first glance, the question of how Marlowe's *Tamburlaine* plays influenced Shakespeare's *Henry V* a decade after they were composed might seem far-fetched. But that is only because the answer is neither obvious nor, in its complexity, wholly definite. What is obvious is that, for Shakespeare, Marlowe's poetic and dramatic legacy lived on long after his death in 1593. As we have seen thus far, the proof resides in some strong responses from Shakespeare, ranging variously from allusions, echoes, and overt parody to important similarities in style, situations, and characterization. Also, the seven or eight dramas in which Shakespeare quotes actual lines from Marlowe's poems and plays all appear to have been composed and first performed after 1593.[1] Looked at collectively, the evidence indicates not only that Shakespeare had a wide experience of Marlowe's works—that is, both his drama and poetry,[2] but that he continued to be influenced by them until the final years of his career. We should therefore not be surprised in examining *Henry V*, written in 1599, to discover that some of the seeds of influence have germinated and blossomed well after they were first planted and that the roots run deep.

Nor should it surprise us to find that, as the distance in time from Marlowe's death lengthened, a crucial change occurred in Shakespeare's attitude toward his former associate's works. Specifically, as he became more sure-footed in composing his plays, his absorption of Marlowe's influence deepened, enhancing both his creative intelligence and artistic authority. There is no evidence to suggest that Shakespeare was ever daunted or inhibited by Marlowe's achievements and reputation. Consequently, I do not mean to suggest that the plays indicate that, at a certain, definable point in his life, Shakespeare suddenly stopped using Marlowe as something of a whipping boy to compensate for his insecurities as a writer. The dating of the plays is too uncertain to suggest so specific a point, much less so specific and harsh a psychological profile; although, to be sure, by the time Shakespeare writes the tragedies, he is no longer even gently parodying Marlowe. I do mean to suggest that, however steady any progression in Shakespeare's attitude toward Marlowe may have been, we can be sure only that his mood varies—say, from clear parody in *2 Henry IV* to a more jovial type of parody in *The Merry Wives of Windsor* to an acceptance of significant influence in *Richard II*, *The Merchant of Venice*, and *Henry V*. What undermines the definiteness of a progression is that *The Merry Wives* may have been written (or revised) after *Henry V*.

In *Richard II*, *The Merchant of Venice*, *2 Henry IV*, *As You Like It*, and *The Merry Wives of Windsor*, Shakespeare echoes presumably well-known lines from Marlowe's plays and poems partly in order to link himself with an eminently successful fellow playwright and partly to indicate just the opposite—his individuality as wordsmith and, by extension, his individuality as dramatist and poet. In declaring his creative independence, some have thought he may also be revealing his insecurity as a competing writer and, perhaps, some envy, but, as we saw in discussing *The Merchant of Venice*, such a conclusion is impossible to ascertain. It would be more accurate to say that in *Henry V*, *King Lear*, and *Antony and Cleopatra* Shakespeare seems increasingly secure in his creative powers, a writer less engaged in an ostensible emulation of Marlowe's legacy than in a mature acceptance of it. I am not positing that, at the time of *Henry V*, Shakespeare felt as secure as a dramatist as he would feel in later plays; his defensiveness about his artistry in the choruses of *Henry V* makes this clear. But with regard to Marlowe's legacy, the portrayal of Henry V, especially in its easy reliance on the Tamburlainian prototype, does suggest a greater confidence in his playwriting abilities. In *Henry V*, *King Lear*, and *Antony and Cleopatra*, he does not take individual lines from his rival's works and place them in a comically derisive context. Instead, with greater detachment, he shifts the focus of his interest to Marlowe's artistic skills and to the dramaturgical sources of his success. Specifically in light of the *Tamburlaine* plays, he accepts what literary history confirms is for him—as well as for other sixteenth- and seventeenth-century dramatists such as Robert Greene, George Peele, and Ben Jonson—the deepest and most pervasive element of Marlowe's influence: the commanding portrayals of the Tamburlainian overreacher.[3]

That Marlowe followed his first *Tamburlaine* play with a second suggests the strong impact his protagonist had on the imagination of his original audiences and the immediate widespread popularity of this figure, two facts of which Shakespeare could hardly have been unaware. Moreover, it seems natural enough that, both as an enterprising playwright seeking knowledge about what makes his fellow dramatist a success and as a member of Marlowe's audience himself, one particularly well endowed with a responsive imagination, Shakespeare would have been drawn to the two plays and to a character of such magnitude. But Marlowe's influence goes beyond these interests. Without a trace of the attitude of a patronizing, small-minded rival, Shakespeare appears in *Henry V* to accept the figure of the overreacher as a pervasive influence, even if he has modified him to suit his own dramaturgical needs and developing tastes. Shakespeare has moved beyond presenting this zealously ambitious figure as a single-dimensional Hotspur or simply as the brief opportunity for comedy that Morocco provided in *The Merchant of Venice*, although, as we shall see, the figure of Pistol offers one last reminder of how Shakespeare can make use of a comic Tamburlaine. In *Henry V*, on the whole, Shakespeare affirms through his protagonist the characterization of Tamburlaine as a prototype, and, implicitly, acknowledges the prototype as part of an imposing dramaturgical inheritance to which he can rightfully and proudly lay claim.[4] In addition, he is confident enough about himself as playwright to build on this inheritance and to give it his own stamp of individuality, not only in *Henry V*, but, later, in such plays as *King Lear* and *Antony and Cleopatra*. Throughout his career, Shakespeare's continuing response to Marlowe's legacy is complex and ever changing. Because he is a delayed reactor, his influence from Marlowe is never that of a slavish imitator. If he often seems indifferent to what we would call the "content" of Marlowe's plays, it is because he does not respond to them in that particular categorical way—as content. Nor does he sustain so single-minded a perspective in his response. He reveals instead a multiconsciousness that plays host to several perspectives, including those that expand, deepen, and reject situations, characterizations, and aspects of style in Marlowe's texts, those that reverse themselves, and those that dissipate with the passage of time. *Henry V* is simply the first play in the chronology of plays as we know it that suggests both an acceptance and an affirmation of a powerful, dominant element in the Marlovian legacy.

II

The changes in Shakespeare's attitude toward Marlowe's work that surface in *Henry V* can be placed in a broader chronological context. We need only understand, as mentioned above, that in the span of time from *Richard II* to *King Lear* there was a major reversal in Shakespeare's overall perspective. We can see the difference sharply once we examine in *Richard II* and *King Lear* the use of Faustus's cry of amazement at the sight of the spirit of Helen of Troy: "Was this the face that launched a thousand ships / And burnt the topless towers of Ilium" (*Doctor Faustus*, V, i, 89–90 [A-Text]; V, i, 93–94 [B-Text]).[5] Whereas in *Richard II* the imitation is blatantly parodic and, ultimately, self-advertising, in *King Lear* it is unself-conscious and deftly integrated into the playtext.[6] In the first play, when the king is forced to abdicate the throne, Shakespeare noticeably undermines Marlowe's lines through Richard's excessive repetition of them and through the grating mechanization of his delivery. In an unrestrained, melodramatic self-display, the king asks rhetorically:

> Was this face the face
> That every day under his household roof
> Did keep ten thousand men? Was this the face
> That like the sun did make beholders wink?
> Is this the face which faced so many follies
> That was at last outfaced by Bolingbroke? (*Richard II*, IV, i, 281–86)

The heavy punning on the word "face" helps to make the parody of Faustus's question patently obvious—although, as is always the case with parody, not without validating the impact of the originating text. Here, in characterizing Richard's self-absorption through linguistic strategies, Shakespeare belittles Marlowe's effectiveness with language by caricaturing his extravagance and intensity. At the same time, in carrying Faustus's awed response cleverly to a ridiculous extreme, he asserts his own ability with words. In *King Lear*, however, where a king's face is also being scrutinized, the dramatist feels little need to prove himself a first-rate wielder of words and public showman. Cordelia asks herself the following questions about her father as she watches him sleep:

> Was this a face
> To be opposed against the jarring winds?
> [To stand against the deep dread-bolted thunder?
> In the most terrible and nimble stroke
> Of quick cross lightning to watch, poor perdu,
> With this thin helm?] (IV, vii, 32–37)

Preceding each of the three infinitives ("To be," "To stand," and "to watch") is "Was this a face." But in contradistinction to the hammering repetitions of Richard, Cordelia underplays Faustus's question, letting the rhetoric of the second and third questions imply rather than state its presence as it establishes emotional continuity and gathers strength. Her words are able to recall the tone and import of Faustus's question without focusing on its style. Shakespeare is thereby able to bring Faustus's thoroughly human wonder to bear on the poignancy of this reconciliation scene. Through the graceful reminder of the well-known line, he suggests Marlowe's grandeur, emphasis, affecting directness, and, perhaps most of all, his fresh evocation of a genuine reaction to an astonishing event. Shakespeare evokes Marlowe here without being afraid to acknowledge him as an influence, however much he may have actually resisted his influence in other plays or tried to indicate through parody that there was little to be influenced by. He evokes him, too, with the implicit understanding that he wishes the imposing weight of the respected Renaissance theatrical tradition in epic language and syntax, sparked by Marlowe, to add stature and dignity unobtrusively to the drama he is writing. Apparently, Shakespeare now sees himself as a serious contributor to a developing tradition. At the time of *Richard II*, he was still on the outside looking in, clambering to make his mark.

Perhaps the change in perspective from a tentative resistance to a decisive acceptance can be said to be the cause of what James Shapiro has in mind when he talks about *Henry V* as the "successful containment of Marlowe's early heroical history, *Tamburlaine*."[7] Shapiro tries to account for why, although Shakespeare rejected the paradigm of the heroical history in writing the *Henry VI* plays in 1589, he did not when he wrote *Henry V* a decade later. He concludes that similar political conditions induced Shakespeare to follow Marlowe's path.[8] Whether this is in fact so, the question remains: "Can one maintain that the *Tamburlaine* plays themselves are a likely influence on *Henry V*?" Shapiro lists in summary fashion five parallels that critics have noted between the *Tamburlaine* plays and *Henry V*:

1. "the protagonists' successive conquests in the face of overwhelming odds"
2. "the choruses that orient our response to the ensuing action"
3. "the heroes' treatment of followers first as 'band[s] of brothers,' then as subjects"

4.   "moments of unexpected and unwarranted cruelty"

5.   "Shakespeare's appropriation of the endings of both parts of *Tamburlaine* at
the conclusion of *Henry V*" (i.e., the marriages of Zenocrate and Katherine and the
failure of the sons to inherit the qualities that made their fathers so successful).[9]

Of these parallels, the fourth seems to me the most convincing: Tamburlaine's tough-
mindedness at Damascus (1 *Tamburlaine*, V, i, 64–134) and Henry's at Harfleur
(*Henry V*, III, iii, 1–43) come immediately to mind. It could be argued that the first
three parallels are derived from storytelling traditions that make them unexceptional
and that the final parallel seems forced.   Apparently, Shapiro also seems to think
the fourth parallel is the most convincing, because it is the only one he develops.[10]
However many parallels one wishes to accept as true, the inescapable implication is
that, by means of his dramatization of Henry, Shakespeare validates Tamburlaine's
heroics.

Rather than expand on Shapiro's argument that the *Tamburlaine* plays and *Henry
V* are heroical histories or on the list of five parallels, I want to take the argument for
influence in another direction.   If we look at the Prologue to the first *Tamburlaine*
play and at the Prologue to Act I of *Henry V*, we can see that both writers are strongly
concerned with the artistry of their plays and, specifically, with the effects on their
audiences of their innovations in language and genre.   *Henry V* reveals the same
strong artistic consciousness about itself that Marlowe sanctions in his Prologue to
Tamburlaine.   Scornful and irreverent, the frequently quoted Prologue is critical of
the impoverished poetic language of Marlowe's native theatrical heritage:

> From jigging veins of rhyming mother-wits,
> And such conceits as clownage keeps in pay,
> We'll lead you to the stately tent of war,
> Where you shall hear the Scythian Tamburlaine
> Threat'ning the world with high astounding terms,
> And scourging kingdoms with his conquering sword.
> View but his picture in this tragic glass,
> And then applaud his fortunes as you please. (1 *Tamburlaine*, Prologue)

In relation to genre, Marlowe suggests that he is going to combine the best elements
of the two most acclaimed types of the classical and medieval past, established long
before the native tradition of "rhyming mother-wits," to present an epic tragedy.   In
order to give to his characters and their actions the majestic expansiveness necessary
to invest the play with epic qualities, he tells us that his protagonist, already made
larger than life through well-known historical accounts,[11] will threaten the world,
not in fourteeners (Poulter's Measure) but in "high astounding terms."   The phrase
"tragic glass" suggests tragedy in the medieval sense of a fall from high estate and
"glass," in particular, the moralizing mirror tradition. But, in the light of the amoral
behavior of Tamburlaine that follows, the phrase seems mock serious.[12]   The word
"tragic" cannot be said to apply in any sense to the first Tamburlaine play.[13]   It can be
applied to the second only by stretching the meaning of medieval tragedy as a fall from

high estate; usually, however, the "fall" occurs before the end of one's life and is not simply the result of natural causes leading to death.[14] Nor do the two plays present us with moral lessons; we understand that they want us to wonder at Tamburlaine's uninhibited assertiveness but they do not assume a didactic mode that encourages us to make the leap to adopt it ourselves any more than they warn us of the inevitability of dire consequences from ruthless acts. It could more easily and persuasively be argued that Marlowe actually undermines the conventions of didactic tragedy in the *Tamburlaine* plays, much as he undermines idealized portrayals of romantic love in *Hero and Leander*. By disappointing the preconditioned expectations of his original audiences, Marlowe not only subverted their propensity for self-deception but enabled them to become receptive to fresh thinking and feeling. The *Tamburlaine* plays jolted these audiences into a pleasurable new state of awareness by overturning their expectation of the successes and failures of a prince who, according to the mirror tradition, was subject to prescribed sociomoral codes. The effect was chiefly aesthetic, not moral, even if we conclude that Marlowe was, in a sense, moralizing in asserting his aesthetic perspective. In addition, the departures from the assertions of the Prologue bespeak an aesthetic rather than a moral consciousness. One key example of the way in which Marlowe overturns his audiences' expectations, both in the *Tamburlaine* plays and *Hero and Leander*, occurs when he dramatizes the dark notion that ultimate reality for those on earth means that neither justice nor compassion can become practicable virtues: Tamburlaine is never punished for his savage acts of ruthlessness; and sexual love "is not full of pity (as men say) / But deaf and cruel where he means to prey" (*Hero and Leander*, 771–72). Ultimate reality is amoral. Struggles for power, not just causes, make up its essence. In substituting hard, cold realism for the standard expectations of each genre strictly defined, Marlowe opens the door to a blurring of precise distinctions.

By the time Shakespeare writes *Henry V*, the categories of the genres of Marlowe's day have exploded into many types and subtypes, as the remarks of Polonius humorously inform us (*Hamlet*, II, ii, 339–44). The two chronicle plays of Tamburlaine that Marlowe seems to have redefined as an epic if not as a tragedy had developed as a genre in Shakespeare's mind into a more general and even more amorphous category which in *Henry V* he calls "history" (Prologue, 32), a category inclusive enough to encompass large doses of broadly comic material as well as tragic elements.[15] His tendency not to be restricted by preformed definitions of the genre within which he was working is, at the very least, reinforced by what he had seen demonstrated in the *Tamburlaine* plays. Whether Marlowe actually influenced the formation of Shakespeare's ideas of genre or only gave support to notions Shakespeare already had formed, both dramatists show themselves strongly aware of their tools and both, in effect, assert the importance of these tools. With an eagerness that is downright Marlovian, Shakespeare helps to solidify and build on the tradition of artistic consciousness that he finds in his former fellow dramatist.

Shakespeare's Prologue is itself a demonstration of the high astounding terms needed to give epic grandeur to the serious scenes of *Henry V*:

O for a Muse of fire, that would ascend
The brightest heaven of invention;
A kingdom for a stage, princes to act
And monarchs to behold the swelling scene!
Then should the warlike Harry, like himself,
Assume the port of Mars, and at his heels,
Leashed in like hounds, should famine, sword, and fire
Crouch for employment. But pardon, gentles all,
The flat unraisèd spirits that hath dared
On this unworthy scaffold to bring forth
So great an object. Can this cockpit hold
The vasty fields of France? Or may we cram
Within this wooden O the very casques
That did affright the air at Agincourt?
O, pardon! since a crooked figure may
Attest in little place a million;
And let us, ciphers to this great accompt,
On your imaginary forces work. (*Henry V*, Prologue, 1–18)

In this initial half of the Prologue, Shakespeare strives for an epic tone through: the conventional appeal to a muse (1); the classical epithets "warlike" (5) and "vasty" (12); the wholly decorative mythological allusion expressed with considerable formality (6); the high-toned allegorical imagery (6–8); the Marlovian hyperbole (3–8); the elevated language (e.g., 10, 12, 13); the emphatic expressive mode (3–4); the inverted syntax (5–8), including suspended constructions (e.g, 17–18), to create a formal, Latinate tone; the rhetorical repetition of "should" (5 and 7); and the serious word play (15–18). Both prologues try to arouse their audiences by announcing that something new in drama is about to take place. Each writer appeals to the imagination of his audiences, although Shakespeare more directly, elaborately, and insistently. Put differently, Marlowe and Shakespeare both express a strong awareness of artistic cause and effect, an awareness that, as their dramatic techniques reveal, is in abundant evidence throughout each of the *Tamburlaine* plays and *Henry V*. At the very least, Marlowe's confidence about reforging the language of dramatic tradition and his breaking down of some conventional barriers of genre must have provided a model for Shakespeare and encouraged him to freely express, also in a prologue, his similarly strong artistic consciousness and identical interest in language and genre. The difference is that Shakespeare takes a more instructive stance than Marlowe: he first declares that there is no theater large enough to house the epic subject except by symbolic representation and, then, concludes that in order for such representation to take place effectively, the audience members must use *their* imaginations.

Central to the artistic concerns of Marlowe in the *Tamburlaine* plays and Shakespeare in *Henry V* is the characterization of the protagonist. For each writer, nothing contributes as much to the dramatic potency of their plays as capturing the ways in which their protagonists outstrip ordinary human beings. If that means that, because some of the actions of the conquering warrior leaders seem inhumane, an audience's spontaneous aesthetic responses and their conditioned moral responses come into conflict, then, from the perspective of playwrights interested in sustaining dramatic tension, the artistry of their plays is smoothly at work. As audience members, we naturally want to gain control over our response to the protagonists by assigning them a categorical designation, one that enables our aesthetic and moral responses to intermingle happily. A wise dramatist plays on that desire. Whether we consider Tamburlaine an awesome hero, a ruthless barbarian, or a canny strategist able to don whatever role circumstances warrant, we remain interested in assigning him to a category, in "getting a fix" on him.[16] But we are prevented from doing so because our perspective on him changes, sometimes alternating between a wondrous acclamation and a fervent denunciation. Our perspective depends largely upon his use of language and the use of language by others who talk about and characterize him, usually in relation to his actions. Although Shakespeare possesses the same intent of using language to govern the effectiveness of his epic protagonist, he also relies—more than Marlowe—on the drama of the situation to generate aesthetic interest. The same Marlovian aesthetic principle of avoiding easy categorization and the same concentration on the protagonist's and others' linguistic strategies are at work in the characterization of Henry V. One difference, however, is that Henry is less dependent on the words of others to form his self-image, however momentary. As a result, he seems more self-reliant and becomes more exalted in our eyes than Tamburlaine. But then Tamburlaine began as a shepherd and Henry V as the son of a king. Even so, in both plays the dramatists purposefully unsettle the audience's desire to experience a fixed, idealized image of the protagonists in order to create and sustain dramatic tension.

At times, the *Tamburlaine* plays and *Henry V* set in conflict a military perspective,[17] understood as principled, and a humane perspective, viewed as natural but sometimes misguided, to sustain the tension and to remind us that making definitive final judgments on the protagonist's behavior is impossible, even if we find the attempt intellectually interesting and aesthetically exhilarating. The chief way in which Tamburlaine and Zenocrate are set in opposition in Marlowe's two plays is through this conflict of military and humane perspectives. Zenocrate's distress at the consequences of war and of the imprisonment of Bajazeth and Zabina in the first play (1 V, i, 319–71) are matched by her desires that Tamburlaine forego warring and have a more balanced expectation of his sons' military propensities in the second (2 I, iii, 1–111). Probably the most emphatic example of the conflict occurs within Tamburlaine himself in the first play when, after ordering that the virgins of Damascus and others be put to the sword, he abruptly begins an extended soliloquy on beauty (V, i, 64–190). Ultimately, Tamburlaine is attracted to the power of beauty more than to beauty itself and, as someone interested in always proving himself extraordinary, to his sensitivity to it as proof of "The highest reaches of a human wit" (168). Disavowing that anything "effeminate and faint" (177) can be associated with this exalted imaginative power—in fact, claiming that it is essential to the superiority of a hero-warrior (178–82), he prides himself on possessing it and, yet, at being able to hold his response to it in check (183–90). That he is able to control his response gives him ultimate power and, in the Marlovian scheme of values, makes for an idealized blend of opposing forces that the Tamburlaine of the second play seems incapable of understanding, let alone sustaining.

The same irresolvable conflict of sensibilities between the heroic ruler and military commander on the one hand, and the private person, on the other, appears, in *Henry V*. But here the king, not just the playwright, is consistently aware of this pervasive conflict, as he indicates in his argument with Williams (IV, i, 84–214). That this conflict cannot be satisfactorily resolved reminds us that neither writer asks his audiences—during the performance at any rate—to rigorously exercise their rational faculties so that they can come to judgments about the protagonists or, conversely, to merely affirm the stereotypes or clichéd notions of such extraordinary figures that they have brought with them to the theater. The writers ask, instead, that their audiences acknowledge the man but champion the hero, that they wonder at the hero's epic feats without trying to reconcile his defects, although Shakespeare goes farther down the path of reconciliation than does Marlowe. The three plays (*Tamburlaine* 1 and 2 and *Henry V*) suggest that these ambivalences absurdly but naturally coexist.[18] If, because of the resulting confusion of our aesthetic and moral responses, we become detached enough to perceive a troubling moral dilemma in the protagonists' unreconciled flaws and heroics—always remembering that it is by no means a certainty that the contradictoriness of our aesthetic and moral responses was precisely the same for the Elizabethans—it is not necessary to automatically assume, as some have done, that the dramatists are themselves in an ethical quandary. What we can more securely assume is that they are demonstrating a clear control and a sophisticated sense of sound dramaturgical artistry. That both writers make use of ambivalence suggests that they understand well that not playing to audiences' complacent expectations and desires is the best way to gain their attention and keep them engaged.[19] In effect, Marlowe and Shakespeare's practice acknowledges that ambivalence leads ultimately to ambiguity and that the process constitutes a major artistic device in holding an audience's attention. As I have already suggested in previous chapters, Shakespeare could not have missed the effectiveness of this technique in the *Tamburlaine* plays. We will see shortly how strongly the device influenced the portrayal of ambiguity in the characterization of Henry V.[20]

Every student of Marlowe knows that the self-consciousness about spoken language expressed in the Prologue to *Tamburlaine* manifests itself in both plays.[21] But there is a difference. Part 2 seems to be *conscious of* rather than *self-conscious about* the language it uses. In Part 1, from Mycetes' opening lines on the importance of "great and thund'ring speech" (I, i, 3), to the "working words" (II, iv, 25) that Tamburlaine uses to win over foes, to the speech on beauty (discussed above) in which the shepherd-turned-warrior is aware that "Fair is too foul an epithet" (V, i, 136), Marlowe reveals through the characters a self-consciousness about the play's undisguised exploration of the power of language to control its hearers; so aware are we of the textual focus on the power of language that when Tamburlaine says, "I speak it, and my words are oracles" (III, iii, 102), we are inclined to think metadramatically that his self-consciousness is also Marlowe's in promoting the effectiveness of *his* "high astounding terms." In Part 2, the "working words" of the playtext speak only for themselves, whether through Orcanes' tough talk (I, i, 25–44), Callapine's unctuous but sensuously captivating description of the rewards that lie in wait for Almeda for helping him escape (I, ii, 19–53), Tamburlaine's lamentations at the death of Zenocrate (II, iv, 1–37, 78–118), or, as he lies dying, the warrior leader's speeches which, through their geographical sweep and classical similes (V, iii, 115–158 and 224–48, respectively), are indicative climactically of an epic magnitude and an awesome magniloquence. Some of this difference may simply be Marlowe's greater confidence after the success of Part 1. Another aspect may be the result of his desire to continue with a style that asks not to be engrossing but to be admired, because he feels that "wounding the world with wonder" (2 *Tamburlaine*, II, iv, 82)[22] is what made the language and syntax of Part 1 such a success. Still another element may be Tamburlaine's degeneration as an epic military figure. If his actions in Part 1 can be justified as proper military behavior—and it is by no means clear to many readers that they can be—certainly not all of his actions in Part 2 can be. His burning of the town in which Zenocrate died and his stabbing of his son Calyphas stand out as heinously barbaric acts. They reflect a man whose emotions are so out of control that his epic stature is diminished, even though, remarkably, at his death he and his followers behave as if it were not. Rather than requesting us to see the man whole or to attempt to come to a moral conclusion about him, the play asks us in the end to be awed by his single-mindedness and his achievements as a military hero. The words of Tamburlaine's followers only reinforce the focus on his lifelong power, his conquests, and the widespread amazement at them. The two plays present a world without moral coherence but a world in which wonders, perceived aesthetically, do exist, as long as we remain detached enough to appreciate them. By drawing attention to themselves as style, the language and syntax become the primary means of creating the detachment from content that enables our awe.

Language and syntax serve an equally important function in *Henry V*, in which, as in the *Tamburlaine* plays, they draw attention to themselves as stylistic artifice—in theory, keeping us detached enough so that we can obey Shakespeare's imperative to the audience: "play with your fancies" (III, Chorus, 7). We also have to be self-aware enough to know when the "performance" needs to be eked out (III, Chorus, 35) and that, in turn, means—as it frequently means in the *Tamburlaine* plays—having something of the detached, godlike perspective of the author as he views the hero and the world of potential moral coherence that he inhabits. Like Marlowe, only more extensively, Shakespeare implies that a detached, self-aware perspective will better enable us to glorify and wonder at the protagonist than will an utterly absorbed perspective. And, in fact, we do need some measure of detachment to enable us to glorify and wonder at both protagonists. But this does not mean that we are so busy being awed that we overlook their weaknesses. In fact, the differences between Tamburlaine and Henry are more clearly marked by their vices than by their virtues. Henry's major reformation takes place while he is still prince, but even as king he is not without flaws, and they are ameliorated only to the extent to which we are invited to understand how the conditions of his roles as king and military leader denature him of his humanity. Unlike Tamburlaine, however, he never murders a son and, unlike the world Tamburlaine inhabits, his world sanctions the principle of moral unity, even if some audiences and readers understand the latter only as evidence of the politics of manipulation and hypocrisy. We may find it difficult to accept the King's view of the war on France as a religious crusade and an honorable righting of an ancient wrong or to understand some of his secular actions as a Christian king and commander-in-chief of the invading forces. If we look with the eyes of one within the world of the play, at times, instead of seeming virtuous, he seems duplicitous. For example, he is neither consistent nor clear in his motives for invading France. In his own self-interest, he overlooks the self-interest of the Archbishop and Bishop who persuade him of the legitimacy of his claim to the French throne (I, ii). Although he says emphatically, "We are no tyrant, but a Christian king" (I, ii, 242), in the harshness of some of his declarations (e.g., at Harfleur), we may suspect that there is more of a tyrant than he admits to. In his message to the Dauphin and in his declarations to Mountjoy he seems to push aside his original, legal reasons for invading France, thereby raising questions about the consistency and clarity of his motives (I, ii, 260–98; III, vi, 111–64; IV, vii, 82–127). The following lines, for instance, contain Henry's response to the Ambassador of France who has brought tennis balls in scorn from the Dauphin; in their egotism and ferocity, Henry's words raise questions about the true nature of his motives as a Christian king:

> I will dazzle all the eyes of France,
> Yea, strike the Dauphin blind to look on us.
> And tell the pleasant prince this mock of his
> Hath turned his balls to gunstones, and his soul
> Shall stand sore chargèd for the wasteful vengeance
> That shall fly with them; for many a thousand widows
> Shall this his mock mock out of their dear husbands,
> Mock mothers from their sons, mock castles down;
> And some are yet ungotten and unborn
> That shall have cause to curse the Dauphin's scorn. (I, ii, 280–89)

The charged language makes one wonder exactly what is behind Henry's desire to invade France. Is it an exclamation of self-interest and personal animosity, the consequences be damned? Or is Shakespeare trying to make him sound authoritative in the epic manner of a Tamburlaine? Both characters know that on certain public occasions (e.g., in response to the public insult Henry has just received) some epically heroic vaunting may be required. A more blatant example of a tyrannical state of mind seems to occur when Henry orders the killing of the French prisoners (IV, vi, 35–38) and only later talks about it as the appropriate punishment for the French soldiers' slaying of the English camp boys (IV, vii, 54–64).[23]

If we look from outside the world of the play at the process of composition, we may feel that Henry's apparent duplicity is, in actuality, evidence of Shakespeare's artistic naïveté in his characterization of the king, of his being overly ambitious in trying to bestow on Henry the qualities of both a heroic king and an ordinary (in the best sense) human being and in trying to reconcile the exacting demands of the kingship and military leadership with his humanity. The playwright has taken Marlowe's dramatization of the conflicting demands of the protagonist's professional and personal lives and deepened it. Whereas Marlowe does not try to reconcile the two, Shakespeare, more optimistic, does, much as he attempted to do in 1 *Henry IV* when Hal tried to link his frivolous activities with his responsibilities as future king.[24] In *A Midsummer Night's Dream*, Shakespeare avoided the conflict, patently manipulating the plot so that the reason and imagination, linked respectively with the establishment of professional and private values functioned in separate locales, the court and the woods; despite the realistic implication that these two basic categories of consciousness will forever be incompatible and, of necessity, will clash, never once did Shakespeare allow the communal interests of the reasoning mind (namely, Duke Theseus's) to come into serious conflict with the private interests of the imagination. In *Richard II*, he faced the conflict head on and, as a consequence, Richard, who was never able to make the necessary adjustments to his duties as ruler, was destroyed.

In *Henry V*, Shakespeare again appears to be trying to reconcile the opposing demands. And, naturally, he depends upon the power of the language to do it, especially when an event goes well beyond the needs of plot and characterization. We see the idea of the conflict and its resolution being developed most fully when the King goes in disguise among his soldiers (IV, i); the import of the scene depends mostly upon language, not action. He discusses with Bates, Court, and Williams the obligations of the King to his subjects (IV, i, 84–214), ultimately evading Williams' question of the justice of war (IV, i, 130–42), and, then, in the soliloquy on Ceremony which immediately follows, the differences between himself and ordinary folk (IV, i, 222–76). Running counter to the king's reduction of the distinction between "private men" (IV, i, 229) and himself to a simple notion of Ceremony are his eloquent manner of speech, demonstrated in the soliloquy, and his heroic qualities, enumerated and enhanced throughout the play, beginning with the Archbishop of Canterbury's elaborate encomium (I, i, 24–69). The difficulty here for theatergoers and readers has been in determining whether the king's evasiveness in responding to Williams's serious moral issues and his oversimplification of the differences between himself as king and his subjects are an accurate reflection of his character and the play's issues or whether Shakespeare is trying to satisfy too many aims at once and, in the process, inadvertently undermining the character of the king and the complexity of the ideas of the play. What causes the problem is the continual idealization of Henry as hero, whether on the throne or on the battlefield. It is difficult to retain one's humanity in the face of such idealization. Moreover, Shakespeare is by instinct too much of a psychological realist to paint a wholly idealized portrait. The Antony of *Antony and Cleopatra* is both a more daring and illuminating portrait of a hero, largely because the play faces squarely the ambivalence and ambiguity of Antony's public and private roles and the conflict between the Roman and Egyptian perspectives on those roles.

In glorifying Henry, Shakespeare is responding not only to the familiar tradition behind Henry the hero king but to the Tamburlaine of Marlowe's first play. Marlowe's second Tamburlaine play contains the problem that Shakespeare faces of trying to invest the protagonist with a humanity that also allows him to survive as a hero. To exemplify the Marlovian ingredients in the magnification of Henry's heroic traits, we need only listen to the Chorus just before the Battle of Agincourt. In the following excerpt, the Chorus places special emphasis on the king's heroic ability to inspire his men to create an uncommonly strong comradeship so that they demonstrate a power in battle that supersedes all numerical odds. It is the manner, not the substance, that takes us back to the *Tamburlaine* plays—in particular, the intensive diction ("plucks"),[25] an imposing abstraction and cosmological detail in combination with elevated language ("A largess universal, like the sun"), the formal, grandiloquent personifications (44–45), the epic imperative ("Behold"), emphatic rhythms, repeated word sounds, and the sonorous resonance of open vowel sounds:

> every wretch, pining and pale before,
> Beholding him, plucks comfort from his looks.
> A largess universal, like the sun.
> His liberal eye doth give to every one,
> Thawing cold fear, that mean and gentle all
> Behold, as may unworthiness define,
> A little touch of Harry in the night. (IV, Chorus, 41–47)

Surely, something more than Ceremony separates Henry from "private men" (IV, i, 229). His ability to inspire his soldiers to do feats they never thought themselves capable of is the stuff of which legends are made.[26] The language of the speech contains a Marlovian excess, beginning with the hyperbolic "every," that typifies the deliberate artifice often used to characterize Henry. Just as in the *Tamburlaine* plays, artifice is used here to remove the protagonist from the ranks of ordinary people. The difference resides in the emotional content of Shakespeare's language. Hyperbole is used here, as it is not in the *Tamburlaine* plays, to suggest the intense *emotional* bond that the tireless king inspires in his men, a bond that galvanizes their energies and becomes the source of their epic military power.

Another indication of what Shakespeare has learned from Marlowe's artistic manipulation of language and detail, as well as how he differs from his predecessor, can be seen by examining Exeter's adulatory description of Henry (II, iv, 97–112). The King of France asks Exeter what will happen if he does not abide by Henry's demands. Exeter is blunt in reply:

> Bloody constraint; for if you hide the crown
> Even in your hearts, there will he rake for it.
> *Therefore in fierce tempest is he coming,*
> *In thunder and in earthquake, like a Jove;*
> That if requiring fail, he will compel;
> And bids you, in the bowels of the Lord,
> Deliver up the crown, and to take mercy
> On the poor souls for whom this hungry war
> Opens his vasty jaws; and on your head
> Turning the widows' tears, the orphans' cries,

The dead men's blood, the privèd maidens' groans,
For husbands, fathers, and betrothèd lovers
That shall be swallowed in this controversy. (II, iv, 97–109; my italics)

To be sure, Shakespeare is treating English history here, as Marlowe in the *Tamburlaine* plays is not. In fact, one key element lacking in Marlowe's plays—an entire emotional dimension—is precisely the patriotic connection found in *Henry V*. In the passage above, the two italicized lines are the most Marlovian. The metaphorical combination of an exalted mythological figure, the king of the gods no less, and an intense natural force, a "fierce tempest," to suggest Henry's power is typical of the yoking of superlatively strong mythological and natural elements to characterize the protagonist's power in the *Tamburlaine* plays.[27] So, too, are the inversion, the harsh word sounds, the heavy rhythms in conjunction with the repetition of the same word ("in") for emphasis, and the ostensible syntactic artifice which removes the form of statement as far as possible from common expression. Shakespeare has learned from Marlowe to make his lines "mighty." What differentiates him from Marlowe is his emotionally connotative language. Whereas Marlowe is always able to turn up the volume, sometimes lapsing into bombast, Shakespeare expresses his individuality by varying and enriching the emotional texture of his language and syntax. I do not mean to suggest that Shakespearean drama is without bombast and that Shakespeare invariably invests his language with emotional connotations, but relatively speaking, Marlowe's effectiveness is with language and details that directly appeal more to the head than the heart. At his best, Shakespeare is just the opposite.

III

In characterizing Marlowe's influence on the characterization and style of *Henry V*, I am not discounting the many other sources of influence on Shakespeare.[28] But the similarities between the *Tamburlaine* plays and *Henry V* are striking enough to suggest that Shakespeare's attraction to Marlowe's forthright interest in artistry, once he fully accepted the attraction, was both inspiring and liberating. As we have observed, Shakespeare was so encouraged by some of the strategies of characterization and style he discovered in Marlowe's two texts that he made use of them in his own play, boldly and imaginatively building on his contemporary's experiments with language and genre. In affirming Marlowe's strategies, his strong concern for artistry, and his venturesomeness, Shakespeare helped to establish a tradition in English drama that esteemed as crucial an attention to aesthetic effectiveness.[29]

   In addition to becoming aware of Marlowe's influence on the serious, high-toned aspects of characterization and style in *Henry V*, we also find Shakespeare's continuing realization of the comic possibilities of the Tamburlainian prototype, a development of his semi-comic characterization of Hotspur and his comic characterization of the Prince of Morocco as Tamburlainian warrior heroes. Ben Jonson is widely recognized as having developed to a fuller extent than Shakespeare the comic possibilities of this figure with such characters as Volpone and Sir Epicure Mammon,[30] but he might not have been encouraged to do so without Shakespeare's earlier examples. Pistol is Shakespeare's most vivid contribution to the developing tradition in characterization that took advantage of the comic richness latent in the Marlovian prototype. Even before the Pistol of 2 *Henry IV* and *Henry V*, Shakespeare had invested such figures as Sampson in *Romeo and Juliet*,[31] the Prince of Morocco in *The Merchant of Venice*, and Hotspur in 1 *Henry IV* with the comedy of the braggadocio, a figure discernible in Marlowe's boastful overreacher. We first meet Pistol in the fourth scene of the second act of 2 *Henry IV*. Immediately before his appearance he is identified as a "swaggerer" by Hostess Quickly and Doll Tearsheet (II, iv, 69–104). Therefore, when he actually appears, we are not surprised to see that he is a comic version of Tamburlaine and that the two women have assisted in setting him up as that. In fact, Pistol's role as a comic Tamburlaine seems to be his chief reason for being. Although he appears briefly in two other scenes of the play (V, iii and V, v), his "big" moment occurs when he repeats Tamburlaine's words to comic effect,[32] parodying Tamburlaine's well-known imperative, "Holla, ye pampered jades of Asia! / What, can ye draw but twenty miles a day" (2 *Tamburlaine*, IV, iv, 1–2):

> … Shall pack horses
> And hollow pampered jades of Asia,
> Which cannot go but thirty mile a day,
> Compare with Caesars, and with Cannibals,
> And Trojan Greeks? (2 *Henry IV*, II, iv, 157–61)

In identifying himself with the warrior hero, Pistol comically inflates Marlowe's already excessive language, increasing the mileage from twenty to thirty (159), and in the end garbles the sense of Tamburlaine's sarcastic address to Trebizon and Soria, the two kingly "jades" drawing his chariot. Shakespeare's transformation of "Holla" into the adjective "hollow" suggests that he had read Marlowe's play, not simply seen it performed in the theater, because the change emanates from a visual rather than an auditory response to the word.

We meet Pistol again in *Henry V* in which he first serves as a comic counterpoint to the king: whereas the king, like Tamburlaine, does what he says he is going to do, Pistol is all talk. As the young boy, Falstaff's former page, remarks, "For Pistol, he hath a killing tongue and a quiet sword; by the means whereof 'a breaks words and keeps whole weapons" (III, ii, 32–35). Later in the play, the boy's criticism of Pistol invokes even more forcefully a moral frame of reference:

> I did never know so full a voice issue from so empty a heart; but the saying is true, "The empty vessel makes the greatest sound." Bardolph and Nym had ten times more valor than this roaring devil i' th' old play that every one may pare his nails with a wooden dagger; and they are both hanged; and so would this be, if he durst steal anything adventurously. (IV, iv, 68–74)

These words set in opposition "valor" as a virtue and the absence of it as a vice. In securing the argument, the boy links Pistol with the devil or Vice figure of the morality plays of the past (70–72). By this point in the play, Shakespeare appears to be no longer governed by an interest in making Pistol a parody of the Tamburlaine prototype. He is instead involved in setting him in opposition to the serious Tamburlaine prototype into which Henry has steadily been developing. This opposition is made clear when Pistol demonstrates a lack of responsibility as a soldier (III, ii, 1–52) and, later, when he goes to Fluellen to ask his help in breaking the rules to prevent Bardolph from being punished for stealing (III, vi, 12–84), in this latter scene, it is Gower who moralizes on the type of "a gull, a fool, a rogue" (III, vi, 66) Pistol is. This moral context is established well before the scene in which Henry in disguise wanders among the soldiers and encounters Pistol. Here, the king sees the irony of the cowardly Pistol's "fierceness" (IV, i, 63). At the same time, Pistol contributes to the idealization of Henry by praising the king (IV, i, 44–48). In other words, Pistol has become a functional character, one used to suit the artistic needs of the play at the moment. No longer is he a purely comic figure, someone whom we respond to without invoking a moral frame of reference. Apart from serving the functions of the moment, he has become someone who undermines a virtue that the play celebrates: devotion to the military cause and, hence, to the country. Like Tamburlaine, Henry is devoted to a principle that takes precedent over his private life, even though in Acts IV and V Shakespeare tries to develop Henry's human qualities. Pistol, by contrast, is incapable of action that is not self-serving and, even then, he is more talk than action. He leaves the play having been justly cudgelled by Fluellen (V, i, 1–85) with Gower delivering the final moral denunciation: "Go, go. You are a counterfeit cowardly knave … dare [you] not avouch in your deeds any of your words" (V, i, 66; 69–70). Whether Shakespeare intended it, the development of Pistol into a minor figure of evil is a commentary on just how uninteresting the Tamburlaine prototype becomes if characterized as a one-trick pony. It may also help to explain why the protagonist of the second part of *Tamburlaine* degenerates from an epic figure into a figure who is clearly flawed. As usual, the flaw for Marlowe seems to emanate from an excess of emotion, the inability to control it. For Shakespeare in *Henry V*, emotion becomes the means to humanize and balance the otherwise overly rational and businesslike personality of the king—as the wooing of Katherine makes clear.

After *Henry V*, the influence on Shakespeare of the Tamburlainian prototype continues until the end of his career, but it does not emerge again as the object of parody. King Lear shows some of the same tireless energy that one finds in Tamburlaine. He also shows in his language a similar intensity and majesty but, as I remarked earlier in differentiating the language of the *Tamburlaine* plays and *Henry V*, the words are suffused with densely emotional connotations as Tamburlaine's are not. The following pair of passages reveals the two protagonists at a moment when they are thoroughly angry with one of their children. The differences in the employment of language and its effect are telling. Standing before a group of soldiers, military leaders, and two of his sons with their prisoners, Tamburlaine calls for his third son Calyphas:

> But where's this coward villain, not my son,
> But traitor to my name and majesty?

He goes and brings him out.
Image of sloth, and picture of a slave,
The obloquy and scorn of my renown,
How may my heart, thus fired with mine eyes,
Wounded with shame and kill'd with discontent,
Shroud any thought may hold my striving hands
From martial justice on thy wretched soul? (2 *Tamburlaine*, IV, i, 89–96)

Tamburlaine's rejection of Calyphas appears to be caused by his perception of how badly his son's inaction and unmanliness reflect on him—wholly a matter of ego, it would seem, since the son unquestionably is not a replica of the father. We are left with a strong impression of Tamburlaine's self-centeredness and narrow-mindedness. In the next passage, Lear is raging against his daughter Goneril:

Lear: Hear, Nature, hear; dear goddess, hear:
             Suspend thy purpose if thou didst intend
             To make this creature fruitful.
             Into her womb convey sterility,
             Dry up in her the organs of increase,
             And from her derogate body never spring
             A babe to honor her. If she must teem,
             Create her child of spleen, that it may live
             And be a thwart disnatured torment to her.
             Let it stamp wrinkles in her brow of youth,
             With cadent tears fret channels in her cheeks,
             Turn all her mother's pains and benefits
             To laughter and contempt, that she may feel
             How sharper than a serpent's tooth it is
             To have a thankless child. (*King Lear*, I, iv, 271–85)

Unlike Tamburlaine, Lear talks about himself only indirectly, in the final three lines of the passage. Moreover, he dramatizes his wishes for Goneril, presenting two scenarios, one in which Goneril is sterile and one in which she has a "thankless child." Tamburlaine makes use of the situation at hand to praise his militarily successful sons and then by contrast to call upon his third son to step forward so that he can attack him—at first only verbally. In talking primarily about himself and in using the language of formal address, Tamburlaine is excessive (e.g., 92–94), enough so that our attention moves past the substance of what he speaks to the manner in which he speaks it. We notice the parallel phrasing in "Image of sloth, and picture of a slave" and again in "Wounded with shame and kill'd with discontent," and we hear a man detachedly making pronouncements, not conveying genuine anguish. The undisguised artifice in the language gives us the sense that it is calculated and has been rehearsed. Consequently, we stand apart listening to Tamburlaine's words and do not look feelingly with his eyes. By contrast, Shakespeare builds on the immediate situation of Lear's frustration as a parent and a king by portraying two other dramatic situations, both under the guise of addressing a prayer to the goddess Nature. As a result, the emotional character of the language increases and enriches the felt effect through the layered complexity of the dramatic situations. Moreover, the language itself is more emotionally connotative than Marlowe's. The speech, in the semblance of a prayer, is really a curse, forcefully conveyed through a string of imperatives. The language is a jolting combination of words that are particular and general on the one hand and concrete and abstract on the other. In union with the overall situation of Goneril's severity, Albany's bewilderment, and Lear's encroaching madness, the prayer to Nature is at once a suppression and a transference of Lear's fury against the loneliness of one raging against the dying of the light, a loneliness, though in part self-inflicted, that speaks to everyone's fear of the loss of human bonds and of physical decay. Beyond moral considerations of Lear's rightness or wrongness, we feel an elderly man's desperation in the face of age and the sharp edge of the serpent's tooth as it severs his connection with a daughter. It is of course unfair to compare the relative detachment we feel in Tamburlaine's words with the engagement we feel in Lear's. Apart from the differences in the two dramatists' experience and other possible sources for Lear's behavior, there are major differences in perspective and context. Even so, both are using language of a high order—for example, "obloquy" (2 *Tamburlaine*, IV, i, 92) and "derogate" (*King Lear*, I, iv, 276)—to magnify the commonplace occurrence of parental frustration.

In addition to the aspects of Tamburlaine in Lear, there are elements attributed to figures as wide-ranging as Coriolanus and Prospero. In the plays thought to be written after 1599, however, the figure who most reflects the Tamburlainian prototype, taken seriously, is the Antony of *Antony and Cleopatra*. Like Tamburlaine, Antony's heroic actions match his words. Both men unmetaphor what at first appear to be hyperbolic statements by making them literal through their actions. That is because for both heroes, "hyperboles" are a realistic norm: Early in their relationship, Tamburlaine tells Zenocrate that he will offer her his "martial prizes" and then himself (1 *Tamburlaine*, I, ii, 102–5) and, by the end of the first play, as they are about to marry, he crowns her Queen of Persia and of "all the kingdoms and dominions / That late the power of Tamburlaine subdu'd" (1 *Tamburlaine*, V, i, 508–9). By the same token, Antony sends his messenger from Rome to say to Cleopatra: "To mend the petty present, I will piece / Her opulent throne with kingdoms" (*Antony and Cleopatra*, I, v, 45–46) and, later, as Octavius Caesar tells us, Antony has given Cleopatra "the stablishment of Egypt, made her / Of lower Syria, Cyprus, Lydia, / Absolute queen" (*Antony and Cleopatra*, III, vi, 9–11).

Living psychologically in the world of demi-gods, both Tamburlaine and Antony manifest the power of the conquering hero. Each is magnified and idealized but, betrayed by the force of emotion,[33] not allowed finally to become an exemplary model of behavior. They are figures more to be wondered at than reduced and contained in commonplace moral categories. Marlowe's deliberate ambiguity about the sources of Tamburlaine's power as a military hero is echoed in Shakespeare's portrayal of Antony's "greatness." Whether one regards Menaphon's physical description of Tamburlaine as an indication of the source of his astonishing feats and power (1 II, i, 7–30) or listens to Tamburlaine's well-known statement of Epicurean materialism to Cosroe (1 II, vii, 12–29), neither speech identifies the sources of Tamburlaine's magnificence. In the latter speech, Tamburlaine says that "Our souls" (21) propel us to power, wealth, and fame. The surprise here, as usual, is in not hearing what we expect to hear: he does not say that *God* propels us or our souls, nor does he say that our "perfect bliss and sole felicity" (28) are a *heavenly* "crown" (29). Like Homer, who is wise enough to suggest the effects rather than the causes of Helen's beauty, Marlowe attributes the origin of Tamburlaine's acclaim to the soul, an ambiguous catchall. When we first hear about Antony's military achievements, in the opening speech of the Roman play, they are similarly shrouded in ambiguity:

> those his goodly eyes
> That o'er the files and musters of the war
> Have glowed like plated Mars... (*Antony and Cleopatra*, I, i, 2–4)

> His captain's heart,
> Which in the scuffles of great fights hath burst
> The buckles on his breast... (*Antony and Cleopatra*, I, i, 6–8)

The language is suggestive and emotionally evocative, not definitive: "goodly," "glowed like plated Mars," "captain's heart," "burst / The buckles." It would be difficult to reduce the metaphors of this speech to literal statements, although they educe Antony's amazing ability to inspire his men and his tremendous exertion of energy in battle. If the style and tone of these lines have their roots in the language of the *Tamburlaine* plays, as I believe they do, one also notices how the context of the comments of Antony's two followers on Cleopatra undercuts the afflatus, giving a complexity that Marlowe's portrayal lacks. Even so, both writers understand the value of ambiguity in kindling the imagination. If the protagonist is to be writ large, it is more effective if the audience and not the writer does it.

·I have tried to show in this chapter that *Henry V* reveals Shakespeare moving beyond the mere belittlement of the Tamburlainian prototype. Both Marlowe and Shakespeare are intensely interested in the mechanics of their artistry as a means for increasing the dramatic effectiveness of their plays. Inspired by Marlowe's achievements, Shakespeare sees that, from the artistic perspective of an imaginative imitator, there are serious and comic sides to Tamburlaine and that he can make use of both within a single play, stretching the boundaries of the chronicle history beyond Marlowe's but not without realizing, as Marlowe realized,[34] that rigid categorizations of genre and an unfettered imagination simply will not work together in harmony.

What, then, is Marlowe's strongest overall influence on Shakespeare from the *Tamburlaine* plays? Assuredly, it is in the acknowledgment of a model that sanctions the primacy of an *artistic* consciousness and demonstrates its effectiveness, given that primacy. In his Prologue and in the two plays that follow, Marlowe leaves Shakespeare with a record that both liberates and inspires his heir's artistic consciousness. Once ignited, Shakespeare's consciousness assimilates Marlowe's stylistic innovations and uses them as incentives for innovations of his own. In the process, he solidifies a tradition in the craftsmanship of language and syntax. Moreover, he accepts

Tamburlaine as a prototype and sees in the prototype both serious and comic possibilities. If *Henry V* causes confusion in its readers, it is because in the excitement of reveling in the delights of his own artistic consciousness, Shakespeare tries to accomplish too much. But it signals the first time in the chronology of his plays as we know it that the word "influence" has significant depth.

Notes

1 As I mentioned in the first chapter, *Doctor Faustus*, V, i, 89 [A-text]; V, i, 93 [B-Text], is twitted in *Richard II*, IV, i, 281–86 (composed and first performed between 1595–97) and then made serious use of in *Troilus and Cressida*, II, ii, 81–83 (composed and first performed between 1601–1603) and in *King Lear*, IV, vii, 32–37 (composed and first performed between 1598–1606); *The Jew of Malta*, II, i, 47–54 is echoed in *The Merchant of Venice*, II, viii, 15–17 (composed and first performed between 1594–98); 2 *Tamburlaine*, IV, iv, 1–2 is parodied in 2 *Henry IV*, II, iv, 157–61 (composed and first performed between 1596–1598); "The Passionate Shepherd to His Love" is parodied in *The Merry Wives of Windsor*, III, i, 16–28 (composed and first performed between 1597–1602); *Hero and Leander*, 176 is rendered comic in *As You Like It*, III, v, 82 (composed and first performed between 1598–1600); and *The Massacre At Paris*, xxii, 67 is echoed seriously in *Julius Caesar*, II, ii, 28 (composed and first performed between 1598–99), unless it was the compilers of Marlowe's text that borrowed the line from *Julius Caesar* (see *Christopher Marlowe: The Plays and Their Sources*, ed. Vivien Thomas and William Tydeman [New York: Routledge, 1994], 258–59). See also my comments on *The Massacre At Paris* and *Julius Caesar* in Chapter 2.

2 It is very likely that, in addition to seeing the plays staged, Shakespeare had a reading knowledge of some of them.

3 See Peter Berek, "*Tamburlaine*'s Weak Sons: Imitation as Interpretation before 1593," *Renaissance Drama* n.s., 13 (1982): 55–82, who states that 10 of the 38 extant plays written for the public theater between 1587 and 1593 "show clear debts to *Tamburlaine*" (58). The plays are Greene's *Alphonsus King of Aragon* (1587), Peele's *Battle of Alcazar* (1589), the anonymous *Locrine* (1591), the anonymous *The Taming of a Shrew* (1589), Greene's *Orlando Furioso* (1591), *The Wars of Cyrus* (1588), Lodge's and Greene's *A Looking-Glass for London and England* (1590), Lodge's *Wounds of Civil War* (1588), *Selimus* (1592) and Shakespeare's *Henry VI* plays. Clare Harraway in *Re-citing Marlowe: Approaches to the Drama* (Burlington, VT: Ashgate, 2000), 101 and n. 34 (107), cites this same article to make a similar point.

4 Maurice Charney, "The Voice of Marlowe's Tamburlaine in Early Shakespeare," *Comparative Drama* 31:2 (Summer 1997): 213–23, finds little in Henry V that recalls Tamburlaine: "Like *Tamburlaine*, *Henry V* is a conqueror play but with an important difference. The authentic voice of Marlowe's Tamburlaine is not heard in Henry V, nor in Prince Hal in the preceding plays of the tetralogy. Instead Hotspur seems to echo the heroic vaunting mode of Tamburlaine, but in an almost parodic form" (220). I agree with these statements but, as I go on to argue, feel that influence extends beyond "the authentic voice of Marlowe's Tamburlaine."

5 See also my discussions of these lines in Chapters 1 and 4.

6 *Troilus and Cressida* was probably written around 1602 and already we can see in II, ii, 81–83 that Shakespeare is no longer eager to parody Marlowe's lines:

> Is she worth keeping? Why, she is a pearl
> Whose price hath launched above a thousand ships
> And turned crowned kings to merchants.

As I will discuss a bit later in the text, one can, of course, also see that Shakespeare's shift in attitude to an acceptance of elements of the Tamburlainian prototype may have influenced the portrayal of Lear's remarkable *élan vital*.

7   James Shapiro, *Rival Playwrights: Marlowe, Jonson, Shakespeare* (New York: Columbia University Press, 1991), 96.

8   Ibid., 96–100.

9   Ibid., 100–101. Apart from Shapiro, the critic who has compared the two plays most extensively is Roy Battenhouse, "The Relation of Henry V to Tamburlaine," *Shakespeare Survey* 27 (1974): 71–79. Battenhouse is particularly effective in demonstrating how un-Christian a Christian king Henry is (e.g., 72, 74). His chief focus, however, is on the parallels and differences between the two *Tamburlaine* plays and *Henry V*. He does not deal with the former as sources for the latter.

10   Shapiro, *Rival Playwrights*, 100.

11   See Thomas and Tydeman, eds, *Christopher Marlowe*, 69–168, who include among the 14 texts they present, excerpts from several historical accounts.

12   Stephen Greenblatt comments in *Renaissance Self-Fashioning: From More to Shakespeare* (Chicago: University of Chicago Press, 1980), 202: "*Tamburlaine* repeatedly teases its audience with the *form* of the cautionary tale, only to violate the convention. All of the signals of the tragic are produced, but the play stubbornly, radically, refuses to become a tragedy." I am not sure what Greenblatt means in his hyperbolic statement, "All of the signals of the tragic are produced." But, given an audience's sense of poetic justice in addition to its conventional sense of justice, it might well be fearful that Tamburlaine could fall from his high estate at any time.

13   If Marlowe wrote the Prologue *after* he wrote the plays, then the phrase "tragic glass" is even more strongly ironic than if he wrote it before writing them. The difference is between an intentional and an unintentional irony.

14   I can find no causal relationship in the text between Tamburlaine's burning of "the Turkish Alcoran" (2, V, i, 171) and his decline and eventual death.

15   The word "tragic" is used here in the sense of calamitous which is, of course, more inclusive than a medieval understanding of the term.

16   For a summary of the critical controversy that emerges from our inability to categorize Tamburlaine, see Ian McAdam, *The Irony of Identity: Self and Imagination in the Drama of Christopher Marlowe* (Newark: University of Delaware Press, 1999), 73–76.

17   Two books helpful in placing the *Tamburlaine* plays and *Henry V* in the military context of the 1590s are: Nina Taunton, *1590s Drama and Militarism: Portrayals of War in Marlowe, Chapman and Shakespeare's "Henry V"* (Burlington, VT: Ashgate, 2001) and Alan Shepard, *Marlowe's Soldiers: Rhetorics of Masculinity in the Age of the Armada* (Burlington, VT: Ashgate, 2002).

18   In an essay entitled "Marlowe and the 'Comic Distance'" in *Christopher Marlowe*, ed. Brian Morris (New York: Hill and Wang, 1968), 47–64, J.R. Mulryne and Stephen Fender discuss the ambivalence of our response, our simultaneous attraction and repulsion to Tamburlaine, as a way of achieving comic distance (52–56). To explain "comic," they quote from an essay on Kafka by Eliseo Vivas: "Generally speaking, a comic grasp of the world rests on the perception by the writer of a moral duality which elicits from the reader

a 'comic' response as the only means of freeing himself from the conflict towards values to which he is attached and yet towards which he cannot justify his attachment satisfactorily" (53). Such a process in the psychology of response clearly obviates the necessity for categorizing our attitude toward Tamburlaine as one of either sympathy or blame.

19   For a more extensive discussion of the use of this crucial artistic device in portraying Tamburlaine, see Robert A. Logan, "Violence, Terrorism, and War in Marlowe's *Tamburlaine* Plays," in *War and Words: Horror and Heroism in the Literature of Warfare*, ed. Sara Munson Deats, Lagretta Tallent Lenker, and Merry G. Perry (Lanham, MD: Rowman and Littlefield, 2004), 65–81.

20   At the forefront of those critics who view ambiguity as an artistic strategy is Sara Munson Deats in her essay, "Henry V: Christian King or Model Machiavel," in *War and Words*, 83–101.

21   For an interesting discussion of a quite different perspective on Tamburlaine's language, which nevertheless comes to some of the same conclusions I come to, see Emily C. Bartels, *Spectacles of Strangeness: Imperialism, Alienation, and Marlowe* (Philadelphia: University of Pennsylvania Press, 1993), 53–81. Bartels finds Tamburlaine's words "embedded within an imperialist exchange in ways that are finally self-consuming rather than self-sustaining" (66); "while mystifying and aggrandizing terms can construct a differentiated, sovereign self, they ultimately cannot sustain it" (80). I agree with these conclusions about Tamburlaine's discourse and think that they also reveal some important characteristics of Marlowe's artistic consciousness and linguistic strategies, as I go on to discuss.

22   It is conceivable that Tamburlaine's "wounding the world with wonder" becomes Hamlet's "wonder-wounded hearers" (*Hamlet*, V, i, 247).

23   There is some question as to whether this repeated order (IV, vi, 36–38 and IV, vii, 58–60) reflects a corruption in the text.

24   See, for example, Hal's well-known soliloquy in I, ii, 183–205 in which he gives moral justification to his behavior through the fundamental aesthetic principle of contrast.

25   One is reminded of Hotspur's well-known Tamburlainian avowal: "By heaven, methinks it were an easy leap / To *pluck* bright honor from the pale-faced moon" (1 *Henry IV*, I, iii, 201–2; my italics).

26   We shall see in the chapter that follows that Antony possesses this same ability to inspire people to outdo themselves and not just his comrades in battle; he inspires Cleopatra to commit suicide and join him in death. The very fact of the play is a testament to how this trait becomes the stuff of which legends are made.

27   For example, 1 I, ii, 172–209; 1 II, vii, 12–29; 1 IV, ii, 30–55; 2 I, iii, 153–71; 2 III, iv, 45–68; and 2 IV, iii, 114–33.

28   These include, of course, the anonymous play, *The Famous Victories of Henry V*, and the chroniclers Holinshed and Hall.

29   See the Appendix to this chapter.

30   For a full treatment of the links between Marlowe and Jonson in style and characterization, see Shapiro, *Rival Playwrights*, 39–73.

31   I am reminded of an essay by Joseph A. Porter, "Marlowe, Shakespeare, and the Canonization of Heterosexuality," in *Displacing Homophobia: Gay Male Perspectives in Literature and Culture*, ed. Ronald R. Butters, John M. Clum, and Michael Moon (Durham, NC: Duke University Press, 1989), 127–47, in which the author tries to make the case that Mercutio "plays the major and indeed virtually the sole part in Shakespeare's processing of the challenge presented by Marlowe's sexuality" (132). Porter is convincing in his discussion of the continuing emulation of Marlowe by Shakespeare after Marlowe's death,

but his emphasis on the way in which Mercutio represents Shakespeare's coming to terms with Marlowe's homoeroticism leads him to underplay other Marlovian elements in the play such as Sampson and the experiments with language.

32 Pistol is also used to make fun of George Peele when in II, iv, 145 and 159–60 he quotes from Peele's lost play, *The Turkish Mahomet and Hiren The Fair Greek* and in II, iv, 263 quotes from Peele's *Battle of Alcazar*.

33 As usual, however, Marlowe places a negative value on emotion, seeming to fear its destructive power, whereas Shakespeare sees it as essentially positive, the basis for human mutuality. Antony's emotional nature is complex but, on the whole, Shakespeare affirms it. It is at its most destructive when it becomes a measure of the triumvir's frustration.

34 I am thinking of the contradiction between the phrase "tragic glass" in the Prologue and the absence of either tragic elements or a moralizing glass in the two plays that follow.

Appendix

As everyone interested in literary history knows, Shakespeare's accomplishment in promoting aesthetic effectiveness as a priority leads to Ben Jonson's strongly proclaimed sense of tradition, his high estimation of his place in it, and his unabashed self-promotion as dramatist and poet. The "Conversations with Drummond" and "Discoveries" suggest that Jonson was himself a Tamburlaine in lording his technical proficiency as a writer over that of contemporaries and predecessors; we are all familiar with some of his pronouncements and their absoluteness:

> He [Jonson] was better versed and knew more in Greek and Latin, than all the poets in England and quintessence their brains. (1, 149)

> ... Donne, for not keeping of accent, deserved hanging. (1, 133)

> ... Shakespeare wanted art. ... (1, 133)

> He cursed Petrarch for redacting verses to sonnets, which he said were like that tyrant's bed, where some who were too short were racked, others too long cut short. (1, 133–34)

> Spenser, in affecting the ancients, writ no language .... (8, 618)[1]

It is Jonson, too, who, after sniping at Shakespeare's lack of artistry in the "Conversations," acknowledges in the poem written for the First Folio of Shakespeare (1623) that the playwright's "art doth give the fashion" (l, 58):

> For a good Poet's made, as well as born.
> And such wert thou. Look how the father's face
> Lives in his issue, even so, the race
> Of *Shakespeare's* mind, and manners brightly shines
> In his well turned and true filed lines:
> In each of which, he seems to shake a lance,
> As brandished at the eyes of ignorance. ("To The Memory of My Beloved The Author, Mr. William Shakespeare, And What He Hath Left Us," 64–70)[2]

In understanding the "Conversations," we need to remember that neither Jonson nor Drummond knew that the latter's rough notes would be published and recorded for posterity and that the relationship between the two men was not entirely sympathetic. Moreover, the statement that "Shakespeare wanted art" is probably best understood as a comment on Shakespeare's lack of fastidiousness rather than as a general reflection on his lack of art.[3] As the poem contributed to the First Folio edition suggests, and as we have seen in *Henry V*, Shakespeare was unusually conscious of his artistry, whether successful or not. The kind of lapses Jonson mentions have less to do with artistry than with factual realism and, very likely, bothered *him* more than they would bother most readers and spectators. The following is a familiar example of a lapse Jonson found in *The Winter's Tale*: "Shakespeare, in a play, brought in a number of men saying they had suffered shipwreck in Bohemia, where there is no sea near by some 100 miles."[4] For all his accuracy, I am not persuaded that, given the effectiveness of the scenes in Bohemia, Jonson could convince many readers or an audience that this was an *artistic* lapse. But it does indicate how strong his sensitivity to all matters that might come under the heading of artistry is. Finally, it is also Jonson who, in taking himself and his profession seriously enough to collect his writing and publish it in 1616, was the first English author to point with pride to his achievements—some thought with presumptuousness—by using the word "works" in his title: *The Works of Benjamin Jonson.* Marlowe's Prologue to *Tamburlaine* undoubtedly set in motion a heightened awareness of the writer's artistry that both Shakespeare and Jonson warmly received, thereby securing the tradition of conscious artistry, not just in drama but in poetry, that has prevailed undiminished ever since.

Notes

1   All quotations from Jonson are from the edition of C.H. Herford and Percy and Evelyn Simpson, *Ben Jonson* (Oxford: Clarendon Press, 1925–52), 11 vols. The spelling of the quotations is modernized. The first four quotations are from the "Conversations with Drummond" and the fifth is from "Discoveries." The parentheses contain volume and page numbers.

2   *H & S*, 8, 392.

3   Jonson's fastidiousness is not limited to realistic detail. We may also remember such statements from the "Conversations" as "he [Jonson] wrote all his [verses] first in prose, for so his master Camden had learned him" (*H & S*, 1, 143).

4   *H & S*, 1, 138, Section 12.

Chapter 7

Making the Haunt His:
Dido, Queen of Carthage as a Precursor
to *Antony and Cleopatra*

In imagining himself and Cleopatra in the Elysian Fields after their deaths, Antony declares the couple's preeminence, exclaiming, "Dido and her Aeneas shall want troops, / And all the haunt be ours" (*Ant.*, IV, xiv, 53–54).[1] By analogy, this statement can be said to represent the traditionally accepted judgment of critics and scholars who, in making connections between *Antony and Cleopatra* and *Dido, Queen of Carthage*, assert the superiority of Shakespeare's play. But, because this evaluative perspective is reductive, it raises the question of the place of such an aim in a study of influence.

Both plays portray powerful, well-known conflicts in which public duty and private affairs of the heart vie for control. The four lovers in these conflicts, already made famous through legend, possess the status of demigods.[2] As such, they not only heighten the importance of the conflicts but elevate the dramatic focus of the two plays, making all the more significant their intricate contexts of moral, psychological, and political issues. Even so, *Dido* has suffered from charges of weak characterization and undramatic structuring, a colorless reworking of earlier versions of the story, while *Antony and Cleopatra*, for all its ambiguity, has usually been viewed as an indelible portrayal of enduring love: genuine, vibrant, and engagingly complicated. Part of the justification for this difference has been that Marlowe apparently wrote *Dido* early in his career, whereas *Antony* was written late, well after Shakespeare had learned a good bit about dramaturgy from writing many successful plays. To be sure, *Antony* was composed ca.1606–1607, a time when, as Shakespeare looked beyond the troubling events and dire consequences he had portrayed in the tragedies to elements of serenity and resolution in the final four romances, his artistic sensibility—seasoned, refined, and complex—manifested itself with full multiconsciousness. But critics and readers have gone beyond this obvious difference to make use of similarities in genre, characterization, and situation as evidence of the inferiority of *Dido*. Thus, it is no surprise that, speaking judgmentally, "all the haunt" has been Shakespeare's.

In adopting this perspective, however, one severely limits discussion, even prematurely closing it off. Set against this reductive tendency, fortunately, is the constant, irrepressible desire of students of Marlowe and Shakespeare to develop a richer understanding of the links between the two plays. Consequently, more fruitful than repeated evaluations is the increasing awareness, visible during the second half of the twentieth century, that, for the success of his play, Shakespeare not only owes a significant debt to Marlowe generally but to *Dido* specifically.[3] Late twentieth-century discussions of *Dido* as a sophisticated, controlled piece of artistry,[4] together with an increased understanding of some basic cultural notions of late sixteenth-century England—that is, sexual differences, gender roles, and the sources of political and personal power,[5] have raised *Dido*'s stock and positioned interpreters of Marlowe and Shakespeare so that they are now able to develop a complex, intertextual understanding of the play's influence on *Antony*.[6] The possibility of fresh critical perspectives not only effectively calls into question the worth of an evaluation but suggests that for Shakespeare there are important sources of interest in *Dido*, whether conscious or not, which scholars and critics, as they explore more fully late sixteenth-century culture, have yet to consider.[7] Therefore, we need to ask in a more encompassing sense than has been asked in the past, "What might Shakespeare, as he was writing *Antony and Cleopatra*, have found in *Dido* valuable enough to influence him fifteen to twenty years after it was composed?"

In answering this question, we would do well to keep in mind, as we saw in the first chapter, that Marlowe's theatrical activities while working at the Rose and seeing his fellow playwright on something like a daily basis had to have made a strong impression on Shakespeare when he was most impressionable—up through the early 1590s (and even earlier if McMillin and MacLean's suppositions are correct).[8] Moreover, *Dido* was first published and made available as a written text in 1594, a time when Shakespeare's interest in and first-hand knowledge of Marlowe's plays and legacy were undoubtedly keen. Thus, whatever viewing experiences Shakespeare might have had of *Dido* may well have been abetted by his reader's knowledge of the play—especially since we know that the playwright was as voracious in his reading as he was in his involvement with multiple aspects of the theater. The most conclusive evidence of support for the likelihood of his reading knowledge of the play comes, of course, from the verbal echoes of *Dido* in *Antony and Cleopatra*. To these and important related matters, we now turn.

I   Stylistic Influences

Scholars have duly listed several similarities between *Dido* and *Antony* in language, situation, and mood.[9] In discussing direct sources, they have not mentioned some prominent verbal parallels, including "man of men" (*Dido*, III, iii, 26 and *Ant.*, I, v, 72); "I must prevent him; wishing will not serve" (*Dido*, IV, iv, 104) and "Wishers were ever fools" (*Ant.*, IV, xv, 38); and, in the sense of practicing deceitful collusion with, "Pack'd" /"Packed" (*Dido*, IV, iv, 127 and *Ant.*, IV, xiv, 19). A striking similarity in situation, also not mentioned, occurs when the right-hand men of Aeneas and Antony decry the debilitating effects of love on their leaders (e.g., Achates in *Dido*, IV, iii, 31–36 and Enobarbus in *Ant.*, III, vii, 1–15; III, xiii, 1–12 and 29–46), thereby increasing the tension between the pleasures of love and the responsibilities of honor in both plays.[10] It is such resemblances that patently strengthen the case for Shakespeare's familiarity with *Dido*.

In addition to the more or less definite similarities enumerated, scholars have not been remiss in delineating the nebulous parallels revealed in the use of like devices of artistry and like elements in the content of the tales: "a similar 'feel' in the substance of the poetry," as, for example, in the imagery of vastness;[11] and a kinship in "the *dramatic* power"[12] of the two plays, based on supposed similarities of story, character, and, as the following quotation exemplifies, rhetoric: "above all the quality and dramatic effect of Dido's sublime erotic rhetoric informs the inner life and movement of Cleopatra's poetic imagination."[13] With this third quotation, one is left to ask, "Is Dido's rhetoric 'erotic,' let alone 'sublime,' and how does it inform 'the inner life and movement of Cleopatra's poetic imagination,' whatever that phrase may encompass?" All of the above quotations reveal that the links between the two plays often tend to be arrived at impressionistically rather than analytically and can be too vague to be of much help in drawing meaningful conclusions. In their enthusiasm for establishing parallels, scholars have frequently lost sight of key differences between sources and analogues, sources and influences, and influences and similarities. This means that, ultimately, they have lost sight of the larger purpose for drawing comparisons, the *implications* of the likenesses—and of the differences as well. The influence of *Dido* on *Antony and Cleopatra*, and, more generally, of Marlowe on Shakespeare, is both broader and deeper than a list of likenesses suggests, whether the items on the list are definite or only impressionistic. Most important, both the specific and general influences on *Antony and Cleopatra* have more to do with dramatic technique than ideas and attitudes, and, with a freshly invented fusion of different kinds of language—a throwback to the fusion of epic, hyperbolic, idealizing language with which Marlowe clearly intended to awe his audiences.[14] As we shall see, examining the influence through an intertextual comparison of the two plays yields some surprises about the commonly held notions of Marlowe as an overreacher and iconoclast and Shakespeare as a conservative and traditionalist.

Some of the verbal links between the two plays have seemed forced. They include such paired passages as the following. In the first, Dido tempts Aeneas with suggestive sensory details and lyricism:

> I'll give thee tackling made of rivelled gold
> Wound on the barks of odoriferous trees:
> Oars of massy ivory, full of holes,
> Through which the water shall delight to play. (*Dido*, III, i, 115–18)

In the second passage, supposedly originating in the first, Enobarbus describes—with equal attention to the sensory, auditory, and rhythmic effects—Cleopatra's trip down the Cydnus to meet Antony:

> … the oars were silver,
> Which to the tune of flutes kept stroke, and made
> The water which they beat to follow faster,
> As amorous of their strokes. (*Ant.*, II, ii, 204–7)

Both passages contain oars and use the pathetic fallacy to suggest the harmony that exists between the oars and the water through which they travel. Yet, Enobarbus's words do not enable us to specify a direct stylistic influence from *Dido*—in part, because the details differ from Marlowe's. The single detail in common is the oars, but they have been made of a different substance, silver rather than ivory. Even more conclusively, Shakespeare so closely models the passage on the description in North's translation of Plutarch, including the silver oars, that it would be illogical to seek a less obvious influence.[15]

The passage does, however, tacitly acknowledge a broader and deeper parallel, for it reveals an important stylistic way in which Shakespeare concurs with Marlowe: like many contemporary writers, among them Sidney in his *Arcadia* and Spenser in *The Faerie Queene* and *Epithalamion*, both playwrights integrate rhetorical artifice with sensuous perfection as a stately means of conveying sentiment, intensified, idealized, and glorified. In its undisguised artifice, the resulting language detaches us emotionally and asks to be admired as creative endeavor. We stand in awe of the writer's artistic achievement rather than becoming so deeply moved by the words and dramatic situations of Dido and Enobarbus that we can see only through their eyes. Content apart, then, for each writer the style itself consciously signifies exalted feeling. The difference is that Marlowe's language requires a more cerebral, less directly emotional and less emotionally engaged response than Shakespeare's. As the paired passages above reflect, whereas Marlowe is complicated and ornate ("rivelled gold / Wound on the barks"), remotely abstract and generalized ("rivelled," "odoriferous," "massy," "water shall delight to play"), and fulsome, Shakespeare is simple ("the oars were silver" as opposed to "Oars of massy ivory, full of holes") and directly emotional in portraying an action that suggests the eager impulsiveness of love ("the oars ... kept stroke, and made / The water which they beat to follow faster"); he is also without Marlowe's copiousness of adjectives, adjectives that, in being general and abstract, require a cerebral act of understanding before they can be particularized by the imagination and given emotional weight. More generally, whereas Marlowe's focus is descriptive, Shakespeare's is dramatic and situational. In addition, the dramatic aim of each passage differs: if Marlowe is interested in capturing the intense power of Dido's love, Shakespeare is interested in conveying the elusive sources of Cleopatra's ability to captivate. That is, Marlowe strives to portray the *effects* of sexual attraction, whereas Shakespeare attempts to suggest its *causes*. In Dido's lyrical outburst, we stand apart and wonder at the power of her love, as well as at Marlowe's talent for conveying it. Shakespeare, on the other hand, invites us to project imaginatively into the impulsiveness of one caught in the mysterious throes of sexual attraction. In its undisguised artifice, however, the personification of the swirling water as a lover and the silver oars as the beloved object partly detaches us, and, in doing so, lets us know that we are also being asked to admire the cleverness of the writer.

In a second set of paired passages, the latter is again commonly supposed to have derived from the former: during an anguished moment of self-reflection, Aeneas cries out, "I may not dure this female drudgery: / To sea, Aeneas, find out Italy" (IV, iii, 55–56); Antony, in an even more deeply anguished moment, laments, "these strong Egyptian fetters I must break, / Or lose myself in dotage" (I, ii, 115–16). Both plays portray heroes who waver between the conflicting claims of love and duty; consequently, there are bound to be some similarities in situation and in commonplace psychological reactions. But neither the similarity here nor the language in the lines from *Antony and Cleopatra* gives evidence of a direct source. Instead, the responses of the two heroes bring to mind a standard, gender-biased, Renaissance complaint: that, in acting upon their romantic desires, women lead men off their moral course and that, naturally enough but less blameworthy, men are extremely susceptible. Writers often make use of this moral predicament by creating a tension-building dilemma intended to engage and sustain the interest of theatergoers and readers.

If this pairing of passages tells us little about the origins of Shakespeare's language, it does tell us something about a similarity in dramatic technique. The two heroes are governed not only by psychological forces within, which draw them to love, but also by forces outside themselves and beyond their control. For Aeneas, the external forces are represented ultimately by fate with the gods acting as potent intermediaries.[16] For Antony, however, the external forces are represented not only by fate, made known by the Soothsayer, but by the body politic and "the strong necessity of time" (*Ant.*, I, iii, 42). The conflict of external and internal forces produces in *Dido* and *Antony* a need for mediating between these opposed forces, for balancing opposites, which, apart from its personal and political consequences within the worlds of the two plays, reflects dramaturgically a technique essential to creating effective dramatic tension, as both writers know and, of course, as Shakespeare had seen well demonstrated in Marlowe.

In *Dido* and *Antony*, the attempt to balance opposites, whether between specific internal and external forces, private desires (love) and public responsibility (duty), or irrational and rational mental states, provides opportunities for spectacle, often through pointed oppositions.[17] Both plays establish contrasts between private moments of introspection and public scenes of splendor; the court at Carthage is no less unrestrained, lavish, and bountiful than the court at Alexandria. There are similar contrasts in setting—court vs. country in *Dido* and Rome vs. Egypt in *Antony*; in costumes—ragged and royal garb in *Dido* and military (Roman) and holiday (Egyptian) dress in *Antony*; and in the number and movements of characters on stage (blocking).[18] In addition to the spectacles created through visual contrasts are those created through auditory contrasts—in music composed for the plays[19] and, as we shall see, in language. Moreover, both plays conclude with spectacles that provide contrasts in Dido's and Cleopatra's behaviors as we have come to know them, oppositions meant to intensify our experience of their deaths. Marlowe captures our interest through the impact of Dido's self-immolation and the unexpected, non-Virgilian deaths of Iarbus and Anna (which have struck some critics and readers as unnecessary, even excessive). Shakespeare dignifies Cleopatra's death, transforming it into a play within a play with Cleopatra as director, set designer, costumer, and lead actor, while investing it with a ritualistic grandeur. Like Marlowe, he enhances the spectacle with the unexpected deaths of Iras and Charmian. It is clear that Marlowe and Shakespeare both understand the value of spectacle in keeping an audience's sensory and emotional faculties engaged. What is less clear is the extent to which Shakespeare was influenced by Marlowe's use of this device.

Even if examining the verbal parallels between *Dido* and *Antony* either reveals little about Marlowe's influence on Shakespeare or tells us what is obvious about the relationship of linguistic sources in *Antony*, examining the function of style in each play brings us closer to revealing the extent of Marlowe's influence and its significance. For example, the use of the heroic-romantic idiom of *Antony and Cleopatra* appears to originate in such plays of "high astounding terms" as *Dido* and, perhaps even more so, the two *Tamburlaine* plays. Reuben Brower comments that "Marlowe's *Dido, Queen of Carthage* ... offered the most likely example for the Shakespearian blend in *Antony and Cleopatra* of the Virgilian heroic and the Ovidian erotic,"[20] and he earlier defines the heroic idiom in *Dido* as "partly Virgilian, partly medieval," the medieval deriving from Lydgate in *The Falls of Princes*.[21] If what is heroic in Marlowe and Shakespeare derives from a combination of classical and medieval texts, what is exaltedly romantic in Shakespeare seems to derive from Marlowe's enthusiastic hyperbole, mighty superlatives, and idealized sentiments. To take a familiar example:

> Our souls, whose faculties can comprehend
> The wondrous architecture of the world,
> And measure every wand'ring planet's course,
> Still climbing after knowledge infinite
> And always moving as the restless spheres,
> Wills us to wear ourselves and never rest
> Until we reach the ripest fruit of all,
> That perfect bliss and sole felicity,
> The sweet fruition of an earthly crown. (1 *Tamburlaine*, II, vii, 21–29)

This passage celebrates the romance of power with a joyous *élan*; that the emotion directed toward an abstract idea is as strong as that directed toward a human being can be understood as generally characteristic of the impersonality of Marlowe's characters and the depersonalization of their sentiments. What emerges finally in *Antony* can be exemplified by any number of passages, but the following one makes both the attachment to Marlowe and the separation from him patently clear. Antony has just won a battle he did not expect to win and, in returning to Alexandria, expresses his gratitude to his men and ecstatically greets his queen:

> I thank you all,
> For doughty-handed are you, and have fought
> Not as you served the cause, but as 't had been
> Each man's like mine: you have shown all Hectors.
> Enter the city, clip your wives, your friends,
> Tell them your feats, whilst they with joyful tears
> Wash the congealment from your wounds, and kiss
> The honored gashes whole ... (IV, viii, 4–11)

O thou day o' th' world,
Chain mine armed neck; leap thou, attire and all,
Through proof of harness to my heart, and there
Ride on the pants triumphing! (IV, viii, 13–16)

The epithet "doughty-handed," the hyperbolic "all Hectors," the epic diction ("clip" and "feats"), and the extravagance of lines 9–11 are characteristics frequently found in the two *Tamburlaine* plays and *Dido*. The cosmological address to Cleopatra as "day o' th' world" and the heavy, emphatic rhythms can be linked to similar elements in Menaphon's description of Tamburlaine as a semi-divine figure (1 *Tamburlaine*, II, i, 7–30). Moreover, in both writers, the ability of a character to make literal what commonly seems hyperbolic, usually an ability associated exclusively with the gods, distinguishes the heroes from ordinary people. What Shakespeare has added to Marlowe's verse is lyrical intensity, imperatives that give a powerful sense of action and transmit strong, genuine personal feelings from the addresser to the addressees.

The difference between the depersonalized dramatic verse of Marlowe's characters and the personalized verse of Shakespeare's throws into relief a glaring difference between the use of the heroic-romantic idiom in *Antony and Cleopatra* and, before its metamorphosis in the imagination of Shakespeare, its use in Marlowe. In *Dido* and the two *Tamburlaine* plays, characterization is often subservient to style and disjoined from it, whereas in *Antony and Cleopatra* style usually works in an integrated manner to define character—probably, in part at least, because of Shakespeare's greater experience and maturity as a playwright. In *Dido*, the style of Aeneas's lengthy description of the Fall of Troy (II, i, 121–288) draws attention to itself as a heroic mode of expression but not as a revelation of character. That is not to say that *what* is being said (content), not *how* it is being said (style), does not reveal something about Aeneas—as, for example, his tendency to flee rather than fight, deserting three women in Troy, even if his actions can be whitewashed by our knowledge of the stringent demands of fate which are controlling him. Our ability to separate content and style in Marlowe's play, in contradistinction to Shakespeare's in which the two are more often securely fused, is itself significant in characterizing a Marlovian artistic habit of mind. The speech is a dramatic narrative—formal, authoritative, Latinate ("A man compact of craft and perjury" [144]), emphatic, embellished with the artifice of "high astounding terms" and characteristic Marlovian excess:

Frighted with this confusèd noise, I rose,
And looking from a turret might behold
Young infants swimming in their parents' blood,
Headless carcasses piled up in heaps,
Virgins half-dead, dragged by their golden hair
And with main force flung on a ring of pikes,
Old men with swords thrust through their aged sides,
Kneeling for mercy to a Greekish lad,
Who with steel pole-axes dashed out their brains. (II, i, 191–99)

In *Antony and Cleopatra,* characters are similarly used as mouthpieces, to help establish a certain tone (e.g., of grandeur, majesty, lyricism) and convey an elevated attitude toward someone or something. But (often at the same time) Shakespeare uses style to reveal character as, for example, in Antony's statements of Marlovian extravagance, beginning with his speech "Let Rome in Tiber melt" (I, i, 33–40), and especially at those moments when hyperbole asserts itself as the norm. Antony's stylistic excesses, in fact, accurately portray his larger-than-life, heroic generosity, what Cleopatra glorifies as his "bounty" (V, ii, 87). In one instance (already mentioned in another connection in the preceding chapter), Antony sends Cleopatra an "orient pearl" with the following message:

> Say the firm Roman to great Egypt sends
> This treasure of an oyster; at whose foot,
> To mend the petty present, I will piece
> Her opulent throne with kingdoms. All the East,
> Say thou, shall call her mistress. (I, v, 43–47)

This sounds as if it were merely the extravagant flattery of an enthusiastic but absent lover, more style than substance. We later find, however, that Antony gives Cleopatra the rule of Egypt, lower Syria, Cyprus, and Lydia, thereby actually piecing "her opulent throne with kingdoms" and showing himself to be as much of a hero in love as he is in war. To establish his semi-divine status, he unmetaphors what we understood as metaphor, making literal what we initially took to be hyperbole. Thus, style is used in the definition and continual redefinition of character, as well as in the establishment of the epic dimensions of the play's heroic-romantic world.

We can readily acknowledge that *Antony and Cleopatra* was strongly affected by the Marlovian style of epic grandeur, majestic amplitude, hyperbole, and sharp emphasis and that this style might well have derived not only from *Dido* but also from the two *Tamburlaine* plays and *Hero and Leander* (e.g., 94–118).[22] To this list of legacies might be added Marlowe's strongly charged language; his fresh images— plentiful, richly suggestive, and wide-ranging; an authoritatively emphatic syntax; strongly assertive rhythms; and the imposing resonance of the many open vowels. All of these elements serve to produce a resounding grandiloquence that, similar to its function in Marlowe's works, suggests the epic stature of Antony and Cleopatra and the world over which they preside. The differences between the two writers lie in the emotional effects of their writing. Emotionally, Shakespeare's text is more direct, more deeply suggestive and evocative, and more diverse than Marlowe's.

If we stand back from particular influences, we can see that the strongest influence of Marlowe's style is in what we might call his employment of the spectacle of language. Marlowe creates verbal spectacles to give *Dido* a forcefulness, both epic and dramatic in tone, undoubtedly intended to awe an audience. In the following passage, Dido makes her last attempt to prevent Aeneas from leaving Carthage:

> And wilt thou not be moved with Dido's words?
> Thy mother was no goddess, perjured man,

Nor Dardanus the author of thy stock;
But thou art sprung from Scythian Caucasus,
And tigers of Hyrcania gave thee suck. (V, i, 155–59)

O serpent that came creeping from the shore
And I for pity harboured in my bosom,
Wilt thou now slay me with thy venomed sting
And hiss at Dido for preserving thee? (V, i, 165–68)

Dido's question before she begins to belittle Aeneas alerts us to the power of her "words" (155)—which so forcefully create verbal spectacles, images of suckling tigers and an envenomed serpent—and to Marlowe as the wordsmith behind them. Shakespeare apparently finds Marlowe impressively successful at awing his audience, because he strives in *Antony and Cleopatra*, also through a forcefulness both epic and dramatic in tone, to make of his audience "wonder-wounded hearers" (*Hamlet*, V, i, 246). Having been surprised by Caesar's men, a wrathful Cleopatra vows to kill herself:

> Know, sir [Proculeius], that I
> Will not wait pinioned at your master's court,
> Nor once be chastised with the sober eye
> Of dull Octavia. Shall they hoist me up,
> And show me to the shouting varletry
> Of censuring Rome? Rather a ditch in Egypt
> Be gentle grave unto me! Rather on Nilus' mud
> Lay me stark-nak'd and let the waterflies
> Blow me into abhorring! Rather make
> My country's high pyramides my gibbet,
> And hang me up in chains! (V, ii, 52–62)

Although the frame of reference of the images in these two angry outbursts differs— Marlowe's being clearly more bookish, more detached from character and situation (i.e., longer on analogy than on what is being analogized), and more in the mode of pronouncements—each writer has put language and syntax on display. As a result, the audience is instilled with enough detachment to admire the achievement of the stylistic spectacles without becoming completely absorbed emotionally by the content and, hence, wholly caught up by an engaged, feeling projection into the anger of the speakers.

As noted above, an inevitable consequence logically or, rather, psychologically results from the detachment encountered during stylistic spectacles: in both plays, detachment disengages members of the reading or viewing audience so that they no longer look with the eyes of the characters from within the world of the drama; instead, viewing from without, they possess a freedom to stand as much in awe of the writers as of the figures being portrayed. Provided with these conditions of response, the medium not only allows self-congratulation but also invites the audience to make comparisons with other writers and works in the same tradition. Aeneas's description of the Fall of Troy (II, i, 121–288), his last exchange with Dido (V, i, 83–183), and Dido's final speech (V, i, 292–313) all provide clear examples, especially when Marlowe foregrounds the epic tradition he associates himself with by having Dido quote in Latin from the *Aeneid* (V, i, 136–40 and V, i, 310–11 and 313). Antony's speech at the beginning of the play, "Let Rome in Tiber melt" (I, i, 33–40), Enobarbus's description of Cleopatra's first meeting with Antony (II, ii, 200–36), and the Queen's speech as she sets the stage for her suicide and applies the asps to her breast and arm (V, ii, 228–313) all amply demonstrate language that asks to be responded to as spectacle. These speeches, like several others in the play, draw attention to themselves less for their content than for being showpieces of style; consequently, we are made aware of the writing talent behind them, an artist proud enough of his accomplishments to "strut his stuff." That the first and third of these speeches also ask to be responded to as strategies of characterization shows that Shakespeare has gone on to develop the technique he witnessed in Marlowe. In enabling his audience to be both engaged and detached within a single speech, Shakespeare has his cake and eats it, too.

What Shakespeare has clearly rejected in *Dido* is Marlowe's brittleness, his use of language that is more denotative than connotative, language that conveys meaning without deep emotional suggestiveness and evocation, whose appeal is surface and momentary. After Aeneas has left her for the second and last time, Dido, in a frenzied state of heightened emotion, begins to fantasize:

> I'll frame me wings of wax like Icarus,
> And o'er ... [Aeneas'] ... ships will soar unto the sun,
> That they may melt and I fall in his arms.
> Or else I'll make a prayer unto the waves
> That I may swim to him, like Triton's niece;
> O Anna, fetch Arion's harp,
> That I may tice a dolphin to the shore
> And ride upon his back unto my love! (V, i, 243–50)

As in *Hero and Leander*, Marlowe here substitutes mythological allusion for direct emotion and intellectual understanding for feeling. Unlike Dido's fantasies, Cleopatra's imaginings remain earthbound. Whereas Dido's words mark off the boundaries of our imaginative response, Cleopatra's language unleashes it:

> O Charmian!
> Where think'st thou he is now? Stands he, or sits he?
> Or does he walk? Or is he on his horse?
> O happy horse, to bear the weight of Antony!
> Do bravely, horse! For wot'st thou whom thou mov'st?
> The demi-Atlas of this earth, the arm
> And burgonet of men. (I, v, 18–24)

The variety in syntax and the combination of the prosaic and literary in the language invite a response of awe, not so much toward the style as toward the speaker, whereas in Marlowe's passage, we are made more aware of the cleverness of the style than the frustrations of the speaker because they are overarticulated. One detail will suffice to illustrate the point. We have just heard Dido ask Anna to "fetch Arion's harp" so that she may "tice a dolphin to the shore / And ride upon his back unto ... [her] ... love." After Antony dies, Cleopatra initiates the legend of Antony by describing his most admirable characteristics to Dolabella; like Dido, she makes use of the image of a dolphin: "His delights / Were dolphinlike, they showed his back above / The element they lived in" (V, ii, 89–91). Marlowe uses the dolphin to convey the intensity of Dido's feeling, but it is too cute, too pat, and one is aware more of the cloying excess of style than the depth of the Queen's unhappiness. Shakespeare, on the other hand, more practiced and not straining for effect, manages to mingle the extraordinary with the ordinary so as to evoke not only a felt sense of Cleopatra's love and the eloquent tribute it inspires, but a sense of what made Antony superhuman and why the world he and Cleopatra inhabit is, although separate, sometimes equal to that of the gods.

II   Modes of Perception and Their Influence

Poetic and dramatic techniques form only part of *Antony and Cleopatra*'s possible inheritance from *Dido*. Shakespeare seems also to have been aware of Marlowe's interest in modes of perception and developed it for himself. Before examining this influence, it is perhaps helpful to recall that the overall perspective of *Dido* seems resigned, even cynical, whereas that of *Antony* seems cheerfully realistic—at least about living life to the lees. (It is perhaps Octavius Caesar's perspective of hardheaded, cynical realism and his wariness of perceiving unclearly when emotion takes control that comes closest to resembling *Dido*'s perspective.) For Marlowe, for example, sexual passion is portrayed solely as a destructive force, injuring Jupiter, Juno, Dido, Aeneas, Anna, Iarbus, and the Nurse. In *Antony*, it is true that love, in combination with other forces, has a destructive power, as the deaths of the protagonists alone make clear. But because Shakespeare yokes sexual passion with devotion and distinguishes love from lust, we more often view love as a creative, synthetic, binding force which, even if only temporarily, promotes a joyfully felt density of self-fulfillment that little else can duplicate. Likewise, in assuming Marlowe's interest in perception, Shakespeare extricates it from its wholly Marlovian cynical context. Or rather, his two protagonists extricate it, whereas the Romans do not; they share Marlowe's cynical viewpoint and reduce instances of love to lust. Thus, Shakespeare, in effect, dramatizes Marlowe's position through his portrayal of the Romans and, yet, ultimately, he rejects it as a code to live by through the characterizations of Antony and Cleopatra.

At the beginning of *Dido*, Marlowe seems to want to impress upon us how susceptible his characters are to being deceived through what they behold, positing the cause as psychological, not physiological.[23] Aeneas suspects that Venus is "a goddess that delud'st our eyes" by shrouding her beauty in the "borrowed shape" of a Tyrian maid (I, i, 191–92). After she departs, he recognizes her as his mother and laments that "in these shades [she] deceiv'st mine eyes so oft" (I, ii, 244). The play commends neither Venus's tendency to deceive her son nor his to be readily deceived.

Shortly after Aeneas's belated recognition of his mother, suffused with grief at his memory of the fall of Troy and the death of Priam, Aeneas mistakes a statue for a living version of the dead king Priam and Achates tells him: "Thy mind, Aeneas, that would have it so, / Deludes thy eyesight" (II, i, 31–32).[24] The men that Aeneas has lost enter and, at first, Aeneas does not recognize them (II, i, 39–44). Both of these instances make clear that, betrayed by his emotions, Aeneas's grip on reality is none too steady and often vacillating. Marlowe's portrayal of a flawed hero with an interesting psychology is not something Shakespeare overlooked when he came to characterize Antony.

The initial meeting between Dido and Aeneas stresses again the tendency of the eyes to perceive falsely. Ilioneus tells Aeneas of Dido's approach and adds, "view her well" (II, i, 72). Aeneas responds, "Well may I view her, but she sees not me" (II, i, 73). But Dido does see him—although she does not recognize him as Aeneas: "What stranger art thou that dost eye me thus" (II, i, 74). In Aeneas's account of the Fall of Troy, Sinon is characterized as a deceiver who could "force an hundred watchful eyes to sleep" (II, i, 146). The similarity in appearance of Cupid and Ascanius is used to delude Dido, so that she ultimately falls wholeheartedly in love with Aeneas (III, i).[25] These three instances again portray how difficult it can be to locate bedrock reality and how easy it is for someone to prevent another from doing so. Later, Achates warns Aeneas of the deception that comes through the "wanton motions of alluring eyes" (IV, iii, 35), a clear case of the distortion of the supposedly ultimate reality of the gods and fate through sensory and emotional responses. Only when Hermes appears does Aeneas free himself from the deception of a lover's tempting appearance and demeanor and go off to Italy to fulfill his destiny. One gathers from these and other references to deception through the eyes that the play seriously questions a person's ability to perceive even physical reality accurately and further questions whether perception is not seriously impaired, in large part, by the force of the senses and emotion. At best, the play remains skeptical, a dour perspective Shakespeare sought to modify.

The irony of *Dido*'s questioning of one's ability to perceive reality lies in the play's realization that one's limited powers of perception can evidently be as much a blessing as a curse. It is evident throughout the play that the characters enjoy—in fact, thrive on—spectacle almost as much as Marlowe himself does and that spectacle always strives to engage the senses fully, leaving little room for reflection, analysis, and deep emotion. Jupiter delights Ganymede by promising him a spectacle of Juno hanging, bound, "meteor-like 'twixt heaven and earth" (I, i, 13). Soon after, the god provides something of a spectacle by decking out his minion with the very gems that Juno wore on her wedding day. The characters either describe spectacles, as Aeneas does in recounting the Fall of Troy (II, i, 121–303) and as Achates, Iarbus, and Anna do in portraying the storm that sends Dido and Aeneas into the cave (IV, i), or they create spectacles, as Dido does in her feasting of Aeneas (II, i) or as Iarbus does in making a sacrifice to Jove (IV, ii). The spectacle at the climax of the play—the death of Dido and the non-Virgilian deaths of Iarbus and Anna—reveals a dramatic heightening of the *Aeneid*, what Marlowe felt he needed to add in order to intensify the impact. On the one hand, the play presents a wariness of the characters' ability not to be deceived by what they see. Yet, the sensory delights of the eyes seem to provide a chief source of satisfaction for the characters, just as, naturally enough, they must have provided satisfaction for the play's earliest audiences and for Marlowe as dramatist.

If Marlowe's paradoxical depiction of the sorrows and joys of perceiving through the eye reflects a mind so caught up by the inherent ambiguities and contradictions of perception that it is not yet ready to give the problem the kind of consideration that leads to a resolution, Shakespeare's *Antony and Cleopatra* reflects a mind that is ready and even eager to do so. More so than Marlowe, Shakespeare is aware of the difficulty of getting one's bearings when trafficking in several personalities and events concurrently. Antony is continually perplexed by Cleopatra's motives, whether it be when she crosses him (I, iii, 9) as he attempts to return to Rome, runs from the Battle of Actium, or allows Thidias to kiss her hand. Enobarbus condemns Antony with Roman rationality only to find how inadequate it is and to die of a broken heart in his remorse at his betrayal of his friend and leader. And Cleopatra is at times baffled because Antony seems not to understand her motives, even though she works overtime to keep him wondering at her unpredictable ways. Reported actions are similarly obscured. Enobarbus describes the paradoxical nature of Cleopatra's actions:

> I saw her once
> Hop forty paces through the public street;
> And having lost her breath, she spoke, and panted,
> That she did make defect perfection,
> And, breathless, power breathe forth. (II, ii, 230–33)

He goes on to assert that "she makes hungry, / Where most she satisfies" (II, ii, 238–39). Other ironies and paradoxes abound. Antony's ancestor and patron Hercules leaves him (IV, iii) and, yet, Antony goes on to win a battle he was not supposed to win (IV, viii). Cleopatra vows to commit suicide and, yet, hides from Caesar enough valuables to purchase the valuables she has reported to him. Clearly, Shakespeare presents a world of ambiguity and paradox, a world in which flux enables these conditions to flourish. The many instances of moralizing in the play, instead of clarifying matters, only make clearer how clouded our perceptions are. Insofar as it is possible to understand people and events, one's understanding will have to come through the non-rational faculties of apprehension, as the infallibility of the Soothsayer indicates. "I see it in my motion, have it not in my tongue" (II, iii, 13), he declares, and we know that this is the best that anyone in the play can do.

Like Marlowe's characters, Shakespeare's thrive on spectacle. But in *Dido* spectacle usually is of a serious nature, whereas in *Antony* it is also for play and can convey a sense of joy. When Antony and Cleopatra first enter, they are ushered in in a spectacle of magnificence, betokening joyfulness: with a fanfare, with several members of the court, and "with Eunuchs fanning her." Cleopatra's journey on the Cydnus, as Enobarbus portrays it, is pure spectacle, the apotheosis of erotic splendor, calculated to ignite the audience's imagination and augment their wonder. Cleopatra's setting the scene for her death and dressing for the part indicate that, for all the egotism involved, there is also a healthy regard for ritual as a means of enhancing, glorifying, and dignifying the spectacle. Antony and Octavius Caesar are equally conscious of spectacle. They present a contrast in their attitudes toward it, however, and in their participation in it. For Antony, spectacle issues from the heart and reveals personal feelings: as in the public scene in which the hero generously bestows on Cleopatra and her sons the lands he has won (III, vi); or when, in a fit of jealousy, he proclaims that Caesar's messenger Thidias be whipped (III, xiii); or when, in grief, he shakes the hands of his servitors as a gesture of farewell (IV, ii); or when, in a state of ecstasy, he jubilantly returns from a battle he did not expect to win to celebrate with Cleopatra (IV, viii). By contrast, Octavius Caesar knows only the political usefulness of spectacle: as when he hollowly complains to Octavia that her return to Rome lacked spectacle, or when he plans to drag Cleopatra as a trophy through the streets of Rome; even after the deaths of Antony and Cleopatra, he is concerned with how the spectacle of the funeral rites will redound to his "glory" (V, ii, 360–62). From this contrast, we can readily understand Shakespeare's categorical distinction between a non-rational and a rational understanding of spectacle. For the non-rationalist, spectacle is symbolic, a ritual demonstration of genuine feeling, and its importance lies in its enduring content. For the rationalist, the genuineness of the symbolism is of little consequence; it is primarily a stylistic gesture, for show, and its importance adheres in its immediate, momentary practical value. Both writers know that, in actual dramaturgical practice, the two perspectives are not mutually exclusive. Yet, as playwright, Marlowe most frequently seems motivated by a rationalist perspective, whereas Shakespeare more often composes from a non-rationalist perspective and clearly endorses this perspective as superior. The deaths of the two queens perhaps best illustrate the distinction. Marlowe constructs the scene of Dido leaping onto the fire with dramatic shrewdness to maximize climactically the sensationalism of it. Shakespeare invests Cleopatra's death with a ritualism that suggests feelingly the Queen's final demonstration of her infinite variety—in addition to her Egyptian sensuousness and her role as mistress and lover, her Roman resolve and her roles as wife and mother, and, above all, her absolute devotion to her man of men (V, ii, 280–319).

Both Marlowe and Shakespeare portray the problems that characters encounter extracting coherent meaning from other characters' words and actions and forming a consistent, sustainable attitude toward them. And, of course, the difficulties are only compounded for the audience—presumably, not without the writers' awareness of the ability of such difficulties to generate and hold an audience's interest. For *Dido*, the problems grow out of Marlowe's cynical perspective, out of an idealist's unhappy recognition of the severe curtailment of one's power to assert one's will. Unable to assert their will to remain together, Dido fails to understand the depth of Aeneas's commitment to the gods and his fate and Aeneas fails to understand the depth of Dido's commitment to their love. For *Antony and Cleopatra* such misunderstandings, apart from giving the play some explosively dramatic moments, add a wondrous mystery to life and the human condition. Much less eager than Marlowe to portray bitter consequences moralistically, Shakespeare, with cheerful realism, affirms the non-rational faculties and makes a judgment about life that is less moral than aesthetic:

it is better to know the world through the synthetic, creative, non-rational faculties of the mind which can embrace ambiguity and mystery than to try to pluck out the heart of its mystery through the rational faculties of logical, empirical analysis. That does not mean that Shakespeare is unable to accept the unhappiness that life brings; it simply means that he has found a way to make it palatable.

The suicides of Dido and Cleopatra clarify the point. One can argue that Dido dies nobly by taking charge of her life for the first time since she fell in love with Aeneas, her nobility made poignant because she has been victimized: by the gods—Venus and Juno, in particular; by Aeneas; and by Aeneas's destiny—that is, by fate. The trouble with the tragic implications of this ending is that Marlowe does not portray Dido as sympathetic in her victimization. Instead of enabling us to see her plight through her eyes or from the perspective of a compassionate overviewer, he focuses on the unpleasing mechanics of her desperation, her lack of control, and her self-pity (especially at the close of the play: V, i, 128–313). At the end, she seems self-indulgent, someone who too easily gives up on life. We are left to wonder whether this bit of disdainful characterization, in combination with the multiple deaths at the theatrical climax of the play (as distinct from the plot climax), are a hopped-up statement about both the human and extra-human uncontrollable forces that inevitably produce tragedy as well as a desire to conclude the play with a strong climactic spectacle. Cleopatra's suicide, unlike Dido's, is an affirmation. Without a trace of self-pity, she rejects the paltriness of a life without Antony, a life without imagination, drama, or aesthetics, and in a burst of theatrical splendor that assures her perpetuity in legend, dies fully conscious of the irony of her final roles as wife and mother. The two women who die with her view her as heroic: Iras dies of sympathetic vibrations and Charmian by imitating her mistress's suicide with the asp. In their awe at Cleopatra, the two women are transformed, reminding us of Antony's ability to transform his men into "Hectors." If Dido's energy ultimately goes for very little, Cleopatra's vitality does not; through it, she achieves a selfhood that Dido only dreamed of.

We see from the example of the two queens' suicides that Shakespeare has learned from Marlowe what not to do. I will conclude this section by highlighting one antithetical lesson, already glanced at, that Shakespeare could have gleaned from *Dido* or found support for in the play, and by pinpointing two additional lessons. Whereas in *Dido* character is made to serve the demands of the poetic style, in *Antony and Cleopatra* style is used to help define the characters as they develop. These two principles include the use of verbal spectacles: if in *Dido* they serve limited functions as showpieces, in *Antony* they are simultaneously integrated into the overall development of character, actions, and meaning. We have seen in each play that the difficulties of the characters' modes of perception cannot help but interest us. Metadramatically, the styles used to portray these modes reveal each playwright's contrasting views of an accepted perceptual opposition: non-rational versus rational understanding. For Marlowe, perceiving the world emotionally can create mental blindness and disarray and, hence, be dangerous and destructive, as Dido unhappily learns. But for Shakespeare a balanced imbalance between an emotional, involuntary intuitive understanding and a logical, empirical, rational understanding—ideally, with the former leading the latter—needs to be sought, even though it cannot be sustained. Cleopatra best exemplifies this paradoxical imbalance when she dresses for her suicide and, for the last time, speaks to herself and her two attendants (V, ii, 280–98).

A second lesson: in *Dido* the world is controlled by the gods and fate; despite the whimsical nature of the gods, the characters are governed by external forces and everything they do and feel ultimately conforms to those forces. In *Antony and Cleopatra,* there is no such clear-cut causal relationship. The universe is beyond analysis, and we respond to it with a healthy, even profound respect for ambiguity. The difference in perception between the two writers comes partly from the dissimilarity in temperament and partly from how much of life each writer has experienced. The difference makes limpid Marlowe's profound fear of emotion as a way of ever knowing the world and, yet, his earnest desire to try knowing it and his faith in rational understanding as the means. In contradistinction, for Shakespeare reliance on emotion is vital to one's experience of happiness. If emotion clouds our perception of the world, rationally considered, then so be it; emotion gives life its vitality, the sense that we are thoroughly alive. For Shakespeare, the world cannot be perceived in a manner that leads to understanding anyway.

Thirdly, the two plays, because they differ so profoundly in their resolutions, suggest that Shakespeare consciously moved in a direction contrary to that of Marlowe. In particular, the two dramatists perceive the relationship between personal happiness and sociopolitical responsibility quite differently. Although Aeneas is victorious in the sense of fulfilling his ordained public responsibility, one is left feeling the tragedy of a world in which the restrictions imposed on personal happiness can be overwhelmingly harsh and not only for Aeneas. In *Antony and Cleopatra*, although the lovers are forced to commit suicide, they die happily ever after. We are left with a sense that they have achieved the selfhood that Dido and Aeneas never achieved and that such selfhood contains ideal ultimate reality for human beings while they live. No one would claim that Shakespeare gained a mature understanding of selfhood from seeing its absence in *Dido*'s protagonists, but his awareness of what was missing must have been increased and his sensitivity given shape and direction by his familiarity with the play.

If we remember that commentary on Marlowe usually characterizes him as an overreacher and iconoclast and Shakespeare as a conservative and traditionalist, we might well wonder how *Dido* and *Antony* could be used to verify these labels. The truth of the matter is that neither play can be. In fact, the structure of Marlowe's play, despite the un-Virgilian treatment of Aeneas's destiny, the lack of felt sympathy for Dido at her self-immolation, and the unconventional portrayal of gender roles, supports a position which is very much that of the conservative and traditionalist—namely, a moral and political status quo which reflects a commonly held, patriarchal perspective. Aeneas does, after all, accept the call of duty and continue on his way. Shakespeare, on the other hand, refuses to side with society against the individual, with system against instinct, and breaks new ground stylistically, apparently with no small thanks to Marlowe.[26] Dryden was right: the play does present a world well lost for love. In proclaiming this so cheerily, Shakespeare has carried the steady disenchantment with public responsibility evolving in his plays to its iconoclastic limit. In facing and outfacing life through art, *Antony and Cleopatra* shows Shakespeare both accepting and rejecting influences from *Dido, Queen of Carthage* but, ultimately, both to Marlowe's credit and discredit, making the haunt his.

III   Gender Roles and Their Influence

To give an idea of how *Dido* and *Antony* can be seen as part of their cultural contexts and, at the same time, to see how cultural influence intersects with Marlovian influence in *Antony*, one need only compare the two plays' portrayals of manliness, an undeniably powerful ideological agent in the formation of gender roles in early modern culture. As we saw in the discussion of *Edward II* and *Richard II*, Simon Shepherd maintains that, in the early modern period, "Assumed values of sex roles derived from the ideology of manliness"[27] and that "the virtue of manliness lies in a mode of acting, particularly in the relationship between the inner person and public action": "a manly man expresses his emotion in social intervention."[28] Moreover, he believes that the "ideology of manliness, or masculinity, inscribes the individual within interpersonal competition and denigrates emotion without action."[29] In these statements, Shepherd defines heroic manliness as it is presented in the Bible, primarily the Old Testament, and in epics, not the quieter, stoical manliness, also found in the Bible, in both the Old and New Testaments, that happily submits to authority or turns the other cheek. One's idea of manliness is learned rather than instinctive, just as manly behavior is learned rather than natural. Although wholly self-validating, the notion of manliness is essentially a patriarchal social ideal that encourages a strengthening of the political order. More pagan than Christian at its root,[30] the manly "mode" is neither right nor wrong, simply politically effective or ineffective, an assertion of power that lasts, relatively speaking, for only a moment.

In *Dido*, the traditional notion of heroic manliness is overturned by Aeneas's submissiveness and passivity as well as by Dido's dominance and assertiveness. The point was probably underscored dramatically by the company of boy actors who first performed the roles, the Children of Her Majesty's Chapel,[31] because an audience accustomed to viewing men in the roles of men and boys in the roles of women would have noticed three departures from convention: boys in the roles of men, a man (played by a boy) who was not acting manly, and a woman (also played by a boy) who was acting manly. Thus, the audience would have seen a boy acting unconventionally as an adult male (Aeneas) with an uncharacteristic lack of manliness, and a second boy acting conventionally as a female (Dido)—unless he was unconventionally younger than the boy who usually played such roles—with uncharacteristic manliness. Moreover, our common understanding of manliness is subverted at the outset of the play when Jupiter, chief of the gods, allows his passion for Ganymede to control his behavior. This passion is merely self-serving—in Shepherd's sense, "emotion without action."[32] Its manifestation also undercuts the conventional notion that men are by nature more rational than women are and that men are less likely than women to yield to strong, personal desires. As the first scene of the play, the undermining of the conventional portrayal of manliness prepares us for Aeneas's indifference to manly behavior and Dido's willingness to embrace it. Aeneas sees himself as a victim; as he laments—almost whining—to the disguised Venus, his mother,

> ... hapless I, God wot, poor and unknown,
> Do trace these Libyan deserts all despised,
> Exiled forth Europe and wide Asia both,
> And have not any coverture but heaven. (I, i, 227–30)

Violating the "manly" ideal, Aeneas is indecisive about his stay in Carthage. He seems continually to be more played upon than actively playing. For example, he is content to be wooed, to be the object of Dido's sexual desires. Aeneas uses his record of manliness in Troy to impress Dido (II, i, 121–288), and, even though his narration of his actual performance in Troy deviates from the heroic ideal as he leaves three helpless women to their doom—Creusa, Cassandra, and Polyxena—Dido seems not to notice, making the situation all the more ironic when he abandons her.[33] While he is within the precincts of Carthage, Aeneas does little to demonstrate his manliness. Moreover, in departing, he seems weak and duplicitous. Dido, on the other hand, from the beginning appears strong and forthright; in her take-charge manner, only 26 lines after they first meet, she utters a forceful imperative to Aeneas, almost as if he were a child: "Remember who thou art. Speak like thyself. / Humility belongs to common grooms" (II, i, 100–101). She continues in her manly behavior, especially as a wooer who not only initiates but also controls and guides the course of the liaison, liberally bestowing gifts. But, finally, her manliness is to no avail because Aeneas deserts her. As we move toward the end of the play, the purposes behind the behaviors of both Dido and Aeneas as well as their eventual separation seem less within their own control than within that of the gods and fate. Although Dido is attracted to Aeneas from the outset, once Cupid's arrow grazes her, she is to a great degree manipulated by the gods, just as Aeneas is in his forced abandonment of her. But in neither case is their uncharacteristic gender behavior determined by external controls. Ironically, for all the interest generated by unsettling an audience's expectations of gender stereotypes, the play ultimately affirms the patriarchal view of the dominant male. The males have a freedom of choice and they succeed, whether they are Jupiter, Cupid, or Aeneas, although Aeneas's free will is always firmly circumscribed by divine fiat, a fiat that favors males as power brokers.[34] In contrast to the men, the women, whether Juno, Venus, Dido, Anna, or the Nurse, are unable to exert power effectively enough to fulfill their desires, desires which are often made to seem foolish or trivial anyway. By the end of the play, one wonders whether Marlowe's decision to make Dido the foremost protagonist and, through her, to overturn commonplace notions of femininity, whether from literature (e.g., the *Aeneid*) or life, was not primarily for the purpose of keeping the audience engaged. Although these rationales are not mutually exclusive, Dido may dominate the play largely for artistic reasons, not because Marlowe wishes to protest cultural conventions. As I explained in the preceding section, this perspective seems particularly evident at the climax of the play where her demise is depicted as sensation without sympathy.

Superficially, *Dido* and *Antony* appear to be similar. Both plays seem to dramatize from within a familiar patriarchal perspective a reversal of gender roles in which the female assumes a position of dominance and manly assertiveness and the male is castigated for his unmanliness. Both Dido and Cleopatra, for example, attempt to prevent their lovers from leaving them by adopting an aggressive manly attitude toward them. Yet, whereas *Dido* ultimately affirms patriarchal values, *Antony* explodes them. Apparently, Marlowe is caught between the patriarchal dictates of his sources and two pressing desires: to subvert the patriarchal ideology and to provide freshness to the tale by a reversal of gender roles. Conversely, *Antony* ultimately affirms the value of creative independence and individuality in two extraordinary human beings over the patriarchal ideal of sociopolitical well-being and the gender roles needed to be played out to attain the ideal. Shakespeare promotes this view contextually, revealing through the action of the play that, in the world of *realpolitik*, the ideal is forever unattainable. The ideal enables those who proselytize for it to hold the reins of power and control, but always at the expense of denaturing even the most privileged people of their uniqueness and selfhood.

Throughout *Antony and Cleopatra*, Shakespeare's acute sense of the psychology of individual human behavior overrides any support for society's notion of manliness. To be sure, in the play, the inhabitants of Rome and the Romans in Egypt are led to understand manliness as a desirable norm. As the play opens, Philo is lamenting with a moralizing single-mindedness Antony's recent fall from epic grace—in effect, the hero's lack of manliness in having become "a strumpet's fool" (I, i, 13): "this dotage of our general's / O'erflows the measure" (I, i, 1–2). But as the play continues, we come to regard manliness as a hollow virtue, a myth of widespread belief used to unify the Roman empire by making its inhabitants think they all share the same values. It is also used by Octavius Caesar to eliminate his competition (Lepidus, Pompey, and, finally, Antony) and to confer political and military authority on himself as he brings to fruition his personal desire for absolute power and fame through conquest. We see that Philo's standard Roman impression of Antony, for all its intensity and emotional suggestiveness, is superficial in reducing love to mere lust and too simple in thinking that, without Cleopatra, Antony would automatically resume his duties as triumvir and his heroic military activities. In effect, Philo asserts a stereotypical view of manliness as an uncomplicated matter of moral behavior, an easy journey from cause to effect. The remainder of the play works to subvert the shallowness of this view. One might say that, in countering Philo's simple-mindedness, the playtext communicates what Enobarbus, with stark practicality, tells Lepidus: "Every time / Serves for the matter that is then born in't" (II, ii, 9–10). As a consequence, one's behavior is more often motivated by impulse than by precept or by a rational consideration of the rightness of external conditions. Insofar as this psychological pattern is valid, it makes either the absence or presence of a concept of manliness irrelevant.

Antony and Cleopatra both indicate through the independence of their behavior that they understand that manliness is a myth used manipulatively as a tool of political control. Dido apparently understands this as well because, by invoking it, she is able to make Aeneas acquiesce to her will a number of times, beginning with her command upon first learning Aeneas's identity: "Warlike Aeneas, and in these base robes! / Go fetch the garment which Sichaeus ware" (II, i, 79–80).[35] As we can see by the "sweating labor" (I, iii, 93) Cleopatra undergoes to counter the effects of the myth on Antony, she is thoroughly aware of the power of a "Roman thought" (I, ii, 82) to inflict guilt, and she knows that the guilt is the result of Antony's questioning of his manly obligations, what he would call—at those moments when he is accepting the myth as truth—his "honour." Once Antony forms a bond with Cleopatra, instead of seeing public responsibility as a continually satisfying fulfillment of one's manhood, he finds that he is transported into unparalleled states of happiness, moments that erase his sense of aging, outface "the strong necessity of time" (I, iii, 42), and make the Roman myth of ideal manly behavior less relevant. Yet, he is shrewd enough to make use of the myth in his dealings with Octavius when, with a display of jovial manliness, he assumes control of the argument during their meeting in Rome (II, ii) and with Octavia when he plays the manly penitent imbued with rational correctness: "I have not kept my square, but that to come / Shall all be done by th' rule" (II, iii, 6–7). It is not difficult to see why both Antony and Cleopatra quite naturally disregard manliness as a true guiding value.

Unlike Othello who believes that heroic behavior culminates in service to the state (V, ii, 338), including the killing of himself as a final rational act of social justice (V, ii, 352–57), Antony's heroic behavior consists of a galvanization of emotional energies that is instinctive, spontaneous, and ultimately mysterious in origin, much like his experience of loving Cleopatra. His heroics are never gilded over with Othello's noble idealism about serving the political state. Antony is frequently too aware of flux and his advanced position in it and too enmeshed in responding with naturalness and immediacy to the realities of everyday living to act from preformed moralisms. The same holds true for Cleopatra who, for all her sophistication, is not as attuned as Antony to the political usefulness of such ideas as manliness, except in the politics of love. But, then, as Matthew Proser puts it, "Antony's whole effort throughout the play is directed toward reestablishing a past conception of himself which not only he, but the rest of the world, acknowledges."[36] Antony's awareness of his image to "the rest of the world" encourages him not only to make political use of the myth of manliness but, at moments, to believe in the assertiveness of manly behavior as a strong component of heroic endeavor and lasting honorable achievement. Ultimately, Antony never resolves his ambivalent attitude toward manliness, for even at his death, he wants to be remembered as "A Roman, by a Roman / Valiantly vanquished" (IV, xv, 58–9). He understands that the way of the world is to use manliness as a standard of measure and that his achievements after his death, to be seen as achievements, need to be portrayed in a legend of manliness. The world sees events only through the lens of patriarchal values. Both Cleopatra and Shakespeare know that Antony's greatness lies in his magnanimity and his ability to inspire others, whether as a warrior, friend, or lover. Viewed from within or from outside a patriarchal political perspective, only at times does Antony achieve an ideal balance between being the greatest warrior and the greatest lover in the world—as, for example, when he returns to Cleopatra after having won a battle he never expected to win (IV, viii). Here, whether regarded through the manly perspective of the Romans or the feminine perspective of the Egyptians, Antony strikes a balance, speaking exuberant words of romantic passion, considered feminine, cloaked in the heroic language of martial prowess, considered masculine. From the perspective of the play, even more to his credit, he accomplishes the balance unself-consciously. This balance allows him to transcend himself and to redefine his selfhood; it also enables the play to undermine the notion of gender role-playing.

Like Antony, Cleopatra at times achieves what, again viewed from either within or outside a patriarchal perspective, could be considered a balance between conflicting masculine and feminine roles. Shortly after we first encounter Cleopatra, she addresses Antony with decisive imperatives and an all-too-tart logic that could be taken for mock manly bluster, all in an effort to hold him in Egypt with her:

> You must not stay here longer, your dismission
> Is come from Caesar; therefore hear it, Antony.
> Where's Fulvia's process—Caesar's I would say—both?
> Call in the messengers. (I, i, 26–29)

With her customary flair for outrageous irony, Cleopatra crosses gender lines in her gruff, masculine manner, criticizing Antony for not staying within the traditional boundaries of his manly gender role by making his own decisions—in this case, by deciding to reside in Egypt with her. She belittles his anticipated weakness in acceding to the demands of his wife and Caesar to return to Rome; she hopes that if he confronts his feelings of guilt, he will overcome them and remain in Egypt. But, of course, there is little logic to her argument since, by staying in Egypt, he would still be acceding to someone else's demands and, consequently, showing himself to have no more control over his decisions and no more power over others than he would have in returning to Rome. In referring to Antony's much younger fellow triumvir as "the scarce-bearded Caesar" (I, i, 21), Cleopatra indicates that, for her, true manliness, although probably not much reflected upon as yet, is related to sexual maturity.[37] Thus, the standard notion of manliness does not become a self-conscious motive for either her behavior or Antony's—although, as we have seen, his links with the idea of manliness and with manly behavior are more complicated than hers—and certainly not the basis for their most important decisions. In fact, both are so resourceful that they are readily able to respond to the mechanics of existence without recourse to such preconceived ideas or strategies. The "mutual pair" (I, i, 37) is frequently so untroubled by improprieties in distinctions of gender and gender roles that, in playing, as Cleopatra tells us, I "… put my tires and mantles on him, whilst / I wore his sword Philippan" (II, v, 22–23). There is truth to Octavius Caesar's claim that Antony "is not more manlike / Than Cleopatra, nor the queen of Ptolemy / More womanly than he" (I, iv, 5–7) but it is not the snide, moralistic truth implicit in his carping: Antony and Cleopatra are often detached from and superior to such commonplace moralisms and stereotypical thinking. Cleopatra's role-playing is self-determined; remarkably enough, even though she is the ruler of Egypt, the affairs of state never limit her nor do they determine her course of action. Antony is less fortunate. In direct conflict with his feelings for Cleopatra, his personal and professional obligations in Rome produce many moments of anguish, resulting in his political marriage to Octavia and a reaffirmation of his political bond with Octavius. Only when he is with Cleopatra and without a Roman thought can he divest himself of the unnaturalness and lack of self-fulfillment that living in society requires.

At her death, Cleopatra achieves an ideal balance of gender roles, exhibiting manliness—courage, constancy, and nobility—by dying with "Marble" constancy (V, ii, 240) "after the high Roman fashion" (IV, xv, 91), while maintaining a rich femininity as a wife ("Husband, I come"—V, ii, 287) and mother, ironically giving suck to an asp ("Dost thou not see my baby at my breast"—V, ii, 309). Through the dramatization of such ideal actions, the play affirms resourceful, independent behavior involuntarily transcending itself, behavior not mired in notions of masculinity and femininity. The only restrictions on Cleopatra's behavior at this point are the natural limitations of self-fulfillment, which, in this instance, surpass all normal human behavior. Cleopatra is not motivated by a desire to exceed traditional ideas of conduct. But her creator may be, because Cleopatra's ultimate triumph occurs when the traditional ideas of wife and mother, rather than dictating normal human behavior, serve, paradoxically, to show the Queen's rise to a superhuman level. Any triumph of self-fulfillment emanates from one's vitality, which provides all people with their most potent sense of being alive. Such vitality forms the bedrock of happy reality in the play. *Antony and Cleopatra* supports a total involvement with life in all its dimensions, not, as in the case of Octavius Caesar, only ideas about life. Because of this perspective, the play emerges as an extraordinary validation of Shakespeare's own "infinite variety" and "infinite virtue" and, conceivably, the most successful expression of his own selfhood as a dramatist.

The final question is, "What did the Shakespeare of *Antony and Cleopatra* see in Marlowe's unconventional portrayal of manliness in *Dido* that suggests a connection between the two playwrights and their plays?" I would reply that Shakespeare was witness to a surprising reversal of gender roles, a perspective on Dido and Aeneas original with Marlowe, independent of his sources, and, within the world of the play, independent of the influence of gods and fate. Shakespeare carried Marlowe's display of innovativeness and defiance to a happier state of completion, particularly in enlarging the strength of Dido's already strong personality in his characterization of Cleopatra. Accepting Marlowe's view but mitigating his cynicism in delineating a fate that irrevocably governs all to the exclusion of joy, Shakespeare deemphasizes the specific gender roles of Antony and Cleopatra, though not their sexual roles, by making the characteristics of gender in each figure fluid, ambiguous, and even contradictory. In establishing their individuality, he establishes their superiority to such considerations, in part through their awareness of the usefulness of gender roles to manipulate people and situations and, at times, in spite of their own belief in manliness as the measurement of proper behavior. At their best, the protagonists are psychologically free from the confinement of the commonplace notions of gender roles and of the behavior they prescribe. Less conscious of inward psychological freedom than the limitations imposed externally by society and fate, Dido and Aeneas have none of the exhilaration and sense of play so characteristic of Antony and Cleopatra in their gender reversals. Shakespeare establishes for himself the artistic freedom necessary to develop the individuality of Antony and Cleopatra by substituting the forces of society for what *Dido* dramatizes as the forces of fate, although, as the Soothsayer makes clear, the mysterious forces of fate ultimately control all destinies. For Shakespeare, the forces of society can be manifested in human form and can therefore be wrestled with, and the resulting struggle can be heroic and inspiring. But the forces of fate cannot be so manifested.[38] Accepting this premise, Shakespeare creates characters who throw off the shackles of the ironclad fate that ultimately inhibits the actions of Marlowe's characters.[39] Moreover, he brings us as close as he can to viewing an extraordinary man and woman societally unaccommodated—that is, figures as little encumbered by the ordinary, controlling myths of society as possible but, by virtue of their authoritative positions as rulers and their distinctive personalities, able to enjoy myths of their own creation. At their core, Antony and Cleopatra are as deeply desirous of human mutuality, of continuing devotion to one another, as two people can be. They are less successful than Aeneas in prolonging their lives but, in living life to the lees, more successful than either Dido or Aeneas. Marlowe has helped Shakespeare set his priorities, helped him to release his imagination more fully. In doing so, Shakespeare has potently dramatized the joys of imaginative release and the most fulfilling kind of selfhood. But he has also laid out the heavy cost: the ever-victorious and impersonal dictates of society, flux, and death. Unlike Marlowe, he nevertheless affirms the unorthodox point of view of the individual, standing against the orthodox perspective of society. Consequently, in yet one more way, he makes the haunt very much his.

Notes

1   All quotations from *Antony and Cleopatra* are from *William Shakespeare: The Complete Works*, gen. eds Stephen Orgel and A.R. Braunmuller (New York: Penguin Putnam, 2002). All quotations from *The Tragedy of Dido, Queen of Carthage* are from *Christopher Marlowe: The Complete Plays*, ed. Mark Thornton Burnett (London: J.M. Dent, 1999).

2   For a full account of the pre- and post-Virgilian Dido legends that Marlowe drew upon for his conceptions of the lovers, see Mary Elizabeth Smith, *"Love-Kindling Fire": A Study of Christopher Marlowe's "The Tragedy of Dido, Queen of Carthage"* (Salzburg, Austria: Institut für Englische Sprache und Literatur Universität Salzburg, 1977), 6–38. For an analysis of the similarities and differences between Virgil and Marlowe, see the brief discussion in Barbara J. Baines, "Sexual Polarity in the Plays of Christopher Marlowe," *Ball State University Forum* 23:3 (Summer 1982): 4–6, and a more extensive discussion in Sara Munson Deats' *Sex, Gender, and Desire in the Plays of Christopher Marlowe* (Newark: University of Delaware Press, 1997), Chapter 3: "Errant Eros: Transgressions of Sex, Gender, and Desire in Marlowe's *Dido, Queen of Carthage*," 91–102 and 105–15.

3   See the parallels listed by Marvin Spevack, *A New Variorum Edition of Shakespeare: "Antony and Cleopatra"* (New York: The Modern Language Association of America, 1990), 96, 292, 603–5.

4   See Matthew N. Proser, *"Dido, Queen of Carthage* and the Evolution of Marlowe's Dramatic Style" in *"A Poet and a Filthy Play-maker": New Essays on Christopher*

Marlowe, ed. Kenneth Friedenreich, Roma Gill, and Constance B. Kuriyama. (New York: AMS Press, 1988), 83–97; Deats, *Sex, Gender, and Desire*, Chapter 3, 89–90 and 123–24; and Patrick Cheney, *Marlowe's Counterfeit Profession: Ovid, Spenser, Counter-Nationhood* (Toronto: University of Toronto Press, 1997), 100.

5   See Simon Shepherd, *Marlowe and the Politics of Elizabethan Theatre* (New York: St Martin's Press, 1986), 192–96 and 199–201; Emily C. Bartels, *Spectacles of Strangeness: Imperialism, Alienation, and Marlowe* (Philadelphia: University of Pennsylvania Press, 1993), 29–52; and Deats, Chapter 3, 89–124.

6   Maurice Charney's essay, "Marlowe and Shakespeare's African Queens," in *Shakespearean Illuminations*, ed. Jay L. Halio and Hugh Richmond (Newark: University of Delaware Press, 1998), 242–52, presents a fine, fairly recent example of the perspective of one who recognizes that source studies are not simply a matter of verbal resemblances but can be widely encompassing studies of a complex, subtle relationship. See also Chapter 7, "Unstable Proteus: Marlowe and *Antony and Cleopatra*," in Brian Gibbons's *Shakespeare and Multiplicity* (Cambridge: Cambridge University Press, 1993), 182–202.

7   For scholars and critics, one crucial area of preliminary interest, for example, appears to be the conflicting claims of biological determinism and social constructionism in the creation of the human subject. Joseph Carroll, in *Evolution and Literary Theory* (Columbia: University of Missouri Press, 1995), believes that "cultural order results from the interaction among innate biological characteristics and environmental circumstances" (33), that human nature is composed of "an innate structure of evolved characteristics that constrain all cultural order" (39), and that "innate psychological structures—perceptual, rational, and affective—have evolved through an adaptive process of natural selection and that these structures regulate the mental and emotional life of all living organisms, including human beings" (2). Separating himself from the post-structuralists, Carroll adds, "This concept sets itself in irreconcilable opposition to the idea that human beings are blank slates, that the structure of motivations and cognition is infinitely malleable, and that language or culture provides all qualitative content and structure for human experience" (2). Ian McAdam in *The Irony of Identity: Self and Imagination in the Drama of Christopher Marlowe* (Newark, Delaware: University of Delaware Press/Associated University Presses, 1999), 13–43, deals in effect with the same conflict, only he uses Marlowe and his dramas as evidence for his perspective. Like Carroll, McAdam separates himself from the poststructuralists, taking issue with those who would deny essentialism and transhistorical psychological characteristics in understanding writers and their works. McAdam pinpoints the humanistic conflict between self-assertion and self-surrender in Marlowe's plays and links this conflict to religious and ideological conflicts within the playwright himself.

8   See Chapter 1 and the argument of Scott McMillin and Sally-Beth MacLean (*The Queen's Men and their Plays* [Cambridge: Cambridge University Press, 1998], 155–69) that Shakespeare may have worked for a time with the Queen's Men.

9   For example, Thomas P. Harrison, Jr, "Shakespeare and Marlowe's *Dido, Queen of Carthage*" (*Studies in English* [University of Texas], 1956), 57–63, and Janet Adelman, *The Common Liar: An Essay on "Antony and Cleopatra"* (New Haven, CT: Yale University Press, 1973), 76–78 and 173–83. See also my discussion of the influence of *Dido* (as well as Shakespeare's other major influences) on *Antony* in "'High Events as These': Sources, Influences, and the Artistry of *Antony and Cleopatra*" in *Antony and Cleopatra: New Critical Essays*, ed. Sara Munson Deats (New York and London: Routledge, 2005), 164–67.

10   Charney, "African Queens," 247–48, uses some of the same evidence to suggest that love undermines Roman values in both plays.

11   J.B. Steane, *Marlowe: A Critical Study* (Cambridge: Cambridge University Press, 1964), 59.

12   Brian Gibbons, "'Unstable Proteus': *The Tragedy of Dido, Queen of Carthage*" in *Christopher Marlowe*, ed. Brian Morris (New York: Hill and Wang, 1968), 43.

13   Ibid. Gibbons is helpful when he compares the inconstant behavior of the two heroines (43) and less so, apart from what I have already indicated, in telling us that the four protagonists are "continually associated with the elements, and the dramatic poetry exalts them to divine proportions" (43). Had he focused more on style and less on content, he might have strengthened his argument.

14   Janet Adelman says that "both playwrights allow their lovers to posit the value of love largely through the assertive power of a highly metaphoric language" (77), making clear that their love is more valuable than the claims of empire (77–78). As I go on to explain, I think the stylistic affiliation between the two writers is even more extensive.

15   The passage from "The Life of Marcus Antonius" in North's Plutarch which corresponds to *Ant.* II, ii, 201–7 is part of the description of the barge: "… the poope whereof was of gold, the sailes of purple, and the owers of siluer, which kept stroke in rowing after the sounde of the musicke of flutes, howboyes, cithernes, viols, and such other instruments as they played vpon in the barge" (See *Shakespeare*, Spevack ed., 413). Although I disagree with Janet Adelman's view that the passage in Marlowe's play "may well have influenced Enobarbus's description of Cleopatra at Cydnus" (181), I do agree that "the similarity of specific details matters less than the similarity of the descriptive technique" (181).

16   The one exception is Venus's statement to Cupid in II, i, 323–31 in which she says that she wants Cupid to make Dido fall in love with Aeneas so that Dido can aid him whether "… he at last depart to Italy, / Or else in Carthage make his kingly throne" (330–31). Unlike Virgil's Venus and against the decree of fate that Jupiter is abiding by, Venus suggests as a possibility Aeneas's settling in Carthage.

17   Jocelyn Powell, "Marlowe's Spectacle" (*Tulane Drama Review* 8 [1963–64]), 195–210, distinguishes between a "drama of spectacle" and a "drama of character" (195). In the former, "action is image" and in the latter "action is fact" (195). Although the former is associated with the tradition of the morality play and the latter with the more recent tradition of "narrative" theater, Powell feels that Marlowe makes use of both. She defines a drama of spectacle as "communicative, not simply decorative" and adds, "Dramatic spectacle is all that is implied by persons *acting*, the whole visual effect of players moving in a decorated or undecorated space with appropriate properties and costumes" (195). In my use of the term spectacle, I mean not only what Powell means by a "drama of spectacle" but also something that is especially, even emphatically eye- or ear-catching, a dramatic public display that is intended to be unusual and to stun. It is "communicative" in Powell's sense that "action is image," but, apart from its initial attack on the senses, it may also express something of the dramatist's overall intention.

18   For a discussion of the staging of *Dido* as a play which "cannot … be understood except as a play for boys" (the Children of Her Majesty's Chapel, by whom the play was first performed) and one in which the "movement of the action unfolds through balance and contrast," see Mary Elizabeth Smith, "*Love-Kindling Fire*," 170.

19   In *Dido*, there are allusions to music that give some sense of what kind of music might be composed and where it might be added—as, for example, just before Dido and Aeneas enter the cave and Dido says:

> What more than Delian music do I hear,
> That calls my soul from forth his living seat
> To move unto the measures of delight? (III, iv, 51–3)

In *Antony*, some of the musical effects are explicitly indicated in the text—as, for example, the initial fanfare ushering in Antony and Cleopatra (I, i), the music for the party on board Pompey's galley (II, vii), and the music of the oboes ("hautboys") as the "god Hercules, whom Antony loved, / Now leaves him" (IV, iii, 15–16).

20 Reuben A. Brower, *Hero and Saint: Shakespeare and the Graeco-Roman Heroic Tradition* (Oxford: Oxford University Press, 1971), 352. Brower gives as examples *Dido*, III, iv, 56–57 and V, i, 243–50.

21 Ibid., 113 and n. 2.

22 This reference to *Hero and Leander* is based on the edition of Mark Thornton Burnett, *Christopher Marlowe: The Complete Poems* (London: J.M. Dent, 2000).

23 In talking about the reliability of eyesight in *Doctor Faustus*, Fred B. Tromley, *Playing with Desire: Christopher Marlowe and the Art of Tantalization* (Toronto: University of Toronto Press, 1998), says that events in the play suggest "that reality is not necessarily apparent to the senses, and that what is visible is not necessarily real" (142). The same perceptual ambiguity holds true for *Dido*.

24 On these scenes, Mary Elizabeth Smith comments: "Marlowe makes more than Virgil does of Venus' 'borrowed shape.' Aeneas' eyesight is deluded by the costume, as it is also by Priam's statue—appearance is not reality; nothing is certain. Thus the image provides a link with the theme of illusion and reality which runs through the play" ("*Love-Kindling Fire*,"113). Ian McAdam takes a more psychological approach to the latter incident: "I suggest the statue scene involves an attempt at 'transmuting internalization' of an idealized self-object by which Aeneas can fill in a missing psychic structure. The ambivalence of the scene does increase our sympathy, for we recognize at once both Aeneas's weakness and his attempts to compensate for it" (*Irony of Identity*, 54).

25 Dido's treatment of Aeneas up until Cupid wounds her with his arrow suggests that she is strongly attracted to him: she seats him next to her and gives him her husband's robe, banqueting him and urging him to tell his story. Cupid turns the attraction into a near obsession.

26 The opening remarks of Terry Eagleton, *William Shakespeare* (New York: Basil Blackwell, 1986), are appropriate here: "Even those who know very little about Shakespeare might be vaguely aware that his plays value social order and stability, and that they are written with an extraordinary eloquence, one metaphor breeding another in an apparently unstaunchable flow of what modern theorists might call 'textual productivity'. The problem is that these two aspects of Shakespeare are in potential conflict with one another. ... His belief in social stability is jeopardized by the very language in which it is articulated" (1).

27 Shepherd, 197.

28 Ibid.

29 Shepherd, 198.

30 The Judeo-Christian heritage, in so far as it subscribed to submission to authority and turning the other cheek, was in conflict with the heroic tradition, which subscribed to aggressive, often amoral action.

31 See Gibbons, *Shakespeare and Multiplicity*, 185, who briefly discusses Marlowe's intention to write the play for boy-actors.

32 See Deats, *Sex, Gender, and Desire*, Chapter 3: "Errant Eros: Transgressions of Sex, Gender, and Desire in Marlowe's *Dido, Queen of Carthage*," for a fine, full treatment of questions of sex, gender, and sexuality in the play, including the departures from the *Aeneid* and the *Heroides* that make Marlowe's differences patently clear.

33 See Deats, 111–12, who suggests that Aeneas's abandonment of these three women prefigures his abandonment of Dido and that all four actions diminish his valor. The notion of weaknesses and evil traits in Aeneas is more in line with the medieval portrayals of Aeneas than the classical ones. See Gibbons, *Shakespeare and Multiplicity*, 191.

34 Aeneas acknowledges his limited freedom of choice when he says in a soliloquy,

> Jove wills it so, my mother wills it so;
> Let my Phoenissa grant, and then I go.
> Grant she or no, Aeneas must away. (*Dido*, IV, iii, 5–7)

Later, he tells Dido, quoting from the *Aeneid*, IV, 360–61:

> Desine meque tuis incendere teque querelis;
> Italiam non sponte sequor.
> [Cease to inflame me and yourself by your lamentations;
> it is not of my own will that I make for Italy.] (*Dido*, V, i, 139–40)

35 Alan Shepard, *Marlowe's Soldiers: Rhetorics of Masculinity in the Age of the Armada* (Burlington, VT: Ashgate, 2002), 62–71, understands as well Dido's manipulation of Aeneas through a commonly shared fiction. Building on Emily C. Bartels's idea of Dido as a key element in Marlowe's questioning of imperialistic forces in the play (in *Spectacles of Strangeness*, 29–30), Shepard argues, "Dido simultaneously colonizes Aeneas and is colonized by the fictions that also drive her to admire him" (64). She plays upon "the integrity of his martial persona" (63).

36 *The Heroic Image in Five Shakespearean Tragedies* (Princeton, NJ: Princeton University Press, 1965), 182.

37 We see the same simple equation in the scene between the eunuch Mardian and Cleopatra (I, v, 8–34). By the end of the play, after Antony's death, the phrase "My man of men" (I, v, 72) takes on a much deeper, richer meaning. But, even then, manliness has a meaning that is less social than personal and individual, for she equates it with Antony's incomparably heroic characteristics.

38 In his book *Shakespeare's Tragic Cosmos* (Cambridge: Cambridge University Press, 1991), T. McAlindon comments: "*Antony and Cleopatra* ... may be called a tragedy of Fortune, where Fortune is conceived, not a cruel and meaningless mischance, nor as a retributive agent of divine providence, but as a manifestation of inevitable change in the cyclic order of history and nature; and where the tragic effect stems mainly from a perception that what has been swept away in the process of change is irreplaceable—two of Nature's masterpieces 'which not to have been blest withal would have discredited' humanity (I.ii.148–9)" (223–4).

39 I see the Soothsayer not only as a spokesman for fate but, arguably, even more significantly as a representative of the authenticity and superiority of one's intuition.

Chapter 8

"Glutted with Conceit":
Imprints of *Doctor Faustus* on *Macbeth* and *The Tempest*

I

The following chapter focuses on the portion of the legacy of *Doctor Faustus* found in Shakespeare's last works. Specifically, it explores the possibilities of the influence of Marlowe's drama in *Macbeth* and *The Tempest*, including metadramatic connections between *Doctor Faustus* and Shakespeare's two plays. I am basing my exploration on the premise that an influence embedded in Shakespeare's consciousness as firmly and deeply as Marlowe's does not simply wither and die but, over time, extends its roots and develops. A well-known example of Shakespeare's keeping older plays in his head for many years is *The Chronicle of King Leir*, first performed in 1594 and usually cited as a source for *King Lear*, first performed in 1606.[1] Thus, the question of whether Shakespeare could have made use of *Doctor Faustus* years later seems to me a non-issue.

Few would dispute Shakespeare's familiarity with *Doctor Faustus*, even if the degree to which it influenced him is still heavily in contention. Nor is *Doctor Faustus* the only play Shakespeare knew with Faustian reminders. There is, for instance, the popular play, *The Merry Devil of Edmonton*, clearly indebted to Marlowe's drama and on the stage between the 1602 revival of *Doctor Faustus* and the 1605–1606 debut of *Macbeth*. Whether one agrees that the parallels between *Doctor Faustus* and *Macbeth* and *The Tempest* are specifically the result of Shakespeare's absorption of Marlowe's play or the result of other influences, the process of examining the plays for influence helps to establish the lines of continuity in the development of drama at the end of the 1600s and beginning of the 1700s. Records of the earliest productions of *Doctor Faustus* indicate that it enjoyed an unusual popularity.[2] Moreover, whatever other versions of the play may have existed, the variations in the 1616 B-Text from the 1604 A-Text tell us that it was so well received initially that the response provided Marlowe, his collaborator(s), his reviser(s), or some combination thereof with strong incentives to enhance the original script—principally, by adding comic antics and displays of magic. Shakespeare could not have missed either the initial impact of the play or its continuing popularity. Furthermore, as I have already observed, Shakespeare appears to have been captivated by Faustus's exclamation, "Was this the face that launched a thousand ships."[3] His adaptation of this line in *Richard II*, *Troilus and Cressida*, and

King Lear indicates that its emphatic rhythm, hyperbolic sentiment, and wondering tone lingered in his imagination with undiminished force. In continuing to make use of the line, he also reflects a confidence that its familiarity was widespread enough to produce resonances in his audiences some 10 to 15 years after *Doctor Faustus* was composed and first performed.[4] The abiding popularity of the play provided Shakespeare's imagination with renewed opportunities for ruminating on the agony of damnation and the fascination of magic and for transforming both of these subjects for use in his own dramas.

The two late plays of Shakespeare that seem to bear the most obvious marks of *Doctor Faustus* are *Macbeth* and *The Tempest*. There is no clear critical consensus, however, on the extent of the influence. For most scholars, the dispute focuses on how strong a debt, especially an indirect debt, each of the plays owes. In surveying criticism on this subject, I find that the degree of influence *Doctor Faustus* exerts, especially on *The Tempest*, has produced contradictory assessments. For example, James Shapiro believes that Shakespeare's "engagement with Marlowe appears to come to an end, around the turn of the century"[5] and, consequently, that neither *Macbeth* nor *The Tempest* reveals a Marlovian inheritance. Marjorie Garber posits indebtedness to *Doctor Faustus* in *Macbeth* but evidently not in *The Tempest*.[6] Jonathan Bate also perceives some links between Marlowe's play and *Macbeth*, but, apparently, locates even stronger links between the concern with magic in *Doctor Faustus* and that in *The Tempest* and, more particularly, a significant verbal parallel between the two plays:

> When Prospero says 'I'll drown my book', he is clearly echoing Faustus' last unfulfilled promise, 'I'll burn my books'. The fact that the quotation bobs up to the surface of *The Tempest* shows that Shakespeare is still haunted by Marlowe.[7]

David Lucking and David Young both support the connection between *Doctor Faustus* and *The Tempest*; like Bate, Lucking notes the same specific verbal "transmutation" in "I'll drown my book."[8] I am less sure of the inevitability of the verbal echo than are Bate and Lucking, but I do agree with all three critics that, even in this very late play, "Shakespeare is still haunted by Marlowe." Moreover, in all probability, there is at least a grain of truth in Bate's emphatic overstatement that "Shakespeare … only became Shakespeare because of the death of Marlowe."[9]

Critics and students of Renaissance drama have been quick to point out that the similarities between *Doctor Faustus* and *Macbeth* begin with a consideration of the plays as studies in damnation.[10] As such, their protagonists have much in common, not only in their sore and afflicted psychologies but in the inexorability of the conditions they bring upon themselves.[11] The terrible irony for both figures is that, whereas they each seek a liberation of sorts, the terms in which they envision it, including the means by which they hope to achieve it, preclude the possibility of ever attaining it. This irony is compounded in both plays by presenting the paradox of a villain endowed with heroic capabilities. Whether Marlowe actually provided the impetus for Shakespeare or simply reinforced and encouraged Shakespeare's own inclinations, or, less likely, whether Shakespeare came upon the notion independently, the portrayal of the villain-hero is clearly a dramaturgical device that each writer valued highly.[12] C.L. Barber states that, "In dramatizing blasphemy, Marlowe also made it something else, a heroic enterprise."[13] The same could be said of Shakespeare in *Macbeth*. There, Macbeth's "blasphemy" in murdering Duncan is an "enterprise" that, because of the protagonist's strong misgivings, requires a concentration of Promethean energy and a prodigious psychoethical upheaval. It is followed by Macbeth's frenetic attempts to quell all disruptive enemy forces, without and within; in this, he is as much an overreacher and as relentless as Tamburlaine. In undertaking the murder of Duncan and in reacting to its consequences, Macbeth adduces some of the same heroic attributes that he is credited with by the Captain when, at the beginning of the play, the latter extols to the King the focused energies and courageous persistence of the warrior leader (I, ii, 16–41).[14] Thus, inextricably bound up with the doomed endeavor of Macbeth, as well as Faustus, are the actions of a villain-hero. Anticipating Milton's defense of true heroism in *Paradise Lost* as an inward struggle, not simply battles,[15] both figures participate in a psychological contest of enormous moral proportions and the most agonizing of consequences.

The progression of influence of the villain-hero from Marlowe to Shakespeare begins with Tamburlaine whose oscillation between acts of heroism and villainy is still, arguably, the chief source of critical controversy in the two plays, especially for those who wish to resolve and thereby oversimplify the combination of apparently contradictory actions in the Scythian conquerer.[16] Faustus follows in Tamburlaine's footsteps, because his efforts as blasphemer are viewed at times as Promethean;[17] Richard III, whose energies and daring are as astonishing as his evil acts are heinous, follows from the characterizations of Tamburlaine and Faustus and leads eventually to the most complex representation of the villain-hero in Macbeth.[18] In each case, we see heroic elements in the protagonists that we admire even as we disapprove morally of their characters and their sorrowful missions. That is, our aesthetic response of wonder runs counter to our ethical response and on separate tracks. Critics have certainly not been shy about commenting on this ambivalence. A recent example is Lawrence Danson who notes that "the complexity of audience response to Marlowe's Edward, torn as it is between moral judgement and dramatic sympathy, will also mark our response to Shakespeare's tragic characters."[19] Danson gives as two of his examples Macbeth and his wife. He then pinpoints our contradictory response to Faustus and declares that Marlowe, like Shakespeare, in evoking such a reaction, reinvents the genre of tragedy.[20] The implication is that Marlowe inspired Shakespeare to be boldly inventive in similarly reinventing the genre of tragedy.

One additional trait, common to both Faustus and Macbeth and frequently commented upon, is that each has feelings of guilt and repentance even before he has consigned his soul to the devil; and each continues to repent as he is selling his soul as well as long after he has sealed the bargain. This complication creates a welcome density in our emotional attitude toward the protagonists, for we watch the slow deaths of the two men's souls take place well before they are dead physically. As aesthetically attractive and morally appalling as their journeys are meant to seem, both figures make their descent into evil knowingly—that is, they understand well that what they are doing lacks reason and, yet, their ineluctable hunger for the power of a control associated only with immortal figures drives them on. There are other similarities between Faustus and Macbeth that we will need to consider, but, for the moment, it is enough to say that Shakespeare could not have helped being influenced by *Doctor Faustus*, both in a personal and professional sense. Not only would the play have captured his imagination through its psychomoral focus and high astounding terms, appealing to tendencies that we recognize as naturally compatible with Shakespeare's own temperament, but the play's popularity and the strength of its hold on its earliest audiences, induced by so fundamental and universal a moral conflict, must have made him take professional notice as well. I shall go on to argue that the chief interest in *Doctor Faustus* for Shakespeare lay in its successful dramaturgical strategies. But its psychoethical subject and its *donnée*—namely, the struggle between the aspirations of an extraordinary human being and the impersonal, omnipotent forces that constrain him—influenced the playwright more than those same two elements in any of Marlowe's other plays.

As for the influence of *Doctor Faustus* on *The Tempest*, here the imprint is more clearly doctrinal. Each play expresses a strong interest in magic and the magician as representations of the imagination, and each play features a protagonist who is a magician, and, from a metadramatic perspective, also a playwright.[21] Because of its interest in black magic and supernatural forces, *Macbeth*, too, can be linked with *Doctor Faustus*. In dramatizing the relationship between magical powers and the superior force of fate, *The Tempest* can be seen as a logical outgrowth of both earlier plays.[22] *Doctor Faustus* and *The Tempest* feature protagonists who are magicians, although they are ostensibly on opposite sides of the fence since Faustus is fascinated with necromancy and Prospero absorbed in white or natural magic.[23] Early in Marlowe's play, the Evil Angel encourages Faustus to enter into

> ... that famous art
> Wherein all nature's treasury [treasure—B-Text] is contained.
> Be thou on earth as Jove is in the sky,
> Lord and commander of these elements. (A-Text: I, i, 76–79; B-Text: I, i, 73–76)

Spurred on by this exhortation, Faustus imagines his powers as a magician and exclaims, "How am I glutted with conceit of this" (A-Text: I, i, 80; B-Text I, i, 77). But the exhortation contains confusion. Neither the Evil Angel nor Faustus gives a hint that becoming "Lord and commander of these elements" conforms to the religiomoral aim of white, not black magic. Nor, on the contrary, do they indicate that they are purposely undermining a conventional belief. According to Pico della Mirandola in his *Oration on the Dignity of Man* (1486), because white magic has the power to command spirits and demons, it "brings forth into the open the miracles concealed in the recesses of the world, in the depths of nature and in the storehouses and mysteries of God," enabling the magician to "wed earth and heaven, that is ... lower things to the endowments and powers of higher things."[24] Conversely, in black magic, the magician is subservient to hellish demons and usually works on their behalf.[25] Thus, Faustus has subordinated himself to a much more exacting taskmaster than the God he rejects. By selecting black rather than white magic, he has also limited the chances for the "omnipotence" (A-Text: I, i, 56; B-Text: I, i, 54) that he initially sought. Whether Marlowe deliberately and subversively creates confusion through the ambiguity of the Evil Angel's words and Faustus's immediate affirmation, the jumbling of attributes of white and black magic reflects a popular notion of magic that was no clearer in the early modern period than it is now.

The intoxication that Faustus conveys when he says, "How am I glutted with conceit of this," is a psychological state that Macbeth and Prospero similarly experience as they thrill to the acquisition of unlimited power: Macbeth in his "vaulting ambition" (*Macbeth*, I, vii, 27) and Prospero in "being transported / And rapt in secret studies" (*The Tempest*, I, ii, 76–77). One can imagine that Marlowe and Shakespeare themselves experienced something similar as they set about, with the absolute power of a god, to people the worlds of their plays, select the events, and position them in movements of time. It is a state, however, that in the plays we are invited to regard with ambivalence, for, as exhilarating as it is for each protagonist to experience and for an audience to watch and hear, in all three cases the characters cross the line into self-indulgence and become self-destructive: Faustus sells his soul for power; Macbeth sells his for a throne; and, in order to empower himself as a magician, Prospero neglects his political responsibilities, not only making himself and his daughter vulnerable to his enemies but ensuring that they suffer the consequences. In reflecting on the ambivalence in our response to the glutted emotional state of each aspirer, we are led to consider the uses and abuses of the imagination and, ultimately, the functions and powers of the imagination in the two dramatists themselves.[26] As Alvin Kernan expresses it, "Shakespeare is following Marlowe in using the magician to prefigure the playwright."[27] But before exploring such implications and assessing Shakespeare's debt to Marlowe, let us examine Marlowe's play and attempt to locate in it what Shakespeare might have discovered and admitted as an influence when he composed *Macbeth* and, later, *The Tempest*.

II   *Doctor Faustus* and *Macbeth*

Perhaps the most obvious and surely the strongest influence that *Doctor Faustus* exerted on the Shakespeare who authored the tragedies is the intense psychological portrayal of the protagonist's agony immediately before his death (Act V, Scene ii of both the A- and B-Texts). Because this scene broke new ground in English drama with an absorbing, emotionally realistic portrayal of the internal workings of a character undergoing angst and because it so well suited the playwright's own aesthetic inclinations—presenting a figure in a soliloquizing mode wrestling with the most crucial of ethical issues—it is no surprise that Shakespeare adopted and refined the technique years before he came to characterize Macbeth. It may well be that Marlowe's single most important characterological gift to Shakespeare was his interiorization of character in *Doctor Faustus*.

In addition to this major parallel in technique, there are other, significant similarities between the two playwrights in portraying their protagonists. For both Faustus and Macbeth, the wrenching pain of the punishments they experience is as horrifying as the crimes that initiated their retribution. With self-loathing, they each live through the isolation, the degradation, and the utter despair of the conditions that they have brought upon themselves. That is, they experience hell as a state of mind. Marlowe and Shakespeare have both prepared us for such internalized portrayals. With genuine credibility, Marlowe places a strong focus on Faustus's psychology by having him disbelieve Mephistopheles's candid characterization of Hell as a place

> Within the bowels of these elements,
> Where we are tortured and remain for ever.
> Hell hath no limits, nor is circumscribed
> In one self place, for where we are is hell,
> And where hell is must we ever be (A-Text: II, i, 22–26; B-Text: II, i, 122–26)

Mephistopheles says, in effect, that hell is a mental state, independent of geographical location. Macbeth inadvertently conveys a sentiment similar to that characterized by Mephistopheles when, in the following soliloquy, he says:

> If it were done when 'tis done, then 'twere well
> It were done quickly. If th' assassination
> Could trammel up the consequence, and catch
> With his surcease success, that but this blow
> Might be the be-all and the end-all—here,
> But here upon this bank and shoal of time,
> We'd jump the life to come. (I, vii, 1–7)

He goes on to explain why the murderous act will *not* "trammel up the consequence," and the rest of the play dramatizes with bitter irony the mental hell that ensues. Both plays focus centrally on the operations of the psyche in the throes of damnation. Thus, that hell is a state of mind, intensified by being in a continuum, is manifested dramaturgically by such actions as Faustus's inability to call upon God to help him (A-Text: II, iii, 18–25; B-Text: II, iii, 18–23) and Macbeth's difficulty in saying "amen" (II, ii, 22–32). In both instances, reliable Christian conventions yield to the complications of psychological distress.

Augmenting the psychological hell that each man experiences are fears of the quickness with which time passes and destruction approaches. In both dramas, the writers exploit our subjective sense of rapidly passing time as a structural device to produce tension. Some might argue that we are perhaps less aware of this fear in *Doctor Faustus* than in *Macbeth*, because Marlowe is busy throughout the middle of the play with Faustus's pranksterish demonstrations of power. But others could counter that we know the specific limits of Faustus's mortality soon after the beginning of the play—24 years. We know, too, the elusive speed with which a dramatist can telescope the action of a play and that we can be manipulated to feel this brevity, because, like

Faustus, we are subjectively focused on objective time. Together, these elements in our consciousness not only allow the tension evoked by the fatalistic threat to Fausus to be sustained even when it is not being portrayed, but they actually augment it. Thus, we move closer to the edge of our seats nervously anticipating Faustus's excruciating end at the fatal moment of reckoning.

In *Macbeth*, the protagonist seems preoccupied with the passage of calendar or clock time and the events that it brings only as they bear on his future existence. Moreover, he is deeply frustrated by his inability to govern these events, as well as the impersonal forces ruling them. Macbeth's feverish desire to gain some control over the future by abandoning life in the present bespeaks an inner imperative to act as a god, as if he existed outside of historical time but had the power to order the events in it—a trait he shares even more with Tamburlaine than with Faustus. As a result, he becomes increasingly anxious to act in a manner that assures him of a meaningful future, a future in which external events can be made subjectively satisfying and, at last, provide a mental calm and contentment.[28] His anxiety only increases as he finds this fantasy beyond his reach. Macbeth's strongly psychic involvement with the dynamics of time and his single-minded focus on the future culminate in his reaction to the news of his wife's death and in the well-known, cynical, grim soliloquy that immediately follows. His reaction to Lady Macbeth's death reveals the depth of his obsession with the future; it is almost comic in its blunt, witty, callous extremism: "She should have died hereafter: / There would have been a time for such a word" ([i.e., as "dead"—V, v, 16]—V, v, 17–18). The soliloquy is further evidence of his insensitivity to the present:

> Tomorrow, and tomorrow, and tomorrow
> Creeps in this petty pace from day to day
> To the last syllable of recorded time,
> And all our yesterdays have lighted fools
> The way to dusty death. Out, out brief candle!
> Life's but a walking shadow, a poor player
> That struts and frets his hour upon the stage
> And then is heard no more. It is a tale
> Told by an idiot, full of sound and fury,
> Signifying nothing. (V, v, 19–28)

It is as if Macbeth's investment in future time and, yet, perpetual disillusionment with what it brings, has made him numb to the rhythms and substantive reality of present time. The utter despair and the weariness he feels in the face of his existence, along with the bleakness of his vision, convey a perspective on passing time that everyone, inescapably, has felt in some measure; consequently, his plight tugs at our emotions as forcefully as does Faustus's agonizing moral dilemma over repentance and salvation just before he dies (A- and B-Text: V, ii). The irony of Macbeth's tragic waste of time is brought home emphatically and finally when, at the beginning of the last speech of the play, Malcolm says, "We shall not spend a large expense of time / Before we reckon with your several loves / And make us even with you" (V, viii, 60–62). In contrast to Macbeth, Malcolm appreciates the value of present time.

Macbeth ends on a modestly optimistic note,[29] as *Doctor Faustus* does not, because, in contradistinction to his kingly predecessor, Malcolm intends to invest present time with positive meaning. His good intentions, however, do not palliate what for many audiences and readers remains Shakespeare's darkest tragedy.

The leaden feeling we experience at the ends of both *Doctor Faustus* and *Macbeth* may in part be the result of the plays' having brought us into so vivid an awareness of the destructiveness of passing time and of fears of our own mortality. Through the portrayals of the protagonists' final despondency at the oppressiveness of advancing time, we become imbued with despair at the ultimate futility of life itself. For all human beings, good or evil, death is, of course, the harshest and most ugly truth of ultimate reality. To undergo a psychic death before the physical one, as Faustus and Macbeth do, only intensifies the agony. Looked at one way, life is an imaginative construct that, because of all-obliterating death, is of necessity filled with actions "signifying nothing." By reminding us of this as they forcefully engage our emotions, both dramatists make us undergo with wrenching authenticity the severe consequences of their protagonists' calamitous decisions and the terrifying impersonal forces that facilitate and magnify those consequences. In both plays, we are made to participate imaginatively in the destructiveness of time's ceaseless advances as it forces the protagonists into death. We are thereby made to feel their helplessness in the face of time's omnipotence and to confront the knowledge that their helplessness will ultimately be ours. Because *Doctor Faustus* guided its audiences through the psychology of dying with such emotional power and effectiveness, Shakespeare was able to augment that power and his effectiveness in *Macbeth*.

Not surprisingly, Shakespeare was little influenced by the cheerless, Christianized world that Marlowe presents in *Doctor Faustus*; but he was influenced by the *donnée* and other artistic strategies of the play. The milieux of the two plays are very different, but they both contain extraordinary figures who cannot discover a way to exploit their unique talents, because they cannot connect with the impersonal forces that govern them. Faustus is unable to find his way to God and salvation and Macbeth is unable to fathom the ambiguity of the Witches and their relevance to the events of time. Increasingly, the two protagonists evoke in us a keen disappointment, especially because of our sense of what they might have become. Although we may be quick to judge Faustus as sinful and Macbeth as evil, we nevertheless feel compassion for both of them at the torturous ends of their lives. In manipulating a contradictory response to the plights of these characters, Marlowe and Shakespeare, as we have just seen, tap into our awareness of two of humankind's most fundamental fears, accelerating time and our own mortality, thereby forcefully heightening the sympathy as well as the ambivalence we feel. The two playwrights must have sensed that, by creating ambivalence between our rational moral judgment and our non-rational sympathy, they were equipping their plays with a means for producing the strongest dramatic tension possible. Thus, we can surmise that, at the very least, the divided response to Faustus in his anguish, in combination with the discord provided by the *donnée* of Marlowe's play, presented Shakespeare with a model for an indelibly powerful transmission of deeply felt conflict.

In his well-known essay on *Doctor Faustus*, "The Forme of Faustus Fortunes Good or Bad," C.L. Barber posits that in his speech to Helen of Troy Faustus is "hoping to find the holy in the profane."[30] Richard Wheeler enlarges this notion when he comments:

> Barber argued that tensions in Elizabethan culture about relationship to divinity and worship, set loose in the theater by the disruptive action of *Tamburlaine* and made explicit in the tragic action of *Doctor Faustus*, also shaped the tragic art of Kyd and Shakespeare, in which *the drive toward a sacred dimension of human experience is pursued in a fundamentally secular world.*[31] (my italics)

Although neither says so specifically, Wheeler and Barber would undoubtedly agree that, in spite of the difference in circumstances, *Macbeth* mirrors *Doctor Faustus* in its drive toward a secularized but nevertheless sacred dimension of human experience. Both Faustus and Macbeth galvanize their energies heroically as they try to make their demonic experience into the equivalent of one that is sacred and divine. Through an act of psychological transference, they seek absolute control, trying to transcend their mortal and secular limitations in order to arrive at a kind of immortality in mortality. What gives poignancy to their struggles is the aloofness of Faustus's God,[32] who appears to be immune to the scholar's *cris de coeur*,[33] and the combined forces of an impersonal fate and the cryptic Witches who, in all their terrible goofiness, seem most to enjoy toying sadistically with Macbeth.[34]

Approached from the perspective of the new historicists, both Faustus and Macbeth remain permanently entrenched in the moral orthodoxy they appear to oppose: "they simply reverse the paradigms and embrace what the society brands as evil."[35] As a consequence, we observe that the heroic aspects of their demonic behavior originate in the very orthodoxy they are trying to liberate themselves from. As we have already learned in the discussion of *Dido, Queen of Carthage* and *Antony and Cleopatra*, Marlowe's depiction of rebellious figures in an unidealized political world is more congenial to Shakespeare's perceptions later rather than early in his career. Aaron and Richard III live in worlds in which an ideal of political well-being still exists; Antony and Cleopatra, Macbeth, and Prospero do not. Therefore, like Faustus, they appear all the more heroic even as they appear all the more foolishly unrealistic for separating themselves from an increasingly imperfect world.

It is time to direct our attention more exclusively to aesthetic matters and to focus on what I am contending reveals how Marlowe most forcibly influenced Shakespeare. We have noted that Faustus's address to Helen of Troy (A-Text: V, i, 91–110; B-Text: V, i, 94–113) haunted Shakespeare's imagination throughout his career. His capacity for being haunted by Marlowe's language in its various forms and arrangements is probably more far-reaching and deeper than we will ever know.[36] It is, therefore, perhaps not unreasonable to think that the line describing Zenocrate from Tamburlaine's well-known soliloquy, "'Fair' is too foul an epithet for thee" (1 *Tamburlaine*, V, i, 136), finds its way into *Macbeth* first as part of the Witches' chant, "Fair is foul, and foul is fair" (I, i, 12), and later as Macbeth's comment to Banquo, "So foul and fair a day I have not seen" (I, iii, 38). Shakespeare's sensitivity to language cannot be overestimated.[37] It would be just like him to remember a play on words and to play on that play on words, not because he is one-upping Marlowe, but for the sheer joy of indulging in a playful paradox that, at the same time, serves two important dramatic functions: it helps to characterize the Witches as powerful, ominous creatures who are beyond our understanding and to create an atmosphere in which nothing is stable—indeed, one in which people and situations can seem or actually be the opposite of what they appear to be.

The world of instability and unnaturalness in *Macbeth* is given early dramatic expression by both the Witches and Macbeth in their linguistic play with "fair" and "foul." A scene whose chief purpose appears to be to expand this notion dramatically occurs at the end of Act II with the figures of the Old Man and Ross; in speaking of the prodigies in nature on the night of Duncan's murder, they describe a world turned upside down:

Old Man:	Threescore and ten I can remember well;
	Within the volume of which time I have seen
	Hours dreadful and things strange, but this sore night
	Hath trifled former knowings.
Ross:	Ha, good father,
	Thou seest the heavens, as troubled with man's act,
	Threatens his bloody stage. By th' clock 'tis day,
	And yet dark night strangles the traveling lamp.
	Is't night's predominance, or the day's shame,
	That darkness does the face of earth entomb
	When living light should kiss it?
Old Man:	'Tis unnatural,
	Even like the deed that's done. On Tuesday last
	A falcon, tow'ring in her pride of place
	Was by a mousing owl hawked at and killed.
Ross:	And Duncan's horses—a thing most strange and certain—
	Beauteous and swift, the minions of their race,
	Turned wild in nature, broke their stalls, flung out,
	Contending 'gainst obedience, as they would make
	War with mankind.
Old Man:	'Tis said they ate each other.
Ross:	They did so, to th' amazement of mine eyes
	That looked upon't. (II, iv, 1–20)

The metaphor of life as a play in lines 5–6 is a commonplace but in this context, seen from a heavenly perspective, generalized as "man's act," and with the vivid phrasing of "his bloody stage," it boldly calls to mind the author-dramatist's frame of reference and reminds us that Shakespeare is thoroughly conscious of his artistry in peopling the world of the play and well aware that, as playwright, he is able to assume the role of God the Creator. The same frame of reference recurs when, in Macbeth's final soliloquy (already quoted in full), Shakespeare employs the following theatrical metaphor: "Life's but a walking shadow, a poor player / That struts his hour upon the stage / And then is heard no more" (V, v, 24–26). Behind this declaration lies the ambivalence of the playwright who feels not only the superiority and satisfactions of creating drama but also the finality of death and being "heard no more."

In suggesting Shakespeare's strong awareness of his professional role as a dramatist, these self-reflexive metaphors encompass his self-fashioned responsibilities to his artistry—responsibilities of which he may not have been wholly conscious. His overall pervasive attention to artistry, in combination with the scene between the choral figures of the Old Man and Ross as a further dramatization and intensification of the instability and unnaturalness suggested by the earlier uses of the fair-foul, foul-fair paradox, leads me back to Tamburlaine's reference to "fair" and "foul." The description by the Old Man and Ross could conceivably have originated in Tamburlaine's words, thereby illuminating how the original context of the 'fair'-'foul' paradox could have had a definite influence on Shakespeare. From what one can surmise of the operations of Shakespeare's aesthetic consciousness, the notion that Tamburlaine's words had an indirect influence on the Old Man and Ross's description seems highly possible and maybe even probable. Ultimately, determining that this particular influence finds or does not find its way from Part 1 of *Tamburlaine* to *Macbeth* is of less importance than recognizing that such a journey can be understood as paradigmatic of the course of Marlowe's influence on Shakespeare's psychology of composition at its most subtle and elusive. As a paradigm, such a journey reveals an unseen pervasiveness in the influence of Marlowe on Shakespeare throughout his career. Although the journey is difficult to chart, it does suggest what Marlowe's influence can beget during a given period of Shakespearean composition.

In commenting on the following words of Lady Macbeth as she gives thanks to Duncan for honoring the Macbeth "house" with his presence, Frank Kermode speaks pejoratively of Shakespeare's complication of simple expressions through an "excess of energy":[38]

> All our service
> In every point twice done, and then done double,
> Were poor and single business to contend
> Against those honors deep and broad wherewith
> Your majesty loads our house. (I, vi, 15–18)

Kermode writes:

> Lady Macbeth's arithmetical measuring of gratitude—even if multiplied by two and then again by two our service would only count as one, given your generosity—is reflected in the doublings of the verse; she goes on to repeat her sums like an accountant (25–28) ["Your servants ever / Have theirs, themselves, and what is theirs, in compt, / To make their audit at your Highness' pleasure, / Still to return your own."]. On many occasions Shakespeare, needing a simple expression, cannot avoid complicating it in this way, as if by an excess of energy, but they should be distinguished from passages in which that energy is full and properly employed; and one of the greatest of these is Macbeth's soliloquy at the beginning of I.vii.[39]

Kermode completes his point by quoting all 28 lines of the soliloquy ("If it were done when 'tis done ..."). Although he is being critical of Shakespeare, disclosing the cause of an uncontrolled moment in the playwright's act of composition, Kermode has here identified the harmonious blending of exuberance, inventiveness, and indelible memory that lead to Shakespeare's unique linguistic feats. It is the blending process that links Shakespeare with a similar propensity in Marlowe and explains why he would have been so receptive to Marlowe's linguistic resourcefulness and to his freedom in manipulating language. Kermode's phrase "an excess of energy" can also be understood as Shakespeare's being "glutted with conceit." This emotional state, despite any flaws it produces, enables both Marlowe and Shakespeare to experiment with the poetics of dramatic language and, in the case of the latter, opens channels able to transmit Marlowe's influence.

One of the sticking points in the criticism of both Marlowe and Shakespeare has always been the degree to which we can psychoanalyze the characters. Realistic at some moments, symbolic or representational at others, or both at the same time, characterizations can seem contradictory, ambiguous, and truncated. The characters of Faustus and Macbeth are good examples of all three qualities. Faustus's contradictoriness is understandable when he is caught between the opposing viewpoints of the Good Angel and the Bad Angel; we recognize the reality of the psychological struggle between conflicting internal forces. What is less understandable is how little Faustus seems to know of the four branches of knowledge he has presumably mastered: philosophy, science, law, and religion. For example, although he cites Aristotle when he reads, "*Bene disserere est finis logices*" (A- and B-Texts: I, i, 7) and translates it, "Is to dispute well logic's chiefest end" (A- and B-Texts: I, i, 8), he is actually quoting from the Ciceronian *Dialecticae* of the anti-Aristotelian Peter Ramus.[40] How are we to understand Faustus's psychology here? Is the confusion simply the result of Marlowe's not having checked his sources before setting pen to paper and, therefore, not intended to perplex us but simply to suggest Faustus's intellectual superiority? Lawrence Danson explains this particular contradiction by positing that the "intellectual subtext" of the speech is "that the letter kills but the spirit gives life" and that "Faustus mistakes the end of logic because he neglects its full context; he sees the art's letter but not its spirit."[41] Danson feels that this is Faustus's failure as a human being rather than as a scholar and that his "repeated error has been in failing to grasp the 'chiefest end' of *any* human endeavor."[42] The generalized nature of this explanation seems to me to blur the contradiction evident in Faustus's supposed and actual learning, because, whereas Danson's generalizations may be readily accepted as often true, they do not account for Faustus's confusion of specific texts here. Thus, the contradiction remains, as does our perplexity about whether it is dramatically purposeful.

A longstanding example of ambiguity for critics has been the question of who is responsible for pulling Faustus down when he tries to leap up to his God. Answers range from Faustus's self-inflicted despair to the aloofness of an impersonal God. The attempts to assign a clear and definite cause have only led to further controversy. However one may choose to answer the question,[43] unlike the perplexing contradiction in Faustus's erroneous attribution of a source (cited above), the ambiguity is powerfully effective in creating tension throughout the play. Even though the pact with the devil has been signed in blood, the appearances of the Good Angel, the fact that Mephistopheles feels it necessary to constantly monitor Faustus and hover over him, and the appearance of the Old Man all offer some slight hope that Faustus can seek salvation. Thus, the ambiguity persists to sustain the dramatic tension.

What has seemed truncated in the portrayal of Faustus—and I do not mean the term as an indication of a defect in Marlowe's artistry—is the relative innocuousness of his deviltry. As many critics have noted, his sin of pride apart, we lack examples of the kind of violence and evil that we find in Macbeth. Most of the time Faustus is delighting in pranks and we are on his side—whether he is engaged in antipapal antics (A- and B-Texts: III, i) or in placing horns on an unnamed knight (A-Text: IV, i) or on Benvolio (B-Text: IV, i). It is his darker side that seems to be missing. With one notable exception, he is never vindictive, mean, nasty, or evil in ways that would make him totally morally repugnant to us: After the appearance of the Old Man (A-Text: V, i, 31–60; B-Text: V, i, 33–63), Faustus, in a bitterly conflicted state, asks Mephistopheles to "torment" (A-Text: V, i, 74; B-Text: V, i, 78) the Old Man. Mephistopheles responds that he can torment his body but not his soul. What Faustus means by "torment" is more a reflection of his displaced anger at his own contradictory state than his anger at the Old Man.[44] Our sympathy for Faustus and our fears for him override a simple condemnation of him as a sinister cohort of the devil. In summary, then, to write off the contradiction, ambiguity, and truncation of the play as artistic defects would be to misunderstand the usefulness of these elements[45] as dramaturgical devices and as part of the Marlovian aesthetic for effective drama.

The portrayals of Macbeth and his wife exemplify the same three elements. As is immediately apparent, the context of the play is more explicitly secular. The most basic contradiction in Macbeth leads to the question of how a man who is heroic, noble, deeply sensitive, and of such refined moral sensibilities can knowingly give himself over to so many hateful, callous evil acts. From the playwright's dramaturgical perspective, the question is, how can a criminal be effectively cast in the role of a tragic hero?[46] By "effectively," I mean with both psychological and dramatic credibility. There is no clear answer, of course.[47] We are as prevented from assigning real motives to Macbeth as we are from understanding the nature of his ambition. He has sold his soul for a crown, but, as critics have pointed out,[48] he lacks interest in the kingship he acquires. Thus, contradiction is compounded with ambiguity. However, what may be seen as a logical weakness may also be viewed as an artistic strength, for, as both Marlowe and Shakespeare must have sensed, with clarity can come disinterest, a lack of engagement.

The aspect of Macbeth's characterization that seems most truncated is his relationship with his wife.[49] At the beginning of the play, she has a powerful effect on him. She seems appropriately organized, controlled (and controlling), detached, alert, shrewd, practical, resourceful, a spur to him. She is a model of the manliness to which Macbeth aspires in his role as murderer and unregenerate criminal:

> Come, you spirits
> That tend on mortal thoughts, unsex me here,
> And fill me from the crown to the toe topfull
> Of direst cruelty. Make thick my blood;
> Stop up th' access and passage to remorse,
> That no compunctious visitings of nature
> Shake my fell purpose nor keep peace betweeen
> Th' effect and it. Come to my woman's breasts
> And take my milk for gall, you murd'ring ministers,
> Wherever in your sightless substances
> You wait on nature's mischief. (I, v, 39–49)

> I have given suck, and know
> How tender 'tis to love the babe that milks me:
> I would, while it was smiling in my face,
> Have plucked my nipple from his boneless gums
> And dashed the brains out, had I so sworn as you [Macbeth]
> Have done to this. (I, vii, 54–59)

But—and it is an enormous "but"—when it comes to murdering Duncan, she murmurs to herself, "Had he not resembled / My father as he slept, I had done't" (II, ii, 12–13). Moreover, apparently she has to take a drink (or two) to fortify and embolden herself to play her relatively minor role in the slaying (II, ii, 1–2). Macbeth never hears her utter the words about the resemblance, so we never hear him respond to it or to her overall queasiness about the murder. By the time she dies, he has fallen so deeply into a depressed, obsessed state that he can only growl about the inconvenience of the timing of her death and, then, perhaps as a momentary refuge from the pain of her death and from the continuing horrors of his own situation, move to a generalized soliloquy (V, v, 17–28). Although she seems to be living her life for him and through him, he is too self-involved to reveal more than an early dependence upon her. As the play develops, their estrangement increases. Like all of Shakespeare's characters for whom life becomes intolerable, she goes mad, a desperate, penultimate act of self-protection. We are left to imagine what initially attracted Macbeth to her and how the relationship advanced to the stage of dependence with which we begin the play.

We can now understand how the characterizations in both *Doctor Faustus* and *Macbeth* raise the important question about Elizabethan and Jacobean drama asked above: To what extent can apparently incomplete psychological characterizations be directly related to the playwright's need to have characters behave as they do because they are controlled by the artistic demands of plot and action and to what extent is an audience free to try to understand their inconsistent behavior through realistic, commonsense psychology? The answer to this question suggests that flexibility is required on the part of audiences as they shift from representational to realistic modes of perception and, further, acknowledge the possibility of both modes' presence simultaneously in a character. Such flexibility also presupposes an understanding and a welcoming of experimentation and new developments in dramaturgical technique—both of which early modern audiences apparently relished.

Apart from the impact of conventions on Marlowe and Shakespeare, conventions that they helped to shape even as they were being shaped by them, is the influence of artistic individuality. One of the most evident truths about Shakespeare's aesthetic sensibility is that he ultimately privileges situations over characters, even though the two are not necessarily mutually exclusive. The best test for this is his poetry where, even though the form does not necessarily invite him to do so, he thinks situationally—*Venus and Adonis*, *The Rape of Lucrece*, and the Sonnets in particular.[50] This is not characteristic of the Marlowe of the *Tamburlaine* plays (the first especially) where the desire for "high astounding terms" dominates the concern with situation. It is characteristic, however, of the Marlowe of *Doctor Faustus*, especially at the beginning and the end of the play, where, not only does the situation of a potentially heroic figure in conflict with the Judeo-Christian moral norm predominate, but, because the situation intensifies rather than advances, Marlowe is able to give more attention to the psychologizing of a character than he has heretofore. We have a subtle and complicated understanding of the sources of Faustus's anguish beyond that of any of Marlowe's other characterizations primarily because we see more deeply into Faustus's emotional nature. Shakespeare undoubtedly recognized Marlowe's experimentation here. He saw in this play the impressive portrayal of psychological cause and effect, but he also saw an unparalleled blending of situation and character. He must have recognized that, with the death scene of Faustus in particular, Marlowe was providing a new standard for evoking emotional depths in an audience. At the very least, Marlowe must have reinforced Shakespeare's own natural inclinations toward psychologizing, a consequence that affirms anew the strength and importance of their remarkable aesthetic bond.

III   *Doctor Faustus* and *The Tempest*

For Marlowe in *Doctor Faustus*, magic consists of what in the twenty-first century we understand as a combination of science and fantasy. However, for sixteenth- and seventeenth-century minds, influenced by a complex of Hermetic ideas and the thinking of Pico della Mirandola, Marsilio Ficino, and especially Giordano Bruno, magic encompassed the material and spiritual worlds and on every social level was believed in, practiced, and widely revered.[51] Consequently, the magician was highly esteemed. As James Robinson Howe explains it, the magician not only links old and new science and philosophy but "is the embodiment of the ideal qualities of man, as the Renaissance saw them. He represents deep religion and philosophy tied to practical ability in this world."[52] Because Faustus espouses necromancy, he understandably falls short of the ideal; yet, paradoxically, he associates "honour" with the study of necromancy, suggesting that his initial self-image was that of a white magician:

O, what a world of profit and delight,
Of power, of *honour*, of omnipotence
Is promised to the studious artisan! (A-Text: I, i, 55–57; B-Text: I, i, 53–55; my italics)

Once he makes his pact with the devil, he turns away from acting as a magician to practicing what, strictly speaking, must be identified as witchcraft.[53] Even so, he can never quite forget his instinctive aspirations as a white magician, for he continues to act the part whenever, as I discussed earlier, he tries to find "the holy in the profane," as he does in his response to Helen. Like Macbeth, he has to suppress good to embrace evil, and we are always aware of what he might have been had his inclinations toward good prevailed.

William Blackburn points out[54] that Faustus confuses the two types of magic as they are clearly set forth by Pico della Mirandola: *goetia* (witchcraft) which is demonic and involves subservience to the powers of evil and *magia* which asserts the superiority of the magician to all spirits and demons (they are in fact subservient to him) and seeks "the utter perfection of natural philosophy."[55] Blackburn's view is that Faustus reveals his ignorance of magic, evident particularly in his conjuring,[56] and that "ignorance of magic is a central metaphor in the play because … it is really an ignorance of the proper way to use language."[57] Thus, he concludes, Faustus "tends to confuse language and reality, his words with those things to which they refer."[58] The argument Blackburn presents would be more persuasive if it explained why the Evil Angel also reveals the same ignorance when he urges Faustus to indulge in *magia* and become, like Jove, lord and commander of the natural elements (A-Text: I, i, 76–79; B-Text: I, i, 73–76). Ultimately, I am more willing than Blackburn to attribute the cause of the confusion about magic to Marlowe than to Faustus.

Unlike Faustus, Prospero comes close to portraying the ideal of the magician,[59] even if he seems not to satisfy Howe's criterion of "deep religion," for he has the most crucial attribute of the magus: "the unifying mind which sees into the essence of things."[60] Prospero has a mind that rises above feelings of personal animosity, discarding superficies to assert the union of proper ethical and social values. Ironically, Prospero supports the conventional values of a society from which he willingly isolated himself and, at the end of the play, to which he is reluctant to return. At the risk of psychological impairment, in returning to Milan he has made a noble gesture on behalf of society, thereby proving that "the unifying mind" requires a serious humbling of the ego. In reaching into the "essence" of social morality, Prospero has had to abjure his magic, the study of which, paradoxically, enabled his unifying mind. Shakespeare appears to be exalting moral idealism on the one hand and subverting it with psychological realism on the other, leaving the characterization and the values of the play deliberately in a tantalizing state of ambiguity.

At first, thinking of himself as a magician, Faustus seems eager to acquire the grandeur that attaches itself to the figure of the magus, but, at the same time, his deepest, controlling motivation is, unquestionably, a goal to which the magus did not aspire, the desire for unlimited power: "A sound [i.e., effective] magician is a mighty god" (A-Text: I, i, 64) or "A sound magician is a demigod" (B-Text: I, i, 61).[61] Faustus describes the wished-for outcome of this driving force in the most encompassing of terms, not only pertaining to the earth but to the cosmos: "All things that move between the quiet poles [the motionless poles of the universe] / Shall be at my command" (A-Text: I, i, 59–60; B-Text: I, i, 56–57). In an exhortation quoted above (A-Text: I, i, 76–79; B-Text: I, i, 73–76), the Evil Angel reduces and makes more specific the scholar's aims; he urges Faustus to achieve what we would understand as a scientific mastery of the four basic "elements" of nature—earth, air, fire, and water—and, presumably, the laws and processes of nature which govern the elements' myriad combinations. The advice of the Evil Angel is strikingly similar to the ultimate aims, if not the inductive means, of Descartes when, in his *Discourse on Method* (1637), he advocates a pragmatic over a speculative knowledge. Descartes suggests that through such useful knowledge, we can learn about

> the force and actions of fire, water, air, of the stars, of the heavens, and of all the bodies that surround us—knowing them as distinctly as we know the various crafts of our artisans—we may in the same fashion employ them in all the uses for which they are suited, *thus rendering ourselves the masters and possessors of nature.*[62] (my italics)

The italicized final phrase, understood less cosmologically, could be taken as Faustus's chief goal as the Evil Angel states it. Ironically, Faustus's evil is Descartes's good and, as the history of intellectual currents of thought has proved, especially with regard to science, ours as well. As it turns out, Faustus's power is considerably less than he hoped for, and he is deflected from his lofty goal of control in the universe, for his achievements are the consequence of relatively innocuous fantasies rather than scientific endeavors, beginning with the parade of sins and ending with the grapes brought instantaneously from another part of the world to satisfy the longings of the pregnant Duchess of Vanholt. In an anguished moment, Faustus commands Mephistopheles to torment or perhaps even kill the Old Man. But Faustus never commits violent crimes and, therefore, never uses his magic powers to escape punishment; nor does he ever object to Mephistopheles's failure to live up to their bargain.[63] Compared with the evil nature of the Duke of Guise or of Macbeth, his wickedness is very bland pudding.

Because of his activities as a magician, Faustus has been likened to Prospero,[64] even though their perspectives differ considerably. For Prospero, happily self-involved, magic is an engrossing scholarly project, one, he discovers, that can be used to promote moral well-being and serve practical ends. More heady and more eager for absolute power, Faustus finds in magic a means for engaging in incantations and making a pact with the devil in order to fulfill his fantasy of creating for himself a world of profit and delight.[65] However, psychologically, the two men share similarities. While in Milan as its ruler, Prospero becomes as "glutted with conceit" of the powers of magic as Faustus does. Thus, both magicians, in their most exhilarating moments of suffusion in magic, reveal an egotistical pride that blinds them to a more pressing reality.

In spite of the obvious difference of focus between Faustus's necromancy and Prospero's white magic, some of their actions are similar. The most specific parallel is the snatching of the food at the "banquet" in each play—from the Pope and his entourage in *Doctor Faustus* (A-Text: III, i, 60–87; B-Text: III, ii, 29–90) and from Alonso, Gonzalo, Sebastian, and Antonio in *The Tempest* (III, iii, 18–82). Ironically,

Marlowe's earliest audiences would have cheered Faustus's anti-Catholic antics and considered them moral, although, generally speaking, Faustus is an amoral magician. Prospero, on the other hand, despite the prickly elements in his personality, always works toward moral ends; he never runs the risk of blasphemy, even when he is, in effect, playing God. From an early modern religious perspective and in accordance with the dictates of honorable white magic, what he is doing would be understood as an attempt to please God. Taking a purely secular perspective, Shakespeare portrays Prospero as a magician who uses his powers to free Ariel from the spell of Sycorax, to control Caliban in order to inculcate him with something more than brute instinct, and to secure an appropriate husband for his daughter. Moreover, even though his magical powers do not appear to extend beyond the island, once the royal party arrives, instead of acting out of anger and merely seeking revenge, he takes advantage of the opportunity to forgive Alonso, Sebastian, and Antonio and to try to revive in them some semblance of an ethical consciousness. As he says to Ariel:

> Though with their [his enemies'] high wrongs I am struck to th' quick,
> Yet with my nobler reason 'gainst my fury
> Do I take part. The rarer action is
> In virtue than in vengeance. They being penitent,
> The sole drift of my purpose doth extend
> Not a frown further. (V, i, 25–30)

Prospero's eventual abandonment of his magic ("… this rough magic / I here abjure"— V, i, 50–51) and his departure from the island not only suggest that his intentions are honorable and have always been so, but that, like Faustus, he is forced to succumb to "the strong necessity of time" (*Antony and Cleopatra*, I, iii, 42) and to renounce the pleasures that his imaginative engrossment with magic brings. From the perspective of maintaining the stability of society, such pleasures are considered dangerously self-indulgent. Thus, he relinquishes his individuality as a magician and as a father to reenter society as a political leader and, in arranging for the marriage of his daughter, to meet the conventional demands of society. But, sadly, returning to society is returning to a place "where / Every third thought shall be my grave" (310–11)—certainly not a ringing endorsement of his new corporate existence. Considered from the viewpoint of a humanist, bringing down the curtain on the protagonist's magical powers in both *Doctor Faustus* and *The Tempest* signals the beginning of a final, direct confrontation with what the two plays recognize, as I suggested earlier, as the most ugly and fearful aspect of ultimate reality for human beings, the descent into death.[66] Neither playtext embraces the solution to the passage of time and death offered by orthodox Christianity—namely, salvation—but, given the presence of its religious and moral atmosphere, *Doctor Faustus* has more trouble exorcising the possibility than *The Tempest*.

Symbolically, the manifestations of magic in both dramas represent the results of a free play of the protagonists' imaginations and the absoluteness of their power. Joel Altman points out that, strictly speaking, the knowledge of magic is not dependent upon possessing an imagination.[67] Both Faustus and Prospero claim that the knowledge of magic is achieved through study, not imaginative rumination. In a passage already quoted, Faustus exalts the knowledge open to "the studious artisan" (A-Text: I, i, 55–57; B-Text: I, i, 53–55) and Prospero tells Miranda:

> the liberal arts
> … being all my study,
> The government I cast upon my brother
> And to my state grew stranger, being transported
> And rapt in secret studies. (I, ii, 73–77)

> I thus neglecting worldly ends, all dedicated
> To closeness, and the bettering of my mind
> With that which, but by being so retired,
> O'erprized all popular rate. … (I, ii, 89–92)

But, once Marlowe and Shakespeare have indicated that Faustus and Prospero have mastered a knowledge of magic, they associate their protagonists' practice of magic with the imagination. Altman and Ian McAdam have both argued, although on different grounds, that Marlowe establishes a discernible link between magic and imagination.[68] For Altman, Marlowe conflates magic and poetry, because both use the imagination to invent reality;[69] he feels that "Marlowe is testing the viability of an imagination that seeks to liberate itself from the trap of a fallen history and reassert its dominion over nature."[70] In establishing the link between magic and imagination, McAdam takes his argument in a universalized, humanistic direction (different from mine). He tells us that in *Doctor Faustus*, "the false power of the play—magic—may thus be seen as a symbol of the imagination."[71] As such, Faustus's failure is his lack of imaginative response to human experience: "This failure arises in part from an excessive confidence in words, as if the poetic imagination gives one direct access to worldly power."[72] McAdam concentrates on Marlowe's continuing interest in the failure of the imagination; Altman would agree with his position, although, as we have just seen, he comes to it by a different route.

That Shakespeare follows in Marlowe's footsteps in linking magic with the imagination is patently suggested by Prospero's commentary upon the masque that he directs for the benefit of Ferdinand and Miranda (IV, i, 148–63), beginning "Our revels now are ended," and by his summary of his magical feats as he abjures his "rough magic" (V, i, 33–57). In both speeches, the feats of a magician merge with the acts of imagination of the playwright, a representation that has readily enabled critics and students of Shakespeare to interpret the speeches from the playwright's perspective as, in part, self-referential. If we also regard the practice of magic in *Doctor Faustus* and *The Tempest* as a symbol of the imagination in happy psychic operation, whatever other associations this practice may evoke as a symbol of deleterious consequences and, ultimately, failure in Faustus and Prospero, we see that performing magic feats can be a source of joy. Initially, Faustus is "glutted with conceit" and Prospero "transported" and "rapt"; in addition, and more pragmatically, the imagination proves to be highly useful to both figures. But it can also be abusive—knowingly or unknowingly. Faustus is aware of its abusive potential because his magical powers are tied securely to the devil as his treatment of the Old Man and Benvolio attest (in the B-Text: IV, ii, 67–95); but, generally, he does not cruelly maltreat others in his use of it. Prospero is unintentionally injurious in risking his and Miranda's lives as a result of his absorption in the study of magic, and he can be hurtful with his powers as a means of keeping Caliban under control; but he, too, is not gratuitously cruel. Insofar as Faustus and Prospero unwittingly deceive themselves through their involvement with their magical powers, they are self-abusive. Faustus, with Mephistopheles's help, also deceives himself knowingly, for he does not want to face the truth of either damnation or salvation. In imposing such a restriction on himself as he exercises his powers of magic, Faustus evinces a limited and, hence, defective imagination. Without realizing it, Prospero allows magic to become an all-consuming obsession until he arrives on the island, where it also becomes a necessity for neutralizing the black magic of Sycorax and for creating civil order out of chaos. Both men find in magic a means for escaping from a conventional public life, and both are aware that their imaginative flight is deliberate.

In each play, the figure of the magician or magus can be seen to stand for the author who, in playing God the Creator, uses his imagination to become glutted with conceit. Thus, inescapably, Doctor Faustus and Prospero reflect to some extent Marlowe and Shakespeare as creators. I say, "to some extent" because Marlowe and Shakespeare as writers of dramatic fiction have greater autonomy in exercising their imaginations in art than either Faustus or Prospero who, as magicians, appear to have stringent obligations to the communities of which they are a part.[73] Thus, Faustus maintains self-control, not becoming a fiend and creating havoc in his world, and Prospero establishes order in the small island community over which he presides. If it is not unusual in literary criticism to find manipulators of magic likened to writers manipulating the products of their imagination to enthrall an audience, it is less common to discover writers providing commentary on their own artistic endeavors through the figure of a magus.[74] Faustus, who defies the norms and attempts to reinvent orthodox reality, is an extension of Marlowe the writer who challenges traditional theatrical and literary norms in the *Tamburlaine* plays and subverts standard ethical, gender, and sociopolitical norms in works as diverse as *Dido, Queen of Carthage*, *The Massacre At Paris*, *Edward II*, and *Hero and Leander*. However, Faustus also serves as a counterpoint to his creator. The magician's self-imposed limitations are not the playwright's nor is the paltriness of his imagination Marlowe's, except, as Altman declares, "in the structure itself, where for the first time Marlowe reverts to the moral frame technique of the older drama, so that his action proper is 'contained' in a way that it has never been before."[75] Unlike Marlowe, Faustus relies more on accepted traditions than on spontaneous inventions in plying his imagination—in a sense, more on the book than the word. But, like Marlowe, Faustus understands the importance of the imagination in those creative endeavors that give meaning to existence. At the same time, also like Marlowe, he makes clear the limitations of the imagination in achieving and sustaining power.

In the case of Prospero as a surrogate for Shakespeare's commentary on his art, there exists a long, sentimental critical tradition of associating the Duke with the playwright readying himself for retirement from the theatrical world of London. As everyone acknowledges, this tradition is occasioned by Prospero's two most well-known speeches, referred to already—the first, uttered after the masque he produces for the benefit of Ferdinand and Miranda: "Our revels now are ended ..." (IV, i, 148–63) and the second, when he promises to "abjure" "this rough magic" and "drown" his "book" (V, i, 33–57). More important than this association is Shakespeare's self-reflexive employment of Prospero to comment upon the powers and function of the creative imagination and how they can be stifled by society. This concern is certainly not new to Shakespeare's dramas. As we saw in Chapter 6, it takes us back to a similar concern in *A Midsummer Night's Dream*. There, Shakespeare sets society, represented by the court and associated with reason and the establishment of social values, in opposition to nature, represented by the woods and linked with the imagination and the acting out of personal, individual values. During the course of the play, Shakespeare never allows the imagination to be seriously hampered by reason and society. But we nevertheless see the potential for serious conflict, indicated by Theseus's insistence upon controlling the imagination: when he tells Hermia she must look with her father's eyes and marry Demetrius (I, i), when he scoffs at the imagination of the lover, lunatic, and poet (V, i, 2–22), and when he allows the imagination of the newlyweds to be unleashed only after the mechanicals' play: "Lovers to bed; 'tis almost fairy time" (V, i, 356). Shakespeare's self-reflection in *A Midsummer Night's Dream*, as in *The Tempest* (but more distantly), comes in the wake of his early awareness of Marlowe's boldness in standing back to assess and even admire his accomplishments as a playwright. This boldness is reflected not only in the self-advertising Prologue to the first *Tamburlaine* play and "The general welcomes [the first part of] Tamburlaine received" from its audiences, noted in the Prologue to the second *Tamburlaine* play [line 1], but also in the innovative employment of heroic language and a mix of the genres of epic and tragedy strongly in evidence in the two *Tamburlaine* plays (discussed in Chapter 6).

Magicians and dramatists both revel in their ability to express themselves imaginatively and in the momentary sense of omnipotence that such ability provides. Faustus tells us as much when he says, "How am I glutted with conceit of this." We know from Prospero's near obsession with magic before he was set adrift and from his reluctance to break his wand and abjure his magic that he has been similarly affected, and we see evidence of the intense emotional nature that makes his obsession possible when he tells Ferdinand and Miranda that he wants to retire to his cell in order "To still my beating mind" (IV, iv, 163). However, as I have just argued, both Faustus and Prospero become too caught up in their "conceit"—so much so that they involuntarily deceive themselves.[76] Apart from the reasons already given, an involvement with magic as magic and magic as imagination is for each protagonist a way of escaping from the unpleasantness of mortality. We watch Faustus cut himself off from all hope of salvation, and we agonize at the inexorability, bleakness, and severity of the death that he is facing, augmented by our knowledge of the permanence of his suffering in the terrors of Hell. Prospero's sad, valedictory mood and his awareness of his aging ("my old brain"—IV, i, 159) tell us that his involvement with magic, no longer just a refuge from a nasty world of politics and public life in Milan, has become a buffer against the fact of his mortality and his increasing awareness of physical decay. I am in full agreement with Reuben A. Brower who finds that "The key metaphor of the play is 'change'"[77] in the sense of metamorphosis or transformation or "transshifting states of being."[78] Within this category, the form of change that brings most sadness, of course, is Prospero's aging and his very reluctant return to a way of life that he is no more suited for than are Edward II and Richard II;[79] like the two kings, his individuality and temperament thrive better in private than in public surroundings. Thus, Faustus and Prospero exercise their imaginations in feats of magic partly to deceive themselves about the encroachments of time.[80] They use their imaginations to outface time psychologically, to provide a temporary respite from thoughts about the power of time to destroy, and to avoid confronting the physical evidences of time's puissance. In portraying their protagonists' act of inventing a reality, Marlowe and Shakespeare convey psychological understanding rather than moralistic judgments, perhaps because they are sympathetic to the desire to defy the onslaught of time and because, as writers, they are so strongly predisposed to delight in the act of imaginative creation itself. Yet, they are clearly not oblivious to the ability of the imagination to deceive through uncontrollable excess and to inflict involuntary self-abuse, whether on magicians or playwrights.

The Duke of Guise and Macbeth offer two better examples of the imagination as an instrument of abuse than either Faustus or Prospero. Like Faustus and Prospero, they promote some self-abuse without being conscious of it. But they also use their imaginations in their abuse of others. Whereas the Duke seems obsessed with mayhem, even demented, Macbeth seems obsessed with destroying all potential foes in order to make his control absolute and thereby gain some peace of mind—given his moral sensibility, a contradiction in itself. Macbeth needs peace of mind as much from the terrible nightmares and visions that afflict his conscience as from the harassment of his enemies; he suffers as only an essentially moral person could suffer. For both the Duke of Guise and Macbeth, the imagination is the agent of abuse. We have already seen how the imagination of the Duke of Guise, defective though it is, is instrumental in perpetrating atrocities. The same is true of Macbeth except that his imagination and conscience continue to terrorize him even as he becomes a hardened killer (e.g., in III, iv, 131–45 and IV, i, 168–77). The origin of Macbeth's desire to become king is ultimately obscure, especially because, as we have seen, he takes so little interest in the kingship once he attains it. Because he has a sensibility that we like to think belongs with a person of honor and nobility, we are made to feel that he is wrenching his most natural inclinations to change himself into the monster he becomes, and we lament the tragic waste. In his case, the imagination becomes a weapon for causing as much pain to himself as to others, and, perhaps on some level, the pain is self-inflicted as punishment for his crimes. The theatrical success of the characterization results from Shakespeare's ability to give greater depth, ambiguity, and psychological realism to the figure of the villain-hero than he has done before or had seen Marlowe do. Macbeth lives in a secular world of uncertainty and mystery, as the Witches signify. Faustus lives in an orthodox religious world of certainty and limitation, although not as much as he thinks. In the exploratory spirit of the dramatic kind that Altman identifies as *questio*,[81] Marlowe appears to be questioning how forgiving the God who rules the universe is, as well as the ambiguities and contradictions inherent in religious belief. But, rightly or wrongly, as hero or villain, Faustus himself does not seem to be questioning. Given his status as a scholar, a man who presumably thrives on intellectual curiosity, this is especially ironic and tragic.

On the whole, Marlowe and Shakespeare are less skeptical and less ambivalent about the function and powers of the imagination than those who are not artists might be. To writers, understandably, the diverse workings and salutary effects of a proliferating imagination far outweigh its abuses. Given the success of the *Tamburlaine* plays and *Doctor Faustus*, Shakespeare must have marveled at the dramaturgical possibilities of the imagination as he saw them manifested by Marlowe. Even at the end of his career, we sense Shakespeare's enthusiasm for feats of imagination. We hear in Prospero the thrill of recalling the accomplishments of the imagination:

> I have bedimmed
> The noontide sun, called forth the mutinous winds,
> And 'twixt the green sea and the azured vault
> Set roaring war; to the dread rattling thunder
> Have I given fire and rifted Jove's stout oak
> With his own bolt; the strong-based promontory
> Have I made shake and by the spurs plucked up
> The pine and cedar; graves at my command
> Have waked their sleepers, oped, and let 'em forth
> By my so potent art. (V, i, 41–50)

The simple stateliness and pride expressed here are entirely in keeping with Prospero's reflections on his art—that is, until he mentions opening graves (48–49). This action asks to be understood metadramatically, for it seems to apply more to Shakespeare than to Prospero, especially when one considers the famous historical figures the playwright's English and Roman histories have portrayed.[82] Marlowe never had the chance to assess the powers of the creative imagination at the end of a long career, but I suspect that he would have felt similarly: that for any and all of its inadequacies, the imagination well merits glorification.

IV   Conclusion

Down through the centuries, until our own day, *Doctor Faustus* has remained Marlowe's most popular play. The *Tamburlaine* plays had an unprecedented, instantaneous popularity that extended into the early seventeenth century, thanks in part to Ben Jonson's continuing interest in the warrior leader and his language,[83] but *Doctor Faustus* has persisted in inspiring playwrights from the seventeenth century to the twenty-first, and, beginning with the twentieth century, screenwriters as well.[84] If *Doctor Faustus* continues to have such a strong impact over four centuries after it was written, it is certainly not surprising that Shakespeare was deeply influenced by the play and that it held a firm, even subtle place in his artistic imagination throughout his career. Nor is it surprising that, in writing *Macbeth*, Shakespeare still looked to *Doctor Faustus* for a model of the psychology of a figure damned and writhing in agony.

For examples of dramas that portrayed the figure of a magus, Shakespeare had principally *Friar Bacon and Friar Bungay* and *Doctor Faustus*.[85] Of course, he also had access to the *Tamburlaine* plays that Howe maintains embodied the spirit of the magus, especially as Giordano Bruno set it forth. By the time he came to write *The Tempest*, Shakespeare knew well how to reconfigure the magician to suit his own needs. If, within the markedly different context of *The Tempest*, Marlowe's influence seems generalized and broad, it is because the play is a testament to Shakespeare's creative independence, his mature artistry, and his boldness of imagination. Similar to his use of Barabas when he came to compose Shylock, in *The Tempest* Shakespeare looks to Marlowe less for dramaturgical technique than for an example of a specific type of figure, in this case a potent magician, that he could rework in creating his magus. In addition, *The Tempest* affirms Marlowe's dramatization of the ineluctable desire, joys, and yet the inevitable sadness of living a life of unrestricted imagination. We see that Shakespeare could draw upon Marlowe without fearing any loss of creative individuality and with utter ease could confidently present a magician who, though metadramatically similar, is in important ways quite the opposite of Faustus: Prospero is less concerned with acquiring power; he shows no confusion in his understanding of white and black magic; and he has the forcefulness that Faustus, in his tendency to be influenced and manipulated by others, lacks. Even so, Shakespeare finds in Faustus a figure with an unusual capacity for control and a symbol of the imagination; and he undoubtedly perceives the dramatic effectiveness of portraying a world in which time acts as an indomitable hostile force.

That *Macbeth* and *The Tempest* choose to develop such strikingly different aspects of *Doctor Faustus* shows the extent to which Marlowe's influence became deeply embedded in Shakespeare's creative intelligence. One might have expected Marlowe's influence to diminish with the passing years, but, as Shakespeare's career progressed, the influence seems only to have manifested itself with greater profundity, breadth, and complexity. Because of its subtlety, it also becomes more elusive; but it certainly cannot be ignored. *The Tempest* reveals a highly probable indication of the increased range of Marlowe's influence, the result of Shakespeare's having had many years to muse upon productions of *Doctor Faustus*. Another indication of the increased strength of Marlowe's influence, as this chapter has already intimated, is that, in absorbing *Doctor Faustus*, Shakespeare reveals himself to be open to an influence of more than dramaturgical techniques and language. For the first time, elements of substance in the conflict of the play and in psychological characteristics of the chief protagonist interest him.

What is particularly striking about the three plays under discussion is their wariness of the powers of the imagination. In the discussion of *The Massacre At Paris*, *Titus Andronicus*, and *Richard III*, we discovered a similar wariness; clearly, for both writers, the subject was of abiding interest. All six plays view the imagination as a potentially destructive force on humankind in its ability to deceive and to promote narcissism, and they understand its potency as a weapon for destroying others. In the hands of a playwright, the imagination is clearly less lethal. It may lead to self-deception and self-indulgence but not to sustained self-absorption, because the dramatist is protected by his sense of the needs of a live audience. The failure of Faustus's imagination and that of Macbeth are quite different: whereas Faustus's is constricted, Macbeth's is excessive. Prospero's, however, is largely under control once he is on the island and therefore suggestive of a golden mean between the two extremes. But this idealization does not extend to the island generally, for the imagination proves to be unruly and malevolent as it evinces itself in the political ambitions of Antonio and Sebastian and in the comic triumvirate of Stephano, Trinculo, and Caliban.

By the time we reach the conclusions of the three plays, we are left with a stronger sense of the weaknesses of the imagination than of its strengths, because we have been looking through the eyes of an inhabitant of the world of those plays, just as Marlowe and Shakespeare intended. If, however, we perceive self-reflectively with the eyes of the two authors, we revel in the artistic powers of the creative imagination and in its life-affirming capability. Moreover, we take delight in those moments when, glutted with conceit, a local habitation is created out of airy nothing, *ex nihilo*. Marlowe's boldness of imagination proved to be an unparalleled inspiration for Shakespeare. Because Shakespeare lived so much longer, the influence of Marlowe had the opportunity of becoming both subtle and significant. Consequently, assuming the perspective of late Shakespeare, who, over the course of his career found Marlowe's daring imagination a continuing source of inspiration, our understanding and appreciation of Marlowe's greatness grows even stronger, and Shakespeare's tacit tribute becomes our vocal one.

As critics, we are now in a position to realize that the most important Marlovian contribution to Shakespeare's artistry was an inventiveness with various forms of dramaturgical ambiguities; and, like Mephistopheles, both of these playwrights resolutely refused to resolve these ambiguities. As many critics have pointed out and I have echoed, the three plays under examination here provide abundant evidence of purposeful ambiguity. Both writers were aware that clarity of cause and effect in characterization and action could leave an audience passive and their imaginations dormant. They knew with equal certainty that ambiguity engages, teases, and evokes audiences' imaginations, inviting them to participate actively in the production of the play. The Chorus in *Henry V* exhorts the audience to, "Piece out our [the author's, the actors', and the production crew's] imperfections with your thoughts" (Prologue 23); ambiguity makes a similar demand on an audience. The recognition that ambiguity is such a powerful artistic device forms one of the strongest aesthetic bonds between the two writers and the reason why we continue to watch their plays on the stage and screen and to scrutinize their texts in the classroom. As men of a rapidly developing theater in an increasingly commercial society, Marlowe and Shakespeare undoubtedly worked at understanding what would most capture and sustain the interests of their audiences. Luckily, in experimenting with ambiguity, they hit upon a device that would suffice "not of an age but for all time." Jonson's words suggest his own sense of literary tradition writ large. This sense, as well as a good many qualities of his own work, indicates not only that learning from other writers was essential in establishing one's place in a literary tradition; it also openly confirms that just as surely as Jonson was bound to Marlowe and Shakespeare, they were bound to each other. That the nature of this relationship itself contains ambiguities only ensures our interest in it for all time.

Notes

1   Moreover, Barnabe Barnes knew *Doctor Faustus* well enough in 1607 to influence him in writing *The Devil's Charter*.

2   See David Bevington and Eric Rasmussen's edition of *Doctor Faustus A- and B-texts (1604, 1616): Christopher Marlowe and His Collaborator and Revisers* (Manchester, UK: Manchester University Press, 1993), 48–49, for a survey of the earliest recorded performances of the play. See also Frances A. Yates, *The Occult Philosophy in the Elizabethan Age* (London: Routledge and Kegan Paul, 1979), 115, who describes the popularity of the play, mentioning that Henslowe's *Diary* records "over twenty performances" between 1594 and 1597.

3   *Doctor Faustus*, V, i, 91 (A-Text) or V, i, 94 (B-Text). All references to the two texts of *Doctor Faustus* are from the edition by Bevington and Rasmussen. Act, scene, and line numbers of both the A- and B-Texts are included in parentheses in the body of the text.

4   As Jonathan Bate points out in *The Genius of Shakespeare* (Oxford: Oxford University Press, 1998), 129, *Doctor Faustus* is "the one pre-Shakespearean play to endure in the theatrical repertoire." Thus, it is not surprising that Shakespeare could expect his audiences to respond to what many think is its most famous line. Furthermore, in *The Merry Wives of Windsor*, the casualness and familiarity with which Bardolph mentions Marlowe's Faustus suggests that the story of Faustus was widespread and enduring: "they threw me off … in a slough of mire; and set spurs and away, like three German devils, three Doctor Faustuses" (iv, v, 57–59). Interestingly, Bardolph recalls an incident in the 1616 B-text version of *Doctor Faustus* (IV, ii, 79–85), published long after *The Merry Wives of Windsor* was written (c. 1600). This apparent anomaly may indicate that other versions, which included this incident, existed before 1600.

5   James Shapiro, *Rival Playwrights: Marlowe, Jonson, Shakespeare* (New York: Columbia University Press, 1991), 81. In a parenthesis, however, Shapiro does say, "in the Faustian moments of *Macbeth* or *The Tempest* we find no verbal recollections, or parodies of Marlowe's play" (96), but he fails to explore his suggestion of "Faustian moments."

6   Marjorie Garber, "Marlovian Vision / Shakespearean Revision," *Research Opportunities in Renaissance Drama* 22 (1979): 3. Garber concentrates largely on the influence of the two *Tamburlaine* plays on *Henry IV*, Parts 1 and 2, *Henry V*, and *Julius Caesar*. Shapiro, *Rival Playwrights*, 79, endorses her reading of Hal's victory over Hotspur as a metaphor for Shakespeare's dramatic victory over Marlowe. As the chapter "Making the Haunt His" indicates, I prefer a less bellicose metaphor to describe Shakespeare's assertion of his creative individuality during his lifelong association with Marlowe.

7   Bate, *Genius of Shakespeare*, 129.

8   David Lucking, "Our Devils Now Are Ended: A Comparative Analysis of *The Tempest* and *Doctor Faustus*," *The Dalhousie Review* 80 (Summer 2000): 151–67 especially 152 and 163). For a discussion of the "transmutation" of Faustus's "I'll burn my books," see pp. 158–60 and 166. See also David Young, "Where the Bee Sucks: A Triangular

Study of *Doctor Faustus, The Alchemist,* and *The Tempest,*" in *Shakespeare's Romances Reconsidered,* ed. Carol McGinnis Kay and Henry E. Jacobs (Lincoln: University of Nebraska Press, 1978), 149–66 (especially 160–61). Young appears to be less certain of the verbal echo than Bate and Lucking (see Young, 153).

9   Bate, 105.

10 In *Henry VI, Part 2,* the Duchess of Gloucester prefigures Lady Macbeth in her rabid ambition. In having the Duchess arrange a conjuration (I, iv), replete with a witch (Marjorie Jordan), a conjurer (Roger Bolingbroke), and two priests (Sir John Hume and John Southwell), Shakespeare may have been given the incentive, if not the specific details, by the conjurations of Faustus.

11 For an illuminating account of the parallels and differences in the two plays as studies in the Protestant notion of damnation and why they may be considered Christian tragedies, see Richard Waswo, "Damnation, Protestant Style: Macbeth, Faustus, and Christian Tragedy," *The Journal of Medieval and Renaissance Studies* 4 (1974): 63–99.

12 I have already discussed in Chapter 2 ("'Unfelt Imaginations'") the possibility of the Duke of Guise, Aaron, and Richard III as villain-heroes and I have made reference to Clarence Valentine Boyer's *The Villain As Hero In Elizabethan Tragedy* (New York: Russell and Russell, 1914) which, because it uses hero and protagonist interchangeably (3), does not have the same frame of reference for the paradoxical figure that I have.

13 C.L. Barber, *Creating Elizabethan Tragedy: The Theater of Marlowe and Kyd,* ed. and intro. Richard P. Wheeler (Chicago: University of Chicago Press, 1988), 14.

14 All references to Shakespeare's plays are from *William Shakespeare: The Complete Works,* gen. eds Stephen Orgel and A.R. Braunmuller (New York: Penguin Putnam, 2002).

15 *Paradise Lost,* Book 9, Lines 13–47.

16 For an eminently sensible view of Marlowe's dramas as a combination of such paradoxical qualties as heroism and villainy without resolution, see Sara Munson Deats, "Marlowe's Interrogative Drama: *Dido, Tamburlaine, Faustus,* and *Edward II,*" in *Marlowe's Empery: Expanding His Critical Contexts,* ed. Sara M. Deats and Robert A. Logan (Newark: University of Delaware Press, 2002), 107–30. For a provocative discussion of the paradoxical qualities in Macbeth, see Robert B. Heilman's "The Criminal As Tragic Hero: Dramatic Methods," *Shakespeare Survey* 19 (1966): 12–24; Heilman describes our responses to a figure "remarkably endowed with aspects of personality not ordinarily expected in a man committed to evil" (20).

17 For a catalogue and summary of the critics who interpret Faustus as a Promethean hero, see Sara Munson Deats, "*Doctor Faustus*: From Chapbook to Tragedy," *Essays In Literature* 3 (Spring, 1976), 1: 4 and n. 6. See also Patrick Cheney, "Love and Magic in *Doctor Faustus*: Marlowe's Indictment of Spenserian Idealism," *Mosaic* 17:4 (Fall, 1984): 93–109, who, in talking about Faustus, notices that "like Macbeth, Faustus is basically a good man who is tempted by demonic powers to commit evil" (100) and goes on to discuss Faustus as a "hero who becomes an evil magician" (100).

18 In discussing *Macbeth* as a tragedy, T. McAlindon, *Shakespeare's Tragic Cosmos* (Cambridge: Cambridge University Press, 1991), 197–98, establishes Shakespearean links with the *Tamburlaine* plays. He tells us that the notion of ambition in *Macbeth* derives from Marlowe's portrayal of it and that Macbeth, like Tamburlaine, has a "desire not so much for power and wealth as for 'greatness'" (198). I agree that Macbeth's ambition is not a desire for power and wealth, but I am not sure that I would pinpoint it as greatness, although that may be part of it. Macbeth seems to want an untroubled life most immediately and, beyond that, it is difficult to tell.

19   Lawrence Danson, *Shakespeare's Dramatic Genres* (Oxford: Oxford University Press, 2000), 44.

20   Ibid., 45. Later in the book, 117–20, Danson discusses the mix of moral and sympathetic responses to Faustus and to the Richard of *3 Henry VI* and *Richard III*.

21   Alvin B. Kernan has a book on this subject: *The Playwright as Magician: Shakespeare's Image of the Poet in the English Public Theater* (New Haven, CT: Yale University Press, 1979). The most recent essay on the subject is Sara Munson Deats's "'Mark this Show': Magic and Theater in Marlowe's Doctor Faustus," in *Placing the Plays of Christopher Marlowe: Fresh Cultural Contexts*, Chapter 1, ed. Sara M. Deats and Robert A. Logan (forthcoming from Ashgate).

22   See Kurt Tetzeli Von Rosador, "The Power of Magic: From *Endimion* to *The Tempest*," *Shakespeare Survey* 43 (1991): 1–13, who views the progression in the following way: "*Doctor Faustus* formulates the magician's fantastic desires for worldly power; *1 Henry VI* introduces the conflict of rival charismas into a historical setting; *Macbeth* dramatizes this conflict starkly as one of the polar opposition of representatives of charismatic authority: *The Tempest* stages a further turn of the screw by presenting what the literature of demonology had pronounced incompatible and therefore non-existent, the ruler as magician, the magician as ruler" (11).

23   In saying this, I am not overlooking the interest in black magic introduced into the play through Sycorax, a witch who could easily have fit into the group of witches in *Macbeth*.

24   These quotations are included in William Blackburn's discussion of Pico della Mirandola's *Oration on the Dignity of Man* (1486) in "'Heavenly Words': Marlowe's Faustus as a Renaissance Magician," *English Studies in Canada* 4.1 (Spring, 1978): 3.

25   Ibid.

26   As I suggested in the second chapter in the discussion of *The Massacre At Paris*, *Titus Andronicus*, and *Richard III*, the imagination is of major, continuing interest for Marlowe and Shakespeare and, inevitably leads to metadramatic considerations.

27   Kernan, 157.

28   The subject of time in the play is not new to critical discussions. T. McAlindon, 214–19, discusses its all-encompassing significance, how it figures into so much of what the characters do and say. Other critics who treat the subject include M.M. Mahood, *Shakespeare's Wordplay* (London: Methuen, 1957), 131–37; Frederick Turner, *Shakespeare and the Nature of Time: Moral and Philosophical Themes in Some Plays and Poems of William Shakespeare* (Oxford: Oxford University Press, 1971), 1–6 (introduction) and 128–45 (on *Macbeth*); Francois Maquin, "The Breaking of Time: *Richard II*, *Hamlet*, *King Lear*, *Macbeth* (The Hero's Stand In and Against Time)," *Cahiers Elisabethains* 7 (1975): 25–41, but 36–40 for *Macbeth*; Wylie Sypher, *The Ethic of Time: Structures of Experience in Shakespeare* (New York: Seabury Press, 1976), 90–108; and G.F. Waller, *The Strong Necessity of Time: The Philosophy of Time in Shakespeare and Elizabethan Literature* (The Hague: Mouton, 1976), especially pp. 124 and 130–36.

29   Stephen Mullaney, *The Place of the Stage: License, Play, and Power in Renaissance England* (Chicago: University of Chicago Press, 1988), 122, explains how the perspective here is English but "fits the perspective of James as well" (122) before whom, in 1606, the play was performed. Mullaney is particularly perceptive on the multiple perspectives with which one can regard the play within its literary, cultural, and historical contexts and on amphibology as a chief form of ambiguity in the play (122–34).

30   Barber, 104.

31   Ibid., 13.

32   Lawrence Danson, "The Questioner" in *Christopher Marlowe: Modern Critical Views*, ed. Harold Bloom (New York: Chelsea House Publishers, 1986), 202–3, raises the question of who is to blame for Faustus's demise and does not answer it because the play does not: "… just who killed John Faustus is one Marlovian question that remains eternally open" (203). Sara Munson Deats comes to a similar conclusion in the fourth section of "Marlowe's Interrogative Drama," 117–20, in *Marlowe's Empery*. Speaking more generally, Bevington and Rasmussen, 31–32, declare that "the most persuasive criticism about *Doctor Faustus*" (31) has been that which sees that the questions raised are not answered and that the play thrives on its paradoxes and ambiguities.

33   For some readers and critics, what I am calling "aloofness" is taken as downright malevolence. As evidence, they point to the Prologue's description of the conspiring heavens (A-Text: 20–22: B-Text: 19–21) and to Mephistopheles' admission in the B-Text (V, ii, 97–101) that, through diversionary means, he prevented Faustus from leaping up to his God, presumably either under the direction of God or without any interference from Him.

34   See Stephen Greenblatt, "Shakespeare Bewitched," 108–35, in *New Historical Literary Study: Essays On Reproducing Texts, Representing History*, ed. Jeffrey N. Cox and Larry J. Reynolds (Princeton, NJ: Princeton University Press, 1993) who, whether the witches are "imagined as real or imagined as imaginary" (120), sees that "Witchcraft provided Shakespeare with a rich source of imaginative energy, a collective disturbance upon which he could draw to achieve powerful theatrical effects" (121).

35   Stephen Greenblatt, *Renaissance Self-Fashioning: From More to Shakespeare* (Chicago: University of Chicago Press, 1980), 209, is talking about Marlowe's "rebels and skeptics" (209), but the idea applies to Macbeth as well. The parallel is of course understandable since, as we are seeing, a good bit of what Shakespeare achieves in *Macbeth* may well derive from what Marlowe accomplished in *Doctor Faustus*. In *Sexual Dissidence: Augustine to Wilde, Freud to Foucault* (Oxford: Oxford University Press, 1991), Jonathan Dollimore comments on Greenblatt's remarks. He quotes a statement from Greenblatt on *Doctor Faustus*: "'the blasphemy pays homage to the power it insults'" (285) and then adds: "Greenblatt has in mind here that extraordinary moment when Faustus seals his pact with the devil by uttering Christ's dying words on the cross: 'consummatum est'. Creation recoils; his blood congeals. Via the expression of a perverse masochism, with its disturbing mix of abjection and arrogance, this act, in one sense the supreme antithesis of everything Christ dies for—he died after all to save us all—is identified as Christlike. Is not this transgression contained, the unintended reverence paid by the sacrilegious to the sacred?" (285–86). Dollimore's views reinforce Greenblatt's, indicating that the form of rebellion taken by such figures as Faustus and Macbeth is shaped by the orthodoxy they are rebelling against.

36   Garber, 3–8, is especially keen on detecting echoes of Marlowe's language in Shakespeare's plays. Some of her arguments are more convincing than others.

37   In his article, "'Time For Such a Word': Verbal Echoing in *Macbeth*," *Shakespeare Survey* 47 (1994): 153–59, George Walton Williams discusses Shakespeare's sensitivity to language within *Macbeth*. He begins with an examination of the witches' "fair is foul …" and Macbeth's echoing of the paradox (153–54).

38   The phrase is from Kermode's chapter on *Macbeth* in *Shakespeare's Language* (New York: Farrar, Straus and Giroux, 2000), 207.

39   Ibid.

40   See Bevington and Rasmussen, 16–17, who summarize the findings of orthodox criticism

in pointing out the errors in the learning of Faustus, the supposedly learned scholar. See also Blackburn, 6, Lawrence Danson, "The Questioner," 183–205, and David Riggs, *The World of Christopher Marlowe* (New York: Henry Holt, 2005), 238–44.

41 Danson, "The Questioner," 199.

42 Ibid., 201.

43 See Danson, "The Questioner," 202–4, for one critic's answer. Not surprisingly, given what we have already seen of his argument, Danson views the ambiguity as a consequence of Faustus's "aspiration stunted by the narrow scope of a mind that will not climb after knowledge infinite" (204).

44 See also the Old Man's affirmation of God as he exits the play, spurning the devils who harass him unsuccessfully—only in the A-Text: V, i, 109–17. One is even less troubled by the dismemberment of Benvolio in the B-Text, because it smacks of just retribution wittily conceived (see B-Text: IV, ii, 88–92).

45 This of course does not include the aforementioned confusion of texts, but only the purposeful conflict created within Faustus by the Good and Bad Angels.

46 James L. Calderwood also poses this opposition in his discussion of *Macbeth* in *If It Were Done: "Macbeth" and Tragic Action* (Amherst: University of Massachusetts Press, 1986), 50.

47 See Calderwood, *If It Were Done*, 49–53, for an interesting commentary on how the absence of persuasive motives can nevertheless lead to a plausible explanation of Macbeth's behavior. He maintains that "Macbeth 'falls in evil' as other men fall in love" (49). It is a sort of "demonic possession" (51), abetted by such forces as "ambition, 'manliness' and uxoriousness" (51). As we shall see, Calderwood's notion of demonic possession moves in the same direction as my view of the play's consideration of the powers of the enraptured imagination.

48 As Calderwood points out on p. 140, n. 13, R.A. Foakes, "Images of Death: Ambition in *Macbeth*," 7–29, and Brian Morris, "The Kingdom, the Power and the Glory in *Macbeth*," 30–53, both in *Focus on "Macbeth,"* ed. John Russell Brown (London: Routledge and Kegan Paul, 1982), do not find that Macbeth has a strong interest in the kingship. Nor does Norman Rabkin, *Shakespeare and the Problem of Meaning* (Chicago: University of Chicago Press, 1981), 101–10, whom Calderwood also cites.

49 Another kind of example is embodied in Lady Macbeth's statement about her husband's "nature" (I, v, 15): "It is too full o' th' milk of human kindness" (I, v, 16). This is more than we are ever privileged to see. Yet, it is an attribute that Shakespeare includes to thicken our response to the ambivalence of Macbeth's personality.

50 I am thinking of such a sonnet as 73 ("That time of year ...") in which the speaker is considerably older and presumably more frail than Shakespeare himself. The contrast between the speaker, who is near death, and the person to whom he is speaking is set to give the situation a dramatic tension that less of a contrast would certainly not have provided. The situation also enriches the meaning of the final two lines of the sonnet: "This thou perceiv'st, which makes thy love more strong, / To love that well which thou must leave ere long" (13–14). Here, the speaker, under the guise of complimenting the addressee (the Young Man—?), is actually asking for his love or for some stronger demonstration of it. The dramatic situation accentuates this request.

51 For a highly informative, clearly written examination of ideas about magic and the magician during the Renaissance in England and the influence of these ideas on the *Tamburlaine* plays in particular but briefly on Marlowe's other plays as well, see James Robinson Howe, *Marlowe, Tamburlaine, and Magic* (Athens: Ohio University Press, 1976). Howe's

description of the strains of magic in the Renaissance and the currents of intellectual thought about it are summarized in his introductory chapter (3–14). His discussion of the pervasiveness of magic in the Renaissance is on page 24. For a consideration of the notion that "magical beliefs were both widespread and passionately contested in early modern England," see Huston Diehl, *Staging Reform, Reforming the Stage: Protestantism and Popular Theater in Early Modern England* (Ithaca, NY: Cornell University Press, 1997), 128. For a discussion of the influence of Agrippa and his writings on *Doctor Faustus*, see Gareth Roberts, "Necromantic Books: Christopher Marlowe, *Doctor Faustus* and Agrippa of Nettesheim" in *Christopher Marlowe and English Renaissance Culture*, ed. Darryll Grantley and Peter Roberts (Burlington, VT: Ashgate, 1996): 148–71. For an interesting account of the way in which magical thinking serves as the underpinning for several of Shakespeare's notions as far-ranging as his "seeming obsession with threatened female chastity and ... his preoccupation with siege warfare" (11), see Linda Woodbridge, *The Scythe of Saturn: Shakespeare and Magical Thinking* (Urbana: University of Illinois Press, 1994). I must admit that the more I read about magic, the more I agree with Barbara Howard Traister, *Heavenly Necromancers: The Magician in English Renaissance Drama* (Columbia: University of Missouri Press, 1984): "... the study of Renaissance magical theory is enormously complicated by the imprecision of terminology and by variations in kinds of magic, many of which seem to overlap or duplicate one another. Discussions of magic are further obfuscated by a deliberate vagueness on the part of philosophers about their specific beliefs" (8).

52   Howe, 12.

53   One critic who makes such an identification is David Woodman, *White Magic and English Renaissance Drama* (Rutherford, NJ: Fairleigh Dickinson University Press, 1973), 37–38. For an explanation of how Faustus differs from Prospero once he makes his pact with the devil, see Anthony Harris, *Night's Black Agents: Witchcraft and Magic in Seventeenth-Century English Drama* (Manchester, UK: Manchester University Press, 1980), especially pp. 3 and 115–18.

54   Blackburn, 2–7.

55   Blackburn, 3, is here quoting Pico's words in his *Oration on the Dignity of Man* (1486).

56   Ibid., 4–5.

57   Ibid., 6.

58   Ibid., 7.

59   Howe's assessment is the following: "Shakespeare, becoming gradually more and more aware of the grand meaning of art in the theatre, culminates his career with *a glorification of the magus in the character of Prospero*" (138; my italics). For another supportive discussion, see Woodman's chapter (*White Magic and the English Renaissance Drama*) entitled "Prospero as the White Magician," 73–86. For still another, see Cheney, "Love and Magic," 101, who claims that Shakespeare's idealization of Prospero as a magus is like Spenser's idealization of Merlin; both focus on magic and its ability to promote ideal love: "like Merlin, the great magus Prospero uses magic power not to secure a beloved for himself, as Faustus and Subtle do, but to unite other lovers ... [in] an incarnate form of heaven on earth that he presents in his wedding masque" (101).

60   Howe, 12. Howe believes that Marlowe confers on Tamburlaine the attributes of the figure of the magus and that, as a result, in a sixteenth-century context Tamburlaine would have been seen as an ideal man.

61   See Ian McAdam, *The Irony of Identity: Self and Imagination in the Drama of Christopher Marlowe* (Newark: University of Delaware Press, 1999), 124, for a discussion of some

possible implications contained in the differences between the A- and B-Texts' versions of this line.

62 René Descartes, *Discourse on Method* (1637) in *Descartes: Philosophical Writings*, selected and trans. by Norman Kemp Smith (New York: Random House, 1958), 130–31.

63 For the possible traditions behind Faustus's foolishness in not balking at Mephistopheles's violations of the terms of the bargain, see L.T. Fitz, "'More Than Thou Has Wit to Ask': Marlowe's Faustus as Numskull," *Folklore* 88 (1977): 215–19.

64 See, for example, Bevington and Rasmussen, 32–33. See also Matthew N. Proser, *The Gift of Fire: Aggression and the Plays of Christopher Marlowe* (New York: Peter Lang, 1995), 6. Lucking, 151–67, not only sees a correspondence in Faustus's and Prospero's involvement with magic, but also points to a parallel in the way in which the protagonists' magical powers are parodied in the two plays' subplots (160). See also Lisa Hopkins, *Christopher Marlowe: A Literary Life* (New York: Palgrave, 2000), 75, who, among other associations, links the two protagonists' "desire to control seeing and being seen."

65 See the distinctions that McAdam, *Irony of Identity*, 112–13, makes about Faustus's relationship with the devils and the foolishness of his incantation. McAdam reads Faustus's involvement with magic psychologically, as a sign that Faustus's "identity is extremely unstable" (113), and concludes that his "damnation, his descent into hell, may be seen as a theatrical metaphor expressing his inability to resolve the conflict between self-assertion and self-surrender" (113).

66 Earlier in this chapter, I said something similar about the concern with death in *Doctor Faustus* and *Macbeth*. The fact that another parallel can be drawn between *Doctor Faustus* and *The Tempest* not only gives support to the notion of Shakespeare's consistency, showing how haunted he was by the destructiveness of time, but makes even more plausible the influence of Marlowe's dramatization on the artistic consciousness of Shakespeare.

67 Joel B. Altman, *The Tudor Play of Mind: Rhetorical Inquiry and the Development of Elizabethan Drama* (Berkeley: University of California Press, 1978), 374–75 and n. 47.

68 Ibid. and McAdam, 133–40. Like Altman and McAdam, I am interested in Marlowe's concern with the failure of the imagination in *Doctor Faustus* and elsewhere, but I am also interested in its functions, powers, uses, and abuses, seen from the perspective of Marlowe and Shakespeare commenting on themselves professionally.

69 Altman, 374.

70 Ibid., 375.

71 McAdam, 133.

72 Ibid.

73 Compare Altman, 389–90, who makes a similar distinction in his discussion of Tudor drama as "a medium of liberal inquiry" (389). Altman makes the point that "While it is true that logic, rhetoric, and poetry may be applied to both good and evil ends, nonetheless *as arts* they may be cultivated without immediate and obvious reference to external cultural values" (389). The same distinction holds true for drama, with one difference. Given the live audience and the necessity of communicating with it with immediacy, the playwright has a stronger obligation to the community that makes up the audience than the poet does.

74 In addition to Kernan's *The Playwright as Magician* and Deats's "'Mark this Show': Magic and Theater in Marlowe's *Doctor Faustus*," another recent example of a critic who not only makes the connection between magic and imagination but between the magical arts and the dramatic arts is Diehl, 76–80. Closer to my focus, although commenting on a different play, are Sara M. Deats and Lisa S. Starks, "'So Neatly Plotted, and So Well

Perform'd': Villain as Playwright in Marlowe's *The Jew of Malta*," *Theatre Journal* 44 (1992): 375–89. Of course, the chief early proponent for this critical perspective is James L. Calderwood, *Shakespearean Metadrama* (Minneapolis: University of Minnesota Press, 1971).

75 Altman, 272.

76 Lawrence Danson, "Continuity and Character in Shakespeare and Marlowe," *Studies in English Literature, 1500–1900* 26.2 (1986): 217–34, comments that "Faustus uses his magic to produce only illusions of self-transformation" (222). This trait is still another element in the scholar-magician's process of self-deception.

77 Reuben A. Brower, "The Mirror of Analogy: 'The Tempest'" in *The Fields of Light: An Experiment in Critical Reading* (New York: Oxford University Press, 1951), 112.

78 Ibid., 121.

79 One might also compare the cloistering tendencies of the Duke, Angelo, and Isabella in *Measure For Measure*. Each has tried to escape from the world of social and political obligations—ultimately, to no avail.

80 See Lucking, 154–56, who comments on the awareness of the movement of time in the two plays.

81 Altman, 8.

82 The opening of graves at night seems to be a well-known tradition. But it does not always require the powers of a magician. In *A Midsummer Night's Dream*, Puck says, "Now it is the time of night / That the graves, all gaping wide, / Every one lets forth his sprite, / In the churchway paths to glide" (V, i, 371–74); cf. his earlier reference to this tradition in III, ii, 378–87. In *Julius Caesar*, Cassius speaks of "… this dreadful night / That thunders, lightens, opens graves, and roars" (I, iii, 72–73) and Calphurnia tells Caesar that "A lioness hath whelpèd in the streets, / And graves have yawned and yielded up their dead" (II, ii, 17–18). Here, the opening of the graves is an ominous omen. The passages from these two plays do not help us to understand why opening graves has been one of Prospero's activities—unless he simply needs random spirits to accomplish the everyday tasks of making life comfortable or providing entertainment on the island.

83 Shapiro, 52–54 and 57, discusses Jonson's interest in Tamburlaine. I also see Sir Epicure Mammon as a comic response to Tamburlaine. Shapiro's chapter on Marlowe and Jonson (39–73) convincingly explains how strong an influence Marlowe was on Jonson throughout his career.

84 An essay on the connection between *Doctor Faustus* and *Man Fly*, titled "*Man Fly*: Sam Shepard's Adaptation of *Doctor Faustus*," was presented by Professor Johan Callens as part of a Marlowe Society of America session at the Modern Language Association Convention in Washington, DC on December 27, 2000. The movie *Bedazzled*, which first appeared in October, 2000, is yet another contemporary example of the Faustus story retold, this time with the figure of the devil a beautiful and seductive woman.

85 See Traister, 1–2.

Chapter 9

Conclusion: Marlovian Incentives

Throughout the preceding chapters, I have tried to create a balance in which the limitations encountered in tracking Marlowe's influence are offset by the queries and reflections that each study begets. As I have demonstrated, there are degrees of limitation, beginning with obscurity and moving to uncertainty, and they are fluid. In the category of uncertainty belongs such questions as the extent to which *Dido, Queen of Carthage* influenced Shakespeare in depicting the tragic tale of unrequited love in *Troilus and Cressida* and the extent to which the imposing, energetic figure of Tamburlaine may have influenced the vituperative comic characterization of Petruchio in *The Taming of the Shrew*. As the limitations on any given consideration of influence fall away, we are able to shift to the possibility, or, even more securely, to the probability of a Marlovian inheritance. Thus, we are able to accept the probability that Aeneas's narrative recounting of the fall of Troy in *Dido* influenced Shakespeare's decision to recreate the tale in *Hamlet* (II, ii, 386–462)[1] and that *Hero and Leander*, *Tamburlaine*, and *Edward II* influenced the language, syntax, and rhythms of *Romeo and Juliet*.[2] These manifestations of likely influence offer additional support for the conclusion that, contrary to the present-day scholarly notion of Marlowe as his rival, Shakespeare seized on the uninhibited resourcefulness of his fellow playwright with relative insouciance in order to give legitimacy and stature to his own inventiveness.

We have discovered that Shakespeare initially conceived of Marlowe as the Shakespeare of his day. As a result, he was intensely interested in the dramaturgical techniques that promoted Marlowe's success, especially because he perceived that they ensured a continuing audience appeal. Understandably, he showed much less interest in the ideas, values, and points of view expressed in Marlowe's works. Moreover, as the juxtaposition of *Hero and Leander* and *Venus and Adonis* most explicitly demonstrates, he had a quite different temperament. We have also discovered that, apart from the demands of longstanding classical and early modern dramatic conventions and his own inborn talent, Shakespeare felt impelled *throughout* his career to ruminate upon his Marlovian legacy and to reincorporate it. As this study has abundantly shown, the process of assimilation caused Shakespeare ceaselessly to foreground Marlowe's three most powerful influences: his verbal dexterity, his flexibility in reconfiguring standard notions of genre, and his use of ambivalence and ambiguity (commandeered for comic purposes in *Hero and Leander* and for serious and ironic purposes in the dramas). Marlowe's ability overall to fuel the fires of unconventionality in Shakespeare through the boldness of his inventiveness and concomitant proclivity for overturning literary and dramatic conventions could only have encouraged Shakespeare to unleash his own inventiveness in language, genre, and ambiguity with greater confidence and abandon.

In consequence, we have been able to account for a Marlovian influence in promoting Shakespeare's intoxication with words and his discovery of new ways to order them. Interestingly, we have viewed passages in *Titus Andronicus*, *King John*, and *The Merchant of Venice* in which Shakespeare tries to write in the manner of Marlowe. Yet, even in these passages his own stylistic characteristics surface, giving us a solid means for defining the traits that make him and his fellow writer distinctive. We have also understood how Marlowe acted as a catalyst in Shakespeare's disregard of standard expectations in a given genre. A good bit of what creates the problems in the problem plays, however narrowly or widely we apply the phrase, is our inability to categorize or stereotype their genres. Part of Shakespeare's fascination with reworking the conventions of genre must have come from experiencing the variety of genres Marlowe selected as well as his many innovations within those genres.

Without Marlowe's examples to inspire him, Shakespeare might not have developed to such a potent level of effectiveness the device of ambiguity in his portrayals of character and event. For example, in the cases of Richard II, Bolingbroke, Aumerle, Shylock, Henry V, Antony, Cleopatra, Macbeth, and even Prospero, Shakespeare does not allow us to come to a quick and easy resolution in assessing either the characters' moral worth or their underlying motivations, much less fit them into categories. Instead, he creates beguiling conflicts and ambiguities that evoke vacillating reactions of attraction and aversion and, as a major means of sustaining our interest throughout the play, lead to uncertainty in our overall response. Marlowe sets before Shakespeare such exemplars of this technique as Aeneas, Tamburlaine, Faustus, Barabas, and, arguably to a lesser extent, Edward II. Virgil's pious Aeneas becomes Marlowe's passive Aeneas, reluctantly doing his duty by the state, according to the dictates of his destiny, but clumsily betraying Dido in the process. Tamburlaine oscillates between acts of valiant heroism and disturbing violence and resists all our attempts to come to a conclusive ethical attitude toward him. In the case of Faustus, we perceive that he is sinful according to Christian morality but we nevertheless feel sympathy for him and sorrow at his demise. Barabas perplexes us through his lack of motivation and quirkiness. And, although we deplore Edward's irresponsibility, his final fortitude in facing death wins our pity and respect. Shakespeare well understood that to unsettle audiences is to provide them with the richest entertainment possible. It is easy to imagine that Marlowe's models encouraged him and gave him direction as he nurtured this belief.

There is also a related type of ambiguity that, as we have seen, Shakespeare found in Marlowe's works and exploited: the incompatibility and purposeful confusion of a work's simultaneous moral and aesthetic perspectives—that is, an audience's essentially ethical responses, on the one hand, and its non-moral or amoral, sensory and emotional reactions, on the other. Marlowe uses this device in the *Tamburlaine* plays, for example, for even when we disapprove of the warrior leader's ethics, we are impressed by the grandness of his actions and language. In *Antony and Cleopatra*, the Romans give strongly negative moral assessments of Cleopatra and through their categorical denunciations write her off—or try to. But an audience's rational estimation of her ethical defects is undermined and complicated by its non-rational reaction to her person, for even when her behavior is ignoble, an audience stands in awe of her raw energy as it listens to the infinite variety of her words and watches the self-dramatizing spectacles that she orchestrates. For both writers, the conflict of moral and aesthetic responses is intended to demand the fullest possible engagement of audiences and lead ultimately to an ambiguous response that is likely to remain with them even after they leave the theater or finish reading the play or poem.

In surveying Marlowe's influence on Shakespeare as a whole, we see that, in addition to the aesthetics of language, genre, and ambiguity, his modes of characterization commanded Shakespeare's fullest attention. Two devices in particular stand out: First, the internalization of characters, best exemplified by Faustus's agonizing psychomachia at the end of his life; this technique makes it possible for an audience to look *with* the character—that is, through the eyes of the character—rather than (or as well as) detachedly *at* the character, and second, the potentially conventional Marlovian character who breaks the mold to provide fresh instances of unexpected, heterodox attitudes and actions, whether a pair of legendary lovers, a warrior leader, a scholar-magician, a Jew in a corrupt Christian society, a demented villain-hero, or a weak king. Even when Shakespeare uses Marlowe's model primarily to move his own comparable character in an opposite or different direction, as he does with Prospero, he may well be reflecting the influence of Marlowe's accomplishments.

Like Marlowe before him, Shakespeare's strong awareness of dramaturgical techniques made him especially sensitive to the manipulation of his audience's reactions. Evidently sparked by Marlowe's directness and forcefulness in appealing to his audiences' imaginations, by his determined raising of the standards of conventional dramatic fare, and by his commercial success, Shakespeare also trained his audiences to expect and participate in deeper imaginative levels of thinking and feeling than they were accustomed to—most explicitly perhaps in the directives of the Chorus of *Henry V*. Marlowe sets before Shakespeare many examples in which he denies the expectations of audiences as a means of attracting their interest. We have seen how he uses ambiguity to undermine an audience's normal desire to type a character and how Shakespeare adopts and develops this technique. Both dramatists employ another potent means of overturning expectations when they juxtapose dramatizations of historical characters and events with an audience's preformed notions of history. Marlowe revises history in *Dido*, *Edward II*, and *The Massacre At Paris* to create effects of surprise and sensationalism intended to intrigue and even jolt his audiences. Whether this device touched off a natural desire in Shakespeare to write in a more unconventional and daring manner or whether he was already well on his way with the *Henry VI* plays, both dramatists revise history for primarily dramaturgical reasons. On the one hand, altering characters and actions in history gives them greater flexibility, enabling them to structure their plays with improved focus and unity; on the other, they are able to engage their audiences fully and even tantalize them by exploding their preconceived notions of historical figures and events.

Of the two writers' shared interest in similar intellectual subjects, probably the powers, uses, and abuses of the imagination emerge as the most pervasive. There is nothing exceptional about this topic since both men are dramatists and poets who prize the creative imagination as the basis of their talent. Nor is it surprising that they are as alert to the dangers as to the benefits of the imagination and that each writer sustains this interest throughout his career. They both admire the inspiration that the imagination creates but decry its capacity for enabling self-deception. We have also seen that the two men separate their ideas about the course of the imagination in their characters from its course in themselves and, as a facet of their artistry, make use of the implicit differences to draw attention to their own professional accomplishments. So individualized is this trait that it would be difficult to conclude that Marlowe's counterpointing did not have some influence on Shakespeare's.

What further emerge from an investigation of influence are the distinct authorial personalities of the two dramatists. Marlowe is intellectual, clever, innovative, ironic, witty and yet broadly humorous, impersonal, and depersonalizing, someone who takes cover from attacks of emotion by invoking Ovidian myths, epic catalogues, elaborate descriptions, generalized language, and comedy. He strongly distrusts the kind of emotion that involves depth, complexity, and commitment, apparently as much in his authorial self as in his characters. Consequently, he detaches himself from his characters and his characters from each other. If for Shakespeare the quintessence of life comes in living a vital, emotional existence, especially through human bonding, for the less romantic Christopher Marlowe, enjoyment exists in cutting through illusion to find a bedrock of disenchanting reality. Apart from an apparent fascination with various kinds of power, the energy needed to acquire it, and the presence of continual change, Marlowe did not live long enough to come to terms with what he desired for people individually and for his culture as a whole, only what he did not desire. Shakespeare's sunnier temperament, in combination with a longer life that provided him with an opportunity to grapple with issues pertaining to both the individual and society, enabled him to be affirming and to indicate his desires and hopes through his plays and poetry. Thus, in *King Lear*, we see him confront and reject a rational, analytical approach to understanding the injustices of mortal existence and, instead, affirm the non-rational bonds of even a momentary experience of human mutuality.

Shakespeare is not only more deeply emotional than Marlowe but is also more accepting and trusting of emotions. In fact, for Shakespeare, it is only through emotion that a joyous self-fulfillment and complete selfhood can occur, no matter how briefly. If the two writers seem to be linked by their appreciation of human vitality and their realization that the swift passage of time continually changes people and circumstances, they are also separated by a major difference in approach: whereas Marlowe thinks descriptively, Shakespeare thinks situationally. This means that the sources of tension in Marlowe's works often depend more upon the language of speeches than the events of the plot and that just the opposite is true of Shakespeare. Of course, in neither writer is the distinction absolute nor are the two sources of tension mutually exclusive.

It would of course be impossible to encapsulate Marlowe's influence on Shakespeare. The pluralistic attitudes of Shakespeare toward Marlowe are far too wide-ranging, variable, and subtle. We realize, however, that Shakespeare's chief interest is in Marlowe the professional writer and theatrical artisan and does not extend to the man himself. Only occasionally and well into his career does he concern himself with Marlowe's non-aesthetic ideas, beliefs, and practices. We understand, too, as the epigraph to this study can be invoked to suggest, that "eyed awry"—that is, from the perspective of one writer interested in how another uses the tools of his trade to achieve a phenomenal success—we can in fact "distinguish form" in Marlowe's influence on Shakespeare. If, as a means of accounting for influence, we look instead for a legacy in the issues and ideas of their works or in their biographies, perspectives currently more "rightly gazed upon," then the results do indeed "show nothing but confusion." Consequently, in directing ourselves to those pragmatic aesthetic elements most basic and essential to Marlowe and Shakespeare's professional work, especially in the theater, we can view the two writers doing what they do best and what most closely binds them. As such, this perspective enables us to arrive at the fullest possible sense of Shakespeare's Marlowe.

Notes

1   Hamlet asks the Player to recite a speech, "Aeneas' tale to Dido" (II, ii, 387) and he does. Maurice Charney, "Marlowe and Shakespeare's African Queens," in *Shakespearean Illuminations*, ed. Jay L. Halio and Hugh Richmond (Newark: University of Delaware Press, 1998), 242–52, examines the relationship of the passage in *Hamlet* to Virgil and Marlowe. He believes that Hamlet's request for the "excellent play, well digested in the scenes, set down with as much modest as cunning" (II, ii, 380–81) and "Aeneas' tale," a speech from it, are a clear reference to Marlowe's play (244–45) and that Hamlet needs the speech "at this point in the play to provide biting analogies for his own tragic situation" (245). Charney also believes that the speech is "Shakespeare's most extensive discussion of Marlowe. It is a kind of displaced hero worship with many characteristically grudging disclaimers" (245). I agree that the speech pays tribute to Marlowe, especially for a theatrical in-crowd, but I am less sure of the "disclaimers." Even when Shakespeare veers off in a different direction (as with Shylock), he does not conceal the influence of Marlowe (as with Morocco). Clare Harraway *(Re-citing Marlowe: Approaches to Drama* [Burlington, VT: Ashgate, 2000], 122), believes that the Player's speech is a parody of Aeneas's speech in *Dido* on the fall of Troy (II, i, 106–303). Harraway does not explain how and, more importantly, why Shakespeare is parodying the speech from Marlowe's play, but I imagine that she has in mind Aeneas's overwrought language. If it is parody, it is certainly "caviar to the general" (*Hamlet*, II, ii, 377–78), unless one assumes that Aeneas's speech in *Dido* was so well known that an audience would immediately hear a parody in the Player's speech. Harraway believes that "the primary point of connection between Marlowe's text and Shakespeare's is the literal and metaphorical theme of fathers" (122), an idea she goes on to explore (122–38).

2   For example, Juliet's speech at the beginning of *Romeo and Juliet*, III, ii, 1–31 has a Marlovian verve, intensity, and use of mythological detail characteristic of the language of the *Tamburlaine* plays and *Hero and Leander*. Moreover, the opening lines are reminiscent of lines in *Edward II*, IV, iii, 45–49:

Edward: Gallop apace, bright Phoebus, through the sky,
          And dusky night, in rusty iron car,
          Between you both shorten the time, I pray,
          That I may see that most desirèd day
          When we may meet these traitors in the field.

Juliet: Gallop apace, you fiery-footed steeds,
          Towards Phoebus' lodging! Such a wagoner
          As Phaeton would whip you to the west
          And bring in cloudy night immediately.
          Spread thy close curtain, love-performing night,
          That runaways' eyes may wink, and Romeo
          Leap to these arms untalked of and unseen.
          Lovers can see to do their amorous rites
          By their own beauties; or, if love be blind,
          It best agrees with night. Come, civil night,
          Thou sober-suited matron, all in black,
          And learn me how to lose a winning match,
          Played for a pair of stainless maidenhoods.
          Hood my unmanned blood, bating in my cheeks,
          With thy black mantle till strange love grow bold,
          Think true love acted simple modesty.
          Come, night; come, Romeo; come, thou day in night;
          For thou wilt lie upon the wings of night
          Whiter than new snow upon a raven's back.
          Come, gentle night; come, loving, black-browed night;
          Give me my Romeo; and, when I shall die,
          Take him and cut him out in little stars,
          And he will make the face of heaven so fine
          That all the world will be in love with night
          And pay no worship to the garish sun.
          O, I have bought the mansion of a love,
          But not possessed it; and though I am sold,
          Not yet enjoyed. So tedious is this day
          As is the night before some festival
          To an impatient child that hath new robes
          And may not wear them.

Bibliography

Adamson, Jane. "Marlowe, *Hero and Leander*, and the Art of Leaping in Poetry." *The Critical Review* 17 (1974): 59–81.

Adelman, Janet. *The Common Liar: An Essay on "Antony and Cleopatra."* New Haven, CT: Yale University Press, 1973.

Altman, Joel B. *The Tudor Play of Mind: Rhetorical Inquiry and the Development of Elizabethan Drama.* Berkeley: University of California Press, 1978.

Baines, Barbara J. "Sexual Polarity in the Plays of Christopher Marlowe." *Ball State University Forum* 23:3 (Summer 1982): 3–17.

Barber, C.L. *Creating Elizabethan Tragedy: The Theater of Marlowe and Kyd*, ed. and intro. Richard P. Wheeler. Chicago: University of Chicago Press, 1988.

Barroll, J. Leeds. "Antony and Pleasure." *Journal of English and Germanic Philology* 57 (1958): 708–20.

Bartels, Emily C. *Spectacles of Strangeness: Imperialism, Alienation, and Marlowe.* Philadelphia: University of Pennsylvania Press, 1993.

Bate, Jonathan. *The Genius of Shakespeare.* New York: Oxford University Press, 1998.

———. *Shakespeare and Ovid.* Oxford: Clarendon Press, 1993.

Battenhouse, Roy. "The Relation of Henry V to Tamburlaine." *Shakespeare Survey* 27 (1974): 71–79.

Bednarz, James P. "Marlowe and the English Literary Scene." In *The Cambridge Companion to Christopher Marlowe*, ed. Patrick Cheney, 90–105. Cambridge: Cambridge University Press, 2004.

Belsey, Catherine. "Love As Trompe-L'oeil: Taxonomies of Desire." In *"Venus and Adonis": Critical Essays*, ed. Philip C. Kolin, 261–85. New York: Garland Publishing, 1997. First published in *Shakespeare Quarterly* 46 (Fall, 1995): 257–76.

Berek, Peter. "*Tamburlaine*'s Weak Sons: Imitation as Interpretation before 1593." *Renaissance Drama* n.s., 13 (1982): 55–82.

Bieman, Elizabeth. "Comic Rhyme in Marlowe's *Hero and Leander.*" *English Literary Renaissance* 9 (Winter, 1979): 69–77.

Blackburn, William. "'Heavenly Words': Marlowe's Faustus as a Renaissance Magician." *English Studies in Canada* 4.1 (Spring, 1978): 1–14.

Bloom, Harold. *The Anxiety of Influence.* New York: Oxford University Press, 1973. Revised edition, 1997.

Born, Hanspeter. "The Date of 2, 3 *Henry VI*," *Shakespeare Quarterly* 25 (1974): 323–34.

Bowers, Rick. "The Massacre At Paris: Marlowe's Messy Consensus Narrative." In *Marlowe, History, and Sexuality. New Critical Essays on Christopher Marlowe*, ed. Paul Whitfield White, 131–41. New York: AMS Press, 1998.

Boyer, Clarence Valentine. *The Villain As Hero In Elizabethan Tragedy.* New York: Russell and Russell, 1914. Reissued in 1964.

Bradbrook, M.C. *Aspects of Dramatic Form in the English and Irish Renaissance.* Sussex, UK: Harvester Press, 1983.

———. *Shakespeare and Elizabethan Poetry.* London: Chatto and Windus, 1951.

————. "Shakespeare's Recollections of Marlowe." In *Shakespeare's Styles: Essays in honour of Kenneth Muir*, ed. Philip Edwards, Inga-Stina Ewbank, and G.K. Hunter, 191–204. Cambridge: Cambridge University Press, 1980.

Bray, Alan. *Homosexuality in Renaissance England.* London: Gay Men's Press, 1982.

Bredbeck, Gregory W. *Sodomy and Interpretation: Marlowe to Milton.* Ithaca, NY: Cornell University Press, 1991.

Briggs, Julia. "Marlowe's *Massacre At Paris*: A Reconsideration." *Review of English Studies* 34 (1983): 257–78.

Brooke, Nicholas. "Marlowe As Provocative Agent In Shakespeare's Early Plays." *Shakespeare Survey* 14 (1961): 34–44.

Brower, Reuben A. *Fields of Light: An Experiment in Critical Reading.* New York: Oxford University Press, 1951.

————. *Hero and Saint: Shakespeare and the Graeco-Roman Heroic Tradition.* Oxford: Oxford University Press, 1971.

Brown, Georgia E. "Gender and voice in 'Hero and Leander.'" In *Constructing Christopher Marlowe*, ed. J.A. Downie and J.T. Parnell, 148–63. Cambridge: Cambridge University Press, 2000.

Bullough, Geoffrey. *Narrative and Dramatic Sources of Shakespeare.* Vol. I. New York: Columbia University Press, 1957.

Bush, Douglas. "The Influence of Marlowe's *Hero and Leander* on Early Mythological Poems." *Modern Language Notes* 42 (1927): 211–17.

————. *Mythology and the Renaissance Tradition in English Poetry.* Revised edition. New York: Norton, 1963. First published in 1932.

————. "Notes on Marlowe's *Hero and Leander*." *Publications of the Modern Language Association* 44 (1929): 760–64.

Cady, Joseph. "'Masculine Love,' Renaissance Writing, and the 'New Invention' of Homosexuality." In *Homosexuality in Renaissance and Enlightenment England: Literary Presentations in Historical Context*, ed. Claude J. Summers, 9–41. Binghamton, NY: Haworth Press, 1992.

Calderwood, James L. *If It Were Done: "Macbeth" and Tragic Action.* Amherst: University of Massachusetts Press, 1986.

————. "*Love's Labour's Lost*: A Wantoning with Words." *Studies in English Literature* 5 (1965): 317–32.

————. *Shakespearean Metadrama.* Minneapolis: University of Minnesota Press, 1971.

Carroll, D. Allen. "Greene's 'Vpstart Crow' Passage: A Survey of Commentary." *Research Opportunities in Renaissance Drama* 28 (1985): 111–27.

Carroll, Joseph. *Evolution and Literary Theory.* Columbia: University of Missouri Press, 1995.

Cartelli, Thomas. *Marlowe, Shakespeare, and the Economy of Theatrical Experience.* Philadelphia: University of Pennsylvania Press, 1991.

Chambers, E.K. *The Elizabethan Stage.* 4 vols. Oxford: Clarendon Press, 1923.

————. *William Shakespeare: A Study of Facts and Problems.* 2 vols. Oxford: Clarendon Press, 1930.

Charney, Maurice. "Jessica's Turquoise Ring and Abigail's Poisoned Porridge: Shakespeare and Marlowe as Rivals and Imitators." *Renaissance Drama* n.s. 10 (1979): 33–44.

————. "Marlowe and Shakespeare's African Queens." In *Shakespearean Illuminations*, ed. Jay L. Halio and Hugh Richmond, 242–52. Newark: University of Delaware Press, 1998.

———. "Marlowe's *Edward II* as Model for Shakespeare's *Richard II*." *Research Opportunities in Renaissance Drama* 33 (1994): 31–41.

———. "Marlowe's *Hero and Leander* Shows Shakespeare, in *Venus and Adonis*, How to Write an Ovidian Verse Epyllion." In *Marlowe's Empery: Expanding His Critical Contexts*, ed. Sara Munson Deats and Robert A. Logan, 85–94. Newark: University of Delaware Press, 2002.

———. "The Voice of Marlowe's Tamburlaine in Early Shakespeare." *Comparative Drama* 31:2 (Summer, 1997): 213–23.

Cheney, Patrick. "Love and Magic in *Doctor Faustus*: Marlowe's Indictment of Spenserian Idealism." *Mosaic* 17:4 (Fall 1984): 93–109.

———. *Marlowe's Counterfeit Profession: Ovid, Spenser, Counter-Nationhood.* Toronto: University of Toronto Press, 1997.

Clemen, Wolfgang. "Shakespeare and Marlowe." In *Shakespeare 1971: Proceedings of the World Shakespeare Congress*, ed. Clifford Leech and J.M.R. Margeson, 123–32. Toronto: University of Toronto Press, 1972.

Comensoli, Viviana. "Homophobia and the Regulation of Desire: A Psychoanalytic Reading of Marlowe's *Edward II*." *Journal of the History of Sexuality* 4.2 (1993): 175–200.

Danson, Lawrence. "Continuity and Character in Shakespeare and Marlowe." *Studies in English Literature, 1500–1900* 26:2 (1986): 217–34.

———. *The Harmonies of "The Merchant of Venice."* New Haven, CT: Yale University Press, 1978.

———. "The Questioner." In *Christopher Marlowe: Modern Critical Views*, ed. Harold Bloom, 183–205. New York: Chelsea House Publishers, 1986.

———. *Shakespeare's Dramatic Genres.* Oxford: Oxford University Press, 2000.

Deats, Sara Munson. "*Doctor Faustus*: From Chapbook to Tragedy." *Essays In Literature* 3 (Spring, 1976): 3–16.

———. "Henry V: Christian King or Model Machiavel." In *War and Words: Horrors and Hallelujahs*, ed. Sara Munson Deats, Lagretta Tallent Lenker, and Merry G. Perry. Lanham, MD: Rowman and Littlefield, 2004.

———. "'Mark this Show': Magic and Theater in Marlowe's *Doctor Faustus*." In *Placing the Plays of Christopher Marlowe: Fresh Cultural Contexts* (forthcoming from Ashgate).

———. "Marlowe's Interrogative Drama: *Dido, Tamburlaine, Doctor Faustus*, and *Edward II*." In *Marlowe's Empery: Expanding His Critical Contexts*, ed. Sara Munson Deats and Robert A. Logan, 107–30. Newark: University of Delaware Press, 2002.

———. *Sex, Gender, and Desire in The Plays of Christopher Marlowe.* Newark, DE: University of Delaware Press, 1997.

——— and Lisa S. Starks. "'So Neatly Plotted, and So Well Perform'd': Villain as Playwright in Marlowe's *The Jew of Malta*." *Theatre Journal* 44 (1992): 375–89.

Descartes, René. *Discourse on Method* (1637). In *Descartes: Philosophical Writings*, selected and trans. by Norman Kemp Smith. New York: Random House, 1958.

Diehl, Huston. *Staging Reform, Reforming the Stage: Protestantism and Popular Theater in Early Modern England.* Ithaca, NY: Cornell University Press, 1997.

Di Gangi, Mario. *The Homoerotics of Early Modern Drama.* Cambridge: Cambridge University Press, 1997.

Dollimore, Jonathan. *Sexual Dissidence: Augustine to Wilde, Freud to Foucault.* Oxford: Oxford University Press, 1991.

Donne, John. *The Complete Poetry of John Donne*, ed. John T. Shawcross. New York: Doubleday, 1967.

Doran, Madeline. *Endeavors of Art: A Study of Form in Elizabethan Drama.* Madison: The University of Wisconsin Press, 1954.

Dubrow, Heather. *Captive Victors.* Ithaca, NY: Cornell University Press, 1987.

Eagleton, Terry. *William Shakespeare.* Oxford: Basil Blackwell, 1986.

Edelman, Charles. "Which Is The Jew That Shakespeare Knew?: Shylock on the Elizabethan Stage." *Shakespeare Survey* 52 (1999): 99–106.

Elizabethan History Plays, ed. and intro. by William A. Armstrong. London: Oxford University Press, 1965.

Empson, William. "Two Proper Crimes." *The Nation* 163 (1946): 444–45.

Engle, Lars. "'Thrift is Blessing': Exchange and Explanation in *The Merchant of Venice*." *Shakespeare Quarterly* 37 (1986): 20–37.

Eriksen, Roy T. "Anxious Art: Shakespeare's Rivalry with Marlowe." In *Proceedings From the Third Nordic Conference for English Studies*, ed. Ishrat Lindblad, 639–49. Stockholm: Almqvist and Wiksell International, 1987.

Farley-Hills, David. *Shakespeare and the Rival Playwrights 1600–1606.* London: Routledge, 1990.

Felperin, Howard. *The Uses of the Canon: Elizabethan Literature and Contemporary Theory.* Oxford: Oxford University Press, 1990.

Fienberg, Nona. "Thematics of Value in *Venus and Adonis*." *Criticism* 31 (Winter, 1989): 21–32.

Fitz, L.T. "'More Than Thou Has Wit to Ask': Marlowe's Faustus as Numskull." *Folklore* 88 (1977): 215–19.

Foakes, R.A., ed. *Henslowe's Diary.* 2nd edition. Cambridge, England: Cambridge University Press, 2002.

———. "Images of Death: Ambition in *Macbeth*." In *Focus on "Macbeth*," ed. John Russell Brown, 7–29. London: Routledge and Kegan Paul, 1982.

Forker, Charles R. "Marlowe's *Edward II* and its Shakespearean Relatives: The Emergence of a Genre." In *Shakespeare's English Histories: A Quest for Form and Genre*, ed. John W. Velz, 55–90. Binghamton, NY: Medieval and Renaissance Texts and Studies, 1996.

Foucault, Michel. *The History of Sexuality.* Vol. I. New York: Pantheon, 1978.

Fraser, Russell. *Young Shakespeare.* New York: Columbia University Press, 1988.

Garber, Marjorie. "Marlovian Vision/Shakespearean Revision." *Research Opportunities in Renaissance Literature* 22 (1979): 3–9.

Gibbons, Brian. *Shakespeare and Multiplicity.* Cambridge, England: Cambridge University Press, 1993.

———. "'Unstable Proteus': The Tragedy of Dido, Queen of Carthage." In *Christopher Marlowe,* ed. Brian Morris, 27–46. New York: Hill and Wang, 1968.

Grande, Troni Y. *Marlovian Tragedy: The Play of Dilation.* Lewisburg, PA: Bucknell University Press, 1999.

Greenblatt, Stephen. *Renaissance Self-Fashioning: From More to Shakespeare.* Chicago: University of Chicago Press, 1980.

———. "Shakespeare and the Exorcists." In *Shakespeare and the Question of Theory*, ed. Patricia Parker and Geoffrey Hartman. New York: Methuen, 1985.

———. "Shakespeare Bewitched." In *New Historical Literary Study: Essays on Reproducing Texts, Representing History*, ed. Jeffrey N. Cox. and Larry J. Reynolds, 108–35. Princeton, NJ: Princeton University Press, 1993.

———. "Shakespeare's Leap." *The New York Times Magazine*, September 12, 2004, 50–55.

————. *Will in the World: How Shakespeare Became Shakespeare.* New York: W.W. Norton, 2004.

Greene, Robert. *The Life and Complete Works in Prose and Verse of Robert Greene.* 15 vols. New York: Russell and Russell, 1881–86.

Greene, Thomas. *The Light in Troy: Imitation and Discovery in Renaissance Poetry.* New Haven, CT: Yale University Press, 1982.

Grosart, Alexander B. *The Life and Complete Works in Prose and Verse of Robert Greene.* 15 vols. New York: Russell and Russell, 1881–86.

Gross, John. *Shylock: A Legend and Its Legacy.* London: Chatto and Windus, 1992.

Gurr, Andrew. *Playgoing in Shakespeare's London.* 2nd edition. Cambridge: Cambridge University Press, 1996.

Guy-Bray, Stephen. "Homophobia and the Depoliticizing of *Edward II.*" *English Studies in Canada* 17.2 (June 1991): 125–33.

Haber, Judith. "'True-loves Blood': Narrative and Desire in *Hero and Leander.*" *English Literary Renaissance* 28:3 (Autumn, 1998): 372–86.

Harraway, Clare. *Re-citing Marlowe: Approaches to the Drama.* Burlington, VT: Ashgate, 2000.

Harris, Anthony. *Black Agents: Witchcraft and Magic In Seventeenth-Century English Drama.* Manchester: Manchester University Press, 1980.

Harrison, Thomas P., Jr. "Shakespeare and Marlowe's *Dido, Queen of Carthage.*" *Studies in English* (University of Texas) (1956): 57–63.

Hattaway, Michael. "Marlowe and Brecht." In *Christopher Marlowe*, ed. Brian Morris, 112–13. New York: Hill and Wang, 1968.

Heilman, Robert B. "The Criminal as Tragic Hero: Dramatic Methods." *Shakespeare Survey* 19 (1966): 12–24.

Hill, R.F. "Dramatic Techniques and Interpretation in 'Richard II.'" In *Early Shakespeare* [Volume 3 of the Stratford-Upon-Avon Studies], ed. John Russell Brown and Bernard Harris, 101–21. London: Edward Arnold, 1961.

Hillman, Richard. *Shakespeare, Marlowe and the Politics of France.* New York: Palgrave, 2002.

Holinshed, Raphaell. *The Third Volume of Chronicles, Beginning at Duke William The Norman, Commonlie Called the Conqueror; and Descending By Degrees of Yeeres to all the Kings And Queenes of England In their Orderlie Successions ... 1586.* New York: AMS Press, 1965.

Hopkins, Lisa. *Christopher Marlowe: A Literary Life.* New York: Palgrave, 2000.

Howe, James Robinson. *Marlowe, Tamburlaine, and Magic.* Athens: Ohio University Press, 1976.

Hulse, Clark. *Metamorphic Verse: The Elizabethan Minor Epic.* Princeton, NJ: Princeton University Press, 1981.

Hutcheon, Linda. *The Politics of Postmodernism.* London: Routledge, 1989.

Jonson, Ben. *Ben Jonson*, ed. C.H. Herford and Percy and Evelyn Simpson. 11 vols. Oxford: Clarendon Press, 1925–52.

Keach, William. *Elizabethan Erotic Narratives.* New Brunswick, NJ: Rutgers University Press, 1977.

Keats, John. *John Keats: Selected Poems and Letters*, ed. Douglas Bush. Boston: Riverside Press, 1959.

Kermode, Frank. "Preface to *Titus Andronicus.*" In *The Riverside Shakespeare*, gen. ed. G. Blakemore Evans, 1065–68. 2nd edition. Boston: Houghton Mifflin, 1997.

————. *Shakespeare's Language.* New York: Farrar, Straus and Giroux, 2000.

Kernan, Alvin B. *The Playwright as Magician: Shakespeare's Image of the Poet in the English Public Theater.* New Haven, CT: Yale University Press, 1979.

Knutson, Roslyn L. "Marlowe Reruns: Repertorial Commerce and Marlowe's Plays in Revival." In *Marlowe's Empery: Expanding His Critical Contexts*, ed. Sara Munson Deats and Robert A. Logan, 25–42. Newark: University of Delaware Press, 2002.

————. *Playing Companies and Commerce in Shakespeare's Time.* Cambridge: Cambridge University Press, 2001.

Kolin, Philip C. "Venus and/or Adonis Among the Critics." In *"Venus and Adonis": Critical Essays*, ed. Philip C. Kolin, 3–65. New York: Garland, 1997.

Kristeva, Julia. *Revolution in Poetic Language*, trans. Margaret Walker. New York: Columbia University Press, 1984.

Kuriyama, Constance Brown. *Christopher Marlowe: A Renaissance Life.* Ithaca, NY: Cornell University Press, 2002,

Leech, Clifford. *Christopher Marlowe: Poet for The Stage*, ed. Anne Lancashire. New York: AMS Press, 1986.

Levin, Richard. "Another Possible Clue to the Identity of the Rival Poet." *Shakespeare Quarterly* 36 (1985): 213–14.

————. "Another 'Source' for The Alchemist and another Look at Source Studies." *English Literary Renaissance* 28:2 (Spring, 1998): 210–30.

Lindheim, Nancy. "The Shakespearean *Venus and Adonis*." *Shakespeare Quarterly* 37 (Summer 1986): 190–203.

Logan, Robert A. "'High Events as These': Sources, Influences, and the Artistry of *Antony and Cleopatra*." In Antony and Cleopatra: *New Critical Essays*, ed. Sara Munson Deats, 153–74. Routledge: New York and London, 2005.

————. "Perspective in Marlowe's *Hero and Leander*: Engaging our Detachment." In *"A Poet and a Filthy Play-maker": New Essays on Christopher Marlowe*, ed. Kenneth Friedenreich, Roma Gill, and Constance B. Kuriyama, 279–91. New York: AMS Press, Inc., 1988.

————. "Violence, Terrorism, and War in Marlowe's *Tamburlaine* Plays." In *War and Words: Horrors and Hallelujahs*, ed. Sara Munson Deats, Lagretta Tallent Lenker, and Merry G. Perry, 65–81. Lanham, MD: Rowman and Littlefield, 2004.

Lucking, David. "Our Devils Now Are Ended: A Comparative Analysis of *The Tempest* and *Doctor Faustus*." *The Dalhousie Review* 80 (Summer 2000): 151–67.

Lynch Stephen J. *Shakespearean Intertextuality: Studies in Selected Plays and Sources.* Westport, CT: Greenwood Press, 1998.

Mahood, M.M. *Shakespeare's Wordplay.* London: Methuen, 1957.

Maquin, Francois. "The Breaking of Time: *Richard II, Hamlet, King Lear, Macbeth* (The Hero's Stand In and Against Time)." *Cahiers Elisabethains* 7 (1975): 25–41.

Marlowe, Christopher. *Christopher Marlowe: The Complete Plays*, ed. Mark Thornton Burnett. London: J.M. Dent, 1999.

————. *Christopher Marlowe: The Complete Poems*, ed. Mark Thornton Burnett. London: J.M. Dent, 2000.

————. *Christopher Marlowe: The Plays and Their Sources*, ed. Vivien Thomas and William Tydeman. New York: Routledge, 1994.

————. *The Complete Works of Christopher Marlowe*, ed. Fredson T. Bowers. 2 vols. Cambridge: Cambridge University Press, 1975.

————. *"Dido, Queen of Carthage" and "The Massacre At Paris" Christopher Marlowe*, ed. H.J. Oliver. Cambridge, MA: Harvard University Press, 1968.

———. *Doctor Faustus A- and B-texts (1604, 1616): Christopher Marlowe and His Collaborator and Revisers*, ed. David Bevington and Eric Rasmussen. New York: St Martin's Press, 1993.

McAdam, Ian. "Carnal Identity in *The Jew of Malta*." *English Literary Renaissance* 26:1 (Winter, 1966): 46–74.

———. *The Irony of Identity*. Newark: The University of Delaware Press, 1999.

McAlindon, T. *Shakespeare's Tragic Cosmos*. Cambridge: Cambridge University Press, 1991.

McDonald, Joyce Green. "Marlowe's Ganymede." In *Enacting Gender on the English Renaissance Stage*, ed. Viviana Comensoli and Anne Russell, 93–113. Urbana: University of Illinois Press, 1999.

McMillin, Scott and Sally-Beth MacLean. *The Queen's Men and their Plays*. Cambridge: Cambridge University Press, 1998.

Merriam, Thomas. "Influence Alone? More on the Authorship of *Titus Andronicus*." *Notes and Queries* 45:3 (September, 1998): 304–8.

Merrix, Robert P. and Carole Levin. "*Richard II* and *Edward II*: the Structure of Deposition." *The Shakespeare Yearbook* 1 (1990): 1–13.

Morris, Brian. "Comic Method in Marlowe's *Hero and Leander*." In *Christopher Marlowe*, ed. Brian Morris, 113–32. New York: Hill and Wang, 1968.

———. "The Kingdom, the Power and the Glory in *Macbeth*." In *Focus on "Macbeth*," ed. John Russell Brown, 30–53. London: Routledge and Kegan Paul, 1982.

Muir, Kenneth. "Venus and Adonis: Comedy or Tragedy." In *Shakespearean Essays*, ed. Alwin Thaler and Norman Sanders, 1–13. Knoxville: University of Tennessee Press, 1964.

Mullaney, Stephen. *The Place of the Stage: License, Play, and Power in Renaissance England*. Chicago: University of Chicago Press, 1988.

Mulryne, J.R. and Stephen Fender. "Marlowe and the 'Comic Distance.'" In *Christopher Marlowe*, ed. Brian Morris, 47–64. New York: Hill and Wang, 1968.

Nashe, Thomas. *The Works of Thomas Nashe*, ed. R.B. McKerrow. 5 vols. London, 1904–10. Reprinted 1958.

Newman, Karen. "Portia's Ring: Unruly Women and Structures of Exchange in *The Merchant of Venice*." *Shakespeare Quarterly* 38 (1987): 19–33.

Orgel, Stephen. *Impersonations: The Performance of Gender in Shakespeare's England*. Cambridge: Cambridge University Press, 1996.

Patterson, Steve. "The Bankruptcy of Homoerotic Amity in Shakespeare's *Merchant of Venice*." *Shakespeare Quarterly* 50:1 (1999), 9–32.

Pierce, Robert B. "Understanding *The Tempest*." *New Literary History: A Journal of Theory and Interpretation* 30:2 (Spring, 1999): 373–88.

Pigman, George W. "Versions of Imitation in the Renaissance." *Renaissance Quarterly* 33 (1980): 1–32.

Porter Joseph A. "Marlowe, Shakespeare, and the Canonization of Heterosexuality." In *Displacing Homophobia: Gay Male Perspectives in Literature and Culture*, ed. Ronald R. Butters, John M. Clum, and Michael Moon, 127–47. Durham, NC: Duke University Press, 1989.

Potter, David. "Marlowe's *Massacre At Paris* and the Reputation of Henri III of France." In *Christopher Marlowe and English Renaissance Culture*, ed. Darryll Grantley and Peter Roberts, 70–95. Burlington, VT: Ashgate, 1996.

Powell, Jocelyn. "Marlowe's Spectacle." *Tulane Drama Review* 8 (1963–64): 195–210.

Proser, Matthew N. "*Dido, Queen of Carthage* and the Evolution of Marlowe's Dramatic Style." In *"A Poet and a Filthy Play-maker": New Essays on Christopher Marlowe*, ed. Kenneth Friedenreich, Roma Gill, and Constance B. Kuriyama, 83–97. New York: AMS Press, 1988.

———. *The Gift of Fire: Aggression and the Plays of Christopher Marlowe*. New York: Peter Lang, 1995.

———. *The Heroic Image in Five Shakespearean Tragedies*. Princeton, NJ: Princeton University Press, 1965.

Rabkin, Norman. *Shakespeare and the Problem of Meaning*. Chicago: University of Chicago Press, 1981.

Ribner, Irving. "Marlowe and Shakespeare." *Shakespeare Quarterly* 15 (Spring, 1964): 41–53.

Riggs, David. *The World of Christopher Marlowe*. New York: Henry Holt, 2005.

Roberts, Gareth. "Necromantic Books: Christopher Marlowe, *Doctor Faustus* and Agrippa of Nettesheim." In *Christopher Marlowe and English Renaissance Culture*, ed. J.A. Downie and J.T. Parnell, 148–71. Burlington, VT: Ashgate, 1996.

Rossiter, A.P., ed. *"Woodstock": A Moral History.* London: Chatto and Windus, 1946.

Sanders, Wilbur. *The Dramatist and the Received Idea*. Cambridge: Cambridge University Press, 1968.

Shepard, Alan. *Marlowe's Soldiers: Rhetorics of Masculinity in the Age of the Armada*. Burlington, VT: Ashgate, 2002.

Shepherd, Simon. *Marlowe and the Politics of Elizabethan Theatre*. New York: St Martin's Press, 1986.

Shakespeare, William. *The Arden Edition of the Works of William Shakespeare: The Poems*, ed. F.T. Prince. 3rd edition. Cambridge, MA: Harvard University Press, 1960.

———. *A New Variorum Edition of Shakespeare: "Antony and Cleopatra,"* ed. Marvin Spevack. New York: The Modern Language Association of America, 1990.

———. *The Poems*, intro. William Empson. In *The Complete Signet Classic Shakespeare*, gen. ed. Sylvan Barnet, 1667–78. New York: Harcourt Brace Jovanovich, 1972.

———. *The Tragedy of King Richard III*, ed. G. Blakemore Evans. In *William Shakespeare: The Complete Works*, gen. ed. Alfred Harbage. 2nd edition, revised. New York: Viking Press, 1969.

———. *Venus and Adonis*, ed. Hallett Smith. In *The Riverside Shakespeare*, gen. ed. G. Blakemore Evans. 2nd edition. Boston: Houghton Mifflin, 1997.

———. *Venus and Adonis*, ed. Katharine Eisaman Maus. In *The Norton Shakespeare*, gen. ed. Stephen Greenblatt. New York: W.W. Norton, 1997.

———. *Venus and Adonis*, ed. Richard Wilbur. In *William Shakespeare: The Complete Works*, gen. ed. Alfred Harbage. 2nd edition, revised. New York: Viking Press, 1969.

———. *William Shakespeare: The Complete Works*, gen. eds Stephen Orgel and A.R. Braunmuller. New York: Penguin Putnam, 2002.

Shapiro, James. *Rival Playwrights: Marlowe, Jonson, Shakespeare*. New York: Columbia University Press, 1991.

———. *Shakespeare and the Jews*. New York: Columbia University Press, 1996.

Shepard, Alan. *Marlowe's Soldiers: Rhetorics of Masculinity in the Age of the Armada*. Burlington, VT: Ashgate, 2002.

Shepherd, Simon. *Marlowe and the Politics of Elizabethan Theatre*. New York: St Martin's Press, 1986.

Skura, Meredith. "Marlowe's *Edward II*: Penetrating Language in Shakespeare's *Richard II*." *Shakespeare Survey* 50 (1997): 41–55.

Sidney, Sir Philip. *The Prose Works of Sir Philip Sidney*, ed. Albert Feuillerat. 4 vols. Cambridge: Cambridge University Press, 1912. Reprinted with corrections 1962.

Smith, Bruce. *Homosexual Desire in Shakespeare's England: A Cultural Poetics.* Chicago: University of Chicago Press, 1991.

Smith, Hallett. *Elizabethan Poetry.* Cambridge, MA: Harvard University Press, 1952.

Smith, Mary Elizabeth. *"Love-Kindling Fire": A Study of Christopher Marlowe's "The Tragedy of Dido, Queen of Carthage."* Salzburg, Austria: Institut für Englische Sprache und Literatur Universität Salzburg, 1977.

Smith, Robert A.H. *"Julius Caesar* and *The Massacre At Paris."* *Notes and Queries* 44:4 (December 1997): 496–97.

Stapleton, M.L. "Venus As Praeceptor: The *Ars Amatoria* in *Venus and Adonis*." In *"Venus and Adonis": Critical Essays*, ed. Philip Kolin, 309–21. New York: Garland, 1997.

Steane, J.B. *Marlowe: A Critical Study.* Cambridge: Cambridge University Press, 1964.

Summers, Claude. *"Hero and Leander*: The Arbitrariness of Desire." In *Constructing Christopher Marlowe*, ed. J.A. Downie and J.T. Parnell, 133–47. Cambridge: Cambridge University Press, 2000.

Sypher, Wylie. *The Ethic of Time: Structures of Experience in Shakespeare.* New York: The Seabury Press, 1976.

Taunton, Nina. *1590s Drama and Militarism: Portrayals of War in Marlowe, Chapman, and Shakespeare's* Henry V. Burlington, VT: Ashgate, 2001.

Traister, Barbara Howard. *Heavenly Necromancers: The Magician in English Renaissance Drama.* Columbia: University of Missouri Press, 1984.

Tromley, Fred B. *Playing with Desire: Christopher Marlowe and the Art of Tantalization.* Toronto: University of Toronto Press, 1998.

Turner, Frederick. *Shakespeare and the Nature of Time: Moral and Philosophical Themes in Some Plays and Poems of William Shakespeare.* Oxford: Oxford University Press, 1971.

Vickers, Brian. *Shakespeare as Co-Author: A Historical Study of Five Collaborative Plays.* Oxford: Oxford University Press, 2002.

Von Rosador, Kurt Tetzeli. "The Power of Magic: From *Endimion* to *The Tempest*." *Shakespeare Survey* 43 (1991): 1–13.

Waller, G.F. *The Strong Necessity of Time: The Philosophy of Time in Shakespeare and Elizabethan Literature.* The Hague: Mouton, 1976.

Waswo, Richard. "Damnation, Protestant Style: Macbeth, Faustus, and Christian Tragedy." *The Journal of Medieval and Renaissance Studies* 4 (1974), 63–99.

Watkins, W.B.C. *Shakespeare and Spenser.* Princeton, NJ: Princeton University Press, 1950.

Wiggins, Martin. *Shakespeare and the Drama of his Time.* Oxford: Oxford University Press, 2000.

Williams, George Walton. "'Time For Such A Word': Verbal Echoing in *Macbeth*." *Shakespeare Survey* 47 (1994): 153–59.

Wilson, F.P., *"The Massacre At Paris* and *Edward II*." In *Marlowe: A Collection of Critical Essays*, ed. Clifford Leech, 128–37. Englewood Cliffs, NJ: Prentice-Hall, 1964.

Wilson, Richard. "'Writ in Blood': Marlowe and the New Historicists." In *Constructing Christopher Marlowe*, ed. J.A. Downie and J.T. Parnell, 116–32. Cambridge: Cambridge University Press, 2000.

Woodbridge, Linda. *The Scythe of Saturn: Shakespeare and Magical Thinking.* Urbana: University of Illinois Press, 1994.

Woodman, David. *White Magic and English Renaissance Drama.* Rutherford, NJ: Fairleigh Dickinson University Press, 1973.

Yates, Frances A. *The Occult Philosophy in the Elizabethan Age.* London: Routledge and Kegan Paul, 1979.

Young, David. "Where the Bee Sucks: A Triangular Study of *Doctor Faustus*, *The Alchemist*, and *The Tempest*." In *Shakespeare's Romances Reconsidered*, ed. Carol McGinnis Kay and Henry E. Jacobs, 149–66. Lincoln: University of Nebraska Press, 1978.

Index